RICHMOND

NOW YOU!

Richmond

TEACHER'S BOOK 2

WELCOME TO NOW YOU!

Richmond NOW YOU! is a four-level English Secondary course which takes students from A1 to B1+ of the Common European Framework. The course features an eclectic approach which takes the best of the latest developments in ELT teaching methodology and carefully interweaves them within a communicative framework.

Learning threads

The course makes use of these **learning threads** to help streamline the learning and teaching experience and **increase learning efficiency** while also **motivating the students** to connect with the learning process.

Learner-centred approach

Personalisation exercises throughout the course make every student the focus of their own learning journey and help to consolidate language and skills. **Learning to learn tools** provide students with tips and tricks for more effective learning.

Vloggers

In every level of the course the student is accompanied by three vloggers who introduce the context of each unit in their **Vlogs**. The vloggers also narrate the **Culture videos**, creating a cultural link between the unit content and the wider world.

Flipped Learning

There are many tools at the teacher's disposal for implementing Flipped Learning with **NOW YOU!**, such as the fun **Grammar animations** which accompany every grammar point and table. The **Vlogs** with their worksheets also present a great opportunity for introducing the lesson content outside of the classroom.

Project-based Learning

Multi-student **Project tasks** are staged across two units and brought together in a **Final task**. Students recap on the tasks, prepare for a presentation and focus on **21st century skills**. Students are also asked to think carefully about the format of the project and to evaluate themselves and their peers, encouraging **Collaborative Learning**.

Attention to values

Reading content is further explored with speaking tasks, in which students focus on and discuss a specific **Core value**.

Mediation

Project tasks throughout the book and information gap **Pairwork** activities for each unit presented at the end of the book combine unit content with practice of **CEFR mediation** activities and strategies.

External exam preparation

The **Review** pages at the end of each book combine course content with **external exam practice questions**, ensuring students are familiar with the format and can apply their knowledge in an exam context.

For the Student

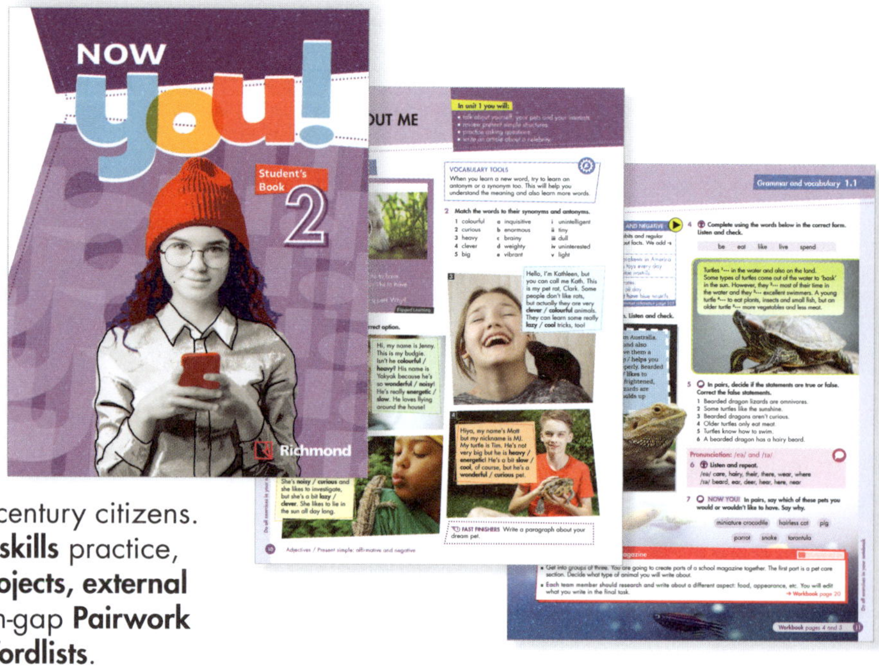

Student's Book

The **NOW YOU! Student's Book** is a dynamic, attractive course book with clear lesson objectives, a wide variety of interesting material for students to engage with and a strong focus on developing skills to help students become confident and competent users of English and well-rounded 21st century citizens. The **Student's Book** includes **integrated skills** practice, **Learning to learn** tools, **Core values, Projects, external exam practice Unit reviews,** information-gap **Pairwork activities,** a **Grammar reference** and **Wordlists**.

Workbook

The **NOW YOU! Workbook** is a **full-colour** resource with more engaging material to complement the **Student's Book**, handy **guided notes pages** for the Writing lessons and Projects, **extra practice for the Grammar reference and Wordlists** and a **Reflect on your learning section** to encourage learner autonomy. Access to **extra interactive practice** based on real-world situations is also available with the **Workbook**.

Workbook Audio

LISTEN ON Spotify

Also available to listen to and download on the **Richmond** *Learning* **Platform**.

All videos and worksheets available on the **Richmond** *Learning* **Platform**

For the Teacher

Teacher's Book

The **Teacher's Book** is your comprehensive guide to teaching **NOW YOU!** and the key methodologies on which the course is based. For each unit of the **Student's Book** there is an **overview** for fast lesson planning, plus complete **teaching notes**, audio **transcripts** and **answer keys** for the student's material.

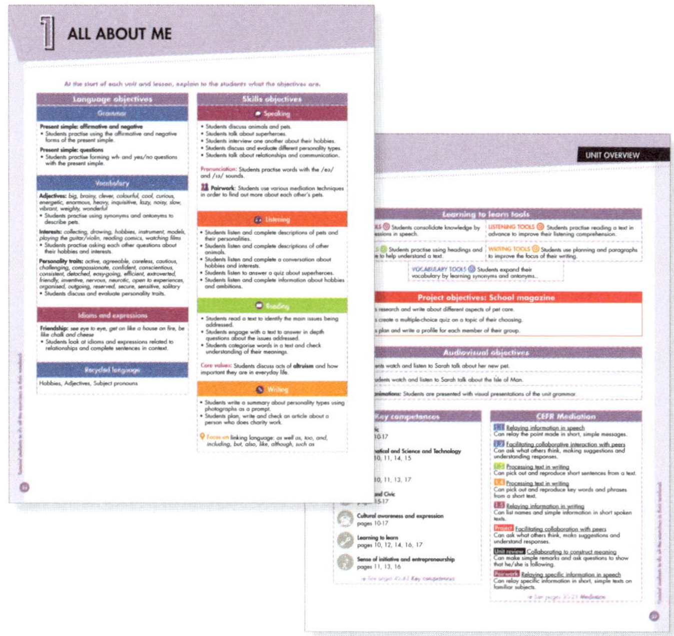

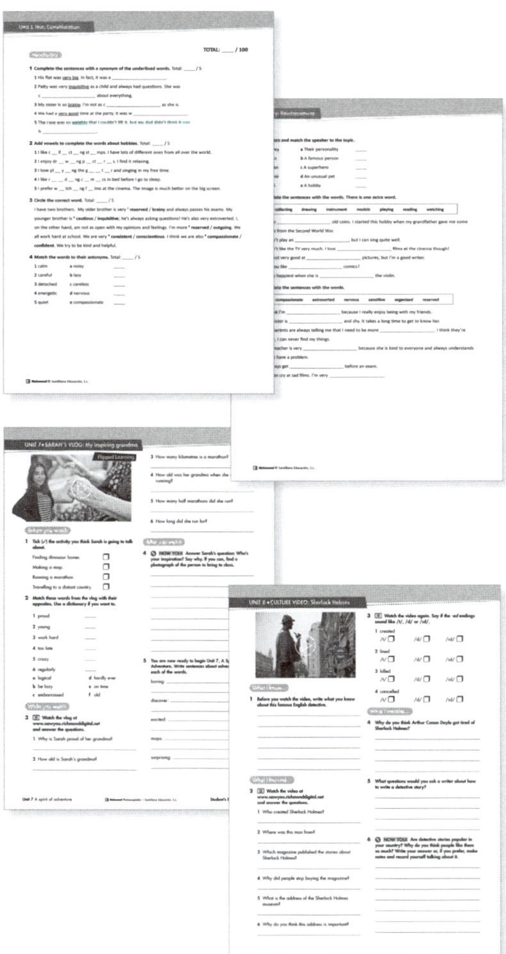

Teacher's Resources

Available on the Richmond*Learning***Platform**

A wide range of ready-to-print and editable material is provided to complement and enhance your teaching.

- **Vocabulary worksheets** at 3 levels of difficulty
- **Grammar worksheets** at 3 levels of difficulty
- **Diagnostic**, **Unit**, **End-of-term** and **End-of-year tests** at 2 levels of difficulty
- **Vlog Flipped Learning worksheets**
- **Culture video worksheets**
- **Essential maps** for each unit

Teacher's Audio

Available on the Richmond*Learning***Platform**

All audio for listening exercises used in the **Student's Book**, **Workbook** and **Teacher's Resources** is available to listen to and download.

All videos and worksheets available on the Richmond*Learning***Platform**

NOW YOU! DIGITAL

For the Student

Student's i-book

The **NOW YOU! Student's i-book** is an online multi-device version of the **Student's Book** to enable students to access the course material at home. It includes:

- All **videos**
- All **Student's Book audio**

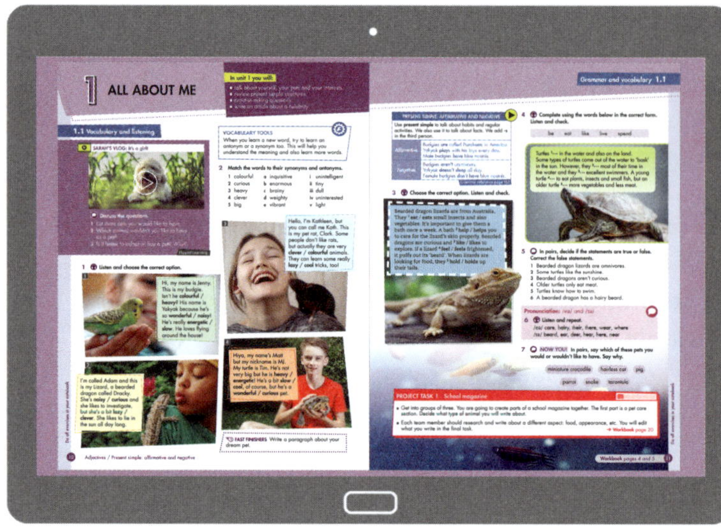

Videos

Three different types of videos (see **Video material** pages 18-19) help teenagers engage with the language in a way that is relevant to their lives outside the classroom.

Vlogs

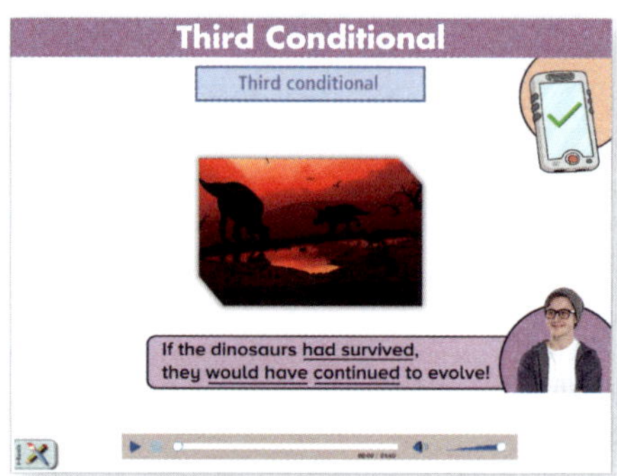

Grammar animations

Culture videos

Student's Interactive Practice

There is also additional interactive practice to consolidate the course content and to develop the concept of English for life. The activities are contextualised in real-world situations. This helps to make the acquisition of language more meaningful for the students.

The **Student's Interactive Practice** includes learning progress and it is ideal for fast finishers or for homework.

Also available to purchase
A fully interactive, **digital version of the Student's Book and Workbook** which provides a complete tracking of the students' progress.

Free App

RICHMOND NOW YOU!

For the Teacher

Offline and online multi-device versions available

Teacher's i-solutions

The **NOW YOU! Teacher's i-solutions** for the classroom include the **Teacher's i-book**, as well as all the resources for the print version of the **Teacher's Book**.

In the **Teacher's i-book** every lesson in the course is presented in the form of a **Learning path**, a step-by step lesson plan that works as a quick lesson guide where the teaching sequence is clear at a glance. All the teaching and learning materials in the course are included and the **resources are colour-coded** to identify what is **core material** and what is **optional**. Teachers can therefore choose activities according to the time available and **tips** for all the material are available **at the click of a button**.

Richmond Test Manager

An online interactive tool to create and assign tests.

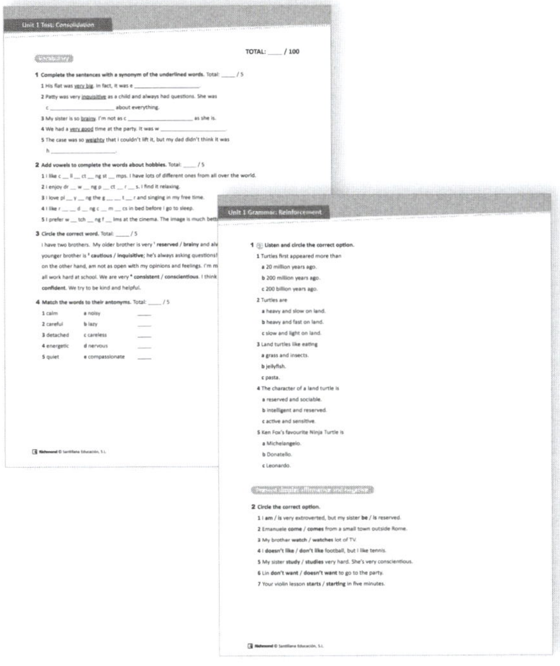

Downloadable material

Teacher's Resources available:

- **Vocabulary worksheets** at 3 levels of difficulty **(PDF and Word format)**
- **Grammar worksheets** at 3 levels of difficulty **(PDF and Word format)**
- **Diagnostic**, **Unit, End-of-term** and **End-of-year tests** at 2 levels of difficulty **(PDF and Word format)**
- **Vlog Flipped Learning worksheets**
- **Culture video worksheets**
- **Essential maps**

All videos and worksheets available on the **Richmond***Learning***Platform**

UNIT WALKTHROUGH

LESSON 1 Grammar, Vocabulary and Listening

1. The **unit menu** outlines the key learning aims of each unit. The four points outline the general communication goal, the central grammar points and the writing task genre. This provides both teacher and student with a clear learning map for the unit.

2. The **lesson focus** tags highlight the main skills focus of each page.

Lessons 1 and 2 provide **grammar**, **vocabulary** and **listening** input. Speaking exercises throughout give students opportunities to practise the key grammar points and vocabulary sets.

Lesson 3 provides **reading** input with a focus on deepening the students' understanding of the unit language in an authentic context.

Lesson 4 guides **writing** output, putting the students' knowledge to practical use.

Lesson 5 is a **culture and communication** page where students are encouraged to recognise their place in global culture and interact with the world around them.

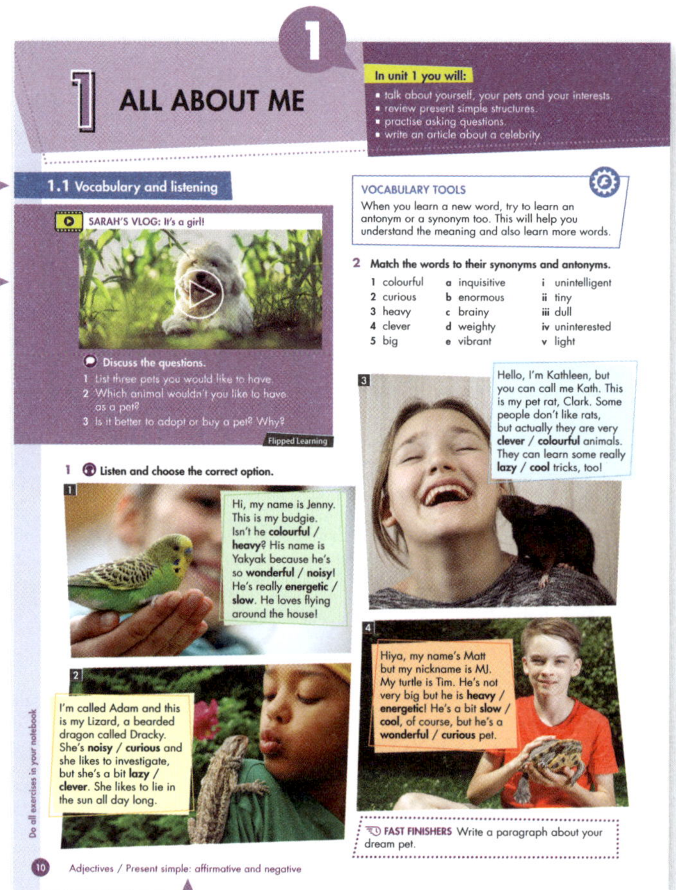

3. Three **vloggers** provide an engaging context for the unit content.
The optional **Flipped Learning** tasks encourage students to take control of their learning by beginning the learning process outside of the classroom. For information about Flipped Learning, see pages 20-23.

These **Vlogs** provide exposure to the unit language aims and can be re-watched in order to capitalise on the content, but students can answer the discussion questions and complete the unit without having watched them.

4. The **lesson objective** clarifies the grammar and vocabulary goals of each lesson. This provides an at-a-glance summary of the lesson for both the teacher and student.

LESSON 1 Grammar, Vocabulary and Listening

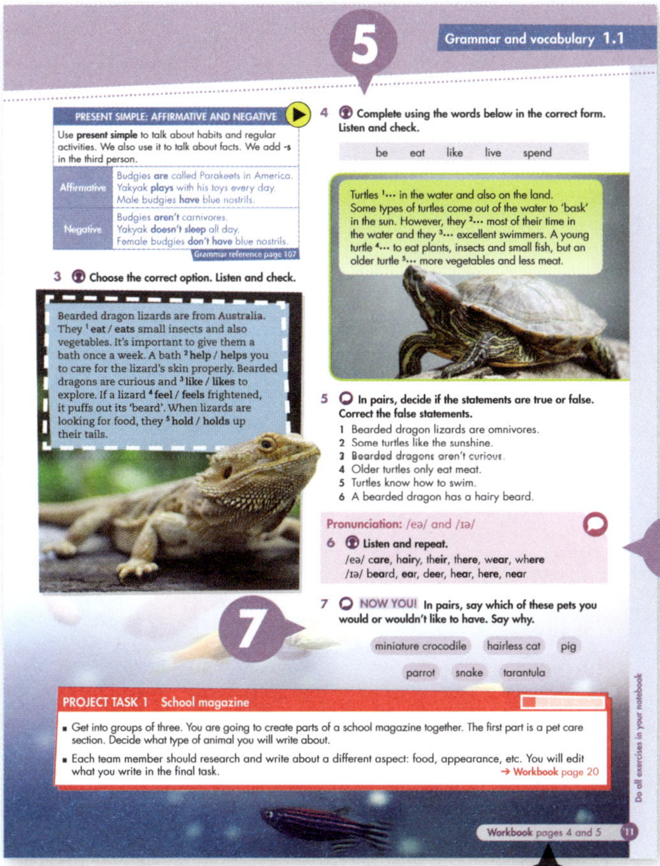

Grammar and vocabulary 1.1

PRESENT SIMPLE: AFFIRMATIVE AND NEGATIVE

Use **present simple** to talk about habits and regular activities. We also use it to talk about facts. We add **-s** in the third person.

Affirmative	Budgies **are** called Parakeets in America. Yakyak **plays** with his toys every day. Male budgies **have** blue nostrils.
Negative	Budgies **aren't** carnivores. Yakyak **doesn't sleep** all day. Female budgies **don't have** blue nostrils.

Grammar reference page 107

3 Choose the correct option. Listen and check.

Bearded dragon lizards are from Australia. They [1] **eat / eats** small insects and also vegetables. It's important to give them a bath once a week. A bath [2] **help / helps** you to care for the lizard's skin properly. Bearded dragons are curious and [3] **like / likes** to explore. If a lizard [4] **feel / feels** frightened, it puffs out its 'beard'. When lizards are looking for food, they [5] **hold / holds** up their tails.

4 Complete using the words below in the correct form. Listen and check.

be eat like live spend

Turtles [1]… in the water and also on the land. Some types of turtles come out of the water to 'bask' in the sun. However, they [2]… most of their time in the water and they [3]… excellent swimmers. A young turtle [4]… to eat plants, insects and small fish, but an older turtle [5]… more vegetables and less meat.

5 In pairs, decide if the statements are true or false. Correct the false statements.

1 Bearded dragon lizards are omnivores.
2 Some turtles like the sunshine.
3 Bearded dragons aren't curious.
4 Older turtles only eat meat.
5 Turtles know how to swim.
6 A bearded dragon has a hairy beard.

Pronunciation: /eə/ and /ɪə/

6 Listen and repeat.
/eə/ **care, hairy, their, there, wear, where**
/ɪə/ **beard, ear, deer, hear, here, near**

7 NOW YOU! In pairs, say which of these pets you would or wouldn't like to have. Say why.

miniature crocodile hairless cat pig parrot snake tarantula

PROJECT TASK 1 School magazine

- Get into groups of three. You are going to create parts of a school magazine together. The first part is a pet care section. Decide what type of animal you will write about.
- Each team member should research and write about a different aspect: food, appearance, etc. You will edit what you write in the final task. → Workbook page 20

Do all exercises in your notebook

Workbook pages 4 and 5 11

5 The **exercises** give students a variety of ways to practise what they are learning.

6 There is a **pronunciation** exercise in each unit to develop students' ability to recognise and produce the different features of spoken English.

7 The **NOW YOU!** exercises at the end of the lesson challenge students to put their knowledge to practical use in the form of personalised speaking or writing exercises.

8 At the end of each lesson students are directed to their **Workbook** for further practice of the unit content.

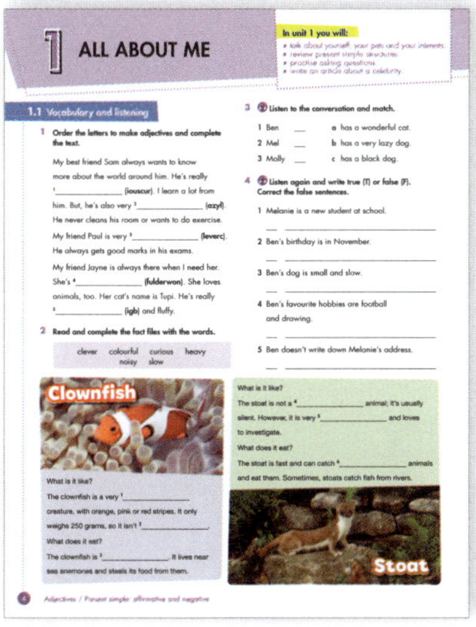

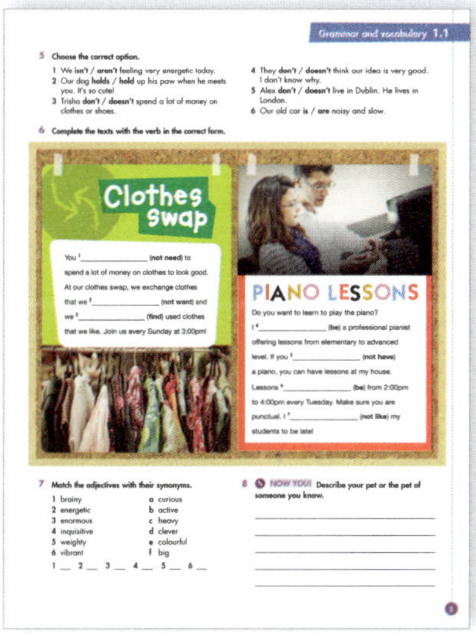

Unit walkthrough

LESSON 2 Grammar, Vocabulary and Listening

1. There is a **Learning to learn tool** for each skill across the unit which gives students strategies to help develop their listening, speaking, reading and writing skills, as well their ability to acquire, retain and use vocabulary.
The colour coding helps students identify the skills at a glance:
   - Listening tools
   - Reading tools
   - Speaking tools
   - Writing tools
   - Vocabulary tools

1.2 Listening and vocabulary

LISTENING TOOLS
Read the text before you listen to help you predict the information that you might hear. This will help you to prepare for the task.

1 Listen and complete.

Ellie: OK, are you ready for the interview questions?
Tamara: Sure!
Ellie: First question: do you have a ¹…?
Tamara: Well, some of my friends call me Tam.
Ellie: And… do you have a ²…?
Tamara: Yup, I have a dog called Jimmy. He's energetic and a bit silly.
Ellie: Ha! True. What's your favourite food?
Tamara: Umm, sausages I think.
Ellie: Yum! What kind of ³… do you like?
Tamara: Erm, I like pop, but I listen to chillout music when I draw.
Ellie: Ah ha! That's the next question. What do you do in your ⁴…?
Tamara: Well, you know I love drawing, but I also ⁵… reading comics and watching action films. I collect stamps and models of superheroes, too! Superman is my favourite.
Ellie: Hmm, I ⁶… Spiderman. So, do you draw every day?
Tamara: Yes! My ⁷… is to be a cartoonist one day. There aren't many female superheroes, so I'm creating one.
Ellie: Cool! What's her superpower?
Tamara: I'm ⁸… yet, but she is very strong and she has X-ray vision.
Ellie: I can't wait to see the film one day!

2 Answer the questions about Tamara.
1 What is her nickname?
2 What is her pet like?
3 What kind of music does she prefer?
4 What are her hobbies?
5 How often does she draw?
6 What is Tamara's dream?

3 NOW YOU! Ask and answer the questions in pairs.
- Do you have a favourite superhero? Who is it? Why?
- What do you think your superhero name would be?
- Which superpower is the best?
- What do you think superheroes do in their free time?

FAST FINISHERS Invent a new superhero and write a paragraph about them.

Do all exercises in your notebook

12 Interests / Present simple: questions

2. Through the unit students are asked to complete a variety of exercises that build on growing knowledge of the unit aims. Special effort has been made to ensure that all the content is visually appealing to students.

3. There is a **Fast finishers** exercise in lessons 1, 2, 3 and 5 to keep stronger students challenged and engaged if they finish the other exercises quickly. These are short, personalised writing exercises that students can complete alone and could keep as part of a language diary.

4. Each grammar lesson contains a **Grammar table** that shows key structures. These tables show clear models which can be used as a quick reference to complete the accompanying exercises.

The connected **Grammar reference** page at the back of the book includes more detailed explanations of both form and use.

LESSON 2 Grammar, Vocabulary and Listening

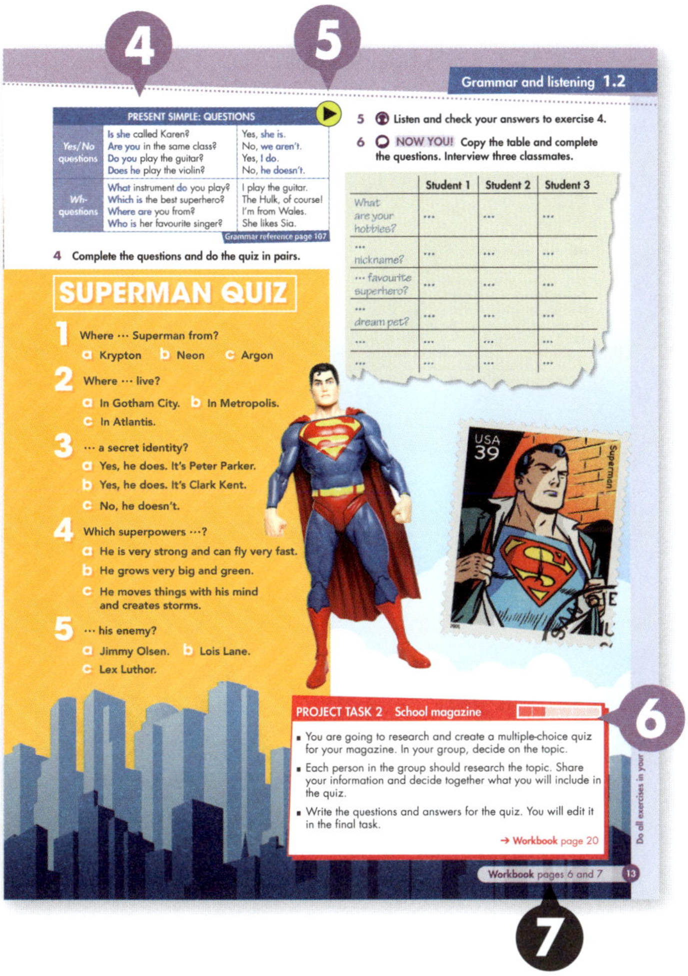
4 5 6 7

Grammar and listening 1.2

PRESENT SIMPLE: QUESTIONS		
Yes/No questions	Is she called Karen? Are you in the same class? Do you play the guitar? Does he play the violin?	Yes, she is. No, we aren't. Yes, I do. No, he doesn't.
Wh- questions	What instrument do you play? Which is the best superhero? Where are you from? Who is her favourite singer?	I play the guitar. The Hulk, of course! I'm from Wales. She likes Sia.

Grammar reference page 107

4 Complete the questions and do the quiz in pairs.

SUPERMAN QUIZ

1 Where ··· Superman from?
a Krypton b Neon c Argon

2 Where ··· live?
a In Gotham City. b In Metropolis. c In Atlantis.

3 ··· a secret identity?
a Yes, he does. It's Peter Parker.
b Yes, he does. It's Clark Kent.
c No, he doesn't.

4 Which superpowers ···?
a He is very strong and can fly very fast.
b He grows very big and green.
c He moves things with his mind and creates storms.

5 ··· his enemy?
a Jimmy Olsen. b Lois Lane. c Lex Luthor.

5 Listen and check your answers to exercise 4.

6 NOW YOU! Copy the table and complete the questions. Interview three classmates.

	Student 1	Student 2	Student 3
What are your hobbies?	···	···	···
··· nickname?	···	···	···
··· favourite superhero?	···	···	···
··· dream pet?	···	···	···
···	···	···	···
···	···	···	···

PROJECT TASK 2 School magazine

- You are going to research and create a multiple-choice quiz for your magazine. In your group, decide on the topic.
- Each person in the group should research the topic. Share your information and decide together what you will include in the quiz.
- Write the questions and answers for the quiz. You will edit it in the final task.

→ Workbook page 20

Do all exercises in your

Workbook pages 6 and 7

13

5 The **Grammar animations** present the grammar in an appealing visual format to help to engage the students and consolidate their understanding of the grammatical structures.
These animations also provide opportunities for **Flipped Learning**.

6 **Project tasks** develop and build towards a final presentation over two units. These tasks draw on the content of the lesson and promote collaborative work. The bar helps students know how many tasks they have completed and have left to complete the project.

In unit 9 students are given **Review tasks** which encourage them to reflect on what they have learnt from units 1 to 9 and develop revision strategies.

The **Teacher's Resources** provide students with worksheets for further practice of both **vocabulary** and **grammar** at their level — ideal for mixed-ability classes. Each worksheet comes at three levels of difficulty:

- Reinforcement — lower level
- Consolidation — course level
- Extension — higher level

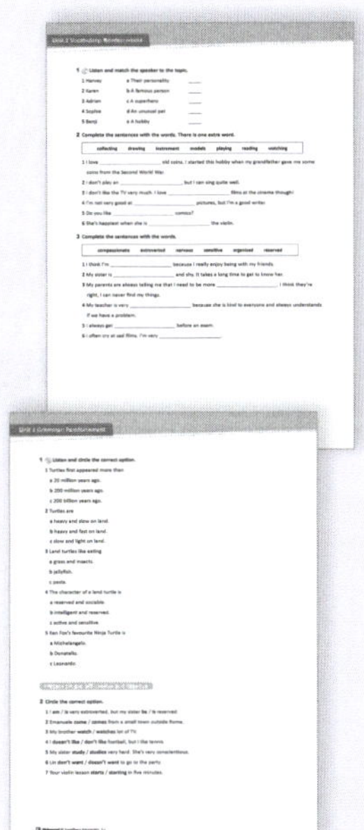

7 Further practice of the lesson content can be found in the **Workbook.**

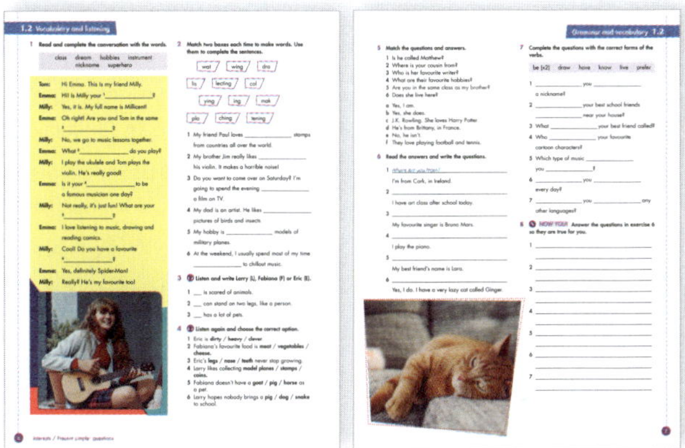

Unit walkthrough

LESSON 3 Reading

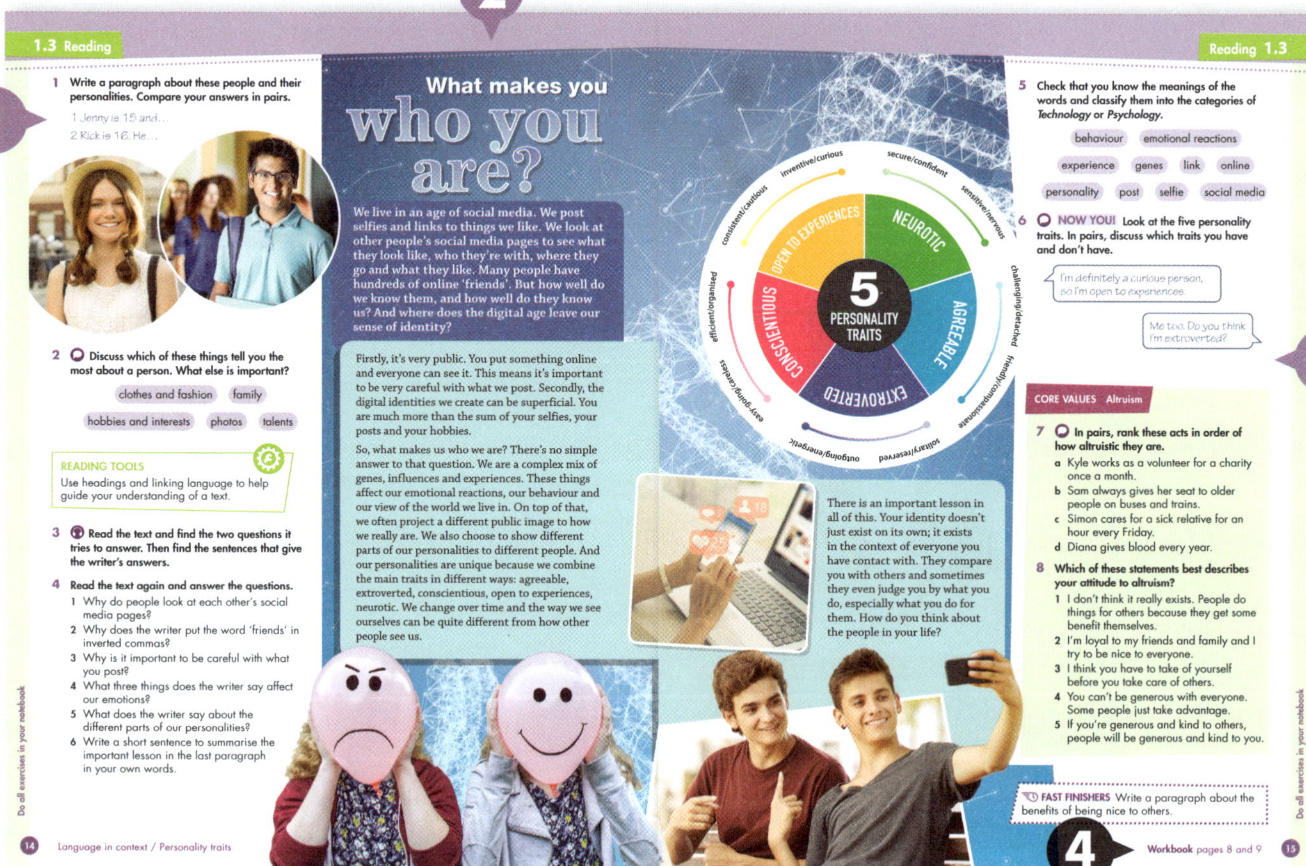
1.3 Reading

1 Write a paragraph about these people and their personalities. Compare your answers in pairs.
1 Jenny is 15 and…
2 Rick is 16. He…

2 Discuss which of these things tell you the most about a person. What else is important?
clothes and fashion | family | hobbies and interests | photos | talents

READING TOOLS
Use headings and linking language to help guide your understanding of a text.

3 Read the text and find the two questions it tries to answer. Then find the sentences that give the writer's answers.

4 Read the text again and answer the questions.
1 Why do people look at each other's social media pages?
2 Why does the writer put the word 'friends' in inverted commas?
3 Why is it important to be careful with what you post?
4 What three things does the writer say affect our emotions?
5 What does the writer say about the different parts of our personalities?
6 Write a short sentence to summarise the important lesson in the last paragraph in your own words.

Do all exercises in your notebook

14 Language in context / Personality traits

What makes you who you are?

We live in an age of social media. We post selfies and links to things we like. We look at other people's social media pages to see what they look like, who they're with, where they go and what they like. Many people have hundreds of online 'friends'. But how well do we know them, and how well do they know us? And where does the digital age leave our sense of identity?

Firstly, it's very public. You put something online and everyone can see it. This means it's important to be very careful with what we post. Secondly, the digital identities we create can be superficial. You are much more than the sum of your selfies, your posts and your hobbies.

So, what makes us who we are? There's no simple answer to that question. We are a complex mix of genes, influences and experiences. These things affect our emotional reactions, our behaviour and our view of the world we live in. On top of that, we often project a different public image to how we really are. We also choose to show different parts of our personalities to different people. And our personalities are unique because we combine the main traits in different ways: agreeable, extroverted, conscientious, open to experiences, neurotic. We change over time and the way we see ourselves can be quite different from how other people see us.

There is an important lesson in all of this. Your identity doesn't just exist on its own; it exists in the context of everyone you have contact with. They compare you with others and sometimes they even judge you by what you do, especially what you do for them. How do you think about the people in your life?

Reading 1.3

5 Check that you know the meanings of the words and classify them into the categories of *Technology* or *Psychology*.
behaviour | emotional reactions | experience | genes | link | online | personality | post | selfie | social media

6 NOW YOU! Look at the five personality traits. In pairs, discuss which traits you have and don't have.
I'm definitely a curious person, so I'm open to experiences.
Me too. Do you think I'm extroverted?

CORE VALUES Altruism

7 In pairs, rank these acts in order of how altruistic they are.
a Kyle works as a volunteer for a charity once a month.
b Sam always gives her seat to older people on buses and trains.
c Simon cares for a sick relative for an hour every Friday.
d Diana gives blood every year.

8 Which of these statements best describes your attitude to altruism?
1 I don't think it really exists. People do things for others because they get some benefit themselves.
2 I'm loyal to my friends and family and I try to be nice to everyone.
3 I think you have to take of yourself before you take care of others.
4 You can't be generous with everyone. Some people just take advantage.
5 If you're generous and kind to others, people will be generous and kind to you.

FAST FINISHERS Write a paragraph about the benefits of being nice to others.

Workbook pages 8 and 9 15

Do all exercises in your notebook

1 The **reading** lesson contains exercises that guide students through the process of effective reading. They include pre-reading exercises, comprehension exercises and follow-up vocabulary and speaking exercises.

2 There are a range of **reading texts** that provide an accessible, authentic context and connect the content of the unit with the world outside the classroom.

3 The **Core values** section provides an opportunity for students to reflect on ideas and beliefs that are considered important in society and the effect these values have on how we behave. The emphasis is on understanding and respecting ourselves and others. This contextualisation of values helps to deepen the students' connection with the reading material and give a clear, communicative resolution to the lesson.

4 More reading practice can be found in the **Workbook**.

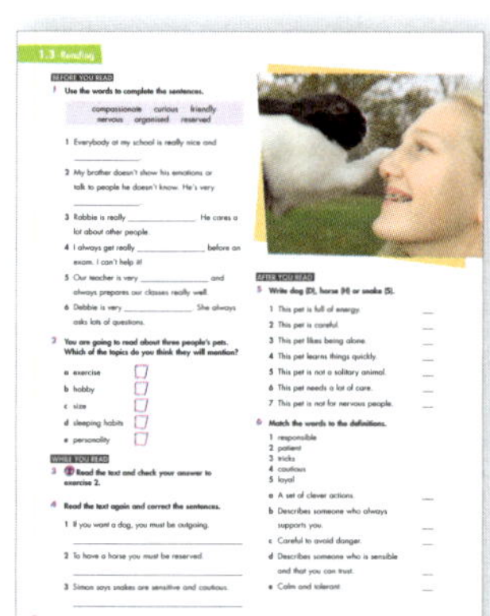

LESSON 4 Writing

1.4 Writing

An article about a celebrity

Focus on linking language

1 Read the descriptions and match with the celebrities.

1 As well as being a successful TV pr... comedian and writer, she is an act... campaigner for animal rights too.
2 He is one of Hong Kong's most famo... and martial arts experts, and contributes to many causes, including the protection of endangered species.
3 She is one of the world's most respected actors, but she also does charity work for organisations like SolarAid.
4 Although he is a famous singer, not everyone knows about his support for the victims of natural disasters such as Typhoon Haiyan in the Philippines.

2 Decide which of the linking words and expressions highlighted are used...
1 to add information.
2 to contrast information.
3 to introduce examples.

3 Read the profile of Bono and answer the questions.
1 What charity work is mentioned?
2 What does the writer think of Bono's contributions?

BONO

Bono, real name Paul Hewson, is the lead singer of U2. He lives in Ireland with his wife Alison. Although he is most famous as the singer of one of the world's best rock bands, he and his wife are also very involved in charity and activism, especially in Africa. They work with organisations that combat poverty and disease, and others that promote fair trade.

Many people say that Bono does it all for publicity, but I don't agree. I think he contributes a lot to making the world a fairer place, and he inspires others to do the same too.

Did you notice?

4 Which of these things does the writer do in the text?
1 Say what Bono is mainly famous for.
2 Give some details about his path to success.
3 Give some details about his charity work.
4 Mention criticisms and address them.
5 Discuss reasons why celebrities do charity work.

NOW YOU! → Workbook page 10

5 PLAN Choose a person who does charity work. Use exercise 4 to plan an article about them.

WRITING TOOLS
Planning your writing in paragraphs gives your text more focus and makes it easier to read.

6 WRITE Write your article. Remember to follow your plan and use linking language.

7 CHECK Check that your writing is clear and that your use of linking language is accurate.

PROJECT TASK 3 School magazine
- You are going to write a profile for each team member and include them in your magazine. Decide together if you will write your own profile or if you will write profiles for each other.
- In your group, make a plan of the information you are going to include in the profiles.
- Write the profiles. You will edit them in the final task. → Workbook page 20

Do all exercises in your notebook

16 An article / Linking language

1 The **Focus on** section gives students an opportunity to revise language they have learnt that will be useful in completing the writing task.

2 A **model text** of the same type required in the writing task provides students with an appropriate scaffold of structure, style and language. The texts are of a range of genres and cover text types and linguistic conventions required in external exams.

3 The **Did you notice?** section highlights contextualised language, style and structural features of the model text for the students to include in their writing.

4 The **NOW YOU!** writing task has **Plan**, **Write** and **Check** exercises to give students a step-by-step guide to producing an appropriate written text, drawing on language they have learnt.

5 The **Workbook** contains a dedicated area per unit for students to complete the writing task. This allows students to build up their own portfolio of writing work.

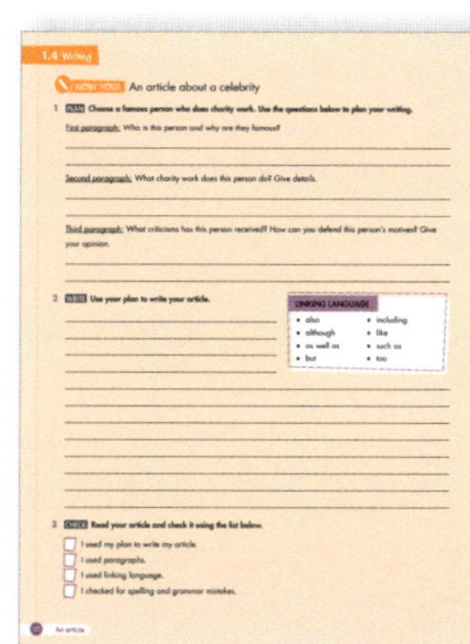

Unit walkthrough

LESSON 5 Culture and Communication

1 The lesson starts with a **Culture video** introduced by the unit vlogger that gives students a window on the world from a cultural perspective using natural language.

As with the **Vlog** at the beginning of the unit, students' responses to the discussion questions will be informed by the content of the video; however, the questions can also be answered by students who have not seen the video.

Understanding of the video is consolidated in the optional **Culture video worksheets** available in the **Teacher's Resources**.

2 Themed sets of **Idioms and expressions** highlight natural, everyday language and phrases. This increases students' confidence by deepening understanding of English as spoken by native speakers and developing fluency.

3 The **Pairwork** exercises provide communicative tasks which practise the target language in line with **CEFR mediation descriptors**. Students analyse, interpret and exchange information using key language from the unit.

Culture and communication 1.5

The Isle of Man

Discuss the questions.
1 Would you like to live on an island? Why?
2 Are there any myths connected to the place where you live?
3 Which special animals can be found in your country?
4 Who is the most famous person in your country's history?

1 Listen and complete the information.

Names: Megan and Matt
Hobby: ··· Dream: ···

Names: ··· Hobby: ···
Dream: Be PE teachers

Idioms and expressions about friendship

Idioms and expressions

2 Match the expressions you heard with the meanings.
1 see eye to eye
2 get on like a house on fire
3 be like chalk and cheese

a When you have a very good friendship with someone.
b When you are very different from someone.
c When you share someone's opinion or view about something.

3 Complete the sentences with the expressions from exercise 2.
1 My grandparents ··· . I don't know how they're so happy together!
2 I always fight with my mum – we never ··· .
3 We ··· from the moment we met, and I knew we were going to be friends.

SPEAKING TOOLS
When you are learning a new expression, use it in lots of short sentences. This will help you to feel more confident with it.

4 NOW YOU! In pairs, talk about…
- what you do when you don't see eye to eye with someone.
- a time when you got on like a house on fire with someone unexpected.
- two people you know that are like chalk and cheese.

Names: ···
Hobby: Skateboarding Dream: ···

PAIRWORK
Student A: go to page 99
Student B: go to page 103

Unit 1 Review • page 90
Wordlist • pages 118–120

Workbook page 11

17

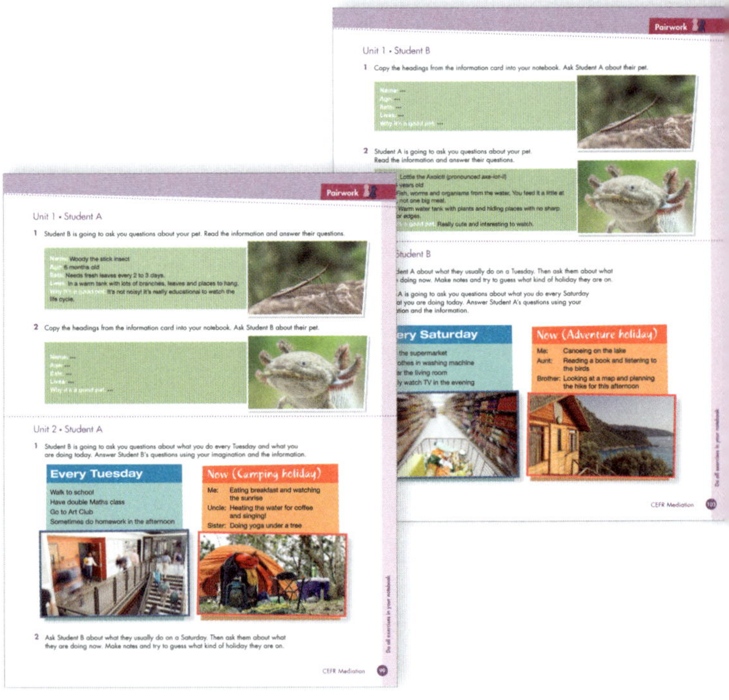

Unit walkthrough

LESSON 5 Culture and Communication

4 The **Unit reviews** help students to revise the language from the unit and practise for external exams. The reading, writing, listening and speaking tasks mirror external exam format and provide comprehensive exam practice.

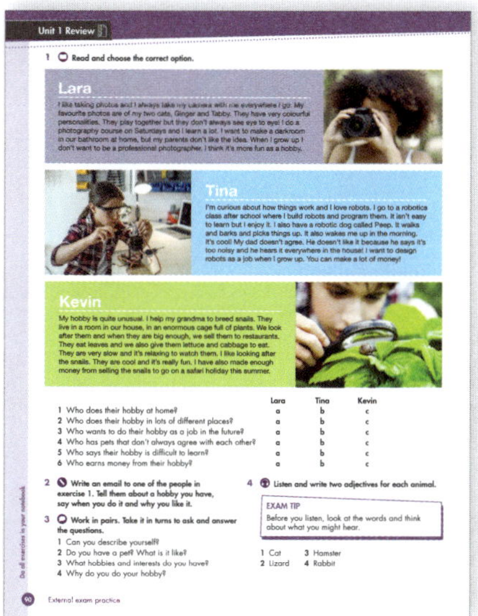

5 The **Wordlist** for each unit helps students to revise the main vocabulary from the unit. The wordlists include key and high frequency words from the unit. There is also an irregular verb list for reference.

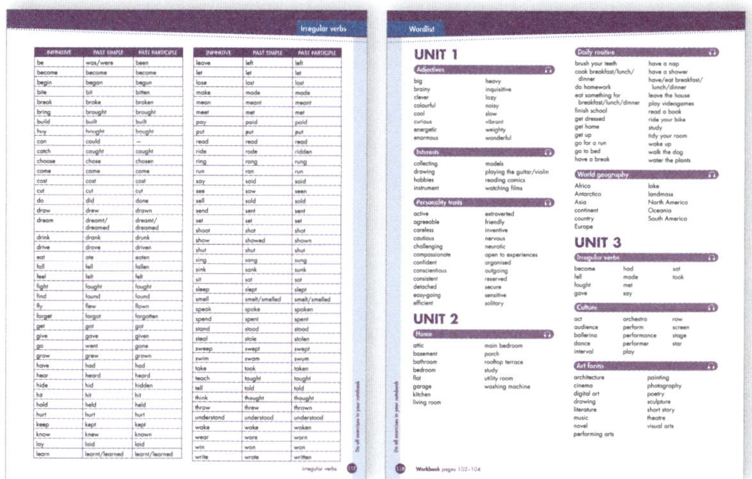

The **Teacher's Resources** contain **tests** which can be used at the end of every unit, term and year. Students can be tested on their knowledge of vocabulary and grammar along with their skills development at two levels of difficulty:

- Consolidation – course level
- Extension – higher level

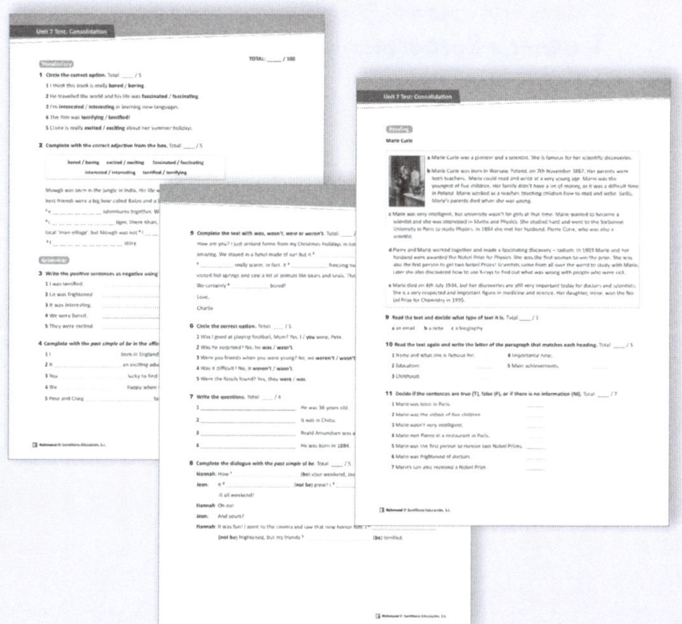

6 In the **Workbook** students will find further practice of the **Idioms and expressions** along with a **Reflect on your learning** table for them to assess their progress using 'I can' statements.

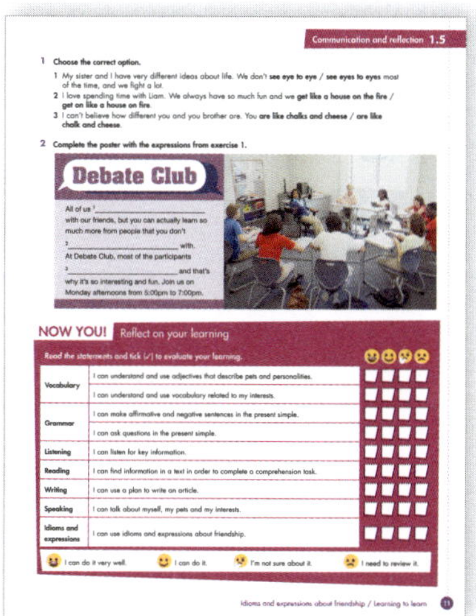

Unit walkthrough

PROJECT

1 At the end of lessons 1, 2, and 4 of each unit students complete a project task. There are six tasks spread over two units. These tasks build towards a final project. The **Recap** section reflects on the six project tasks students have undertaken over the course of these units.
Each of these tasks requires students to apply the knowledge they have acquired in each lesson, which helps boost their motivation.

2 The **Final task** is where students come together to organise, refine and present their work. The projects are conceived as multi-skill activities that develop students' ability to collaborate and to express their knowledge, aptitudes, interests and feelings.

3 The **Useful expressions** are a list of phrases that students can incorporate into the final presentation.

PROJECT: School magazine

RECAP

- In this project, you have researched and written material for a school magazine.
- In **units 1 and 2**, you talked about yourself, your pet, interests, friends and routines. You learnt how to ask questions. You also used the present simple, present continuous and adverbs of frequency to talk about daily life.
- Now you are ready to present your school magazine to the class!

TASK 1	Write pet care instructions.
TASK 2	Research and create a quiz.
TASK 3	Write a profile for each team member.
TASK 4	Interview a person at your school.
TASK 5	Create the perfect daily routine.
TASK 6	Write about daily life in a different country.

FINAL TASK: Complete and present your magazine

- Decide if you will create the magazine by hand or use a computer.
- Look back at the material that you have created. Correct any mistakes and improve it where possible.
- Together, decide how you will present the information on the page and how many pages you will include. Write a final version of the texts and choose photos to go on each of the pages. Look at online magazines to inspire you.
- Create a name for your magazine and design the front cover. Remember to include information about the contents.
- When your magazine is ready, present it to the class. Then exchange the magazines and look at them closely. In your group, choose the best section in each magazine.

USEFUL EXPRESSIONS

- We chose this title because…
- This magazine contains … pages.
- We interviewed … because…
- I think the section about … is the best because…
- So, do we agree that the best section is … ?

21ST CENTURY SKILLS

Negotiating

To negotiate well, try to plan a way that everyone can benefit from the decision. Try to see the other person's point of view and remember to:

✓ be clear and calm.
✓ listen and be respectful.
✓ be ready to compromise.

Do all exercises in your notebook

26 Workbook pages 20 and 21

4 The **21st century skills** box shows students how the soft skills they have developed during the project can be useful to them outside the classroom. This helps the students to see how they can apply broader skills they have developed in the classroom to the real world.

PROJECT

Project • Units 1 and 2

GO BEYOND

ETHICAL MEDIA

Magazines are aimed at readers with a particular common interest, like fashion, sports or photography. Some people buy them regularly, and some people only read them while they wait for the dentist.

Magazines that focus on celebrity gossip, fashion and beauty, however, are often criticised for putting too much emphasis on superficial things. This focus can become unhealthy when it makes people feel negative about themselves, or feel pressured to buy things they can't afford. After all, magazines make most of their money through advertising.

On the other hand, pop culture magazines present up-to-date information about modern day life and bring people with a common interest together. They also encourage people who don't enjoy reading to read more.

Magazines have been around since the 1600s and, although their popularity is decreasing, they will probably be around for a long time to come.

Answer the questions in pairs.

1 Do you read magazines? Which ones?
2 Why do people enjoy reading magazines?
3 Are pop culture magazines superficial? Why?
4 How could magazines be used to help people?

EVALUATION

Answer the questions in your team.

1 Did you disagree with each other while you were making the magazine?
2 How did you solve the disagreements?
3 Did you negotiate with each other?
4 Were all the members of the team happy with the final magazine?

Do all exercises in your notebook.

27

5 The **Evaluation** questions help students to evaluate individual and team performance from the context of the 21st century skills. This process of reflection promotes a thoughtful approach to the learning process.

6 The **Go beyond** section takes a closer look at an aspect of the project theme. This can be used as a vehicle for class discussion or as a fast finishers activity for students who complete the final task ahead of time.

7 In the **Workbook** the students are provided with a **project notes** organiser to complete each of the project tasks. This ensures that students have all the notes and ideas at hand, creating a portfolio of their work which they can look back on for evaluation purposes.

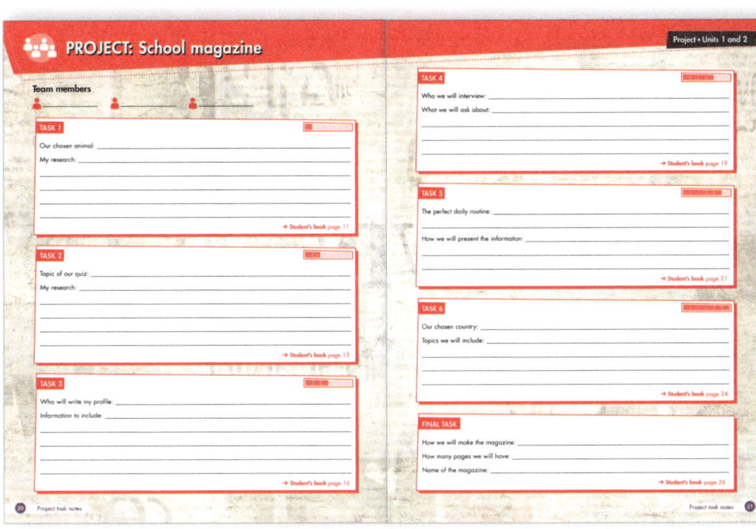
PROJECT: School magazine

Project • Units 1 and 2

Team members

TASK 1
Our chosen animal:
My research:
→ Student's book page 11

TASK 2
Topic of our quiz:
My research:
→ Student's book page 13

TASK 3
Who will write my profile:
Information to include:
→ Student's book page 16

TASK 4
Who we will interview:
What we will ask about:
→ Student's book page 19

TASK 5
The perfect daily routine:
How we will present the information:
→ Student's book page 21

TASK 6
Our chosen country:
Topics we will include:
→ Student's book page 24

FINAL TASK
How we will make the magazine:
How many pages we will have:
Name of the magazine:
→ Student's book page 26

20 Project task notes

Project task notes 21

Video material

The benefits of learning through video

Video is an essential tool in today's ELT classroom and should be embraced as one of the most important resources for learning by both teachers and students alike. Not only does video offer many benefits for students, it is also the **preferred medium of content** for teenagers all over the world. Videos allow students to engage and **connect with English** in a way that written texts do not. This feeling of connection is one of the most **powerful motivational tools** available when learning a language.

Language input and review

Video is a useful tool **for introducing new language** – grammar, vocabulary and functional language. It provides a natural, more complete context for the language, which helps students develop a more **thorough understanding of how the language is used**. Videos give students information about register and pronunciation, as well as lots of audiovisual clues to aid understanding like tone of voice, gestures and facial expressions. This also helps **memory retention**, especially when language is reviewed in subsequent videos. Videos are a very **dynamic review tool**.

Video is also a vital resource for **Flipped Learning**, a dynamic educational model whereby students begin learning new structures by watching a video at home. This is particularly useful for mixed-ability classes because students can learn at their own pace. For more on **Flipped Learning**, see pages 20-23.

Key competences

Video material is also an excellent opportunity to instil **Key competences for lifelong learning**, which encourage students to become responsible citizens in 21st century communities (see **Key competences** pages 42-43). As well as **Linguistic competence**, video helps build these two competences:

- **Cultural awareness and expression:** videos show students how people live and express themselves around the world, thus promoting cultural empathy.
- **Digital competence:** students can gain confidence using digital technologies for learning. This is particularly relevant for students who may be at risk of digital exclusion.

The **videos in NOW YOU!** have **been specifically designed to appeal to teenage students** of English. They are presented in formats that teenagers enjoy and are familiar with. There are three types of video, as outlined below and explained in more detail on the next page.

NOW YOU! videos at a glance

- A **Vlog** about the daily life of the vlogger at the start of every unit.
- **Teacher's Resources** include a **Vlog worksheet** to be completed in class or at home (**Flipped Learning**).

- A **Culture video** narrated by the vlogger to extend the students' knowledge of the world.
- **Teacher's Resources** include a **Culture video worksheet** to be completed in class or for homework.

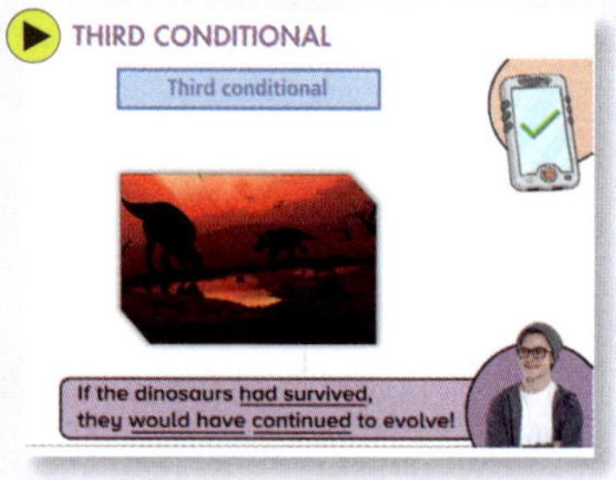

- A **Grammar animation** for every **Grammar table**.
- To be watched either in class or at home (**Flipped Learning**).

How the NOW YOU! videos work

Vlogs and Culture videos

The **Vlogs** and **Culture videos** are used to present and review unit themes and key language, and reflect the way teenagers engage with the world around them. Both videos revolve around **three age-appropriate teenage characters** who are dealing with **authentic, relevant topics** that students can easily identify with. Students hear the unit language being used naturally in context by a native speaker, with visual support from **gifs, emoticons, key words** on screen and, of course, **subtitles**.

The characters' stories evolve throughout the course, from the **Get started!** unit, where students meet the characters, to **Unit 9,** where they say goodbye to them for the summer break. This continuity creates anticipation for the next unit and serves as a memory aid for previous units. There are worksheets to help students get the most out of the videos in the **Teacher's Resources**. Both **Vlog** and **Culture video worksheets** can be used in class and both include exercises to prepare students to watch the videos, to guide them as they watch and to consolidate what they have watched in a way that is personal and accessible to students at all levels of competence. The **Vlog worksheets can also be flipped** (see **Flipped Learning** pages 20-23).

Grammar animations

The **Grammar animations** are a series of fun animations that bring grammar to life for young digital natives. They feature a character called Grammar Gadget, an enthusiastic smartphone in training. It interacts with a group of teenagers on a wide variety of **digital platforms** such as chats and apps. Through their interactions, Grammar Gadget **learns new grammar**, saving it onto its system and **building on it as the level progresses**. Grammar Gadget breaks down each grammar point on screen, so that **students learn along with it**. There are often **multiple grammar animations for each grammar point**. This allows students to focus on each grammar point individually before using them together in subsequent activities. **Like the Vlogs, the Grammar animations can be watched in class or flipped** (see **Flipped Learning** pages 20-23).

All videos and worksheets available on the Richmond*Learning*Platform

Flipped Learning

What is Flipped Learning?

Flipped Learning is an educational model originally developed by Aaron Sams and John Bergmann, two high school teachers in the US, as a strategy for meeting the needs of students who could not attend class. They started by sending them informative videos so that they did not fall behind in their studies. They realised that by providing such videos to all students before class, students could spend class time discussing content, experimenting with the material and receiving assistance from their teachers. Little by little, teachers discovered the benefits and possibilities offered by this model and it was perfected and extended over time.

In a traditional class, teachers first explain new material to their students in the classroom and students subsequently apply that information to class work or homework. In a **Flipped classroom**, this order is reversed or 'flipped'; students first engage with the new material at home and then apply their newly learnt knowledge in the classroom. This approach was born in the digital age and has become increasingly relevant to the challenges facing students preparing to become citizens of the of the 21st century and their teachers. Today, students can access educational content more easily than ever before, and because of this, the teacher's role is no longer merely to transmit content but to be a guide in the education process, awakening the students' curiosity for learning and helping them to develop the skills that will allow them to become more autonomous learners.

Flipped Learning benefits

The benefits of **Flipped Learning** can be divided into three main areas.

Competences and skills

- It develops the student's **Digital competence** and **audio-visual language**.
- It works as an **initial, autonomous evaluation of the student's understanding of vocabulary and grammar**.
- It promotes the development of the student's **Learning to learn competence**.
- It **promotes creativity**.

Methodological and pedagogical

- It allows the teacher to **save class time** and thus significantly increases opportunities to reinforce the key content and **complete tasks in the classroom**.
- It anticipates the context of the lesson and ensures that **each student can work at their own pace** to get ready for the class.
- It maximises the use of the course resources.
- It allows **multidimensional work** through video images and audio to encourage the student's **comprehension** and **memory**.
- It allows the teacher to include a **wider diversity of tasks** that promote different **thinking skills** and richer access to learning.

Emotional

- It helps **build confidence** by giving students a more active role in their own learning.
- It **motivates** students because it brings classroom work into their real lives. This allows students to **link what they are learning to their emotions, feelings and experiences**.
- It **personalises learning** so that each student can access the new content as often as needed without restriction.
- It provides a space for work on content and pronunciation **in a climate of safety and trust**.

Flipped Learning in NOW YOU!

NOW YOU! has two main resources that favour **Flipped Learning**. These resources can be used to promote change in the English classroom in order to **motivate students** to participate actively in their own learning process and take responsibility for it.

They can also be used to anticipate the content of the next lesson. This encourages **meta-learning** and helps the students to be aware of what will happen in the classroom later. This awareness promotes **security** and **confidence** in our students.

The **Vlog** at the start of every unit anticipates and facilitates the introduction of both the unit theme and the new vocabulary in an engaging context.

SARAH'S VLOG: It's a girl

All the **Grammar animations** can be used to anticipate the presentation of the key grammar structure or structures of each unit. **Grammar Gadget** presents the grammar rules in a very **systematic and standardised** way to facilitate the understanding of each rule and improve the **student's long-term learning and memory**.

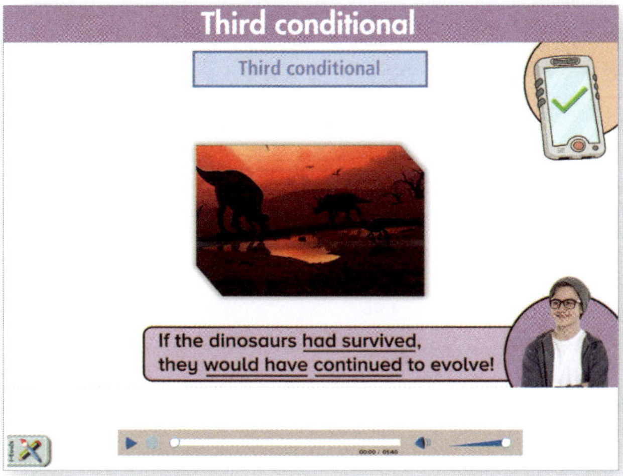

How to get started

Using **Flipped Learning** involves a **commitment on the part of both students and teachers**, each one accepting their role and responsibility. It is advisable that the **starting point** be to **inform the students about this approach** before beginning to use the dynamics of **Flipped Learning** in **NOW YOU!** It is very important that students understand **the benefits that Flipped Learning brings to their global learning process**.

In order to help teachers explain to students how the model works, the **Flipped Learning visual guide** below can be downloaded and printed from the **Richmond*Learning*Platform** to be given out to students during setup.

All the students need to have **access to a computer or mobile device, and internet connection at home**.

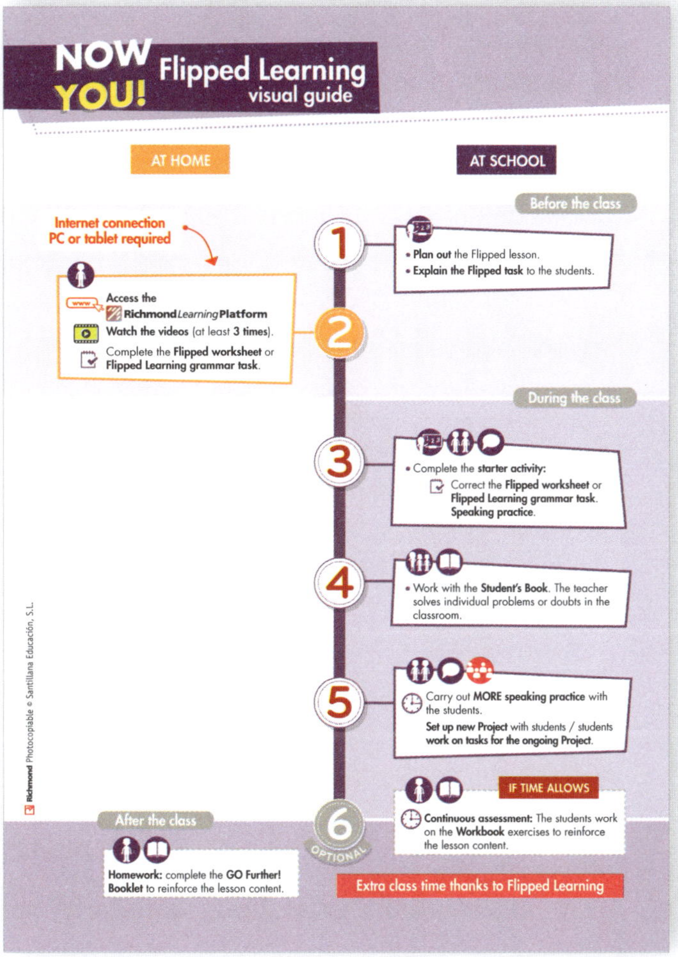

Flipped Learning

How to flip the Vlog

The unit theme is introduced by **watching the Vlog from Lesson 1 at home**. Not only is the content specifically tailored to the relevant age group, the videos are also based on popular formats the students are familiar with and will therefore easily hold their attention.

The videos are available for students on the **Richmond***Learning***Platform**, in a section called **Flipped Learning**. Explain to the students that they have to register on the platform using the **access code included in their Student's Book**. The videos can be viewed from any device, whether it be a computer, mobile or tablet.

SARAH'S VLOG: It's a girl!

Before the start of a new unit, the students take home a task that will promote participation and autonomous learning. **Explain the task** in advance in class as follows:

1 **Give a copy of the Flipped worksheet** to each student so they can complete it at home. Make sure it is clear what they have to do. The worksheets are available for teachers in **PDF** format in the **Teacher's Resources** on the **Richmond***Learning***Platform**.

AT HOME

2 The students read all the exercises to get an overall vision of the task and then **complete the** Before you watch section in the **Flipped worksheet** that was given out in the previous class. These worksheets are also available for the students on the **Richmond***Learning***Platform**.

3 The students watch the **Vlog** at least 3 times:

- **A first time** where the video is played all the way through.
- **A second time** stopping at moments of interest to answer the questions in the While you watch section in the **Flipped worksheet**.
- **A third time** to check that the content has been understood. This time it is also played without stopping and students should be encouraged to practise the pronunciation of key words while they watch it.

If there are students who need to watch the video more than 3 times, encourage them to do so. The important thing is that **each student can work at their own pace and come to the next class prepared.** This approach adapts to the learning process of each student.

4 The students complete the After you watch section in the **Flipped worksheet**. The worksheet must be returned to the classroom so the teacher can check that the initial work with the new unit has been done.

AT SCHOOL

5 Once in the classroom, the starter activity of the unit will be to check that the video has been watched, the **Flipped worksheet** completed, and the content understood. This starter activity practises speaking skills and the students use the completed **Flipped worksheets** to participate.

6 After this starter activity has been carried out, the new content is then used in more complex, communicative and active ways during the rest of the class. Some of the **Student's Book** exercises can then be skipped to save time for the **Project tasks**.

How to flip a grammar lesson

The **animated grammar presentations** in **NOW YOU!** provide **clear step-by-step explanations** for all the grammar rules covered in the course, ensuring **students can work autonomously**.

Any grammar lesson in the Student's Book can be flipped. However, if teachers have already used the Flipped Learning approach for the start of the unit, it is advisable to flip the grammar presentation in Lesson 2. Remember the videos are available for students on the **Richmond***Learning***Platform**, in a section called **Flipped Learning**.

1 **Before the start of Lesson 2**, give students one of these **Flipped Learning grammar** tasks to complete at home:

- Write five true/false sentences using the grammar structure to be shared in class.
- Write five sentences with a word missing for a classmate to complete.
- Write a short dialogue to perform with a classmate in class.
- Write a short quiz of 5 questions and the answers to be shared in class.
- Write a short message for a classmate to reply to using the grammar structure.

AT HOME

2 The students watch the animated grammar presentations before the start of the grammar lesson. Note there may be more than one video for each key grammar structure in the **Student's Book**. The students should **watch each video at least 3 times**:

- **A first time** where they watch the presentation all the way through without stopping.
- **A second time** stopping the presentation several times in order to focus on the most important aspects and write down questions to take to class.
- **A third time** to check that the content has been understood. They watch without stopping while trying to practise the pronunciation and intonation of questions and statements.

If there are students who need to watch the video more than 3 times, encourage them to do so. The important thing is that **each student can work at their own pace and come to the class prepared**. This approach adapts to the learning process of each student.

3 The students **complete** the **Flipped task** that was explained by the teacher in the previous class. The **Flipped task** must be seen in the classroom so the teacher can check the student's understanding of the grammar rule shown in the video(s).

AT SCHOOL

4 When teaching the lesson where the grammar table appears, check that the grammar presentation(s) have been watched at home, the **Flipped task** completed and the content understood.

5 Resolve individual queries and help the students who still have problems with the grammar structures while the rest of their classmates focus on the **Student's Book** exercises individually or in pairs.

Projects

Project-based Learning

Project-based Learning is a method in which students learn through completing real-world projects. The project is completed over a period of time and is an opportunity for students to demonstrate their knowledge and skills and apply them in a practical context, as well as learning from each other.

During the project, the students also learn new skills through the vehicle of the project itself. These skills include not just linguistic skills, but also **higher-order thinking skills** such as **reasoning**, **problem solving** and **critical thinking**, and equally importantly **soft skills** such as **communication** and **collaboration**.

Collaborative Learning

Collaborative Learning is an approach in which groups of learners work together to complete a task, solve a problem or create a product. Collaborative tasks can be outlined and explained to the student; however, the responsibility for checking that tasks are understood and completed appropriately lies with them. Similarly, each participant in the group is responsible for not only their own actions, but the completion of the final product. This in turn encourages exploratory talk within the group into how the work will be completed.

Students are encouraged to **formulate and challenge ideas**, learn to manage and deliver **feedback** and develop **time management skills**. Group members work together to accomplish the shared learning goal, which encourages students to respect the abilities and contributions of their peers.

Unlike more dictated structures of team-based learning, consensus building in collaborative learning relies on cooperation by group members and their identification of the personality types in their group. This method empowers the students to take responsibility for their own learning process and develop their ability to communicate with others.

Project-based Learning and Collaborative Learning in NOW YOU!

Based on the principle that students learn best when engaged in meaningful tasks which involve knowledge, comprehension and production skills, **NOW YOU!** includes many activities which motivate students to use language meaningfully, communicatively and cooperatively.

Each **Project** in **NOW YOU!** is a natural space for **Project-based Learning** and **Collaborative Learning** skills. Students are asked to think carefully about the format of their project and to evaluate themselves and their peers, encouraging them to see the importance of effective collaboration. The tasks draw on the content of the lesson and in this way, students understand the purpose of the target language they are learning rather than understanding it as an isolated verbatim linguistic structure.

By drawing the students' attention to the accumulative nature of their work and the ways in which their own performance affects the members of their group, they also develop metacognitive skills. Students will become aware of their progress, and they will also be presented with concrete examples of how their new knowledge is useful to them.

Challenge-based Learning

Challenge-based Learning is a collaborative experience in which students identify and propose a solution, then implement and evaluate it, finally culminating in a public presentation of a final product. The holistic process encourages students to identify their approach to a problem, develop the material and then reflect on their learning process.

The framework for **Challenge-based Learning** was developed with a focus on real-world challenges. However, this specific skills process can be developed through any task which calls for students to reflect on the key steps involved in solving a problem. Students are called upon to identify an issue, ask appropriate questions to develop their understanding and then develop a method to complete the task. When faced with a challenge, successful groups are able to use their relevant experience, identify and employ available resources, develop a plan and find the best solution to the problem that is posed.

Challenge-based Learning in NOW YOU!

The **Projects** can be used as a vehicle for **developing Challenge-based Learning skills**. In order to do this, the teacher should invert the sequence of the presentation of the project tasks to the students as outlined below. In this way, students are encouraged to understand the importance of both the content and the method by which the final product is created. This will motivate the students' learning experience, help to develop their relevant soft skills and create learner autonomy. This method will also help the students to connect with the language they learn as they begin to understand the learning process as delivering them with useful building blocks for communication and not isolated linguistic content.

Using Challenge-based Learning skills to frame the Project experience

Before beginning each pair of units, direct the students to the **Recap** and **Final task** boxes on the **Project** pages (see the **Project** section of the **Unit walkthrough** on pages 16-17). Promote a discussion either as a class or in small groups about the **Final task** the students will be working towards. Encourage the students to think about the materials, knowledge and the types of personal qualities that will best help them to complete the task.

On page 26 you will find a list detailing ways in which the **Project tasks** can be adapted. This list can be shared with the students, and as a class they can decide the best way to complete the tasks for each particular project.

Once the students have engaged with the **Final task** and method in which they will complete the tasks, direct their attention back to the first lesson of the pair of units. Before you begin teaching each lesson, ask the students to read the contents of the **Project task** box. By framing their learning experience in this way, the students will come to understand their language learning in terms of its real-world application.

Projects

The benefits of projects

Encouraging students to work effectively in groups towards a final product has many benefits. The structured and practical tasks give students an immediate opportunity to practise the language and structures they have learnt during the lesson, which develops their **confidence** and **fluency**. These tasks also improve **motivation** due to the immediate, real world application of skills students have learnt on the page.

Projects provide a natural space for the development of **Mediation skills** (see pages 30-33). As students think together and work together in order to complete a project, they are given a space to grow their **social competence** and **self-esteem**. As students reflect on their contribution to the group's success or failure, they are also made aware of the need for **positive, supportive interactions**. Finally, the structure of the tasks themselves encourage **responsibility, learner independence** and **time management skills**.

How to use NOW YOU! Projects

The **Project tasks** that are woven through **NOW YOU!** can be found at the end of lessons 1, 2 and 5 of each unit. There are six tasks which are then brought together in a **Final task** which can be found on the **Project** pages at the end of the two units. Each **Project task** consolidates the material presented to the students during the lesson.

The instructions included in the task boxes outline the type of group the students will work in for the particular **Project**.Throughout the **Student's Book** there is a combination of group sizes, from pairs to groups of four. This is intended to encourage different group dynamics and avoid students working with the same classmates each time.

The **Projects** are themselves **optional, flexible, integrated** and **adaptable**. They are separated into these six, bitesize tasks so that the students are able to complete the **Project** in a controlled and efficient way, integrated into their class time. The tasks can, however, be used in various ways in class, as outlined in the following list.

Ways to use the Project tasks in class

- Students can complete each **Project task** as indicated in the **Student's Book**, consolidating the content of the lesson and building steadily towards the **Final task**.
- As above, but the teacher can choose to miss out or adapt **Project tasks** as dictated by available class time.
- Students can complete all three **Project tasks** together at the end of each unit as a method of reviewing the content, followed by the **Final task**.
- Students can complete all six **Project tasks** and the **Final task** together in one block of work after the two units.
- Teachers can use a discussion of the **Project tasks** as a vehicle for developing **Challenge-based Learning** skills; students will then complete them using their chosen method.
- All or some of the **Project tasks** can be completed by the groups outside of class time and later brought together or presented in the classroom.
- Alternatively, the **Project tasks** can be avoided altogether, in the case that students do not have available class time. This does not affect the progression of the material in the **Student's Book**.

The Final task

The culmination of the Project is the **Final task**, which consists of a **Recap** and **task summary**, instructions for the **Final Task**, a **Useful expressions** box, **21st century skills** and **Evaluation** boxes and a **Go beyond** section (see the **Project** section of the **Unit walkthrough** on pages 16-17).

The **Recap** section helps students understand the practical use of the grammar and vocabulary structures they have learnt. Similarly, the **task summary** in this initial section helps students to recall the material they have created. Teachers may wish to read this section with their students as they begin **Project task** 1 in order to motivate the students and help them understand their work in relation to the final product.

The **Final task** is the moment when students are encouraged to review, edit and refine the work they have completed over the previous two units. A **Useful expressions** box provides students with relevant language structures that will enable them to present their final product with confidence.

When students have all completed the **Final task**, they are provided with material which encourages them to reflect on their experience. This material can be found in the **21st century skills** and **Evaluation** boxes. For more information on how to use the **21st century skills box**, see pages 28-29. The rubric in the **Evaluation** box directs students to answer the questions included either in their groups after the **Final task** or during the presentations of their peers. This section encourages students to evaluate their individual or group performance and reflect on the learning process.

Finally, the **Go beyond** section includes a short text related to the material that the students have completed in order to bring a broader, real-world context to the content or form of the work they have created. This text can be used to stimulate further class discussion on the **Project** content.

The **Project notes** pages in the **NOW YOU! Workbook** work as an organiser and provide students with a visual presentation of how their work culminates to create the final product. This gradual building of a portfolio of work means that students can also compare their progress over the school year by looking back over the **Projects** they have completed.

21st century skills

What are 21st century skills?

Our world is changing before our eyes. Technological advances, societal and economic developments and a hyper-connected globalisation mean that our students face an exciting yet unpredictable future. The new technologies and types of employment they will encounter are unknown both to them and to us – the adults that shape their education. This poses the question: how can we effectively prepare our students for success in a future we cannot predict?

In answer to this question, educators and academics have identified certain skills as **21st century skills**; that is, soft skills which we can teach our students in order to better prepare them for the future, whatever it may hold.

A quick online search will render multiple definitions of the key **21st century skills**. However, most commonly these are understood in terms of **the 7 Cs**.

The 7 Cs of 21st century skills

- **Collaboration:** Teamwork, adaptability, cooperation, etc.
- **Communication:** Information literacy, ability to share thoughts and ideas, etc.
- **Creativity:** Innovation, productivity, identifying solutions, etc.
- **Critical thinking:** Problem solving, analysis, linking learning across subjects, etc.
- **Career and learning self-reliance:** Responsibility, initiative, self-direction, etc.
- **Computing:** Digital literacy, effective use of electronic tools, etc.
- **Cross-cultural understanding:** Respect for diversity, effective social interaction, etc.

21st century skills in NOW YOU!

Natural spaces for the development of these seven skill sets exist throughout **NOW YOU!**, for example in the **Culture videos** (cross-cultural understanding), **Project tasks** (collaboration) and **NOW YOU! exercises** (communication).

However, a clearly identified **21st century skills box** can be found on the **Project** pages. Here, a specific **21st century skill** that the students have developed during the completion of the **Project tasks** is identified and presented to the student, and the student's attention is drawn to the ways in which it is useful to them outside the classroom. For example, in a **Project** where students are called upon to conduct online research into an individual for a biography, the 21st century skill focus is fact checking.

Teachers who choose not to use the **Project pages** can, however, use this box independently.

In both cases, the teacher should encourage students to read the **21st century skills box** together and discuss their reactions as a class or in small groups. Productive discussion of the themes will include the teacher asking the students to identify their own strengths and weaknesses with regards to the particular skill. Students could also identify ways in which they can develop or apply the skill more effectively in their own lives.

21st century skills from the previous levels are then addressed in the **Get started!** unit of each subsequent level of **NOW YOU!** in order to refresh the student's memory. The connection of the **21st century skill** to a new context also highlights its broader use.

Each skill has been named with the student's understanding in mind, but can also be mapped onto **the 7 Cs** as detailed in the table below.

The benefits of teaching 21st century skills

Aside from the obvious future benefits of teaching students these types of skills, there are also clear implications in terms of **learner motivation**. Encouraging students to recognise and value abilities that are not knowledge-based leads to greater **self-esteem** and **acceptance of diversity**. Furthermore, these skills are intended to promote **learner independence**, develop **positive lifelong learning habits** and place value on **higher-order thinking skills**.

Project	21st century skill	From the 7 Cs
Units 1 & 2: School magazine	Negotiating	Collaboration
Units 3 & 4: Biography	Fact checking	Critical thinking
Units 5 & 6: Invention	Making connections	Creativity
Units 7 & 8: Eco-tourism holiday	Flexibility	Collaboration

CEFR mediation

What is Mediation?

COUNCIL OF EUROPE
CONSEIL DE L'EUROPE

The **Common European Framework of Reference for Languages** (CEFR) in 2001 defined mediation as facilitating cross-linguistic communication; they saw the language learner as a social agent acting between individuals with no common language.

The updated 2018 CEFR, however, gives the skill greater importance and takes a broader interpretation. It sees mediation as those key soft skills required for competent communication, the ability to **reformulate language to facilitate understanding**.

Rather than simply referring to the interpretation or translation of language, mediation is understood as a more meaningful act within the language learning experience. It is an act of interaction that **bridges reception and production**; that interaction can be **between individuals**, **between languages** or **language registers** or in a personal **act of processing language**.

In this way, mediation skills can be developed in a **monolingual learning environment** where use of L1 is not encouraged in the classroom.

The diagram on the next page shows all of the aspects of mediation recognised by the CEFR. There are three main categories of **mediation activities: mediating communication, mediating a text** and **mediating concepts**. Then there are **mediation strategies**, grouped separately because they can be used while doing the mediation activities. As with other skills, there is a range of **CEFR Mediation descriptors** for different levels. For example, in relaying information in speech a language user at B1 level 'can relay specific information given in straightforward informational texts'.

CEFR Mediation in NOW YOU!

NOW YOU! provides opportunities in every lesson for mediation activities and strategies to be developed and has a strong focus on mediation in the **Projects** and **Pairwork** sections.The **overviews** at the beginning of each unit in the **Teaching notes** indicate which **CEFR Mediation descriptors** apply to each lesson (see examples on pages 32-33).

Mediation activities and strategies

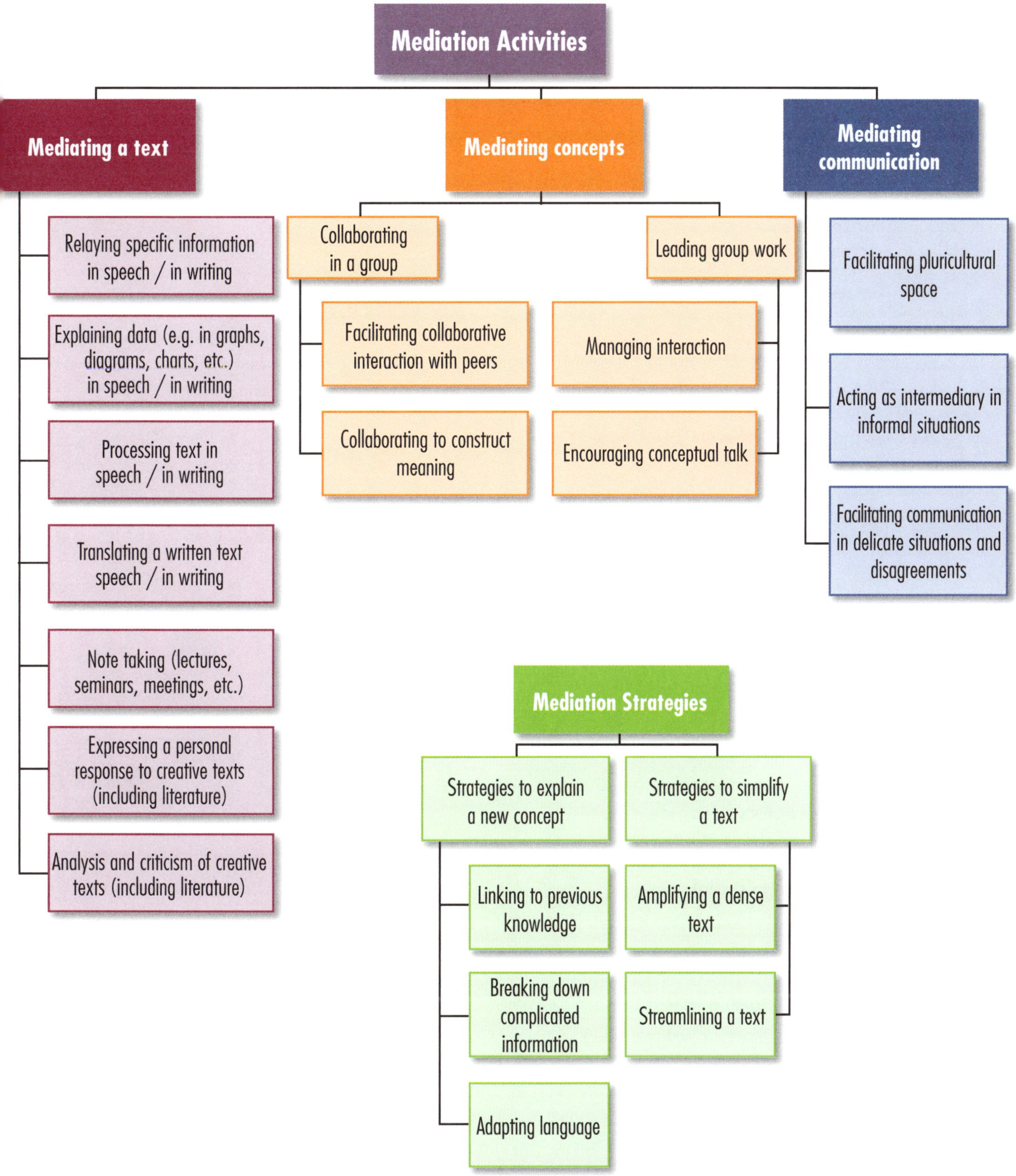

Taken from: Common European Framework of Reference for languages; learning, teaching, assessment Companion volume with new descriptors 2018

CEFR mediation

Main units

All the lessons in the main units of **NOW YOU!** offer students concrete opportunities to develop the **important transferable skills** defined in the **mediation descriptors** in order to become competent, confident communicators, as outlined in the descriptions and examples below.

Lessons 1 & 2 • Grammar, vocabulary & listening

NOW YOU! exercises provide practice for a wide range of mediation skills:
Note-taking
Can make simple notes about familiar subject matter.

Lesson 3 • Reading

Reading lessons develop skills for **mediating a text**:
Expressing a personal response to creative texts
Can describe a character's feelings and explain the reasons for them.
The **Core values** section provides further opportunities:
Facilitating communication in delicate situations and disagreements
Can recognise when difficulties occur in interaction and adapt simple phrases to seek compromise.

Lesson 4 • Writing

Exercises in the **Focus on** and **Did you notice?** sections also develop skills for **mediating a text**:
Processing text in writing
Can pick out and reproduce key words and phrases or short sentences from a short text.

Lesson 5 • Culture and communication

The **Culture video** and **Idioms and expressions** sections provide a space for students to develop skills for **mediating communication**:
Facilitating pluricultural space
Can help to develop a shared communication culture by exchanging information in a simple way about values and attitudes to language and culture.

Projects

The **Project tasks** and the **Final project** are a natural vehicle for Mediation skills concerned with **mediating concepts**; these are further divided into **collaborating in a group** and **leading group work**.

The below tables illustrate the integration of these and other **mediation skills** into the **NOW YOU! Projects**.

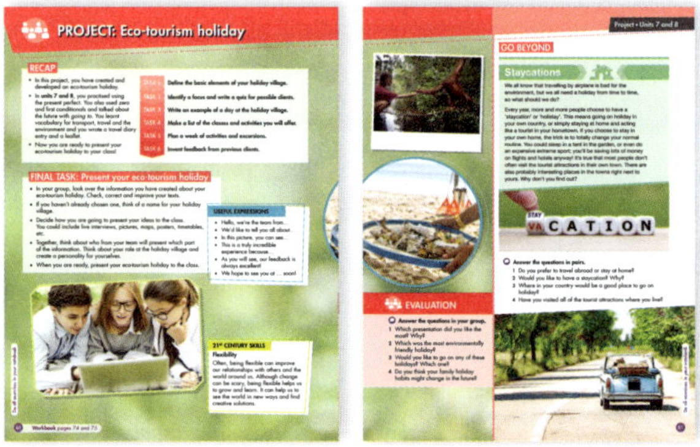

Projects • Student's Book 2	
Project	**A2 / B1 CEFR Mediation descriptors**
Units 1 & 2 School magazine	Processing text in speech Can summarise the main points made during a conversation on a subject of personal or current interest.
Units 3 & 4 Biography	Processing text in writing Can paraphrase short written passages in a simple fashion, using the original text wording and ordering.
Units 5 & 6 Invention	Relaying specific information in speech Can relay the point made in short, clear, simple messages, instructions and announcements.
Units 7 & 8 Eco-tourism holiday	Overall mediation Can convey relevant information contained in clearly structured, short, simple, informational texts.

Pairwork

The communicative, interactive nature of the **Pairwork section** creates a natural space for the development of **Mediation skills**.

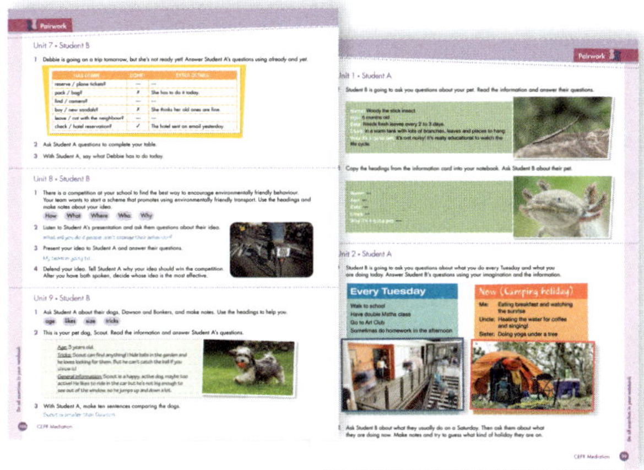

Pairwork • Student's Book 2	
Unit	**A2 / B1 CEFR Mediation descriptors**
Unit 1 Requesting information	Processing text in speech Can summarise the main point(s) in simple, short informational textson familiar topics.
Unit 2 Asking and answering questions	Relaying specific information in speech Can relay specific, relevant information contained in short, simple texts, labels and notices on familiar subjects.
Unit 3 Comparing information	Adapting language Can paraphrase short written passages in a simple fashion, using the original order of the text.
Unit 4 Summarising information	Processing text in speech Can convey the main point(s) contained in clearly structured, short, simple spoken and written texts.
Unit 5 Comparing ideas	Encouraging conceptual talk Can ask what somebody thinks of a certain idea.
Unit 6 Interpreting information	Relaying specific information in writing Can list the main points of short, clear, simple messages and announcements.
Unit 7 Completing information	Overall mediation Can convey the main point(s) involved in short, simple conversations or texts on everyday subjects of immediate interest.
Unit 8 Defending ideas	Facilitating collaborative interaction with peers Can collaborate in simple, practical tasks, asking what others think, making suggestions and understanding responses.
Unit 9 Comparing information	Overall mediation Can convey relevant information contained in clearly structured, short, simple, informational texts.

Plurilingualism

What is plurilingualism?

The **Common European Framework of Reference for Languages** defines plurilingualism as the ability of an individual to call flexibly upon an inter-related repertoire of linguistic experience and strategies to resolve a communicative situation in a given cultural context.

Because it is called on in a given cultural context, the CEFR points out that 'Plurilingualism has itself to be seen in the context of pluriculturalism. Language is not only a major aspect of culture, but also a means of access to cultural manifestations.'

Consequently, an individual will be competent in plurilingualism when he/she develops the ability to use all his/her linguistic knowledge and experience to achieve effective communication with an interlocutor that takes into account their cultural and linguistic background.

Plurilingualism at secondary level

Because of the transversal nature of plurilingualism, it is not considered necessary to define assessable competences at the level of compulsory secondary education, but it is important to **highlight plurilingual strategies** alongside other linguistic competences.

On the basis of the above, in compulsory secondary school we should focus on the development of plurilingualism in two areas:

1 a **knowledge of culture and traditions** in English-speaking regions (mealtimes, customs, habits, etc.)

2 **experience of communicative success** when an individual overcomes his/her fear of oral and written comprehension and expression

Plurilingualism with NOW YOU!

There are several features of **NOW YOU!** that offer students the opportunity to work on developing their plurilingual competences.

Culture and communication

These lessons offer students an opportunity to develop their plurilingual competences by **watching and responding to videos** about various different aspects, features and events of English-speaking cultures throughout the world, including Irish dancing, the Edinburgh Fringe Festival and the American barbecue. The lessons also include listening exercises involving **short talks and conversations** using frequent English **idioms** and a chance to practise the idioms in short **personalised speaking exercises**. Thus both aspects of plurilingualism as outlined above are developed in these lessons.

NOW YOU! exercises and Pairwork

The **NOW YOU! exercises** throughout each unit and the **Pairwork** activities at the end are designed to develop students' ability to communicate effectively in spoken and sometimes written English. In these exercises, students do activities like comparing what they do in their free time, describing other people, using newly acquired expressions in a conversation and writing a description of someone they admire, among others.

Point out to students that these are not just exercises for putting their linguistic knowledge into practice, but also for **building confidence** in and developing their ability to **communicate and interact** with each other using all their linguistic and communicative resources. In the spoken activities, encourage them to participate **without fear of embarrassment** and using whatever language and communicative strategies they have, including **paralinguistic strategies** like gestures and facial expressions, and asking a speaker to slow down to give them the chance to check that they have understood what the speaker is saying.

Projects

The **Projects** require students to collaborate to prepare and then present a final product. Providing students with this challenge **facilitates the transferral of communication strategies** learnt in their own language (and any other languages they speak) over to their English language competence and vice versa. These strategies, which are necessary for effective completion of the project, help build students' ability to communicate more effectively and confidently **in a range of real-life contexts** involving any language.

Other activities you can do in class to develop your students' plurilingual competence include:

- Showing them **TV programmes**, **films** or **plays** with a strong cultural element.
- **Extending speaking activities** in class to include longer class discussions and **other types of discourse** not already featured in the course: role-plays, formal interviews and debates, etc.
- Asking students to **identify similarities in grammar and vocabulary** between English and their own language (and indeed other languages) to help their linguistic ability and confidence.
- Using **digital communications resources** (like Skype, Zoom, Microsoft Teams, etc.) to help develop communication with students from other countries.
- Encouraging students to get involved in **collaborative projects with students or NGOs in other countries** to put the strategies they have learnt into practice in real-life situations.

Literature

What do we mean by literature?

Literature can be defined as the creative production and comprehension of written, spoken and audiovisual texts in an attempt to produce an emotional and/or intellectual reaction in the reader, listener or viewer.

Written literature at secondary level includes novels, short stories, written plays and essays, as well as comics, articles and blog entries.

Oral literature includes all recited or interpreted texts, such as poems, songs, dramatizations (sketches and short plays), and even tongue-twisters, rhymes, sayings and jokes.

Audiovisual literature refers to works that combine images and spoken or written text, such as cartoons, films, series, advertisements, videoclips, trailers, etc.

The benefits of teaching literature at secondary level

Literature provides us all with a **sense of community** and our place within it, and gives us tools to **express ourselves effectively** to other members of the community to **strengthen bonds** between us and help build our **sense of identity**, both individual and communal. Living in a global and multi-lingual community makes this more of a challenge but also more rewarding.

Focusing on English-language literature at secondary school helps students develop this sense of community and their **understanding of the world**, their **own culture** and their **own identity**.

It also helps develop their **skills** in and **enjoyment** of **reading**, **writing** and other forms of communication, as well as stimulating **creativity** and developing **critical thinking**.

At secondary level, students need to learn to **understand** and **assess** a variety of **literary texts** both adapted and authentic, and to be able to **orally reproduce literary texts** (oral literature) both adapted and authentic. They also need to be able to **express themselves** in ways that show an **awareness of literary culture** as defined above.

Literature in NOW YOU!

There are several features of **NOW YOU!** that offer students the opportunity to develop a healthy relationship with literature and to build on their literary skills.

Reading and Writing lessons

In the **Reading** and the **Writing** lessons, students encounter various **different text types**, including articles, stories, blog entries and descriptions of people and artworks, throughout the course. Both lessons provide students with the opportunity to **offer personal responses** to the texts. To help develop their literary skills, use this opportunity to **highlight literary devices and features** of the text, starting with those they found effective and pointing out any that you think worth remarking on. The **Writing lesson** has a specific **Did you notice?** section to help them **develop literary awareness** and to guide them in using relevant features of the model text to produce their own effective writing.

Vlogs and Culture videos

The **Vlogs** and the **Culture videos** are both typical examples of **21st century audiovisual literature**. They also include personal and cultural anecdotes, jokes and sayings to help students develop their knowledge of global literary culture, and the accompanying material gives them the opportunity to share their responses.

To **further exploit** the literary element of these videos videos, prepare extra questions that encourage students to respond to the content with reference to their own experience and cultural and literary knowledge, with a view to **preparing their own videos**, based on the content they have just seen and heard. Give them time to write scripts, prepare questions for other students to answer and then record themselves. Encourage them to include some literary content (even a joke or an anecdote) and to ask questions that require comprehension and interpretation of that content, as well as giving them the chance to express their opinions, feelings and thoughts in response to the videos.

You could also get students to **find a simple literary text** that is related to one of the videos and get them to **recite** or **dramatize** it. This could be a short poem or rap involving rhyme and metre, which help develop good word stress and pronunciation. Encourage supportive and constructive class feedback.

Graded readers

Richmond offers **a wide range of graded readers**, including adaptations of **classic literature** and **original short novels**, each with **audio CD, glossary** and **activities** designed to help comprehension and generate meaningful and informed responses to the content.

You could have your **class choose a reader** for everyone to read and dedicate some class time to do the related activities and discuss the story. We recommend that you encourage them to **discuss excerpts** that they have read or listened to, offering them whatever support they need to do this effectively. Provide them with valid models of literary assessment so that you can help them **develop literary assessment skills**. You could also get students to do **rewriting activities** to help build confidence and as basic training for more **independent writing**. Such tasks could include varying words or phrases, rewriting an excerpt as a different text type (e.g. a play or a speech), writing part of the story from a different character's perspective or writing an alternative ending.

The learning and interest acquired from lessons based around the one reader you chose as a class could then be used as a springboard for students to **each choose a reader or another literary text** to share with the class as a whole or in smaller groups. They could simply **give an assessment** of the work to share and discuss in order to see if it generates interest among their classmates, or perhaps **recite or interpret** it and prepare activities for their classmates to do in response. Encourage them to find something of particular interest to them individually and in any format and using whatever platforms they want, as long as it doesn't make it impractical for them to share their assessment in class.

Mixed-ability classes

The basics of Mixed-ability classes

To some extent, all classes are of mixed ability. Students have different levels of **knowledge** as well as **ability** and learn at **different speeds** and in **different ways**. It can be a challenge to manage a class where these differences are pronounced, a challenge that many teachers have to face. Some students may become stressed and demotivated because they find the class difficult while others in the same class are bored or frustrated because they find it easy and perhaps finish exercises very quickly. However, with a bit of planning, a few helpful strategies and judicious use of resources, teaching a mixed-ability group can be very rewarding for teachers and students alike.

Mixed-ability in NOW YOU!

The Student's Book

Collaborative Learning

With its strong focus on **Collaborative Learning**, **NOW YOU!** helps highlight the idea of language as a tool for communication, and communication as a collaborative activity with **all parties taking responsibility** for its success. With this methodology as the basis, the **Student's Book** provides a range of tools to develop students' skills across various levels and abilities.

The **The Projects**, **Pairwork** activities and **NOW YOU! speaking exercises** all help emphasise broader **communicative criteria** rather than just language accuracy as a way to grade speaking performance (see **Assessment** pages 40-41 for ideas on assessment criteria). They also **help identify students' strengths and weaknesses** and to help them recognise them **without fear of judgement**. For these activities, giving confident and strong students roles that enable them to share their knowledge and understanding with others gives students the **opportunity to help each other**. Students who are less confident can be encouraged to ask questions to check their understanding. Additionally, students who are confident in their knowledge are not always right and if other students are **encouraged to question their knowledge** it can help check accuracy, and develop critical thinking skills **and reinforce what students have learnt**.

Make students aware **all roles are important** in any group activity, for example timekeeper, materials distributor, note-taker, spokesperson, a nominated person to keep the group on task, etc. **Let them assign roles** within their groups where possible. This can be based on their strengths at first, but then encourage students to **swap** roles regularly so that all students can **learn a variety of skills** by practising them themselves and by observing their classmates demonstrating them. Offer and encourage support to all members of a group as much as possible.

Mixed-ability classes

Independent Learning

The **Student's Book** also contains tools to allow students to help themselves and to take ownership of their own learning journey.

For students at a lower level, the **Grammar tables** and **animations** provide a reference point when unsure or underconfident against which to check their learning. Similarly, the **Learning to learn tools** offer students strategies for developing their weaker skills. Make sure to always draw students' attention to these tools and encourage independent learning outside of the classroom. For students at a higher level, the **Fast finishers** exercises in lessons 1, 2, 3 and 5 of every unit give further personalised practice for students who finish exercises before the rest of the class. Check the work students produce in these exercises to make sure they are making the most of them and consider asking them to share their work if it could be of interest or use to rest of the class.

Flipped Learning

The integration of the **Flipped Learning** methodology throughout **NOW YOU!** provides students with further opportunities to **take control of their learning**, and to assimilate knowledge **at their own pace** and in their **own way** (see pages 20-23).

The Workbook

The **Workbook** contains lots of extra practice to help students **consolidate their knowledge**, including **more personalised NOW YOU! exercises** for students to write sentences at their own level of complexity to consolidate language points, and specific sections with **extra practice** for the **Grammar reference** and **Wordlist** at each level, which is ideal for mixed-ability classes. It also includes a **Reflect on your learning** section at the end of each unit so that students can **identify their own strengths and weaknesses** and know when and where to ask for guidance.

Teacher's Resources

The **Teacher's Resources** include **Grammar** and **Vocabulary** worksheets for each unit at **three levels**: Revision, Consolidation and Extension, from lowest to highest. There is also a series of tests including a **Diagnostic test** and then **tests at two levels** after each unit, each group of three units and at the end of the year (see **Assessment** pages 40-41). Thus a teacher can **determine their students' levels** at the start of the year and give them **level-appropriate tests** to monitor them throughout the year in a way that gives students a **sense of confidence and progress**. The worksheets are all also **editable** so they can be tailored to the needs of specific students or groups of students.

Assessment

The basics of assessment

In the context of secondary level English language learning, students can be assessed on their performance and progress by **regular tests and exams**, **continuous teacher assessment** and **self-assessment**. In the 21st century language classroom, students should be assessed not only on their language skills, but also on their **ability to use their language skills** in a wider context and on their capacity for **independent learning**, i.e. their ability to learn how to learn.

Assessment in NOW YOU!

Regular tests

The **Richmond Test Manager** offers a comprehensive battery of tests. There is a **Diagnostic test** you can use at the start of the year to assess students' knowledge and use of vocabulary and grammar before they start the course. Then there are **Unit tests**, **End-of-term tests** and an **End-of-year test** to assess students' vocabulary and grammar, as well as their listening, reading and writing skills. These exist at two levels (Consolidation and Extension) and each have a marking scheme that gives a total of 100. There are also **Speaking tests** at the same intervals. These have no marking scheme so as to allow flexibility in using them, but the following criteria could be used to give a mark: overall task completion, fluency, interaction and language (range, appropriacy and accuracy of vocabulary and grammar).

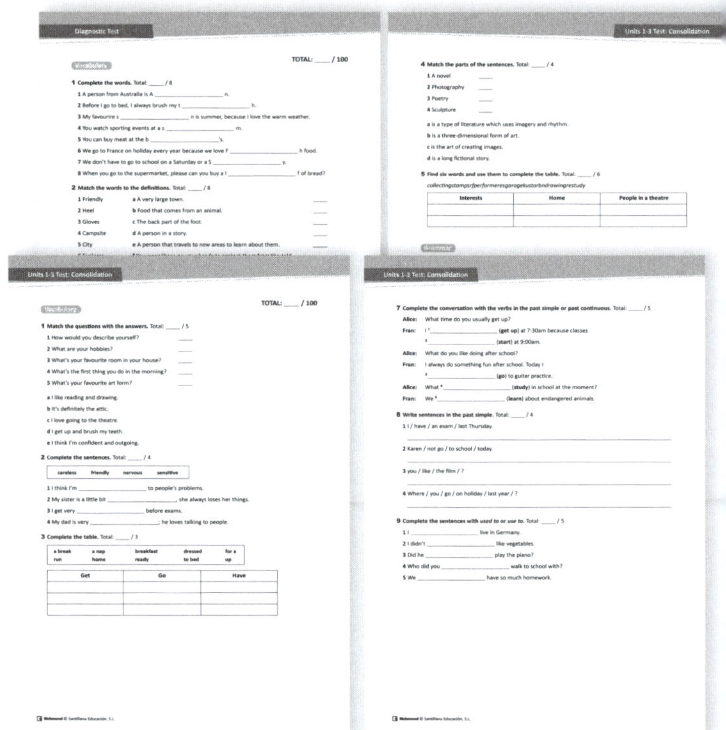

At the end of the main units in the **Student's Book**, there is also a **Review** for every unit. These offer further assessment of the language content of the unit in the **format of external exams** at the appropriate level.

Continuous assessment

For every lesson there is a **Continuous assessment** footer in the **Teacher's book** for the teacher to be mindful of as students go through the lesson. These are connected to the language and skills objectives of the lesson as outlined in the **overviews** at the start of each unit in the **Teaching notes**. It is a good idea to observe and keep records of all of the students' performances as best you can and offer support to those who need it. The **Writing** lessons require students to produce texts that can also be assessed more formally, perhaps using criteria you set specifically for each writing task or more general criteria you apply throughout, such as task completion, structure/linking, style, language range and language accuracy.

Self-assessment

At the end of every unit in the **Workbook**, there is a **Reflect on your learning** section in the **Communication and reflection** lesson. It offers students an opportunity to **assess their own abilities** in the relevant language points and skills areas. Make sure they understand that the purpose of this is to **build their confidence** in their knowledge and use of English and to **help improve** any areas of weakness. Use their assessments to offer material to help them in these areas. The **Teacher's Resources** offer such material at different levels to suit different students' support needs.

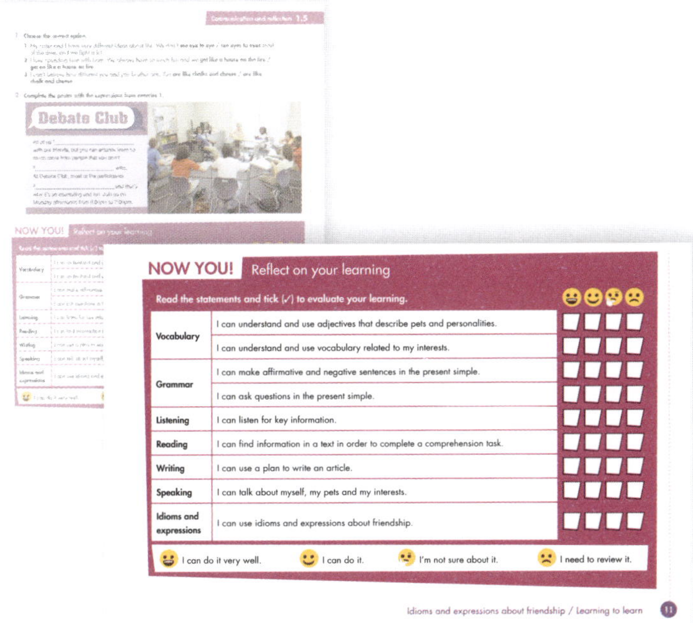

NOW YOU! Reflect on your learning

Read the statements and tick (✓) to evaluate your learning.

		😃	🙂	😕	☹️
Vocabulary	I can understand and use adjectives that describe pets and personalities.				
	I can understand and use vocabulary related to my interests.				
Grammar	I can make affirmative and negative sentences in the present simple.				
	I can ask questions in the present simple.				
Listening	I can listen for key information.				
Reading	I can find information in a text in order to complete a comprehension task.				
Writing	I can use a plan to write an article.				
Speaking	I can talk about myself, my pets and my interests.				
Idioms and expressions	I can use idioms and expressions about friendship.				

😃 I can do it very well. 🙂 I can do it. 😕 I'm not sure about it. ☹️ I need to review it.

Idioms and expressions about friendship / Learning to learn 11

There is also an opportunity for students to self-assess more informally in the **Evaluation** section of the **Project**. These activities allow students to **assess individual and team performance**, as well as their personal experience of bringing the project to completion.

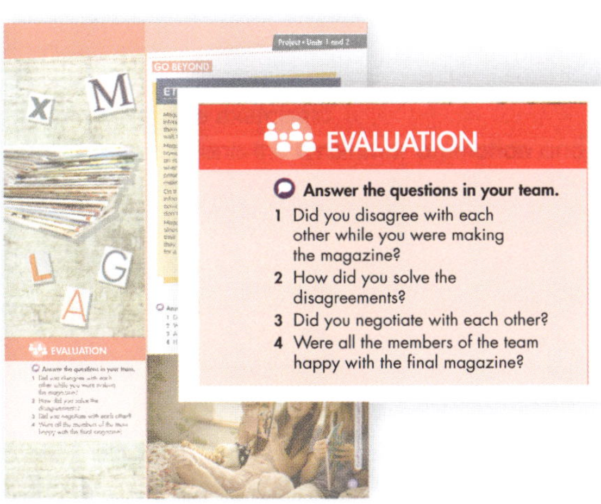

EVALUATION

Answer the questions in your team.

1 Did you disagree with each other while you were making the magazine?
2 How did you solve the disagreements?
3 Did you negotiate with each other?
4 Were all the members of the team happy with the final magazine?

It is a good idea to get students to keep a **self-assessment diary**, and their discussions in the **Project Evaluation** could be an opportune moment for them to start and continue the diary.

This diary could include a range of criteria on which students could assess themselves, including linguistic skills as well as other broader skills that **NOW YOU!** helps teach students.

These include the **21st century skills** on the **Project pages**, **the Core values** in the **Reading lessons**, **Learning to learn tools** throughout the book and **mediation skills** from the unit overviews in the **Teacher's Book**. You could make a list of these and get students to write what knowledge and skills they have acquired and developed, and which they want to work on. Encourage them to write how they feel about their learning and progress too. Collect these diaries at intervals to monitor students' awareness of their abilities, performance and development, as well as their morale and motivation.

Key competences

What are the Key competences?

Key competences combine the **knowledge**, **skills** and **attitudes** necessary to develop and achieve success as well being active **in all areas of social and civic life**. Each of the competences is equally important, and for that reason there are many shared goals which support and underpin one another. The basic skills of language, literacy, numeracy and information and communication technologies provide the foundation blocks for critical thinking, creativity, taking initiative, problem-solving, decision-making and management of feelings.

NOW YOU! works on these **Key competences** as set out by the European Commission.

LC Linguistic competence

This competence develops the use of language as a tool for communication. It involves understanding and producing oral and written messages and requires knowledge of vocabulary and grammar. The focus here is on understanding, expressing and interpreting a range of facts, opinions, thoughts and feelings in a variety of different contexts. Language skills students learn when studying a foreign language can be transferred to their native language and use of other languages, which enhances their plurilingual abilities.

MST Mathematical competence and basic competences in Science and Technology

The use of mathematical thinking to solve problems in everyday situations, scientific knowledge to explain the natural world and an understanding of technological principles are the focus of this competence. An awareness of the world around us and the effect we have on it are at the core. Introducing these competences into the language learning environment enriches the students' learning experience.

DC Digital competence

Digital competence involves the use of information technology as a way of researching, presenting and exchanging information. Students use computers, the internet, the interactive whiteboard, audiovisual material and other multimedia resources to enhance their own learning experience. They also learn to critically evaluate different information technologies and the content they provide access to.

SCC Social and Civic competences

These competences equip students with the necessary skills to participate fully in social and civic life on both a personal and interpersonal level. On a personal level, students focus on those skills needed to function effectively and constructively in everyday life, skills such as being able to know, express and assert themselves. Students also focus on values such as diversity, tolerance and understanding, which will help them become an active part of the local and wider community.

CAE Cultural awareness and expression

Studying a foreign language involves an awareness of the culture of the people that speak it, including their art, their food, their festivals and their customs, as well as a general sense of global culture. By learning about other cultures through reading texts, videos and discussions to share different cultural experiences, students also become more aware of their own culture and learn to express themselves creatively in a way that shows awareness of their cultural context, reinforcing their sense of the world and their place in it.

LL Learning to learn

Students need to develop effective strategies to improve their ability to learn independently. This means trying a variety of strategies to find ones which suit them and their learning styles, evaluating their own progress and thinking of ways to improve their ability to gain new knowledge and skills. Many of these strategies can be transferred to other subjects and learning contexts.

IE Sense of initiative and entrepreneurship

Creativity, innovation, risk-taking and the ability to plan and manage projects in order to achieve objectives form the core of this competence. Collaborative projects give students a range of contexts in which to demonstrate and develop these abilities. Success in this competence gives students skills that are transferable from the classroom directly to the workplace.

Key competences in the Student's Book

Linguistic competence	
Every page of the **Student's Book** is dedicated to this competence.	
Mathematical competence and basic competences in Science and Technology	
Get started page 9 **Unit 1** pages 10, 11, 14, 15 **Unit 2** pages 22-25 **Unit 3** pages 29, 32 **Unit 4** pages 36, 37, 39, 41, 42	**Unit 5** pages 46-55 **Unit 6** pages 57, 60 **Unit 7** pages 64, 65, 68 **Unit 8** pages 72-79 **Unit 9** pages 85-87
Digital competence	
Get started page 6 **Unit 1** pages 10, 11, 13, 17 **Unit 2** pages 18, 19, 21, 25 **Unit 3** pages 28, 29, 31, 35 **Unit 4** pages 36, 37, 39, 43	**Unit 5** pages 46, 47, 49, 53 **Unit 6** pages 54, 55, 57, 61 **Unit 7** pages 64, 65, 67, 71 **Unit 8** pages 72, 73, 75, 79 **Unit 9** pages 82, 83, 85, 89
Social and Civic competences	
Get started pages 6-9 **Unit 1** pages 15-17 **Unit 2** pages 18, 23, 25 **Unit 3** pages 32, 35 **Unit 4** pages 40, 41	**Unit 5** pages 50- 53 **Unit 6** pages 57-60 **Unit 7** pages 69, 71 **Unit 8** pages 72, 73, 75-79 **Unit 9** pages 83-89
Cultural awareness and expression	
Get started pages 6, 9 **Unit 1** pages 10-17 **Unit 2** pages 22, 23, 25 **Unit 3** pages 28-35 **Unit 4** pages 40, 41, 43	**Unit 5** pages 51, 53 **Unit 6** pages 59, 61 **Unit 7** pages 64-71 **Unit 8** pages 72, 73, 75-79 **Unit 9** pages 82-89
Learning to learn	
Get started page 7, **Unit 1** pages 10, 12, 14, 16, 17 **Unit 2** pages 19, 20, 23-25 **Unit 3** pages 28, 30, 32, 34, 35 **Unit 4** pages 36, 38, 40, 42, 43	**Unit 5** pages 46, 49, 50, 52, 53 **Unit 6** pages 56-58, 60, 61 **Unit 7** pages 65, 67, 68, 70, 71 **Unit 8** pages 74-76, 78, 79 **Unit 9** pages 83-84, 87, 89
Sense of initiative and entrepreneurship	
Get started pages 7, 8 **Unit 1** pages 11, 13, 16 **Unit 2** pages 20, 21, 24 **Unit 3** pages 29, 31, 34 **Unit 4** pages 37, 39, 42	**Unit 5** pages 47, 49, 52 **Unit 6** pages 55, 57, 60 **Unit 7** pages 65, 67, 70 **Unit 8** pages 73, 75, 78 **Unit 9** pages 83, 85, 88

CONTENTS NOW YOU! 2

GET STARTED!

At the start of each unit and lesson, explain to the students what the objectives are.

Language objectives

Grammar

There is* and *There are

- Students review and practise *There is* and *There are* to talk about the existence and location of things.

Quantifiers

- Students review and practise quantifiers in questions and answers.

Possessive adjectives

- Students review and practise possessive adjectives.

Subject pronouns

- Students review and practise subject pronouns.

Countable and uncountable nouns

- Students review and practise the use of countable and uncountable nouns.

Demonstrative pronouns

- Students review and practise demonstrative pronouns.

Vocabulary

Clothes and patterns: *belt, boots, cap, flowers/flowery, football strip, gloves, hat, jacket, jeans, jumper, pattern/patterned, scarf, shoes, shorts, skirt, socks, spots/spotty, stripes/stripy, suit, sunglasses, swimsuit, tartan, tie, trainers, trousers*

- Students review the vocabulary for clothes and patterns.

Greetings: *Good morning., How are you today?, I'm very well, thank you., I'd like to introduce…, Nice to meet you., It was lovely to meet you.*

- Students review greetings and introductions.

Hobbies: *basketball, folk music, gardening, pop music, rollerblading, surfing, watching films*

- Students review vocabulary for hobbies.

Food and units of measurement: *banana, bowl, box, bread, butter, cabbage, carrot, cereal, dairy, dish, eggs, fats, fruit, grains, gram, kilo, loaf, meat, milk, oil, protein, rice, salt, snack, spicy, spoonful, vegetarian*

- Students review vocabulary for food and units of measurement.

21st century skills objectives

Collaboration

- Students discuss and reflect on skills needed for effective collaboration.

Communication

- Students discuss and reflect on the importance of good communication skills.

Cultural awareness

- Students discuss and reflect on cultural awareness and culture shock.

Audiovisual objectives

Meet the vloggers: Student's watch and listen to Emma, George and Sarah talk about their summer holidays.

Key competences

LC **Linguistic**
pages 6-9

MST **Mathematical and Science and Technology**
pages 9

DC **Digital**
pages 6

SCC **Social and Civic**
pages 6-9

CAE **Cultural awareness and expression**
pages 6, 9

LL **Learning to learn**
pages 7

IE **Sense of initiative and entrepreneurship**
pages 7, 8

→ See pages 42-43 **Key competences**

CEFR Mediation

Facilitating collaborative interaction with peers
Can make and respond to suggestions and ask if others agree.
Can help work towards a common goal by asking and answering questions.

Relaying information in writing
Can relay specific information contained in spoken texts on familiar subjects..

Collaborating to construct meaning
Can make simple remarks and pose occasional questions to show that he/she is following.
Can make suggestions in a simple way to move the discussion forward.

Encouraging conceptual talk
Can ask what somebody thinks of an idea.

→ See pages 30-33 **Mediation**

Remind students to do all the exercises in their notebook

GET STARTED!

In this unit you will:
- get to know the vloggers.
- review grammar structures you have learnt.
- activate the vocabulary you know.
- reflect on key 21st century skills.

Language review

MEET THE VLOGGERS

1 Discuss the questions.
1 Did you go to a camp during the summer holidays?
2 Do you have friends from a different country?
3 Do you like to try new or unusual kinds of food? Why?
4 What are you looking forward to this year at school?

2 Choose the correct option.

Emma did some [1] **interesting / interested** activities at sports camp this year. She had a great time and made [2] **much / lots of** new friends. The sports camp had [3] **a few / few** different sports, like rugby, football and [4] **tennis / swim**. She also learnt a lot about working in a team with her friends.

3 Complete the text with the verb in the correct form.

Sarah's family [1]… (**not go**) away on holiday this year, they [2]… (**stay**) at home. Sarah is happy because her new neighbours [3]… (**be**) very interesting people. After she [4]… (**break**) the ice, she discovered that they [5]… (**have**) lots of stories to tell her about their lives.

4 Use the words to complete the text.

aware culture fascinating holiday perfect

George went on a fantastic [1]… to South Korea with his family. He found out a lot about Korean [2]… and really enjoyed the food. He learnt that being [3]… of other people's cultures is [4]…, and delicious too! He also learnt how to use chopsticks to eat with; practice makes [5]…!

5 Complete the headings below with information about yourself.

Name: …
What I did in the summer holidays: …
How I feel about this school year: …

6 NOW YOU! Share your answers from exercise 5 in groups of four.

Do all exercises in your notebook

6 Get to know Emma, Sarah and George.

ANSWER KEY

Page 6

1 *Student's own answers*

2
1 interesting
2 lots of
3 a few
4 tennis

3
1 didn't go
2 stayed
3 are
4 broke
5 had

4
1 holiday
2 culture
3 aware
4 fascinating
5 perfect

5 *Student's own answers*

6 *Student's own answers*

LESSON FOCUS

Grammar Present and past simple
Vocabulary Interests, culture and holidays
Speaking Comparing experiences of the summer holidays and feelings about the coming school year.

Resources
Teacher's i-solutions, Student's Book audio, Vlog and worksheets

MEET THE VLOGGERS

Video and worksheet available on the Richmond Learning Platform

- In pairs, ask students to complete the *Before you watch…* exercises on the vlog worksheet.
- Show students the vlog and ask them to complete the *While you watch…* exercises on the worksheet.
- In pairs, students compare answers.
- In small groups, tell students to complete the *After you watch…* exercises on the worksheet.

Warmer

Tell students that you are going to tell them 3 simple things about yourself but that one is not true, and they have to guess the lie. Put the students in pairs or small groups to repeat the activity.

1 Get the students to leave their books closed and dictate the questions. Then get them to open their books and check their questions before asking them in pairs or small groups.

2, 3 and 4 Put students into groups of three. When they've finished, write the answers to all three exercises on the board and get them to write them in their notebooks. Then each group of three could test how much the person who did the exercise remembers of the text with his/her book closed, using their books to prompt him/her. You could also get them to test each other's memory of all of the vloggers by reading facts about them for the others to guess.

5 Encourage students to write as much as they can and help them with any vocabulary they need.

6 NOW YOU! Tell students that a member from each group will give their group's answers to the class and encourage them to give extended answers and to listen carefully to each other.

Remind students to do all the exercises in their notebook

 CONTINUOUS ASSSESMENT Students can understand people writing about different things they did on their summer holidays.

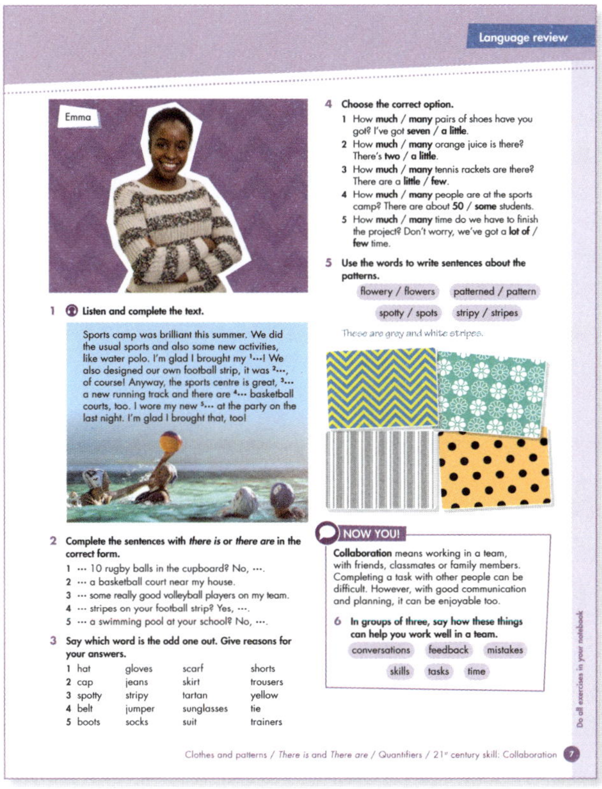
Language review

Emma

1 Listen and complete the text.

Sports camp was brilliant this summer. We did the usual sports and also some new activities, like water polo. I'm glad I brought my [1]…! We also designed our own football strip, it was [2]…, of course! Anyway, the sports centre is great, [3]… a new running track and there are [4]… basketball courts, too. I wore my new [5]… at the party on the last night. I'm glad I brought that, too!

2 Complete the sentences with *there is* or *there are* in the correct form.
1 … 10 rugby balls in the cupboard? No, ….
2 … a basketball court near my house.
3 … some really good volleyball players on my team.
4 … stripes on your football strip? Yes, ….
5 … a swimming pool at your school? No, ….

3 Say which word is the odd one out. Give reasons for your answers.

1 hat	gloves	scarf	shorts
2 cap	jeans	skirt	trousers
3 spotty	stripy	tartan	yellow
4 belt	jumper	sunglasses	tie
5 boots	socks	suit	trainers

4 Choose the correct option.
1 How **much** / **many** pairs of shoes have you got? I've got **seven** / **a little**.
2 How **much** / **many** orange juice is there? There's **two** / **a little**.
3 How **much** / **many** tennis rackets are there? There are a **little** / **few**.
4 How **much** / **many** people are at the sports camp? There are about **50** / **some** students.
5 How **much** / **many** time do we have to finish the project? Don't worry, we've got a **lot of** / **few** time.

5 Use the words to write sentences about the patterns.

flowery / flowers patterned / pattern spotty / spots stripy / stripes

These are grey and white stripes.

NOW YOU!

Collaboration means working in a team, with friends, classmates or family members. Completing a task with other people can be difficult. However, with good communication and planning, it can be enjoyable too.

6 In groups of three, say how these things can help you work well in a team.

conversations feedback mistakes skills tasks time

Do all exercises in your notebook

Clothes and patterns / *There is* and *There are* / Quantifiers / 21st century skill: Collaboration 7

LESSON FOCUS

Grammar *There is* and *There are*; Quantifiers
Vocabulary Clothes and patterns
Listening Listening and completing a text
Speaking A discussion about collaboration
21st Century skill Students discuss and reflect on the skill and value of collaboration and evaluate factors that help us work in teams.

Resources
Teacher's i-solutions, Student's Book audio
Preparation Some photos of celebrities wearing a range of different clothes

Warmer

Put the photos of celebrities where students can see them. Put students in pairs or small groups and ask them to describe one for the others to guess. Alternatively (if the students don't wear a uniform) get them to describe their classmates.

1 1.1 (See page 168 for transcripts) Tell students they will listen to Emma talk about her summer camp and ask what sport the people are playing in the photo (water polo). Give them time to read the text before they listen. Ask if the camp sounds like fun.

2 Point out that there are questions and negative forms in the sentences. Extend the exercise by asking students questions about the sports facilities at your school or in your area.

3 Do the first item as a class to make sure students understand.

4 After students complete the exercise, you could summarise by drawing a table of countable and uncountable nouns and which expressions are used with each category.

5 If any of the celebrity photos involve patterns, extend the exercise by getting students to describe them.

6 NOW YOU! Read the paragraph on collaboration together and ask what difficulties collaboration can bring. For example: some people can dominate, some might not pull their weight, difficulties communicating ideas, making sure everyone's involved, it can be hard to recognise and to make the most of different people's strengths. After students complete the exercise, ask volunteers to tell the class which ideas their group came up with.

ANSWER KEY

Page 7

1
1 swimsuit
2 stripy
3 there is
4 a few
5 jacket

2
1 Are there; there aren't
2 There is
3 There are
4 Are there; there are
5 Is there; there isn't

3
1 shorts – you wear the others in the winter
2 cap – you wear the others on your legs
3 yellow – the others are patterns
4 jumper – the others are accessories
5 suit – the others go on your feet

4
1 many; seven
2 much; a little
3 many; few
4 many; 50
5 much; lot of

5 *Student's own answers*

6 *Student's own answers*

Remind students to do all the exercises in their notebook

CONTINUOUS ASSESSMENT Students can use *There is* and *There are*, and quantifiers and vocabulary for clothes and patterns.

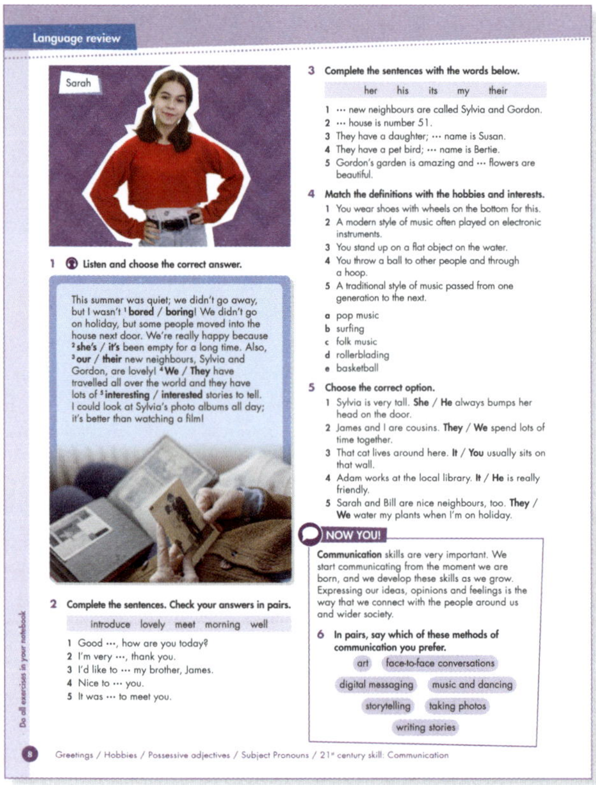

Language review

Sarah

1 Listen and choose the correct answer.

This summer was quiet; we didn't go away, but I wasn't [1] **bored / boring**! We didn't go on holiday, but some people moved into the house next door. We're really happy because [2] **she's / it's** been empty for a long time. Also, [3] **our / their** new neighbours, Sylvia and Gordon, are lovely! [4] **We / They** have travelled all over the world and they have lots of [5] **interesting / interested** stories to tell. I could look at Sylvia's photo albums all day; it's better than watching a film!

2 **Complete the sentences. Check your answers in pairs.**

introduce lovely meet morning well

1 Good ···, how are you today?
2 I'm very ···, thank you.
3 I'd like to ··· my brother, James.
4 Nice to ··· you.
5 It was ··· to meet you.

3 **Complete the sentences with the words below.**

her his its my their

1 ··· new neighbours are called Sylvia and Gordon.
2 ··· house is number 51.
3 They have a daughter; ··· name is Susan.
4 They have a pet bird; ··· name is Bertie.
5 Gordon's garden is amazing and ··· flowers are beautiful.

4 **Match the definitions with the hobbies and interests.**

1 You wear shoes with wheels on the bottom for this.
2 A modern style of music often played on electronic instruments.
3 You stand up on a flat object on the water.
4 You throw a ball to other people and through a hoop.
5 A traditional style of music passed from one generation to the next.

a pop music
b surfing
c folk music
d rollerblading
e basketball

5 **Choose the correct option.**

1 Sylvia is very tall. **She / He** always bumps her head on the door.
2 James and I are cousins. **They / We** spend lots of time together.
3 That cat lives around here. **It / You** usually sits on that wall.
4 Adam works at the local library. **It / He** is really friendly.
5 Sarah and Bill are nice neighbours, too. **They / We** water my plants when I'm on holiday.

NOW YOU!

Communication skills are very important. We start communicating from the moment we are born, and we develop these skills as we grow. Expressing our ideas, opinions and feelings is the way that we connect with the people around us and wider society.

6 **In pairs, say which of these methods of communication you prefer.**

art · face-to-face conversations · digital messaging · music and dancing · storytelling · taking photos · writing stories

Do all exercises in your notebook

8 Greetings / Hobbies / Possessive adjectives / Subject Pronouns / 21st century skill: Communication

ANSWER KEY

Page 8

1 **1** bored
2 it's
3 our
4 They
5 interesting

2 **1** morning
2 well
3 introduce
4 meet
5 lovely

3 **1** my
2 their
3 her
4 its
5 his

4 **1** d **2** a **3** b **4** e **5** c

5 **1** She
2 We
3 It
4 He
5 They

6 *Student's own answers*

LESSON FOCUS

Grammar Possessive adjectives; Subject pronouns
Vocabulary Greetings; Hobbies
Listening Listening to choose options
Speaking A discussion about communication
21st century skill Students discuss and reflect on the importance of communication skills and on their preferred methods of communication.

Resources
Teacher's i-solutions, Student's Book audio

Warmer

Describe a hobby to the class – what you need to do it and what it involves – and have students guess what it is. Students can continue the activity in pairs or small groups.

1 1.2 (See page 168 for transcripts) Tell students they please adjust line spacing Sarah talk about her summer at home. Get them to read the text before they listen and guess the correct option. Ask what you can do during a holiday at home.

2 To extend the exercise, get students to practise the sentences as a short conversation in groups of three, changing some of the words as appropriate and putting on different dramatic voices to make it more interesting for them.

3 Make sure that students understand all the sentences refer to Sylvia and Gordon from the text in exercise 1.

4 Ask students if they like any of the activities mentioned.

5 You could extend this exercise by testing students. Give names for them to find the pronouns for, from their perspective (*Jim – he; My family and I – you; All of you – us*).

6 NOW YOU! Read the paragraph on communication together and ask students to do the exercise, making sure they give reasons for their preferences. Ask volunteers to share their group's preferences and reasons, and discuss as a class what skills are needed for the different means of communication.

Remind students to do all the exercises in their notebook

 CONTINUOUS ASSESSMENT Students can give greetings, recognise and describe hobbies, and use possessive adjectives and subject pronouns

Language review

George

1 Listen and complete the text.

This summer was absolutely amazing. We went on holiday to Seoul, the capital of South Korea! There are so [1]··· interesting buildings to see and cool things to do, but my favourite thing was the food. It's so [2]···, and delicious! There's usually a [3]··· kimchi on the table. Kimchi is a spicy cabbage dish. Often, there isn't [4]··· dairy in Korean food, but there's nearly always [5]··· rice, even for breakfast!

2 Complete the sentences. Compare your answers in pairs.

1 I ate a bowl of cereal for breakfast this morning. I didn't eat ··· rice.
2 No, there ··· any butter on the table.
3 This is a good place to eat because there ··· lots of restaurants nearby.
4 There is ··· meat on the menu, but many dishes are vegetarian.
5 I usually have ··· banana for a snack.

3 Match the units of measurement with the correct food.

1 A box of — a meat.
2 A spoonful of — b oil.
3 A gram of — c bread.
4 A kilo of — d salt.
5 A loaf of — e eggs.

4 Choose the correct option.

1 **These** / **This** are the three best places to visit.
2 Here we are! **That** / **This** is the famous communication tower.
3 **That** / **Those** are my shoes. Take them off!
4 Whose suitcase is **that** / **this**, over there?
5 **These** / **This** isn't our hotel. We got off at the wrong bus stop!

5 Copy and complete the table in pairs.

Grains	Fruit and vegetables	Dairy	Fats	Protein
rice	carrots	milk	···	···
···	···	···	···	···

NOW YOU!

We all know that people around the world look, dress, speak and act differently. **Cultural awareness** helps us to understand these differences and treat others with respect. However, these differences sometimes affect us more than we expect when we travel and can make us experience confusion or anxiety known as 'culture shock'.

6 In groups of four, say how these things affect you when you travel.

buildings clothes food language social rules

Do all exercises in your notebook

Food and units of measurement / Countable and uncountable nouns / Demonstrative pronouns / 21st century skill: Cultural awareness 9

LESSON FOCUS

Grammar Countable and uncountable nouns; Demonstrative pronouns

Vocabulary Food and units of measurement

Listening Listening and completing a text

Speaking A discussion of cultural awareness

21st century skill Students discuss and reflect on cultural awareness and aspects of different cultures that can result in culture shock when travelling.

Resources

Teacher's i-solutions, Student's Book audio

Warmer

Put students in pairs and ask them to talk about their favourite foods. Ask them to tell you about the strangest food they have tried and whether or not they liked it.

1 1.3 (See page 168 for transcripts) Tell students that they will hear George talk about his holiday in Seoul and ask where it is (South Korea). Let them read the text before you play the audio and guess possible answers. Ask them if they know about Korean food and whether they like it or if it appeals to them.

2 Tell students to use only one word in their answers. Ask them to identify all the countable and uncountable nouns in the exercise.

3 Check that students understand the units of measurement and offer different examples to explain ones they don't know.

4 You could draw a table on the board to illustrate which demonstrative pronouns are for singular nouns and which for plural, which are for things close to the speaker and which are for things far away.

5 Give students a time limit and help with any vocabulary they don't know. Elicit examples to put on the board for students to copy.

6 NOW YOU! Read the paragraph on cultural awareness together and ask if any students have experienced culture shock. Encourage students to give specific examples of the things that affect them when they travel or to draw on their imaginations for places they've seen on TV or online. Ask if anyone can think of any useful lessons their country could learn from other cultures.

ANSWER KEY

Page 9

1
1 many
2 healthy
3 bowl of
4 any
5 some

2
1 any
2 isn't
3 are
4 some
5 a

3
1 e
2 b
3 d
4 a
5 c

4
1 These
2 This
3 Those
4 That
5 This

5 *Student's own answers*

6 *Student's own answers*

Remind students to do all the exercises in their notebook

CONTINUOUS ASSESSMENT Students can use countable and uncountable nouns, demonstrative pronouns, vocabulary for food and units of measurement.

1 ALL ABOUT ME

At the start of each unit and lesson, explain to the students what the objectives are.

Language objectives

Grammar

Present simple: affirmative and negative
- Students practise using the affirmative and negative forms of the present simple.

Present simple: questions
- Students practise forming *wh-* and *yes/no* questions with the present simple.

Vocabulary

Adjectives: *big, brainy, clever, colourful, cool, curious, energetic, enormous, heavy, inquisitive, lazy, noisy, slow, vibrant, weighty, wonderful*
- Students practise using synonyms and antonyms to describe pets.

Interests: *collecting, drawing, hobbies, instrument, models, playing the guitar/violin, reading comics, watching films*
- Students practise asking each other questions about their hobbies and interests.

Personality traits: *active, agreeable, careless, cautious, challenging, compassionate, confident, conscientious, consistent, detached, easy-going, efficient, extroverted, friendly, inventive, nervous, neurotic, open to experiences, organised, outgoing, reserved, secure, sensitive, solitary*
- Students discuss and evaluate personality traits.

Idioms and expressions

Friendship: *see eye to eye, get on like a house on fire, be like chalk and cheese*
- Students look at idioms and expressions related to relationships and complete sentences in context.

Recycled language

Hobbies, Adjectives, Subject pronouns

Skills objectives

Speaking

- Students discuss animals and pets.
- Students talk about superheroes.
- Students interview one another about their hobbies.
- Students discuss and evaluate different personality types.
- Students talk about relationships and communication.

Pronunciation: Students practise words with the /eə/ and /ɪə/ sounds.

Pairwork: Students use various mediation techniques in order to find out more about each other's pets.

Listening

- Students listen and complete descriptions of pets and their personalities.
- Students listen and complete descriptions of other animals.
- Students listen and complete a conversation about hobbies and interests.
- Students listen to answer a quiz about superheroes.
- Students listen and complete information about hobbies and ambitions.

Reading

- Students read a text to identify the main issues being addressed.
- Students engage with a text to answer in depth questions about the issues addressed.
- Students categorise words in a text and check understanding of their meanings.

Core values: Students discuss acts of **altruism** and how important they are in everyday life.

Writing

- Students write a summary about personality types using photographs as a prompt.
- Students plan, write and check an article about a person who does charity work.

Focus on linking language: *as well as, too, and, including, but, also, like, although, such as*

Remind students to do all the exercises in their notebook

Learning to learn tools

SPEAKING TOOLS Students consolidate knowledge by using new expressions in speech.	**LISTENING TOOLS** Students practise reading a text in advance to improve their listening comprehension.
READING TOOLS Students practise using headings and linking language to help understand a text.	**WRITING TOOLS** Students use planning and paragraphs to improve the focus of their writing.

VOCABULARY TOOLS Students expand their vocabulary by learning synonyms and antonyms..

Project objectives: School magazine

Task 1 Students research and write about different aspects of pet care.

Task 2 Students create a multiple-choice quiz on a topic of their choosing.

Task 3 Students plan and write a profile for each member of their group.

Audiovisual objectives

Vlog: Students watch and listen to Sarah talk about her new pet.

Culture: Students watch and listen to Sarah talk about the Isle of Man.

Grammar animations: Students are presented with visual presentations of the unit grammar.

Key competences

LC **Linguistic**
pages 10-17

MST **Mathematical and Science and Technology**
pages 10, 11, 14, 15

DC **Digital**
pages 10, 11, 13, 17

SCC **Social and Civic**
pages 15-17

CAE **Cultural awareness and expression**
pages 10-17

LL **Learning to learn**
pages 10, 12, 14, 16, 17

IE **Sense of initiative and entrepreneurship**
pages 11, 13, 16

→ See pages 42-43 **Key competences**

CEFR Mediation

1.1 Relaying information in speech
Can relay the point made in short, simple messages.

1.2 Facilitating collaborative interaction with peers
Can ask what others think, making suggestions and understanding responses.

1.3 Processing text in writing
Can pick out and reproduce short sentences from a text.

1.4 Processing text in writing
Can pick out and reproduce key words and phrases from a short text.

1.5 Relaying information in writing
Can list names and simple information in short spoken texts.

Project Facilitating collaboration with peers
Can ask what others think, make suggestions and understand responses.

Unit review Collaborating to construct meaning
Can make simple remarks and ask questions to show that he/she is following.

Pairwork Relaying specific information in speech
Can relay specific information in short, simple texts on familiar subjects.

→ See pages 30-33 **Mediation**

Remind students to do all the exercises in their notebook

1.1 Vocabulary and listening

1 ALL ABOUT ME

In unit 1 you will:

- talk about yourself, your pets and your interests.
- review present simple structures.
- practise asking questions.
- write an article about a celebrity.

1.1 Vocabulary and listening

SARAH'S VLOG: It's a girl!

Discuss the questions.

1 List three pets you would like to have.
2 Which animal wouldn't you like to have as a pet?
3 Is it better to adopt or buy a pet? Why?

Flipped Learning

1 Listen and choose the correct option.

1 Hi, my name is Jenny. This is my budgie. Isn't he **colourful** / **heavy**? His name is Yakyak because he's so **wonderful** / **noisy**! He's really **energetic** / **slow**. He loves flying around the house!

2 I'm called Adam and this is my Lizard, a bearded dragon called Dracky. She's **noisy** / **curious** and she likes to investigate, but she's a bit **lazy** / **clever**. She likes to lie in the sun all day long.

VOCABULARY TOOLS

When you learn a new word, try to learn an antonym or a synonym too. This will help you understand the meaning and also learn more words.

2 Match the words to their synonyms and antonyms.

1 colourful	a inquisitive	i unintelligent
2 curious	b enormous	ii tiny
3 heavy	c brainy	iii dull
4 clever	d weighty	iv uninterested
5 big	e vibrant	v light

3 Hello, I'm Kathleen, but you can call me Kath. This is my pet rat, Clark. Some people don't like rats, but actually they are very **clever** / **colourful** animals. They can learn some really **lazy** / **cool** tricks, too!

4 Hiya, my name's Matt but my nickname is MJ. My turtle is Tim. He's not very big but he is **heavy** / **energetic**! He's a bit **slow** / **cool**, of course, but he's a **wonderful** / **curious** pet.

FAST FINISHERS Write a paragraph about your dream pet.

Do all exercises in your notebook

10 Adjectives / Present simple: affirmative and negative

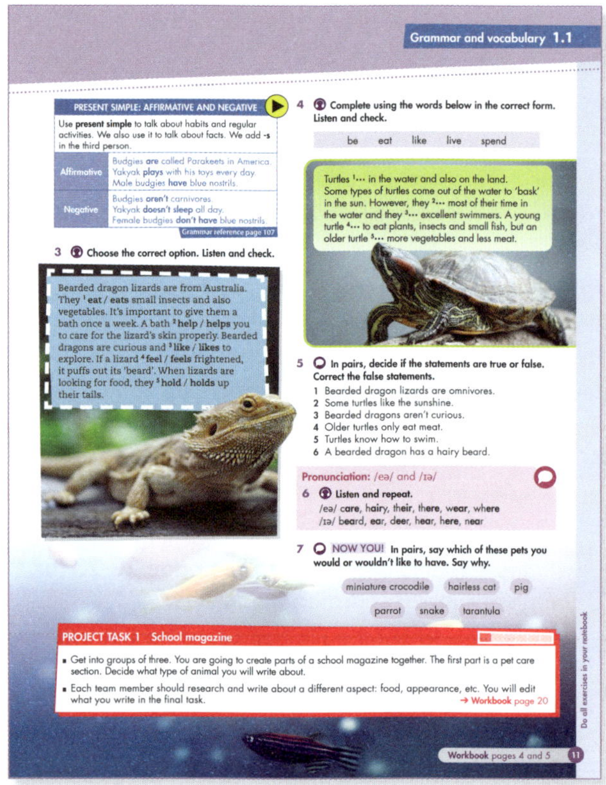

Grammar and vocabulary 1.1

PRESENT SIMPLE: AFFIRMATIVE AND NEGATIVE

Use **present simple** to talk about habits and regular activities. We also use it to talk about facts. We add **-s** in the third person.

Affirmative	Budgies **are** called Parakeets in America. Yakyak **plays** with his toys every day. Male budgies **have** blue nostrils.
Negative	Budgies **aren't** carnivores. Yakyak **doesn't sleep** all day. Female budgies **don't have** blue nostrils.

Grammar reference page 107

3 Choose the correct option. Listen and check.

Bearded dragon lizards are from Australia. They [1] **eat / eats** small insects and also vegetables. It's important to give them a bath once a week. A bath [2] **help / helps** you to care for the lizard's skin properly. Bearded dragons are curious and [3] **like / likes** to explore. If a lizard [4] **feel / feels** frightened, it puffs out its 'beard'. When lizards are looking for food, they [5] **hold / holds** up their tails.

4 Complete using the words below in the correct form. Listen and check.

be eat like live spend

Turtles [1]... in the water and also on the land. Some types of turtles come out of the water to 'bask' in the sun. However, they [2]... most of their time in the water and they [3]... excellent swimmers. A young turtle [4]... to eat plants, insects and small fish, but an older turtle [5]... more vegetables and less meat.

5 In pairs, decide if the statements are true or false. Correct the false statements.

1 Bearded dragon lizards are omnivores.
2 Some turtles like the sunshine.
3 Bearded dragons aren't curious.
4 Older turtles only eat meat.
5 Turtles know how to swim.
6 A bearded dragon has a hairy beard.

Pronunciation: /eə/ and /ɪə/

6 Listen and repeat.

/eə/ **care**, **hairy**, **their**, **there**, **wear**, **where**
/ɪə/ **beard**, **ear**, **deer**, **hear**, **here**, **near**

7 NOW YOU! In pairs, say which of these pets you would or wouldn't like to have. Say why.

miniature crocodile, hairless cat, pig, parrot, snake, tarantula

PROJECT TASK 1 School magazine

- Get into groups of three. You are going to create parts of a school magazine together. The first part is a pet care section. Decide what type of animal you will write about.
- Each team member should research and write about a different aspect: food, appearance, etc. You will edit what you write in the final task. → Workbook page 20

Do all exercises in your notebook

Workbook pages 4 and 5 11

ANSWER KEY

Page 10-11

1
1 colourful; noisy; energetic
2 curious; lazy
3 clever; cool
4 heavy; slow; wonderful

2
1 e iii
2 a iv
3 d v
4 c i
5 b ii

3
1 eat
2 helps
3 like
4 feels
5 hold

4
1 live
2 spend
3 are
4 likes
5 eats

5 *Suggested answers:*
1 True
2 True
3 False
4 False
5 True
6 False

6 *Student's own answers*

7 *Student's own answers*

Remind students to do all the exercises in their notebook

LESSON FOCUS

Grammar Present simple: affirmative and negative
Vocabulary Adjectives
Listening Descriptions of pets and animals
Speaking Discussion of different types of pets
Project task 1 Research and write about different aspects of pet care

Resources
Teacher's i-solutions, Student's Book audio, Vlog and worksheet
Preparation Pictures of different kinds of animals

Flipped Learning

SARAH'S VLOG: Top tutors

- Make sure to set up the **Flipped Learning** work with the students beforehand. **See page 20-23 for complete Flipped Learning guidelines.**
- Ask students to put the **Flipped Learning worksheets** on their desks and walk around to check how many have completed the Flipped task.
- In pairs or small groups, ask students to compare and check the *Before you watch...* and *While you watch...* exercises on the worksheet.
- Show students **Sarah's Vlog** and ask volunteers to provide correct answers and clarify any doubts other students may have.
- Choose three or four students to read aloud their answers to the *After you watch...* exercises on the worksheet and encourage some class discussion.
- Move straight to exercise 1 on page 10.

Warmer

Watch Sarah's Vlog and discuss the questions with the whole class. If you don't have video facilities, simply discuss the questions.

1 1.4 (See page 168 for transcripts) Tell students they are going to listen to people describing their pets. They should pay special attention to the vocabulary used to describe them and their characteristics, as this will be useful in the next exercises.

VOCABULARY TOOLS

Draw on the adjectives students heard in exercise 1 to lead into this **Vocabulary tool** and elicit antonyms and synonyms.

2 Get students to work in pairs to match the synonyms and antonyms, they should discuss how and why they made their choices.

FAST FINISHERS Students can complete this exercise alone or in pairs.

Flipped Learning

PRESENT SIMPLE: AFFIRMATIVE AND NEGATIVE

Draw students' attention to the Grammar table. Remind students that they can use this as a quick reference while completing the exercises.

Show students the **Grammar animation** and/or refer students to the **Grammar reference** on page 107 for further information on form and use.

→ See page 23 for how to flip the **grammar lesson**

3 1.5 (See page 168 for transcripts) Students should read the text and decide on the correct option in the present simple. Indicate that they can refer to the Grammar table to help them do so. Students should then check their answers by listening to the transcript.

4 1.6 (See page 168 for transcripts) Students should develop their use of the present simple by completing the text. They will need to conjugate the verbs in the wordpool. They can continue to refer to the Grammar table to help them do so.

5 Students can be organised into pairs to discuss the questions. They should use knowledge and vocabulary from the listening exercises. Check their understanding of new words.

Pronunciation

6 1.7 (See page 168 for transcripts) Get students to pronounce the individual sound before they say the words.

7 **NOW YOU!** Students should also be encouraged to talk about any pets they already have at home and what they like (or dislike) about having a pet.

PROJECT TASK 1
School magazine

Organise student into teams of 3. For this task they will research and create a pet care guide. They can use the pictures of animals from the warmer to help decide which animal they are going to write about. Remind students that they need to keep their project notes together in their **Workbook** (page 20) or in their own notebook.

→ See pages 24-27 **Projects**

FURTHER PRACTICE

Workbook pages 4-5
- **Grammar reference and practice** pages 84 and 94
- **Wordlist and exercises** pages 99 and 102

Remind students to do all the exercises in their notebook

CONTINUOUS ASSESSMENT Students can use adjectives and the affirmative and negative of the present simple.

1.2 Listening and vocabulary

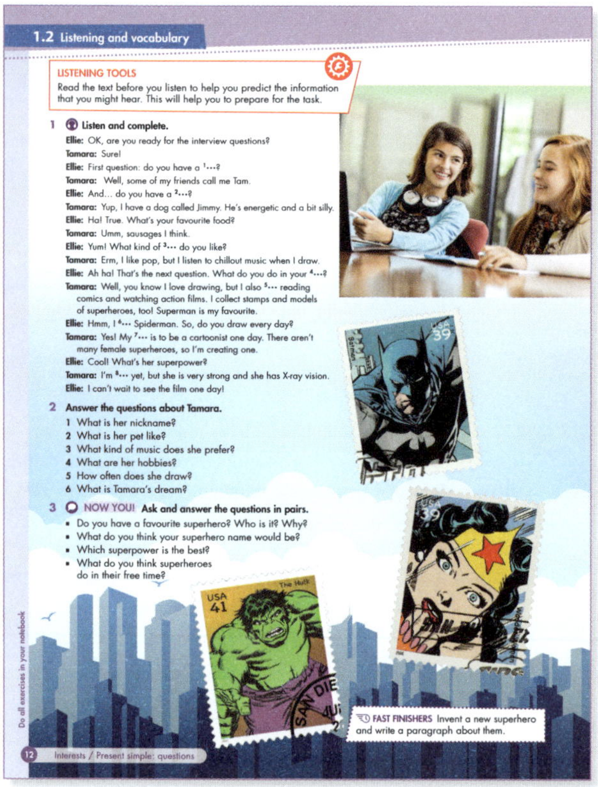

LISTENING TOOLS
Read the text before you listen to help you predict the information that you might hear. This will help you to prepare for the task.

1 Listen and complete.

Ellie: OK, are you ready for the interview questions?
Tamara: Sure!
Ellie: First question: do you have a [1]…?
Tamara: Well, some of my friends call me Tam.
Ellie: And… do you have a [2]…?
Tamara: Yup, I have a dog called Jimmy. He's energetic and a bit silly.
Ellie: Ha! True. What's your favourite food?
Tamara: Umm, sausages I think.
Ellie: Yum! What kind of [3]… do you like?
Tamara: Erm, I like pop, but I listen to chillout music when I draw.
Ellie: Ah ha! That's the next question. What do you do in your [4]…?
Tamara: Well, you know I love drawing, but I also [5]… reading comics and watching action films. I collect stamps and models of superheroes, too! Superman is my favourite.
Ellie: Hmm, I [6]… Spiderman. So, do you draw every day?
Tamara: Yes! My [7]… is to be a cartoonist one day. There aren't many female superheroes, so I'm creating one.
Ellie: Cool! What's her superpower?
Tamara: I'm [8]… yet, but she is very strong and she has X-ray vision.
Ellie: I can't wait to see the film one day!

2 Answer the questions about Tamara.
1 What is her nickname?
2 What is her pet like?
3 What kind of music does she prefer?
4 What are her hobbies?
5 How often does she draw?
6 What is Tamara's dream?

3 NOW YOU! Ask and answer the questions in pairs.
- Do you have a favourite superhero? Who is it? Why?
- What do you think your superhero name would be?
- Which superpower is the best?
- What do you think superheroes do in their free time?

FAST FINISHERS Invent a new superhero and write a paragraph about them.

Do all exercises in your notebook

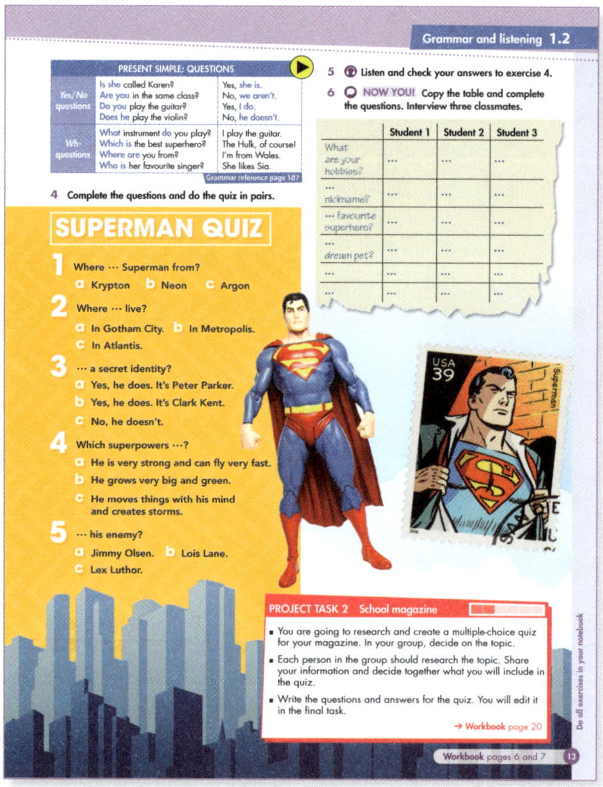

PRESENT SIMPLE: QUESTIONS		
Yes/No questions	Is she called Karen? Are you in the same class? Do you play the guitar? Does he play the violin?	Yes, she is. No, we aren't. Yes, I do. No, he doesn't.
Wh- questions	What instrument do you play? Which is the best superhero? Where are you from? Who is her favourite singer?	I play the guitar. The Hulk, of course! I'm from Wales. She likes Sia.

Grammar reference page 107

4 Complete the questions and do the quiz in pairs.

SUPERMAN QUIZ

1 Where … Superman from?
a Krypton b Neon c Argon

2 Where … live?
a In Gotham City. b In Metropolis. c In Atlantis.

3 … a secret identity?
a Yes, he does. It's Peter Parker.
b Yes, he does. It's Clark Kent.
c No, he doesn't.

4 Which superpowers …?
a He is very strong and can fly very fast.
b He grows very big and green.
c He moves things with his mind and creates storms.

5 … his enemy?
a Jimmy Olsen. b Lois Lane. c Lex Luthor.

5 Listen and check your answers to exercise 4.

6 NOW YOU! Copy the table and complete the questions. Interview three classmates.

	Student 1	Student 2	Student 3
What are your hobbies?	…	…	…
… nickname?	…	…	…
… favourite superhero?	…	…	…
… dream pet?	…	…	…
…	…	…	…
…	…	…	…

PROJECT TASK 2 School magazine
- You are going to research and create a multiple-choice quiz for your magazine. In your group, decide on the topic.
- Each person in the group should research the topic. Share your information and decide together what you will include in the quiz.
- Write the questions and answers for the quiz. You will edit it in the final task.

→ Workbook page 20

Do all exercises in your notebook

ANSWER KEY

Page 12-13

1
1 nickname
2 pet
3 music
4 free time
5 enjoy
6 prefer
7 dream
8 not sure

2
1 Tam
2 energetic and silly
3 pop or chill-out
4 drawing, reading comics, watching action films, collecting stamps and models of superheroes
5 every day
6 to be a cartoonist

3 *Student's own answer*

4
1 a
2 b
3 b
4 a
5 c

5 *Student's own answers*

6 *Student's own answers*

Remind students to do all the exercises in their notebook

LESSON FOCUS

Grammar Present simple: questions
Vocabulary Interests
Listening Conversation about hobbies and interests; Superhero quiz
Speaking Discussion of superheroes, and hobbies and interests
Project task 2 Create a multiple-choice quiz
Resources
Teacher's i-solutions, Student's Book audio
Preparation Research different popular superheroes (names and powers)

Warmer

Ask students what superpowers they know. Try and draw in some of the vocabulary from the exercises that are coming up *(X-ray vision; the ability to fly; very strong; move things with the power of the mind)*. Which superpower would students like to have? What would they use it for? Do students like reading or watching films about superheroes, or do they have different interests? Try and incorporate phrases and vocabulary about hobbies and interests.

LISTENING TOOLS

Draw students' attention to the **Listening tool**. Students should read the text quickly before listening to the conversation. Explain that this will help them to predict the correct information.

1 1.8 (See page 168 for transcripts) Let students know that they should concentrate on the wider context of the conversation so that they will have a better understanding, instead of only listening out for the words to fill in the gaps.

2 Encourage students to answer the questions as full sentences, using the present simple.

3 NOW YOU! As a warmer to the prompt questions, in pairs, students can mime the superhero they admire most and get their partner to guess who it is.

FAST FINISHERS Students can complete this exercise alone or in pairs.

PRESENT SIMPLE: QUESTIONS

Flipped Learning

Draw students' attention to the **Grammar table**. Remind students that they can use this as a quick reference while completing the exercises.

Show students the **Grammar animation** and/or refer students to the **Grammar reference** on page 107 for further information on form and use.

→ See page 23 for how to flip the **grammar lesson**

4 If students don't know very much about Superman, encourage them to interact and work with other pairs to find out the correct answers.

5 1.9 (See page 168 for transcripts) Ask students how many questions they got right. Reward the winning team with the superpower of their choice.

6 NOW YOU! Encourage students to invent questions of their own to add to the table and to be inventive with their own answers.

PROJECT TASK 2
School magazine

Tell students that they will work together to decide the topic for the quiz, but each student should do their own research. Students can use exercise 4 for ideas for creating and structuring the quiz. Remind students that they need to keep their project notes together in their **Workbook** (page 20) or in their own notebook.

→ See pages 24-27 **Projects**

FURTHER PRACTICE

Workbook pages 6-7
- **Grammar reference and practice** pages 84 and 94
- **Wordlist and exercises** pages 99 and 102

Vocabulary and Grammar worksheets available to download and edit from the **Richmond** *Learning* **Platform**

→ See page 38-39 **Mixed-ability classes**

Remind students to do all the exercises in their notebook

CONTINUOUS ASSESSMENT Students can talk about interests and ask and answer questions in the present simple.

1.3 Reading

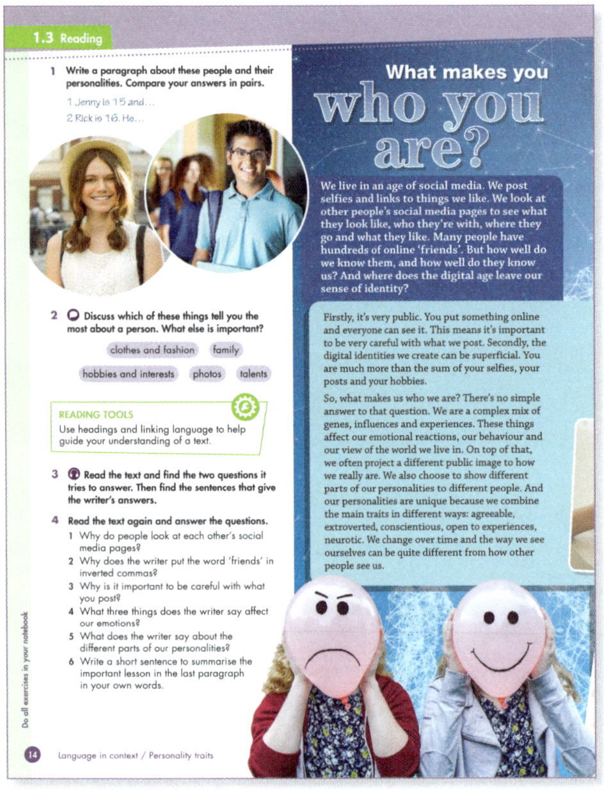

1.3 Reading

1 Write a paragraph about these people and their personalities. Compare your answers in pairs.

1 Jenny is 15 and…

2 Rick is 16. He…

2 Discuss which of these things tell you the most about a person. What else is important?

clothes and fashion | family | hobbies and interests | photos | talents

READING TOOLS
Use headings and linking language to help guide your understanding of a text.

3 Read the text and find the two questions it tries to answer. Then find the sentences that give the writer's answers.

4 Read the text again and answer the questions.
1 Why do people look at each other's social media pages?
2 Why does the writer put the word 'friends' in inverted commas?
3 Why is it important to be careful with what you post?
4 What three things does the writer say affect our emotions?
5 What does the writer say about the different parts of our personalities?
6 Write a short sentence to summarise the important lesson in the last paragraph in your own words.

What makes you who you are?

We live in an age of social media. We post selfies and links to things we like. We look at other people's social media pages to see what they look like, who they're with, where they go and what they like. Many people have hundreds of online 'friends'. But how well do we know them, and how well do they know us? And where does the digital age leave our sense of identity?

Firstly, it's very public. You put something online and everyone can see it. This means it's important to be very careful with what we post. Secondly, the digital identities we create can be superficial. You are much more than the sum of your selfies, your posts and your hobbies.

So, what makes us who we are? There's no simple answer to that question. We are a complex mix of genes, influences and experiences. These things affect our emotional reactions, our behaviour and our view of the world we live in. On top of that, we often project a different public image to how we really are. We also choose to show different parts of our personalities to different people. And our personalities are unique because we combine the main traits in different ways: agreeable, extroverted, conscientious, open to experiences, neurotic. We change over time and the way we see ourselves can be quite different from how other people see us.

Do all exercises in your notebook

14 Language in context / Personality traits

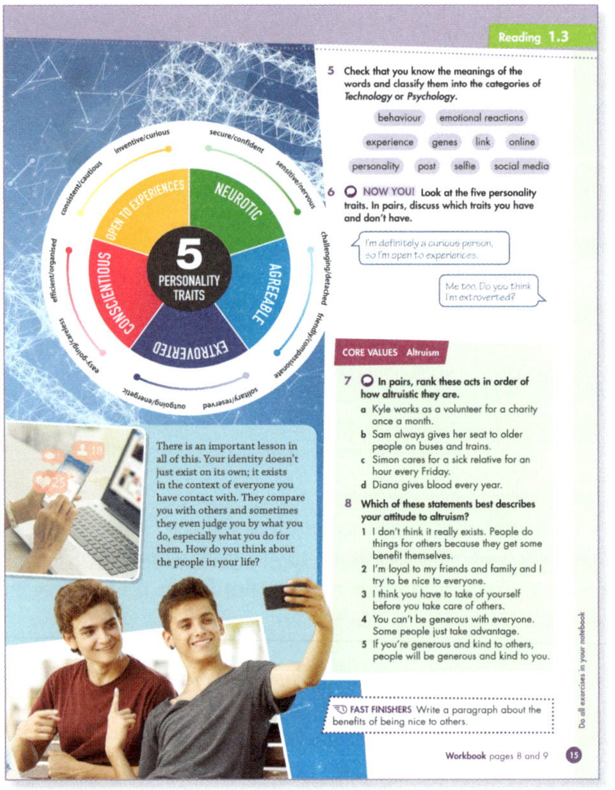

Reading 1.3

There is an important lesson in all of this. Your identity doesn't just exist on its own; it exists in the context of everyone you have contact with. They compare you with others and sometimes they even judge you by what you do, especially what you do for them. How do you think about the people in your life?

5 Check that you know the meanings of the words and classify them into the categories of *Technology* or *Psychology*.

behaviour | emotional reactions | experience | genes | link | online | personality | post | selfie | social media

6 NOW YOU! Look at the five personality traits. In pairs, discuss which traits you have and don't have.

I'm definitely a curious person, so I'm open to experiences.

Me too. Do you think I'm extroverted?

CORE VALUES Altruism

7 In pairs, rank these acts in order of how altruistic they are.
a Kyle works as a volunteer for a charity once a month.
b Sam always gives her seat to older people on buses and trains.
c Simon cares for a sick relative for an hour every Friday.
d Diana gives blood every year.

8 Which of these statements best describes your attitude to altruism?
1 I don't think it really exists. People do things for others because they get some benefit themselves.
2 I'm loyal to my friends and family and I try to be nice to everyone.
3 I think you have to take of yourself before you take care of others.
4 You can't be generous with everyone. Some people just take advantage.
5 If you're generous and kind to others, people will be generous and kind to you.

FAST FINISHERS Write a paragraph about the benefits of being nice to others.

Do all exercises in your notebook

Workbook pages 8 and 9 15

ANSWER KEY

Page 14-15

1 *Student's own answers*

2 *Student's own answers*

3 *Suggested answers:*

Question 1: Where does the digital age leave our sense of identity?

Answer sentences: Firstly, it's very public. Secondly, it can be very superficial.

Question 2: So, what makes us who we are?

Answer sentence: We are all a complex mix of genes and experience that influence our emotional reactions, our behaviour and our view of the world we live in.

4
1 To see what they look like, who they're with, where they go and what they like.
2 Because they're not necessarily real friends.
3 Because everyone can see it.
4 Genes, influences and experiences.
5 We project a different public image to how we really are, we show different sides of our personality to different people.
6 *Suggested answer:* Our identities don't exist on their own, they are affected by the people we come into contact with and how we treat them.

5 **Technology:** link, online, post, selfie, social media

Psychology: behaviour, emotional reactions, experience, genes, personality

6 *Student's own answers*

7 *Student's own answers*

8 *Student's own answers*

LESSON FOCUS

Language in context Personality traits

Core values Altruism

Resources

Teacher's i-solutions, Student's Book audio

Preparation Research some celebrity names

→ See pages 36-37 **Literature**

Warmer

Write the names of around four different celebrities on the board, from politics, sports, the arts or the music industry. Ask students to shout out what they think these people are like, use vocabulary from the reading to guide them *(confident, sensitive, nervous, detached, friendly, reserved)*. Ask students how many of them have met one of these famous people. Discuss the role of social media in how we come to make judgements about people we have never met.

1 Building on the discussion from the warmer, encourage students to use new vocabulary and expressions in their descriptions.

2 Students can work in small groups or pairs. After they have discussed between themselves, write the words from the wordpool on the board and discuss the findings as a class.

READING TOOLS

Tell students to read the Reading tool and encourage them to apply it to the next exercise.

3 1.10 (See page 168 for transcripts) Remind students of the Reading tool and get them to check their answers with the person sitting next to them to make sure they have applied it.

4 In the same pairs give students time to discuss the questions, then ask each pair one of the questions from the list.

5 Write the words technology and psychology on the board and ask students to tell you where to put each word. Check they are correct. Ask students to add extra words from the reading to the categories.

6 NOW YOU! Drill the students with useful expressions and questions in the present simple. Ask them to label someone in their family with one of the five personality traits. Students can then continue in pairs.

CORE VALUES Achievement

7 Remind students about the discussion at the beginning of class and to consider if a person's actions say more about them than other things, like their clothes or their job.

8 After they have discussed in pairs, ask students when they have done something altruistic for another person, and when another person has done something for them. Ask them how both examples made them feel.

FAST FINISHERS Students can complete this exercise alone or in pairs.

FURTHER PRACTICE

Workbook pages 8-9

Remind students to do all the exercises in their notebook

CONTINUOUS ASSESSMENT Students can understand vocabulary for personality traits in a text about identity in a digital age.

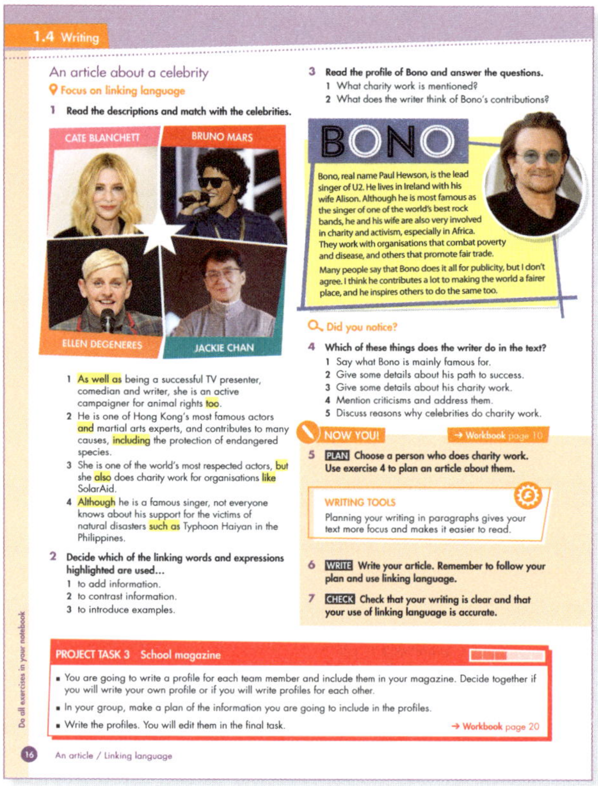

1.4 Writing

An article about a celebrity

Focus on linking language

1 **Read the descriptions and match with the celebrities.**

1 As well as being a successful TV presenter, comedian and writer, she is an active campaigner for animal rights too.
2 He is one of Hong Kong's most famous actors and martial arts experts, and contributes to many causes, including the protection of endangered species.
3 She is one of the world's most respected actors, but she also does charity work for organisations like SolarAid.
4 Although he is a famous singer, not everyone knows about his support for the victims of natural disasters such as Typhoon Haiyan in the Philippines.

2 **Decide which of the linking words and expressions highlighted are used…**
1 to add information.
2 to contrast information.
3 to introduce examples.

3 **Read the profile of Bono and answer the questions.**
1 What charity work is mentioned?
2 What does the writer think of Bono's contributions?

BONO

Bono, real name Paul Hewson, is the lead singer of U2. He lives in Ireland with his wife Alison. Although he is most famous as the singer of one of the world's best rock bands, he and his wife are also very involved in charity and activism, especially in Africa. They work with organisations that combat poverty and disease, and others that promote fair trade.

Many people say that Bono does it all for publicity, but I don't agree. I think he contributes a lot to making the world a fairer place, and he inspires others to do the same too.

Did you notice?

4 **Which of these things does the writer do in the text?**
1 Say what Bono is mainly famous for.
2 Give some details about his path to success.
3 Give some details about his charity work.
4 Mention criticisms and address them.
5 Discuss reasons why celebrities do charity work.

NOW YOU! → Workbook page 10

5 **PLAN Choose a person who does charity work. Use exercise 4 to plan an article about them.**

WRITING TOOLS
Planning your writing in paragraphs gives your text more focus and makes it easier to read.

6 **WRITE Write your article. Remember to follow your plan and use linking language.**

7 **CHECK Check that your writing is clear and that your use of linking language is accurate.**

PROJECT TASK 3 School magazine

- You are going to write a profile for each team member and include them in your magazine. Decide together if you will write your own profile or if you will write profiles for each other.
- In your group, make a plan of the information you are going to include in the profiles.
- Write the profiles. You will edit them in the final task. → Workbook page 20

Do all exercises in your notebook

16 An article / Linking language

ANSWER KEY

Page 16

1
1 Ellen DeGeneres
2 Jackie Chan
3 Cate Blanchett
4 Bruno Mars

2
1 as well as, too, also, and
2 but, although
3 including, like, such as

3
1 Combating poverty and disease, promoting fair trade.
2 They help make the world a fairer place and inspire others to do the same.

4 1, 3, 4

5 *Student's own answers*

6 *Student's own answers*

7 *Student's own answers*

FURTHER PRACTICE

Workbook page 10

LESSON FOCUS

Focus on Linking language
Writing An article about a person who does charity work
Project task 3 Plan and write a profile for each member of their group

Resources
Teacher's i-solutions

Preparation Post-it notes

Warmer

Put students into pairs. Student A writes the name of a celebrity on a post-it without Student B seeing and sticks it on Student B's forehead. Student B guesses the name of the celebrity by asking Student A questions, then they swap roles.

Focus on linking language

1 Ask students to close their books and ask them what they already know about the four celebrities. Reopen the books and do the exercise as a class, see if anyone already knew some of the facts about the celebrities.

2 Write the three headings on the board and ask students which linking words and expressions belong to each category. Leave them on the board so that they can be used for the writing exercise.

3 Get students to read the profile quickly and shout out the answers to the two questions.

Did you notice?

4 Ask the students to reread the profile, this time paying special attention to structure so that they can get ideas for their writing task.

5 **PLAN** Once students have finished their plan, encourage them to talk it through with a partner.

WRITING TOOLS

Draw students' attention to the **Writing tool** and ask them to look back over their plan to make sure that it includes paragraphs.

6 **WRITE** Before students start writing, make a checklist on the board of any elements related to content, structure, language and style that they should bear in mind.

7 **CHECK** Once students have checked their own profiles, they can swap with a partner and check theirs

PROJECT TASK 3
School magazine

Remind students to use linking words in their profiles and to pay attention to structure. Remind students that they need to keep their projects notes together in their **Workbook** (page 20) or in their own notebook.

→ See pages 24-27 **Projects**

Remind students to do all the exercises in their notebook

 CONTINUOUS ASSESSMENT Students can use appropriate linking language to write an article about a celebrity.

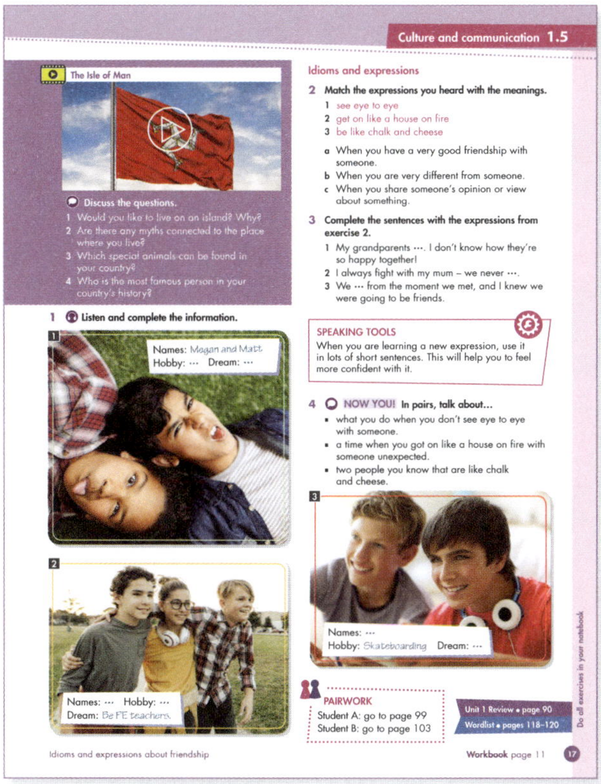
Culture and communication 1.5

The Isle of Man

Discuss the questions.
1 Would you like to live on an island? Why?
2 Are there any myths connected to the place where you live?
3 Which special animals can be found in your country?
4 Who is the most famous person in your country's history?

1 Listen and complete the information.

1 Names: Megan and Matt
Hobby: ··· Dream: ···

2 Names: ··· Hobby: ···
Dream: Be PE teachers.

Idioms and expressions

2 Match the expressions you heard with the meanings.
1 see eye to eye
2 get on like a house on fire
3 be like chalk and cheese
a When you have a very good friendship with someone.
b When you are very different from someone.
c When you share someone's opinion or view about something.

3 Complete the sentences with the expressions from exercise 2.
1 My grandparents ···. I don't know how they're so happy together!
2 I always fight with my mum – we never ···.
3 We ··· from the moment we met, and I knew we were going to be friends.

SPEAKING TOOLS
When you are learning a new expression, use it in lots of short sentences. This will help you to feel more confident with it.

4 NOW YOU! In pairs, talk about...
- what you do when you don't see eye to eye with someone.
- a time when you got on like a house on fire with someone unexpected.
- two people you know that are like chalk and cheese.

3 Names: ···
Hobby: Skateboarding Dream: ···

PAIRWORK
Student A: go to page 99
Student B: go to page 103

Unit 1 Review • page 90
Wordlist • pages 118–120

Do all exercises in your notebook

Idioms and expressions about friendship

Workbook page 11

17

LESSON FOCUS

Idioms and expressions Friendship
Listening Hobbies and ambitions
Speaking Relationships and getting along with people

Resources

Teacher's i-solutions, Student's Book audio, Culture video and worksheet

The Isle of Man

Video and worksheet available on the Richmond*Learning*Platform

- In pairs, ask students to complete the *What I know...* exercises on the **Culture video worksheet**.
- Show students the **Culture video** and ask them to complete the *What I learned...* exercises on the worksheet.
- In pairs, students compare answers.
- In small groups, tell students to complete the *What I wonder...* exercises on the worksheet.

Warmer

Watch the **Culture video** and discuss the questions with the whole class. If you don't have video facilities, simply discuss the questions.

1 1.11 (See page 169 for transcripts) Ask students which pair of friends they think they are most like.

Idioms and expressions

2 Ask students if they guessed the meaning of the phrases from the words used. Explain how the meanings of the expressions can be guessed from the words used.

3 Ask students to think of three examples of people they know that fit the three sentences.

SPEAKING TOOLS

Tell students to read the **Speaking tool** and apply it to exercise 4.

4 NOW YOU! After they have discussed the questions in pairs, ask one student from each pair to tell the class about a time when the other student got along very well with someone, didn't get along with someone, or someone who is very different to them.

PAIRWORK **Student's Book** pages 99 and 103
See **Teacher's Book** page 62 for more information.
→ See pages 30-33 **Mediation**

ANSWER KEY

Page 71

1 **1** Name: Megan and Matt
Hobby: Playing keyboard / guitar.
Dream: Be in a famous band.

2 Name: James, Liz, Ross.
Hobby: Skateboarding.
Dream: Be PE teachers

3 Name: Tom and Alex.
Hobby: Skateboarding
Dream: Be famous scientists

2 **1** c **2** a **3** b

3 **1** are like chalk and cheese
2 see eye to eye
3 got on like a house on fire

4 *Student's own answers*

FURTHER PRACTICE AND UNIT ASSESSSMENT

Unit 1 Review **Student's Book** page 90
Workbook page 11
- Reflect on your learning page 11
- Grammar reference and practice pages 84 and 94
- Wordlist and exercises pages 99 and 102

Tests available to download and edit from the **Richmond*Learning*Platform**

→ See pages 40-41 **Assessment**

Remind students to do all the exercises in their notebook

Unit 1 Review

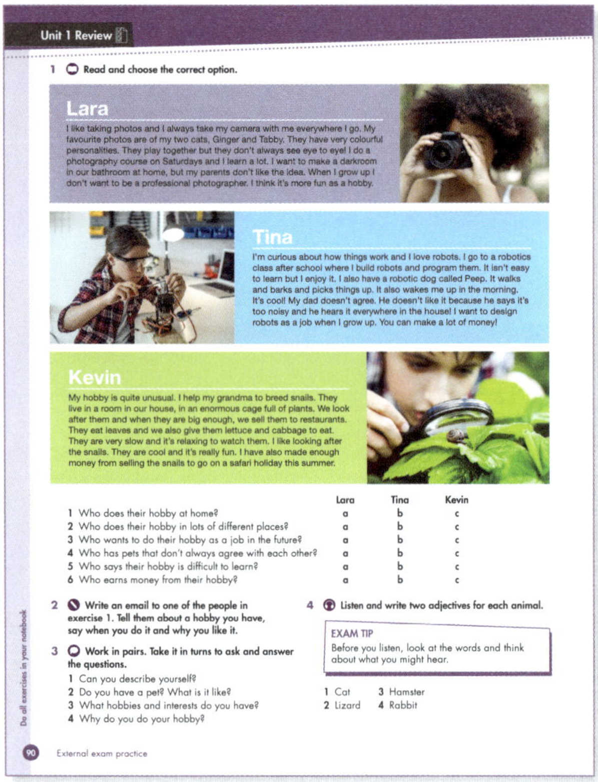

Unit 1 Review

1 Read and choose the correct option.

Lara

I like taking photos and I always take my camera with me everywhere I go. My favourite photos are of my two cats, Ginger and Tabby. They have very colourful personalities. They play together but they don't always see eye to eye! I do a photography course on Saturdays and I learn a lot. I want to make a darkroom in our bathroom at home, but my parents don't like the idea. When I grow up I don't want to be a professional photographer. I think it's more fun as a hobby.

Tina

I'm curious about how things work and I love robots. I go to a robotics class after school where I build robots and program them. It isn't easy to learn but I enjoy it. I also have a robotic dog called Peep. It walks and barks and picks things up. It also wakes me up in the morning. It's cool! My dad doesn't agree. He doesn't like it because he says it's too noisy and he hears it everywhere in the house! I want to design robots as a job when I grow up. You can make a lot of money!

Kevin

My hobby is quite unusual. I help my grandma to breed snails. They live in a room in our house, in an enormous cage full of plants. We look after them and when they are big enough, we sell them to restaurants. They eat leaves and we also give them lettuce and cabbage to eat. They are very slow and it's relaxing to watch them. I like looking after the snails. They are cool and it's really fun. I have also made enough money from selling the snails to go on a safari holiday this summer.

	Lara	Tina	Kevin
1 Who does their hobby at home?	a	b	c
2 Who does their hobby in lots of different places?	a	b	c
3 Who wants to do their hobby as a job in the future?	a	b	c
4 Who has pets that don't always agree with each other?	a	b	c
5 Who says their hobby is difficult to learn?	a	b	c
6 Who earns money from their hobby?	a	b	c

2 Write an email to one of the people in exercise 1. Tell them about a hobby you have, say when you do it and why you like it.

3 Work in pairs. Take it in turns to ask and answer the questions.
1 Can you describe yourself?
2 Do you have a pet? What is it like?
3 What hobbies and interests do you have?
4 Why do you do your hobby?

4 Listen and write two adjectives for each animal.

EXAM TIP
Before you listen, look at the words and think about what you might hear.

1 Cat
2 Lizard
3 Hamster
4 Rabbit

Do all exercises in your notebook

90 External exam practice

Student's Book page 90

ANSWER KEY

See page 179 for transcripts

1 **1** c **2** a **3** b **4** a **5** b **6** c

2 *Student's own answers*

3 *Student's own answers*

4 2.37
1 enormous, noisy
2 energetic, fast
3 lazy, slow
4 curious, light

Pairwork

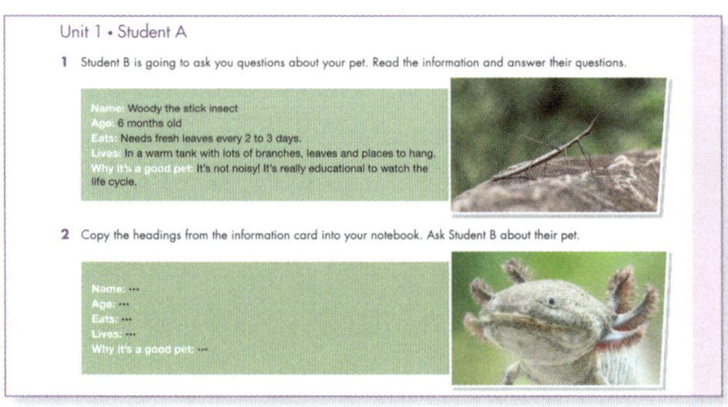

Unit 1 • Student A

1 Student B is going to ask you questions about your pet. Read the information and answer their questions.

Name: Woody the stick insect
Age: 6 months old
Eats: Needs fresh leaves every 2 to 3 days.
Lives: In a warm tank with lots of branches, leaves and places to hang.
Why it's a good pet: It's not noisy! It's really educational to watch the life cycle.

2 Copy the headings from the information card into your notebook. Ask Student B about their pet.

Name: ...
Age: ...
Eats: ...
Lives: ...
Why it's a good pet: ...

Student's Book page 99

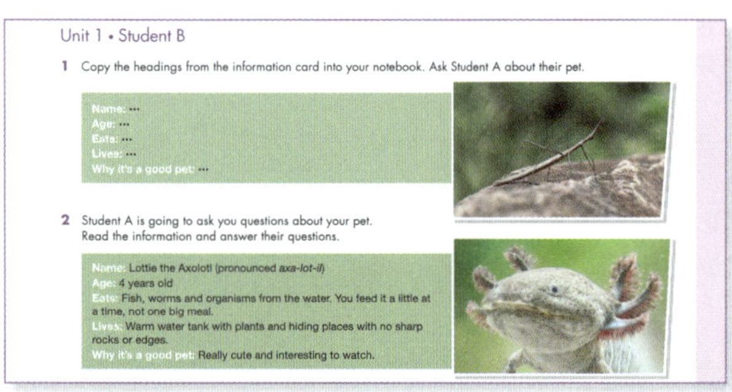

Unit 1 • Student B

1 Copy the headings from the information card into your notebook. Ask Student A about their pet.

Name: ...
Age: ...
Eats: ...
Lives: ...
Why it's a good pet: ...

2 Student A is going to ask you questions about your pet. Read the information and answer their questions.

Name: Lottie the Axolotl (pronounced *axa-lot-il*)
Age: 4 years old
Eats: Fish, worms and organisms from the water. You feed it a little at a time, not one big meal.
Lives: Warm water tank with plants and hiding places with no sharp rocks or edges.
Why it's a good pet: Really cute and interesting to watch.

Student's Book page 103

CEFR MEDIATION DESCRIPTOR

- **Processing text in speech**
  Students can summarise the main point(s) in simple, short informational texts on familiar topics.

- **Requesting information**
  Put the students in pairs, decide who is A and who is B and get them to turn to their corresponding page. Tell them they have the same instructions but different pets and information, and that they can't show each other their page. They need to ask and answer questions about each other's pets in order to understand basic information about each pet.

Grammar reference

Present simple: affirmative and negative

Use **present simple** to talk about habits and regular activities. We also use it to talk about facts. We add **-s** in the third person.	
Affirmative	Budgies **are** called Parakeets in America. Yakyak **plays** with his toys every day. Male budgies **have** blue nostrils
Negative	Budgies **aren't** carnivores Yakyak **doesn't sleep** all day. Female budgies **don't have** blue nostrils.

When we talk about things that happen every day, things that we do regularly, facts or attitudes, we use the **present simple**.

I **get up** at eight o'clock.

My dad **comes** from Ecuador.

I **don't like** football. I **prefer** tennis.

We use the same form of the verb in the **present simple** for ***I***, ***you***, ***we*** and ***they***, and the same form for ***he***, ***she*** and ***it***. In the third person singular, (***he***, ***she*** and ***it***) we add **-s** or ***-es***.

We add **-s** to the end of most verbs that end in **a vowel + a consonant**:

She **plays**, he **knows**, it **rains**

We add ***-es*** if the verb ends in ***-ch***, ***-sh***, ***-ss***, ***-o***, ***-x*** or ***-z***:

He **watches**, she **kisses**, it **buzzes**

If the verb ends in a consonant + ***-y***, the ending is ***-ies***:

It **carries**, he **studies**, she **flies**

We add ***-es*** for ***go*** and ***do***:

She **goes**, it **echoes**, he **does**

We also use the **present simple** to talk about timetables and scheduled events in the near future.

Our flight **leaves** at six in the morning.

Hurry up! Your piano lesson **starts** in an hour.

My friends **arrive** tonight.

The negative forms **don't** and **doesn't** are contractions of ***do not*** and ***does not***. We usually use the contracted forms.

We **don't go** on holiday every year.

School **doesn't start** until September.

Johnny **doesn't like** pineapple. I **don't like** it either.

Don't and ***doesn't*** are used in combination with all verbs, except ***be***.

He **isn't** ready to do.

NOT ~~He doesn't ready to go.~~

Present simple: questions

Yes/No questions	**Is she** called Karen? **Are you** in the same class? **Do you** play the guitar? **Does he** play the violin?	Yes, **she is**. No, **we aren't**. Yes, **I do**. No, **he doesn't**.
Wh- questions	**What** instrument **do** you play? **Which is** the best superhero? **Where are** you from? **Who is** her favourite singer?	I play the guitar. The Hulk! I'm from Wales. She likes Sia.

We use ***do*** or ***does*** to form ***yes/no*** **questions** in the **present simple** with all verbs, except ***be***.

Do you have the time, please?

Does the film seem interesting?

Are you Richard's sister?

NOT ~~Do you are Richard's sister?~~

Do comes before all **subject pronouns** except the third person singular: ***do I?***, ***do you?***, ***do we?***, ***do they?*** For questions with the third person singular, we use **does**: ***does she?***, ***does he?***, ***does it?***

Do you visit your grandparents often?

Does he live in London?

Do they have enough money?

When we want more information than a ***yes/no*** **question** can provide, we add a question word before ***do*** or ***does***.

How often do you visit your grandparents?

Where does he live?

How much money **do** they have?

When we give short answers in the **present simple**, we repeat ***do*** or ***does***, not the main verb.

Do you like Indian food? Yes, I **do**.

NOT ~~Yes, I like.~~

Do all exercises in your notebook

Workbook pages 94–97

Student's Book page 107

Wordlist

UNIT 1

Adjectives

big	heavy
brainy	inquisitive
clever	lazy
colourful	noisy
cool	slow
curious	vibrant
energetic	weighty
enormous	wonderful

Interests

collecting	models
drawing	playing the guitar/violin
hobbies	reading comics
instrument	watching films

Personality traits

active	extroverted
agreeable	friendly
careless	inventive
cautious	nervous
challenging	neurotic
compassionate	open to experiences
confident	organised
conscientious	outgoing
consistent	reserved
detached	secure
easy-going	sensitive
efficient	solitary

Do all exercises in your notebook

Workbook pages 102–104

Student's Book page 118

2.46 2.47 2.48

Remind students to do all the exercises in their notebook

2 DAILY LIFE

At the start of each unit and lesson, explain to the students what the objectives are.

Language objectives

Grammar

Time expressions and adverbs of frequency

- Students practise using time expressions and adverbs of frequency for talking about routine.

Present simple and present continuous

- Students practise using the present simple and the present continuous to talk about actions in the present and habitual actions.

Vocabulary

Home: attic, basement, bathroom, bedroom, flat, garage, kitchen, living room, main bedroom, porch, rooftop terrace, study, utility room, washing machine

- Students use vocabulary related to houses and homes.

Daily routine: brush your teeth, cook breakfast/lunch/dinner, do homework, eat something for breakfast/lunch/dinner, finish school, get dressed, get home, get up, go for a run, go to bed, have a break, have a nap, have a shower, have/eat breakfast/ lunch/dinner, leave the house, play videogames, read a book, ride your bike, study, tidy your room, wake up, walk the dog, water the plants

- Students use common phrasal expressions to describe routines.

World Geography: Africa, Antartica, Asia, continent, country, Europe, lake, landmass, North America, Oceania, South America.

- Students use vocabulary related to geography and the continents.

Idioms and expressions

Sleep: *be a night owl, the early bird gets the worm, sleep like a log*

- Students look at expressions related to sleep and different times of the day and complete sentences in context.

Recycled language

Hobbies, Present simple

Skills objectives

Speaking

- Students talk about their homes.
- Students talk about their routines.
- Students discuss the kind of house they would like to live in.
- Students role play conversations about different routines.
- Students do a quiz about the five continents.
- Students compare and contrast the routines of students from around the world.
- Students create and discuss study plans.

Pronunciation: Students practise words with the /æ/ sound.

Pairwork: Students use various mediation techniques in order to find out more about each other's routines.

Listening

- Students listen to a student talking about his routine and make corrections to the statements.
- Students listen to two friends talking about their habits and complete a table of information.
- Students listen to a description of a daily routine and answer multiple choice questions.
- Students listen and complete a conversation.
- Students listen to students from around the world talking about their routines and complete fact files for each.

Reading

- Students read about the lives of teenagers from around the world and answer questions.
- Students read and complete a text about habits.
- Students read to learn new words and expressions related to daily routine.
- Students read to learn about punctuation.

Core values: Students consider the importance of **routines** in daily life.

Writing

- Students complete and correct sentences and paragraphs describing people's interests and hobbies.
- Students plan, write and check a personal profile of themselves.

Focus on punctuation: *apostrophes, capital letters, commas*

Learning to learn tools

SPEAKING TOOLS Students practise inserting new phrases and expressions into conversation.	**LISTENING TOOLS** Students practise visualising new words to help understand and memorise them.
READING TOOLS Students practise skim reading a text to look for specific information.	**WRITING TOOLS** Students practise reading a text out loud to help place punctuation correctly.

VOCABULARY TOOLS Students use visual prompts to help them remember new vocabulary.

Project objectives: School magazine

Task 4 Students plan an interview with someone from their school about daily routines

Task 5 Students write an article or infographic about the perfect daily routine.

Task 6 Students research and write an article about daily life in a different country.

Audiovisual objectives

Vlog: Students watch and listen to George talk about an exchange student.

Culture: Students watch and listen to George talk about country life in India.

Grammar animations: Students are presented with visual presentations of the unit grammar.

Key competences

LC **Linguistic**
pages 18-25

MST **Mathematical and Science and Technology**
pages 22-25

DC **Digital**
pages 18-19, 21, 25

SCC **Social and Civic**
pages 18, 23, 25

CAE **Cultural awareness and expression**
pages 22-23, 25

LL **Learning to learn**
pages 19-20, 23-25

IE **Sense of initiative and entrepreneurship**
pages 12, 21, 24

→ See pages 42-43 **Key competences**

CEFR Mediation

2.1 Relaying specific information in writing
Can relay in writing specific information in texts on familiar subjects.

2.2 Collaborating to construct meaning
Can express an idea and ask what others think.

2.3 Processing text in writing
Can list relevant information in simple texts about familiar subjects.

2.4 Processing text in speech
Can summarise the main points in short, simple texts.

2.5 Encouraging conceptual talk
Can ask what somebody thinks of a certain idea.

Project Facilitating collaboration with peers
Can ask what others think, make suggestions and understand responses.

Unit review Collaborating to construct meaning
Can make simple remarks and ask questions to show he/she is following.

Pairwork Adapting language
Can repeat the main point of a message using different words to help someone understand.

→ See pages 30-33 **Mediation**

Remind students to do all the exercises in their notebook

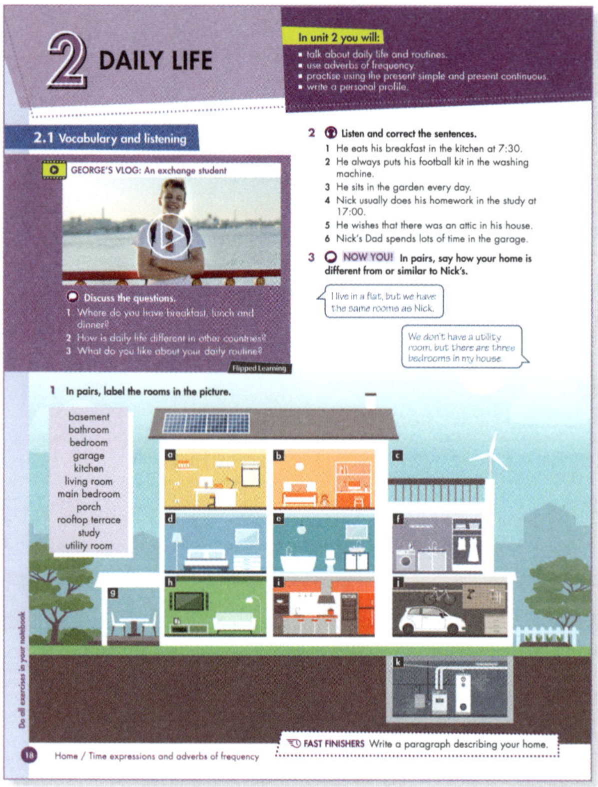
2 DAILY LIFE

In unit 2 you will:
- talk about daily life and routines.
- use adverbs of frequency.
- practise using the present simple and present continuous.
- write a personal profile.

2.1 Vocabulary and listening

GEORGE'S VLOG: An exchange student

Discuss the questions.
1 Where do you have breakfast, lunch and dinner?
2 How is daily life different in other countries?
3 What do you like about your daily routine?

Flipped Learning

1 In pairs, label the rooms in the picture.

basement, bathroom, bedroom, garage, kitchen, living room, main bedroom, porch, rooftop terrace, study, utility room

2 Listen and correct the sentences.
1 He eats his breakfast in the kitchen at 7:30.
2 He always puts his football kit in the washing machine.
3 He sits in the garden every day.
4 Nick usually does his homework in the study at 17:00.
5 He wishes that there was an attic in his house.
6 Nick's Dad spends lots of time in the garage.

3 NOW YOU! In pairs, say how your home is different from or similar to Nick's.

I live in a flat, but we have the same rooms as Nick.

We don't have a utility room, but there are three bedrooms in my house.

FAST FINISHERS Write a paragraph describing your home.

Do all exercises in your notebook

18 Home / Time expressions and adverbs of frequency

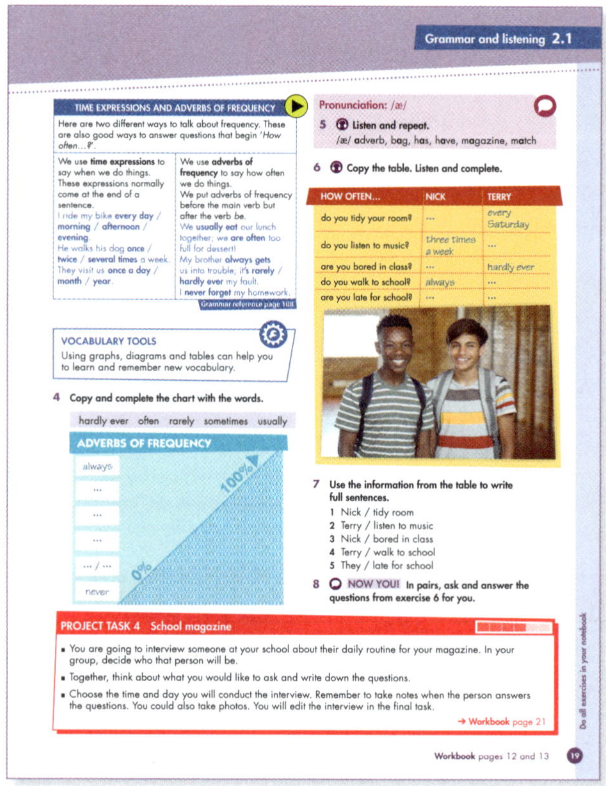
Grammar and listening 2.1

TIME EXPRESSIONS AND ADVERBS OF FREQUENCY

Here are two different ways to talk about frequency. These are also good ways to answer questions that begin 'How often...?'.

We use time expressions to say when we do things. These expressions normally come at the end of a sentence.
I ride my bike every day / morning / afternoon / evening.
He walks his dog once / twice / several times a week.
They visit us once a day / month / year.

We use adverbs of frequency to say how often we do things.
We put adverbs of frequency before the main verb but after the verb be.
We usually eat our lunch together; we are often too full for dessert!
My brother always gets us into trouble; it's rarely / hardly ever my fault.
I never forget my homework.

Grammar reference page 108

VOCABULARY TOOLS
Using graphs, diagrams and tables can help you to learn and remember new vocabulary.

4 Copy and complete the chart with the words.

hardly ever, often, rarely, sometimes, usually

ADVERBS OF FREQUENCY
always, ..., ..., ..., ..., ... / ..., never
100%, 0%

Pronunciation: /æ/
5 Listen and repeat.
/æ/ adverb, bag, has, have, magazine, match

6 Copy the table. Listen and complete.

HOW OFTEN...	NICK	TERRY
do you tidy your room?	...	every Saturday
do you listen to music?	three times a week	...
are you bored in class?	...	hardly ever
do you walk to school?	always	...
are you late for school?	...	...

7 Use the information from the table to write full sentences.
1 Nick / tidy room
2 Terry / listen to music
3 Nick / bored in class
4 Terry / walk to school
5 They / late for school

8 NOW YOU! In pairs, ask and answer the questions from exercise 6 for you.

PROJECT TASK 4 School magazine
- You are going to interview someone at your school about their daily routine for your magazine. In your group, decide who that person will be.
- Together, think about what you would like to ask and write down the questions.
- Choose the time and day you will conduct the interview. Remember to take notes when the person answers the questions. You could also take photos. You will edit the interview in the final task.

→ Workbook page 21

Do all exercises in your notebook

Workbook pages 12 and 13 19

ANSWER KEY

Page 18-19

1

a study
b bedroom
c rooftop terrace
d main bedroom
e bathroom
f utility room
g porch
h living room
i kitchen
j garage
k basement

2

1 He eats his breakfast in the kitchen at 7:00.
2 He sometimes puts his football kit in the washing machine.
3 He sits on the porch every day.
4 Nick does his homework in the kitchen at 17:00.
5 He wishes that there was a basement in his house.
6 Nick's Dad spends lots of time on the rooftop terrace.

3 *Student's own answers*

4

always
usually
often
sometimes
rarely / hardly ever
never

5 *Student's own answers*

6

HOW OFTEN...	NICK	TERRY
do you tidy your room?	several times a week	every Saturday
do you listen to music?	three times a week	rarely
are you bored in class?	all the time	hardly ever
do you walk to school?	always	never
are you late for school?	always	always

7

1 Nick tidies his room several times a week.
2 Terry rarely listens to music.
3 Nick is bored in class all the time.
4 Terry never walks to school.
5 They are always late for school.

8 *Student's own answers*

Remind students to do all the exercises in their notebook

LESSON FOCUS

Grammar Time expressions and adverbs of frequency
Vocabulary Home
Listening Descriptions of routines and habits
Speaking Discussion of daily routines
Project task 4 Plan an interview about daily routine

Resources
Teacher's i-solutions, Student's Book audio, Vlog and worksheet

Preparation Pictures of different unusual of housing (castles, houseboats, apartments, tree houses, etc)

Flipped Learning

GEORGE'S VLOG: An exchange student

- Make sure to set up the **Flipped Learning** work with the students beforehand. **See page 20-23 for complete Flipped Learning guidelines.**
- Ask students to put the **Flipped Learning worksheets** on their desks and walk around to check how many have completed the Flipped task.
- In pairs or small groups, ask students to compare and check the *Before you watch...* and *While you watch...* exercises on the worksheet.
- Show students **George's Vlog** and ask volunteers to provide correct answers and clarify any doubts other students may have.
- Choose three or four students to read aloud their answers to the *After you watch...* exercises on the worksheet and encourage some class discussion.
- Move straight to exercise 1 on page 18.

Warmer

Watch George's Vlog and discuss the questions with the whole class. If you don't have video facilities, simply discuss the questions.

1 Students can complete this alone or in pairs.

2 1.12 (See page 169 for transcripts) Get students to quickly read the sentences in advance to check understanding before listening to the audio.

3 NOW YOU! Encourage students to discuss whether they think Nick's routine would suit them and whether they would like to live in a house like his.

FAST FINISHERS Students can complete this exercise alone or in pairs.

Flipped Learning

TIME EXPRESSIONS AND ADVERBS OF FREQUENCY

Draw students' attention to the **Grammar table**. Remind students that they can use this as a quick reference while completing the exercises.

Show students the **Grammar animation** and/or refer students to the **Grammar reference** on page 108 for further information on form and use.

→ See page 23 for how to flip the **grammar lesson**

VOCABULARY TOOLS

Draw students' attention to the **Vocabulary tool**. Explain how visual prompts can help them to memorise new words and structures.

4 Students can add any other adverbs of frequency that they know. Once completed, get students to cover up the table and test their knowledge using visualisation.

Pronunciation

5 1.13 (See page 169 for transcripts) Get students to pronounce the individual sound before they say the words.

6 1.14 (See page 169 for transcripts) Students can quickly revise the adverbs of frequency from exercise 4 before completing this exercise.

7 Students should use the **Grammar table** to assist them to construct the sentences correctly.

8 NOW YOU! Encourage students to add their own questions about routine to this exercise

PROJECT TASK 4
School magazine

Organise students into teams of 3. Students will choose someone at the school to interview about their daily routine. They should set a time and date for the interview and think about what photos they will need. Remind students that they need to keep their project notes together in their **Workbook** (page 21) or in their own notebook.

→ See pages 24-27 **Projects**

FURTHER PRACTICE

Workbook pages 12-13
- **Grammar reference and practice** pages 85 and 94
- **Wordlist and exercises** pages 99 and 102

Remind students to do all the exercises in their notebook

CONTINUOUS ASSESSMENT Students can talk about the home and use time expressions and adverbs of frequency.

2.2 Listening and vocabulary

LISTENING TOOLS
As you listen, try to create an image in your mind. It will help you to focus and guess the meaning of new words.

1 Listen and choose the correct answer.
1 Billy gets home at
a five o'clock.
b seven o'clock.
c six o'clock.
2 Before Billy goes to bed, he
a walks the dog.
b does his homework.
c reads a book.
3 At 7:00, Emily
a wakes up.
b gets up.
c has a nap.
4 After Emily finishes school, she
a goes for a run.
b has a break.
c tidies her room.
5 Steven has a shower
a in the morning.
b during the day.
c in the evening.
6 Steven's family eats dinner at
a the same time every day.
b a different time every day.
c half past seven.

2 Answer the questions. Listen again and check.
1 When does Billy water the plants?
2 Why does Billy get dressed quickly?
3 Who cooks lunch with Emily?
4 Why does Emily have to wait to brush her teeth?
5 Where does Steven play video games?
6 What time does Steven get up?

3 Complete the sentences for you.
1 I get up at ···.
2 I often eat ··· for breakfast.
3 I leave the house at ···.
4 Every day, I ··· to school. I don't travel by ···.
5 After I finish school, I ···.
6 I usually have dinner at ···.

4 In pairs, say which home you would like to live in and why.

FAST FINISHERS Write a paragraph describing your daily routine.

Do all exercises in your notebook

20 Daily routine / Present simple and present continuous

Grammar and vocabulary 2.2

PRESENT SIMPLE AND PRESENT CONTINUOUS	
Use the **present simple** to express habits, routines and facts. I **go** to classes every day. He **doesn't like** broccoli. **Do** you **walk** to school?	Use the **present continuous** to talk about actions happening at the moment. She **is walking** the dog. I'**m not talking** on the phone. **Are** you **watching** TV right now?

Grammar reference page 108

5 Choose the correct option.
1 At the moment, I **am studying** / **study** English.
2 I **am eating** / **eat** breakfast every day.
3 We often **are doing** / **do** our homework after dinner.
4 I **am going** / **go** to piano class three times a week.
5 He **is having** / **has** a shower right now.
6 They **are riding** / **ride** their bikes to school today.

6 Complete with the verb in the correct form. Listen and check.
Sophie: Hello?
Jane: Hey, it's me.
Sophie: Jane! This is a strange phone number.
Jane: Oh. I 1··· (**have**) a new French phone.
Sophie: Ah! Well thanks for phoning. We miss you!
Jane: I miss you too! But I 2··· (**have**) a great time.
Sophie: Cool! So, what 3··· (**do**) right now?
Jane: I 4··· (**talk**) to you!
Sophie: Don't be silly...
Jane: Sorry. Well, right now I 5··· (**wait**) for my host family.
Sophie: What are they doing?
Jane: They 6··· (**buy**) sandwiches for a picnic this afternoon.
Sophie: Sounds great. How often 7··· (**have**) picnics?
Jane: We 8··· (**have**) a picnic about twice a week.
Sophie: That sounds wonderful. I 9··· (**love**) picnics.
Jane: Oh! I can 10··· (**see**) them now. They 11··· (**come**) back. I've got to go!
Sophie: Have fun and take care.
Jane: OK! Speak soon.

7 Read and complete the sentences with the verb in the correct form.

be buy call decide eat have live visit

Jane 1··· in England, but at the moment she 2··· a family in France. She usually 3··· lunch at home with the host family, but today they 4··· a picnic. The family 5··· sandwiches for the picnic when Jane 6··· to call her sister. Sophie 7··· confused because Jane 8··· from a strange phone number.

8 NOW YOU! In pairs, role-play a similar conversation to the one in exercise 6.

PROJECT TASK 5
School magazine
- You are going to write about the perfect daily routine in your magazine. Together, think about things like sleep, diet, technology, exercise, social life, homework, etc.
- Decide how you will present the information: in an article, timetable, infographic, etc. Create the material. You will edit it in the final task.

→ Workbook page 21

Do all exercises in your notebook

Workbook pages 14 and 15 21

ANSWER KEY

Pages 20-21

1
1 b
2 c
3 a
4 b
5 c
6 b

2
1 Around 7:00.
2 It's cold in the mornings.
3 Her dad.
4 Because the sink is small.
5 At the back of the boat.
6 At 6:30.

3 *Student's own answers*

4 *Student's own answers*

5
1 am studying
2 eat
3 do
4 go
5 is having
6 are riding

6
1 have
2 am having
3 are you doing
4 am talking
5 am waiting
6 are buying
7 do you have
8 have
9 love
10 see
11 are coming

7
1 lives
2 is visiting
3 eats
4 are having
5 is buying
6 decides
7 is
8 is calling

8 *Student's own answers*

Remind students to do all the exercises in their notebook

LESSON FOCUS

Grammar Present simple and present continuous
Vocabulary Daily routine
Listening Descriptions of different routines
Speaking Discussing different types of houses and routines
Project task 5 Write an article or infographic about the perfect daily routine

Resources

Teacher's i-solutions, Student's Book audio

Warmer

Revise grammar from the previous unit (questions in the present simple and present simple: affirmative and negative) by asking students what they have done that day before coming to class. Ask how often they do the things that they mention and encourage them to use adverbs of frequency.

LISTENING TOOLS

Encourage students to read over the **Listening tool** and apply it to the next exercise.

1 1.15 (See page 169 for transcripts) Students should read the questions for exercises 1 and 2 quickly before listening to the audio. They should take notes as they listen, as well as answering the questions.

2 1.16 (See page 170 for transcripts) Students should use their notes from exercise 1 to help with answering the questions. Remind them they will hear the audio one more time.

3 Remind students that they can use the questions in exercises 1 and 2 to help them construct their answers in the present simple and the present continuous, as well as the **Grammar table**.

4 Ask the class to think of more unusual places that people can live. Write them on the board and ask the students if they would like to live there.

FAST FINISHERS Students can complete this exercise alone or in pairs.

PRESENT SIMPLE AND PRESENT CONTINUOUS

Flipped Learning

Draw students' attention to the **Grammar table**. Remind students that they can use this as a quick reference while completing the exercises.

Show students the **Grammar animation** and/or refer students to the **Grammar reference** on page 108 for further information on form and use.

→ See page 23 for how to flip the **grammar lesson**

5 After the students have finished, ask them which sentences are in the present simple and which are in the present continuous.

6 1.17 (See page 170 for transcripts) Remind students to pay attention to the whole conversation and not just the missing words to improve their listening comprehension.

7 Before starting the exercise, tell students to close their books. Read the text out loud and see if they can guess the missing words without the **wordpool**.

8 NOW YOU! In their pairs, one student can imagine they are in another country and the other student should be in Spain.

PROJECT TASK 5
School magazine

Working together students will decide on the perfect daily routine and discuss the best way to present it in the magazine. Remind students that they need to keep their project notes together in their **Workbook** (page 21) or in their own notebook.

→ See pages 24-27 **Projects**

FURTHER PRACTICE

Workbook pages 14-15
- **Grammar reference and practice** pages 85 and 94
- **Wordlist and exercises** pages 99 and 102

Vocabulary and Grammar worksheets available to download and edit from the
Richmond *Learning* **Platform**

→ See pages 38-39 **Mixed-ability classes**

Remind students to do all the exercises in their notebook

CONTINUOUS ASSESSMENT Students can talk about daily routines and use the present simple and present continuous.

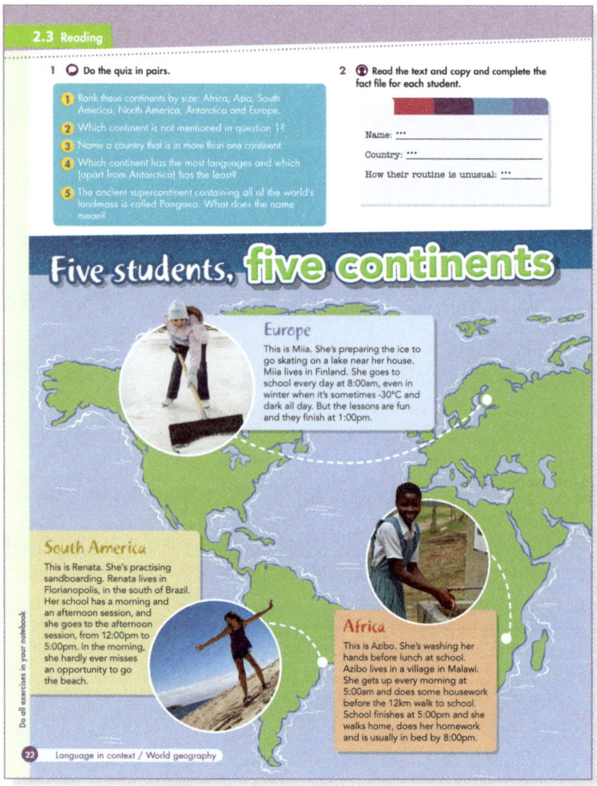

1 Do the quiz in pairs.

1 Rank these continents by size: Africa, Asia, South America, North America, Antarctica and Europe.
2 Which continent is not mentioned in question 1?
3 Name a country that is in more than one continent.
4 Which continent has the most languages and which (apart from Antarctica) has the least?
5 The ancient supercontinent containing all of the world's landmass is called Pangaea. What does the name mean?

2 Read the text and copy and complete the fact file for each student.

Name: ···
Country: ···
How their routine is unusual: ···

Five students, five continents

Europe
This is Miia. She's preparing the ice to go skating on a lake near her house. Miia lives in Finland. She goes to school every day at 8:00am, even in winter when it's sometimes -30°C and dark all day. But the lessons are fun and they finish at 1:00pm.

South America
This is Renata. She's practising sandboarding. Renata lives in Florianopolis, in the south of Brazil. Her school has a morning and an afternoon session, and she goes to the afternoon session, from 12:00pm to 5:00pm. In the morning, she hardly ever misses an opportunity to go the beach.

Africa
This is Azibo. She's washing her hands before lunch at school. Azibo lives in a village in Malawi. She gets up every morning at 5:00am and does some housework before the 12km walk to school. School finishes at 5:00pm and she walks home, does her homework and is usually in bed by 8:00pm.

Do all exercises in your notebook

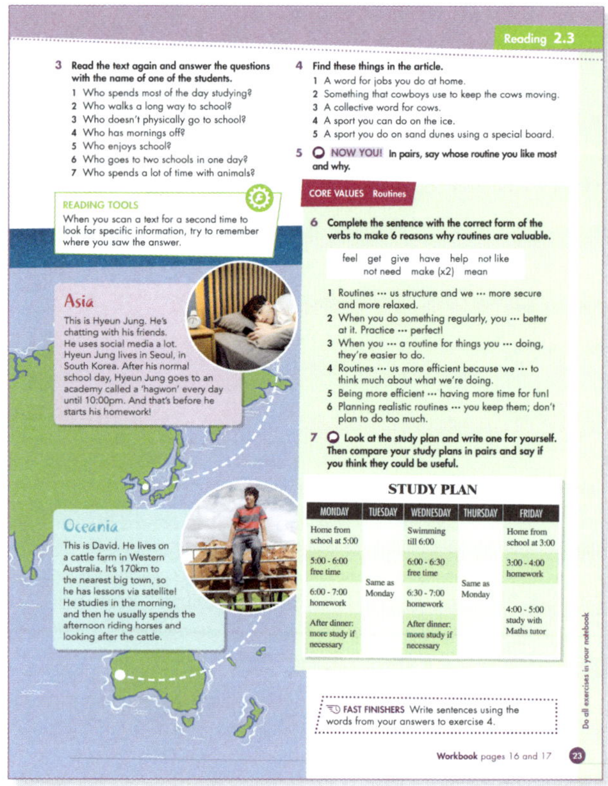

3 Read the text again and answer the questions with the name of one of the students.

1 Who spends most of the day studying?
2 Who walks a long way to school?
3 Who doesn't physically go to school?
4 Who has mornings off?
5 Who enjoys school?
6 Who goes to two schools in one day?
7 Who spends a lot of time with animals?

READING TOOLS
When you scan a text for a second time to look for specific information, try to remember where you saw the answer.

Asia
This is Hyeun Jung. He's chatting with his friends. He uses social media a lot. Hyeun Jung lives in Seoul, in South Korea. After his normal school day, Hyeun Jung goes to an academy called a 'hagwon' every day until 10:00pm. And that's before he starts his homework!

Oceania
This is David. He lives on a cattle farm in Western Australia. It's 170km to the nearest big town, so he has lessons via satellite! He studies in the morning, and then he usually spends the afternoon riding horses and looking after the cattle.

4 Find these things in the article.

1 A word for jobs you do at home.
2 Something that cowboys use to keep the cows moving.
3 A collective word for cows.
4 A sport you can do on the ice.
5 A sport you do on sand dunes using a special board.

5 NOW YOU! In pairs, say whose routine you like most and why.

CORE VALUES Routines

6 Complete the sentence with the correct form of the verbs to make 6 reasons why routines are valuable.

feel get give have help not like not need make (x2) mean

1 Routines ··· us structure and we ··· more secure and more relaxed.
2 When you do something regularly, you ··· better at it. Practice ··· perfect!
3 When you ··· a routine for things you ··· doing, they're easier to do.
4 Routines ··· us more efficient because we ··· to think much about what we're doing.
5 Being more efficient ··· having more time for fun!
6 Planning realistic routines ··· you keep them; don't plan to do too much.

7 Look at the study plan and write one for yourself. Then compare your study plans in pairs and say if you think they could be useful.

STUDY PLAN

MONDAY	TUESDAY	WEDNESDAY	THURSDAY	FRIDAY
Home from school at 5:00	Same as Monday	Swimming till 6:00	Same as Monday	Home from school at 3:00
5:00 - 6:00 free time		6:00 - 6:30 free time		3:00 - 4:00 homework
6:00 - 7:00 homework		6:30 - 7:00 homework		4:00 - 5:00 study with Maths tutor
After dinner: more study if necessary		After dinner: more study if necessary		

FAST FINISHERS Write sentences using the words from your answers to exercise 4.

Do all exercises in your notebook

ANSWER KEY

Pages 22-23

1 *Suggested answers:*

1 Asia, Africa, North America, South America, Antarctica and Europe.
2 Oceania.
3 Egypt (in Africa and Asia), Russia, Turkey, Kazakhstan and Azerbaijan (all in both Europe and Asia).
4 Asia (2,310) and Europe (286).
5 All the land or earth (Pan meaning 'all' and Gaia meaning 'land' or 'earth').

2 **Name:** Miia
Country: Finland
How their routine is unusual: It's sometimes -30°C and dark all day. She finishes school at 1pm.

Name: Renata
Country: Brazil
How their routine is unusual: She goes to the beach most mornings and only has classes in the afternoon.

Name: Azibo
Country: Malawi
How their routine is unusual: She walks 12 km to school.

Name: Hyeun Jung
Country: South Korea
How their routine is unusual: He studies until after 10pm.

Name: David
Country: Australia
How their routine is unusual: He has lessons via satellite.

3 **1** Hyeun Jung **2** Azibo **3** David **4** Renata **5** Miia **6** Hyeun Jung **7** David

4 **1** housework **2** whip **3** cattle **4** (ice) skating **5** sandboarding

5 Student's own answers

6 **1** give; feel **2** get; makes **3** have; don't like **4** make; don't need **5** means **6** help

7 *Student's own answers*

Remind students to do all the exercises in their notebook

LESSON FOCUS
Language in context World geography
Core values Routines

Resources
Teacher's i-solutions, Student's Book audio
Preparation Map of the world

→ See pages 36-37 **Literature**

Warmer

Show the students a map of the world. Ask them which countries they have been to and if there was anything that they found particularly unusual or different to their own country.

1 Students can use the map of the world from the warmer to help them to answer the questions.

2 1.21 (See page 170 for transcripts) Remind students to take notes as they are reading.

3 Encourage students to answer the questions with full sentences, using the present simple.

READING TOOLS

Students can use the tip from the **Reading tool** to help them answer the questions. They should look out for key words to help identify the information they need.

4 Ask students ifthey learned any new vocabulary about routines from the **reading text**. Write these new words on the board so that students can use them for the next exercise.

5 NOW YOU! After the students have discussed in pairs, have a class debate to see which routine students felt was the best one overall.

CORE VALUES Routines

6 Write the verbs from the **wordpool** on the board. After students have finished the exercise, ask students to make further sentences using the verbs.

7 Encourage students to discuss how the plans compare to the perfect daily routine they designed for the **Project task** on page 21, and what things they could do to improve their plans to make them more like the perfect routine.

FAST FINISHERS Students can complete this exercise alone or in pairs.

FURTHER PRACTICE

Workbook pages 16-17

Remind students to do all the exercises in their notebook

CONTINUOUS ASSESSMENT Students can understand vocabulary about world geography in a text about people living in different continents.

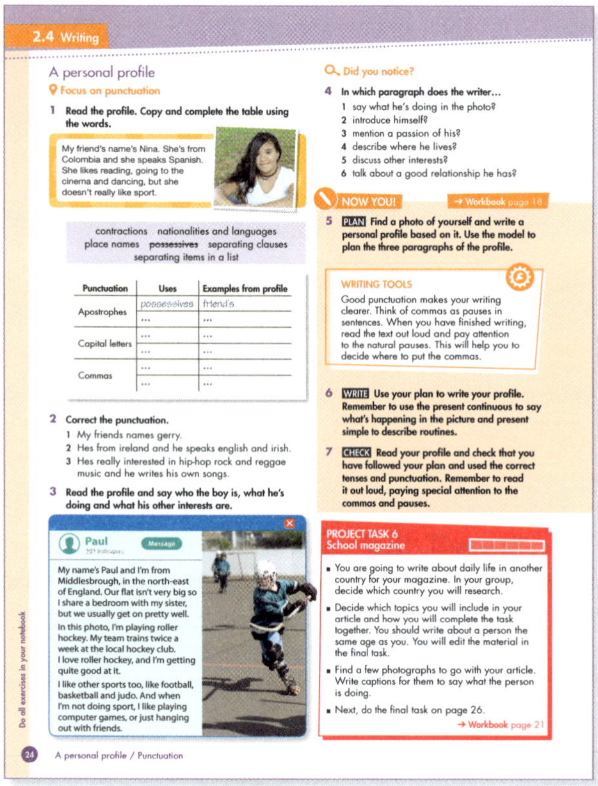

2.4 Writing

A personal profile

Focus on punctuation

1 **Read the profile. Copy and complete the table using the words.**

My friend's name's Nina. She's from Colombia and she speaks Spanish. She likes reading, going to the cinema and dancing, but she doesn't really like sport.

contractions nationalities and languages place names ~~possessives~~ separating clauses separating items in a list

Punctuation	Uses	Examples from profile
Apostrophes	possessives	friend's
	…	…
Capital letters	…	…
	…	…
Commas	…	…
	…	…

2 **Correct the punctuation.**

1 My friends names gerry.
2 Hes from ireland and he speaks english and irish.
3 Hes really interested in hip-hop rock and reggae music and he writes his own songs.

3 **Read the profile and say who the boy is, what he's doing and what his other interests are.**

Paul

Message

My name's Paul and I'm from Middlesbrough, in the north-east of England. Our flat isn't very big so I share a bedroom with my sister, but we usually get on pretty well.

In this photo, I'm playing roller hockey. My team trains twice a week at the local hockey club. I love roller hockey, and I'm getting quite good at it.

I like other sports too, like football, basketball and judo. And when I'm not doing sport, I like playing computer games, or just hanging out with friends.

Did you notice?

4 **In which paragraph does the writer…**

1 say what he's doing in the photo?
2 introduce himself?
3 mention a passion of his?
4 describe where he lives?
5 discuss other interests?
6 talk about a good relationship he has?

NOW YOU! → Workbook page 18

5 PLAN **Find a photo of yourself and write a personal profile based on it. Use the model to plan the three paragraphs of the profile.**

WRITING TOOLS

Good punctuation makes your writing clearer. Think of commas as pauses in sentences. When you have finished writing, read the text out loud and pay attention to the natural pauses. This will help you to decide where to put the commas.

6 WRITE **Use your plan to write your profile. Remember to use the present continuous to say what's happening in the picture and present simple to describe routines.**

7 CHECK **Read your profile and check that you have followed your plan and used the correct tenses and punctuation. Remember to read it out loud, paying special attention to the commas and pauses.**

PROJECT TASK 6
School magazine

- You are going to write about daily life in another country for your magazine. In your group, decide which country you will research.
- Decide which topics you will include in your article and how you will complete the task together. You should write about a person the same age as you. You will edit the material in the final task.
- Find a few photographs to go with your article. Write captions for them to say what the person is doing.
- Next, do the final task on page 26.

→ Workbook page 21

Do all exercises in your notebook

24 A personal profile / Punctuation

ANSWER KEY

Page 24

1

Punctuation	Uses	Examples from profile
Apostrophes	possessives; contractions	friend's; name's
Capital letters	place names; nationalities and languages	Colombia; Spanish
Commas	separating clauses; separating items in a list	but she doesn't really like sport

2
1 My friend's name's Gerry.
2 He's from Ireland and he speaks English and Irish.
3 He's really interested in hip-hop, rock and reggae music, and he writes his own songs.

3 *Suggested answer:*
Paul is from Middlesborough. He's playing roller hockey. He likes sports, playing computer games and hanging out with friends.

4 1 Paragraph 2 2 Paragraph 1 3 Paragraph 2 4 Paragraph 1 5 Paragraph 3 6 Paragraph 1

5 *Student's own answers*

6 *Student's own answers*

7 *Student's own answers*

FURTHER PRACTICE

Workbook page 18

LESSON FOCUS

Focus on Punctuation

Writing Write a personal profile

Project task 6 Research and write an article about daily life in a different country.

Resources

Teacher's i-solutions, Student's Book audio

Warmer

Tell the students they are going to practise using puctuation in this lesson. Ask them to think of and shout out all the different types of punctuation they can think of. Write them on the board and ask the students to define them. If the students have trouble thiking of examples, tell them to scan the texts in the **reading text** in the previous lesson.

Focus on linking language

1 Write the text from the exercise on the board without any punctuation. Ask a student to read it out loud so the class can see how it makes the text hard to understand. Add in the punctuation afterwards so the students can see how it works.

2 Remind students to use the table from exercise 1 to help them.

3 Students can read alone and then discuss the profile with the person sitting next to them.

Did you notice?

4 Discuss with the class whether they think the profile is well structured, or not, and why.

5 PLAN In the planning stage, remind students that they should use a photo of themselves which says something about their interests and daily life.

WRITING TOOLS

Draw students' attention to the **Writing tool** and remind them of the how the text without punctuation sounded in exercise 1. They should read their profiles out loud to check for punctuation errors.

6 WRITE Students can use the grammar reference to help them to write the profile in the present continuous.

7 CHECK Once students have checked their own profiles, they can swap with a partner and check theirs.

PROJECT TASK 6
School magazine

Students should research and write about daily life in a different country. To help them, remind them of the **Core values** exercises on page 23 and their discussion of routines in a different country. Remind students that they need to keep their project notes together in their **Workbook** (page 21) or in their own notebook.

→ See pages 24-27 **Projects**

Remind students to do all the exercises in their notebook

CONTINUOUS ASSESSMENT Students can use appropriate punctuation to write a personal profile.

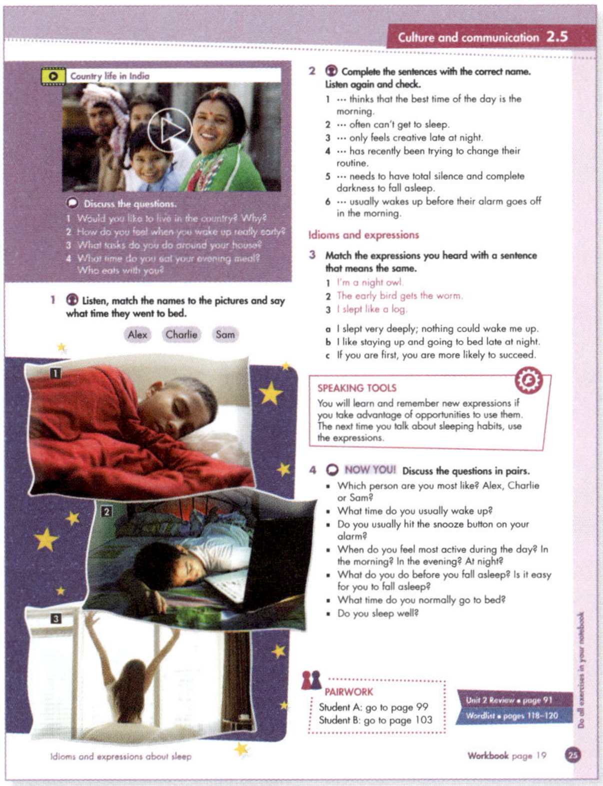

Culture and communication 2.5

Country life in India

Discuss the questions.

1 Would you like to live in the country? Why?
2 How do you feel when you wake up really early?
3 What tasks do you do around your house?
4 What time do you eat your evening meal? Who eats with you?

1 Listen, match the names to the pictures and say what time they went to bed.

Alex Charlie Sam

2 Complete the sentences with the correct name. Listen again and check.

1 ··· thinks that the best time of the day is the morning.
2 ··· often can't get to sleep.
3 ··· only feels creative late at night.
4 ··· has recently been trying to change their routine.
5 ··· needs to have total silence and complete darkness to fall asleep.
6 ··· usually wakes up before their alarm goes off in the morning.

Idioms and expressions

3 Match the expressions you heard with a sentence that means the same.

1 I'm a night owl.
2 The early bird gets the worm.
3 I slept like a log.

a I slept very deeply; nothing could wake me up.
b I like staying up and going to bed late at night.
c If you are first, you are more likely to succeed.

SPEAKING TOOLS
You will learn and remember new expressions if you take advantage of opportunities to use them. The next time you talk about sleeping habits, use the expressions.

4 NOW YOU! Discuss the questions in pairs.

- Which person are you most like? Alex, Charlie or Sam?
- What time do you usually wake up?
- Do you usually hit the snooze button on your alarm?
- When do you feel most active during the day? In the morning? In the evening? At night?
- What do you do before you fall asleep? Is it easy for you to fall asleep?
- What time do you normally go to bed?
- Do you sleep well?

PAIRWORK
Student A: go to page 99
Student B: go to page 103

Unit 2 Review • page 91
Wordlist • pages 118–120

Do all exercises in your notebook

Idioms and expressions about sleep

Workbook page 19 25

LESSON FOCUS

Idioms and expressions Sleep

Listening Teenagers talking about times of the day and sleep

Speaking Discussion of which times of the day are best for doing activities

Resources

Teacher's i-solutions, Student's Book audio, Culture video and worksheet

Country life in India

Video and worksheet available on the Richmond Learning Platform

- In pairs, ask students to complete the *What I know...* exercises on the **Culture video worksheet**.
- Show students the **Culture video** and ask them to complete the *What I learned...* exercises on the worksheet.
- In pairs, students compare answers.
- In small groups, tell students to complete the *What I wonder...* exercises on the worksheet.

Warmer

Watch the **Culture video** and discuss the questions with the whole class. If you don't have video facilities, simply discuss the questions.

1 1.19 (See page 170 for transcripts) Remind students to take notes while they are listening. They will be able to listen to the audio twice.

2 1.20 (See page 170 for transcripts) Ask students which student they are most like.

Idioms and expressions

3 Ask students if they were able to guess the meanings of the idioms from the words they are comprised of, i.e., a log is very still and doesn't move; owls only come out at night.

SPEAKING TOOLS

Draw students' attention to the **Speaking tool** and remind them of the warmer. They should read their profiles out loud to check for punctuation errors.

4 NOW YOU! After students have discussed the questions in pairs, have a conversation with the whole class about sleep. Do students think sleep is cultural? Do people sleep differently in different countries? Where in the world are naps common? What are sleep routines and customs like in the students' country?

PAIRWORK **Student's Book** pages 99 and 103
See **Teacher's Book** page 74 for more information.
→ See pages 30-33 **Mediation**

ANSWER KEY

Page 25

1 **1** Sam
2 Charlie
3 Alex

2 **1** Alex
2 Sam
3 Charlie
4 Sam
5 Charlie
6 Alex

3 **1** b
2 c
3 a

4 *Student's own answers*

FURTHER PRACTICE AND UNIT ASSESSSMENT

Unit 2 Review **Student's Book** page 91
Workbook page 19
- **Reflect on your learning** page 19
- **Grammar reference and practice** pages 85 and 94
- **Wordlist and exercises** pages 99 and 102

Tests available to download and edit from the Richmond Learning Platform

→ See pages 40-41 **Assessment**

Remind students to do all the exercises in their notebook

CONTINUOUS ASSESSMENT Students can use idioms and expressions about sleep.

Unit 2 Review

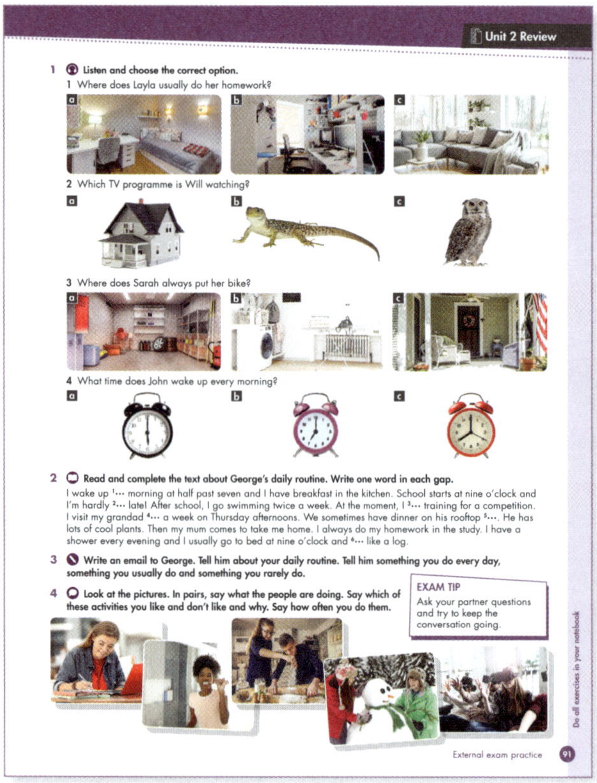

1 Listen and choose the correct option.

1 Where does Layla usually do her homework?

a b c

2 Which TV programme is Will watching?

a b c

3 Where does Sarah always put her bike?

a b c

4 What time does John wake up every morning?

a b c

2 Read and complete the text about George's daily routine. Write one word in each gap.

I wake up [1]… morning at half past seven and I have breakfast in the kitchen. School starts at nine o'clock and I'm hardly [2]… late! After school, I go swimming twice a week. At the moment, I [3]… training for a competition. I visit my grandad [4]… a week on Thursday afternoons. We sometimes have dinner on his rooftop [5]…. He has lots of cool plants. Then my mum comes to take me home. I always do my homework in the study. I have a shower every evening and I usually go to bed at nine o'clock and [6]… like a log.

3 Write an email to George. Tell him about your daily routine. Tell him something you do every day, something you usually do and something you rarely do.

4 Look at the pictures. In pairs, say what the people are doing. Say which of these activities you like and don't like and why. Say how often you do them.

EXAM TIP
Ask your partner questions and try to keep the conversation going.

Do all exercises in your notebook

Student's Book page 91

ANSWER KEY

See pages 179-180 for transcipts

1 2.38

1 b **2** a **3** c **4** c

2

1 every
2 ever
3 am
4 once
5 terrace
6 sleep

3 *Student's own answers*

4 *Student's own answers*

Pairwork

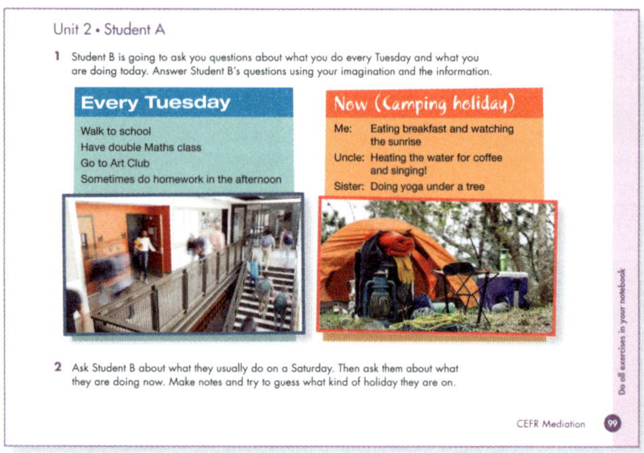
Unit 2 • Student A

1 Student B is going to ask you questions about what you do every Tuesday and what you are doing today. Answer Student B's questions using your imagination and the information.

Every Tuesday

Walk to school
Have double Maths class
Go to Art Club
Sometimes do homework in the afternoon

Now (Camping holiday)

Me: Eating breakfast and watching the sunrise
Uncle: Heating the water for coffee and singing!
Sister: Doing yoga under a tree

2 Ask Student B about what they usually do on a Saturday. Then ask them about what they are doing now. Make notes and try to guess what kind of holiday they are on.

Do all exercises in your notebook

Student's Book page 99

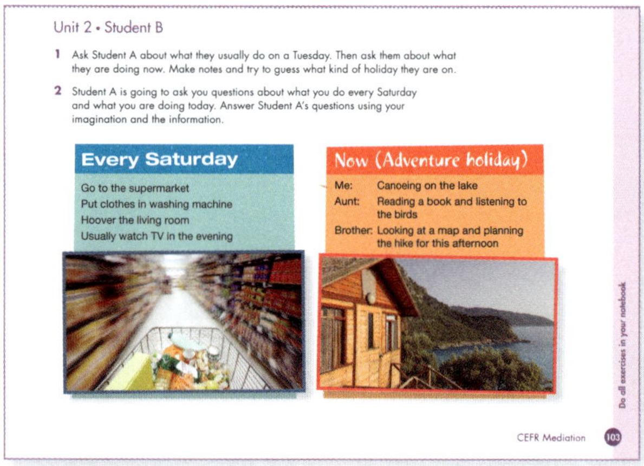
Unit 2 • Student B

1 Ask Student A about what they usually do on a Tuesday. Then ask them about what they are doing now. Make notes and try to guess what kind of holiday they are on.

2 Student A is going to ask you questions about what you do every Saturday and what you are doing today. Answer Student A's questions using your imagination and the information.

Every Saturday

Go to the supermarket
Put clothes in washing machine
Hoover the living room
Usually watch TV in the evening

Now (Adventure holiday)

Me: Canoeing on the lake
Aunt: Reading a book and listening to the birds
Brother: Looking at a map and planning the hike for this afternoon

Do all exercises in your notebook

Student's Book page 103

CEFR MEDIATION DESCRIPTOR

- **Relaying specific information in speech**
  Students can relay specific, relevant information contained in short, simple texts, labels and notices on familiar subjects.

- **Asking and answering questions**
  Put the students in pairs, decide who is A and who is B and get them to turn to their corresponding page. Tell them they have the same instructions but different information and that they can't show each other their pages. They will ask each other questions in order to find out more about their routines. Tell them they should use the information as well as their imagination when deciding on their answers.

Remind students to do all the exercises in their notebook

Unit 2 Grammar reference

Time expressions and adverbs of frequency

Here are two different ways to talk about frequency. These are also good ways to answer questions that begin *How often…?*.

Use **time expressions** to say when we do things. The expressions normally come at the end of a sentence.	Use **adverbs of frequency** to say how often we do things. We put adverbs of frequency before the main verb but after the verb *be*.
I ride my bike **every day** / **morning** / **afternoon** / **evening**. He walks his dog **once** / **twice** / **several times** a week. They visit us **once a day** / **month** / **year**.	We **usually eat** our lunch together; we **are often** too full for dessert! My brother **always gets** us into trouble; it's **rarely** / **hardly ever** my fault. I **never forget** my homework.

Time expressions with ***every*** require a space between ***every*** and the other word.

They meet **every year** at the festival.

Every time I play basketball, my ankle hurts.

I brush my teeth **every day**.

NOT ~~I brush my teeth everyday.~~

We can also put ***usually***, ***often***, ***sometimes*** and ***occasionally*** at the start of a sentence.

I **always** have lunch at school.

Mum doesn't **usually** drive to work.

Sometimes my brother watches TV during dinner.

Present simple and present continuous

Use the **present simple** to express habits, routines and facts.	Use the **present continuous** to talk about actions happening at the moment.
I **go** to classes every day. He **doesn't like** broccoli. **Do** you **walk** to school?	She **is walking** the dog. I**'m not talking** on the phone. **Are** you **watching** TV right now?

The **present continuous** is formed with ***be*** + ***-ing*** form of the verb.

Most verbs → add ***-ing***:
Doing, **playing**, **jumping**

Verbs that end in ***-e*** → drop the ***-e*** and add ***-ing***:
Making, **writing**, **driving**

One-syllable verbs → double the final consonant:
Running, **putting**, **stopping**

We use the **present simple** to talk about regular actions and permanent situations and facts. However, we use the **present continuous** to talk about actions in progress and temporary situations.

Sally's not here right now; she**'s playing** tennis. She **plays** tennis every Friday.

Franz **is speaking** to his mum at the moment. His mum **speaks** English and German.

Do all exercises in your notebook

108 **Workbook** pages 94–97

Student's Book page 108

Wordlist

Wordlist

UNIT 1

UNIT 2

Home

attic
basement
bathroom
bedroom
flat
garage
kitchen
living room
main bedroom
porch
rooftop terrace
study
utility room
washing machine

Daily routine

brush your teeth
cook breakfast/lunch/dinner
do homework
eat something for breakfast/lunch/dinner
finish school
get dressed
get home
get up
go for a run
go to bed
have a break
have a nap
have a shower
have/eat breakfast/lunch/dinner
leave the house
play videogames
read a book
ride your bike
study
tidy your room
wake up
walk the dog
water the plants

World geography

Africa
Antarctica
Asia
continent
country
Europe
lake
landmass
North America
Oceania
South America

UNIT 3

Do all exercises in your notebook

118 **Workbook** pages 102–104

Student's Book page 118

2.49 2.50 2.51

Remind students to do all the exercises in their notebook

PROJECT: School magazine

RECAP

- In this project, you have researched and written material for a school magazine.
- In **units 1 and 2**, you talked about yourself, your pet, interests, friends and routines. You learnt how to ask questions. You also used the present simple, present continuous and adverbs of frequency to talk about daily life.
- Now you are ready to present your school magazine to the class!

TASK 1 **Write pet care instructions.**
TASK 2 **Research and create a quiz.**
TASK 3 **Write a profile for each team member.**
TASK 4 **Interview a person at your school.**
TASK 5 **Create the perfect daily routine.**
TASK 6 **Write about daily life in a different country.**

FINAL TASK: Complete and present your magazine

- Decide if you will create the magazine by hand or use a computer.
- Look back at the material that you have created. Correct any mistakes and improve it where possible.
- Together, decide how you will present the information on the page and how many pages you will include. Write a final version of the texts and choose photos to go on each of the pages. Look at online magazines to inspire you.
- Create a name for your magazine and design the front cover. Remember to include information about the contents.
- When your magazine is ready, present it to the class. Then exchange the magazines and look at them closely. In your group, choose the best section in each magazine.

USEFUL EXPRESSIONS

- We chose this title because…
- This magazine contains … pages.
- We interviewed … because…
- I think the section about … is the best because…
- So, do we agree that the best section is … ?

21ST CENTURY SKILLS

Negotiating

To negotiate well, try to plan a way that everyone can benefit from the decision. Try to see the other person's point of view and remember to:

✓ be clear and calm.
✓ listen and be respectful.
✓ be ready to compromise.

Do all exercises in your notebook

26 **Workbook** pages 20 and 21

EVALUATION

Answer the questions in your team.

1 Did you disagree with each other while you were making the magazine?
2 How did you solve the disagreements?
3 Did you negotiate with each other?
4 Were all the members of the team happy with the final magazine?

Project • Units 1 and 2

GO BEYOND

ETHICAL MEDIA

Magazines are aimed at readers with a particular common interest, like fashion, sports or photography. Some people buy them regularly, and some people only read them while they wait for the dentist.

Magazines that focus on celebrity gossip, fashion and beauty, however, are often criticised for putting too much emphasis on superficial things. This focus can become unhealthy when it makes people feel negative about themselves, or feel pressured to buy things they can't afford. After all, magazines make most of their money through advertising.

On the other hand, pop culture magazines present up-to-date information about modern day life and bring people with a common interest together. They also encourage people who don't enjoy reading to read more.

Magazines have been around since the 1600s and, although their popularity is decreasing, they will probably be around for a long time to come.

Answer the questions in pairs.

1 Do you read magazines? Which ones?
2 Why do people enjoy reading magazines?
3 Are pop culture magazines superficial? Why?
4 How could magazines be used to help people?

Do all exercises in your notebook

27

Workbook project task notes

PROJECT: School magazine

Project • Units 1 and 2

Team members

TASK 1

Our chosen animal: ______

My research: ______

→ Student's book page 11

TASK 2

Topic of our quiz: ______

My research: ______

→ Student's book page 13

TASK 3

Who will write my profile: ______

Information to include: ______

→ Student's book page 16

TASK 4

Who we will interview: ______

What we will ask about: ______

→ Student's book page 19

TASK 5

The perfect daily routine: ______

How we will present the information: ______

→ Student's book page 21

TASK 6

Our chosen country: ______

Topics we will include: ______

→ Student's book page 24

FINAL TASK

How we will make the magazine: ______

How many pages we will have: ______

Name of the magazine: ______

→ Student's book page 26

20 Project task notes

Project task notes 21

Remind students to do all the exercises in their notebook

PROJECT FOCUS

→ See pages 24-27 **Projects**

Skills

- Collaborate to create a school magazine
- Write about pet care
- Research and write a quiz
- Write a personal profile
- Conduct and write up an interview
- Write an article about an ideal daily routine in your country and about daily life in another country
- Edit and correct written texts
- Discuss and evaluate the project
- Read and discuss a text related to the project

CEFR mediation

Facilitating collaborative interaction with peers

Can collaborate in simple practical tasks, asking what others think, making suggestions and understanding responses.

→ See pages 30-33 **Mediation**

Preparation Remind students to bring their work from tasks 1-6 and their notes from the **Workbook** project task notes pages 20-21. Decide how much class time you want to give them to complete their magazines and how long they will have to present them. Make sure students have access to any technology you want to give them the option of using, and/or whatever stationery they might need (e.g. scrap book, glue, scissors, pens). Get them to bring in their self-assessment diaries if you decided you wanted them to keep one.

Recap

Put students in their teams and read through the **Recap** as a class. Draw their attention to the project tasks and the unit objectives and ask which tasks helped achieve which objectives. Make sure they have all the materials and notes that they need (see **Preparation**) for the **Final task**.

Final Task: Complete and present your magazine

Put students into their teams and tell them they are now going to complete and present their magazines. Tell them the time limits you've decided for the two parts of the task. Before starting, direct their attention to the **21st century skill** (see next column).

Read through the steps of the task and make sure every team has the necessary materials. Suggest to students that they make a plan of what they need to decide and when, what tasks need to be done before the magazine is ready and who is going to do each. You could give them a time limit to do this first, just to make sure everyone knows what they're doing.

Monitor groups to make sure everyone is collaborating effectively and only intervene to show interest and praise work or to help if a group is really stuck and students are getting frustrated.

When students are ready to present their magazines, get them to decide if all of the group is going to present it or if they're going to choose a representative. Then when they exchange magazines, make sure each group decides which section is best before handing them on to another group. You could round up with a class vote on which magazines they thought were most interesting, best presented and best written, for example.

21ST CENTURY SKILLS

Read through the text with the students. Ask them how well they think they have negotiated in the project so far and tell them that they will have to continue to negotiate in the **Final task**. Remind them that everyone has the responsibility to hear others and make themselves heard in order to reach an effective consensus

→ See pages 28-29 **21st century skills**

Evaluation

Before students discuss the questions as a group, give them time to prepare notes about their experience during the project. Remind students to be supportive and give constructive criticism if necessary, with ideas on how to do things better next time. Monitor discussions, adding your own feedback where appropriate and noting common observations to then convey to the class as a whole. Have a class discussion about what students have learnt from the project, reminding them of the unit objectives, the **Core values** and the **Learning to learn tools** of units 1 and 2 as well as the **21st Century skills** section of the **Project** pages.

As is suggested in the introductory notes on **Assessment**, the **Evaluation** section of the project could be an opportunity for students to write a diary of self-assessment. This would include short comments on the knowledge and skills they have acquired and developed, those which they want to work on and their feelings about their learning and progress. Encourage them to use the **Evaluation** discussion as a base and to refer to the Reflect on your learning section of the **Workbook** if they have one.

→ See pages 40-41 **Assessment**

Go beyond

Get students to discuss their answers to the questions below the text before reading it and then to read and compare ideas. Open up to a class discussion if there is time.

Remind students to do all the exercises in their notebook

CONTINUOUS ASSESSMENT Students can negotiate respectfully and effectively to produce a magazine as a group.

3 ART FORMS

At the start of each unit and lesson, explain to the students what the objectives are.

Language objectives

Grammar

Past simple
- Students practise the past simple in the affirmative and the negative, and in questions.

Used to
- Students learn how to talk about past habits.

Vocabulary

Irregular verbs: *became, fell, fought, gave, had, made, met, say, sat, took*
- Students learn the past simple forms of irregular verbs.

Culture: *act, audience, ballerina, dance, interval, orchestra, perform, performance, performer, play, row, screen, stage, star*
- Students learn and categorise words related to art and culture

Art forms: *architecture, cinema, digital art, drawing, literature, music, novel, performing arts, painting, photography, poetry, sculpture, short story, theatre, visual arts*
- Students learn vocabulary related to art forms

Idioms and expressions

Likes and dislikes: *not my cup of tea, can't stand something, be crazy about something*

- Students look at idioms and expressions related to likes and dislikes in the context of art.

Recycled language

Adjectives, Irregular verbs, Questions

Skills objectives

Speaking

- Students discuss paintings and famous painters.
- Students test their knowledge of the artworks discussed.
- Students categorise different art forms and discuss new ones.
- Students debate the importance of art in society.
- Students use their imagination and creativity to invent new uses for an everyday object.
- Students talk about the art forms that they like and those that they dislike.

Pronunciation: Students practise question intonation.

Pairwork: Students use various mediation techniques in order to describe and discuss two different styles of paintings.

Listening

- Students listen and complete fact files about famous paintings and painters.
- Students listen in order to write questions.
- Students listen to complete a written text about the theatre.
- Students listen to teenagers talking about their past habits and their new hobbies.
- Students listen and complete sentences with *used to*.
- Students listen to identify key information within a text.
- Students listen to identify opinions about artworks around the world.

Reading

- Students read about different artists and complete sentences about them.
- Students read and complete a text about the theatre.
- Students read a text and answer questions about a famous dancer.
- Students read a text about turning points in the arts and answer questions.
- Students read a text about a famous artist and complete a fact file.

Core values: Students consider the definition of **creativity** and practise using their imagination.

Writing

- Students write sentences about past habits.
- Students plan, write and check a description of a piece of art.

Focus on adjectives to describe artworks; *abstract, beautiful, classical, fantastic, ugly, terrible, etc.*

Learning to learn tools

SPEAKING TOOLS Students practise and memorise new expressions by applying them to their own lives and experiences.	**LISTENING TOOLS** Student practise repeating new words out loud to perfect pronunciation.
READING TOOLS Students practise reading to identify distractors.	**WRITING TOOLS** Students practise writing with an audience in mind to ensure that meaning is clear.

VOCABULARY TOOLS Students practise categorising new words to remember them better.

Project objectives: Biography

Task 1 Students choose a famous person from the past to research.

Task 2 Students make notes about the childhood and daily life of their chosen person.

Task 3 Students research how and why their chosen person became famous.

Audiovisual objectives

Vlog: Students watch and listen to Emma talk about a new painting.

Culture: Students watch and listen to Emma talk about art galleries.

Grammar animations: Students are presented with visual presentations of the unit grammar.

Key competences

LC **Linguistic**
pages 28-35

MST **Mathematical and Science and Technology**
pages 29, 32

DC **Digital**
pages 28, 29, 31, 35

SCC **Social and Civic**
pages 32, 35

CAE **Cultural awareness and expression**
pages 28-35

LL **Learning to learn**
pages 28, 30, 32, 34, 35

IE **Sense of initiative and entrepreneurship**
pages 29, 31, 34

→ See pages 42-43 **Key competences**

CEFR Mediation

3.1 Relaying specific information in writing
Can list the main points of short, spoken texts.

3.2 Relaying specific information in writing
Can relay in writing specific information in spoken texts.

3.3 Processing text in writing
Can summarise the main points in straightforward written texts.

3.4 Processing text in writing
Can collate information and summarise it.

3.5 Encouraging conceptual talk
Can ask what somebody thinks of a certain idea.

Project Processing text in speech
Can collate short pieces of information from several sources and summarise them.

Unit review Collaborating to construct meaning
Can ask someone to give reasons for their views.

Pairwork Streamlining a text
Can highlight the essential information in a text to pass it on.

→ See pages 30-33 **Mediation**

Remind students to do all the exercises in their notebook

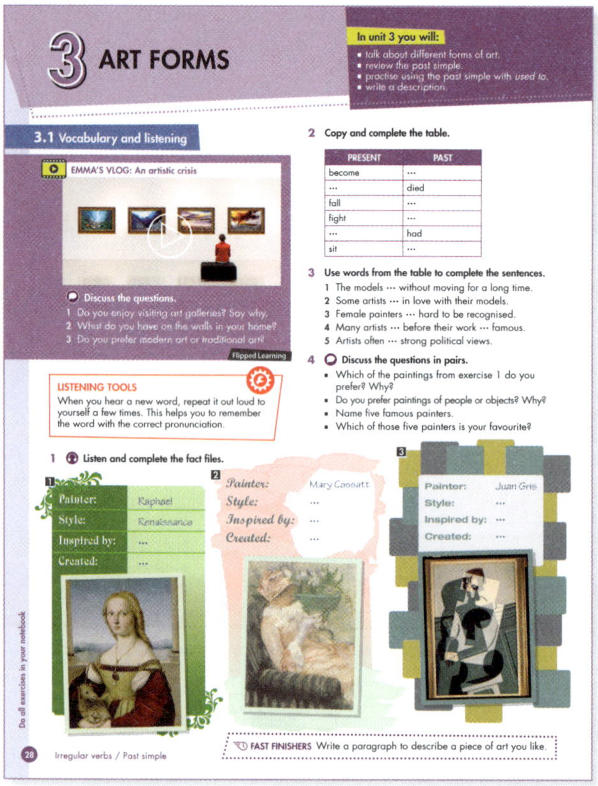

3 ART FORMS

In unit 3 you will:
- talk about different forms of art.
- review the past simple.
- practise using the past simple with *used to*.
- write a description.

3.1 Vocabulary and listening

EMMA'S VLOG: An artistic crisis

Discuss the questions.
1 Do you enjoy visiting art galleries? Say why.
2 What do you have on the walls in your home?
3 Do you prefer modern art or traditional art?

Flipped Learning

LISTENING TOOLS
When you hear a new word, repeat it out loud to yourself a few times. This helps you to remember the word with the correct pronunciation.

1 Listen and complete the fact files.

1	
Painter:	Raphael
Style:	Renaissance
Inspired by:	...
Created:	...

2	
Painter:	Mary Cassatt
Style:	...
Inspired by:	...
Created:	...

3	
Painter:	Juan Gris
Style:	...
Inspired by:	...
Created:	...

2 Copy and complete the table.

PRESENT	PAST
become	...
...	died
fall	...
fight	...
...	had
sit	...

3 Use words from the table to complete the sentences.
1 The models ··· without moving for a long time.
2 Some artists ··· in love with their models.
3 Female painters ··· hard to be recognised.
4 Many artists ··· before their work ··· famous.
5 Artists often ··· strong political views.

4 Discuss the questions in pairs.
- Which of the paintings from exercise 1 do you prefer? Why?
- Do you prefer paintings of people or objects? Why?
- Name five famous painters.
- Which of those five painters is your favourite?

FAST FINISHERS Write a paragraph to describe a piece of art you like.

Do all exercises in your notebook

28 Irregular verbs / Past simple

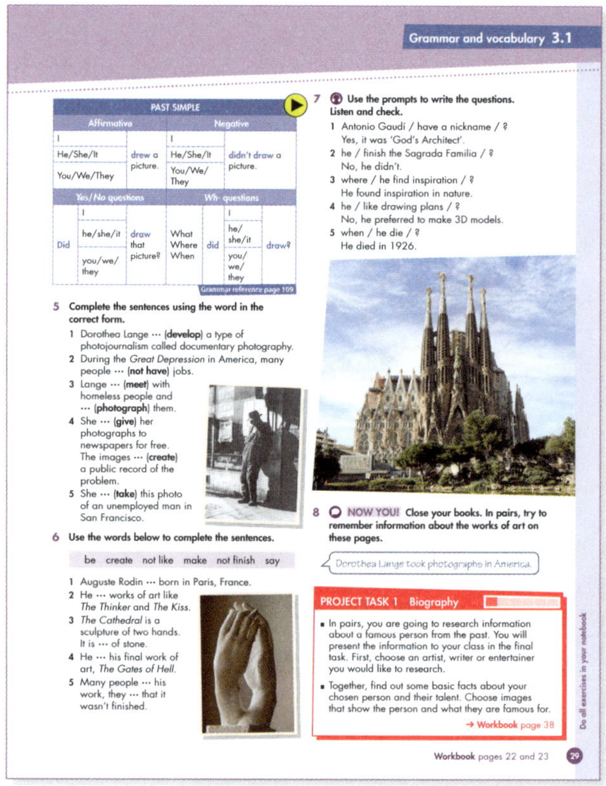

Grammar and vocabulary 3.1

PAST SIMPLE			
Affirmative		Negative	
I He/She/It You/We/They	drew a picture.	I He/She/It You/We/They	didn't draw a picture.
Yes/No questions		Wh- questions	
Did I / he/she/it / you/we/they	draw that picture?	What / Where / When did I / he/she/it / you/we/they	draw?

Grammar reference page 109

5 Complete the sentences using the word in the correct form.
1 Dorothea Lange ··· (develop) a type of photojournalism called documentary photography.
2 During the *Great Depression* in America, many people ··· (not have) jobs.
3 Lange ··· (meet) with homeless people and ··· (photograph) them.
4 She ··· (give) her photographs to newspapers for free. The images ··· (create) a public record of the problem.
5 She ··· (take) this photo of an unemployed man in San Francisco.

6 Use the words below to complete the sentences.

be create not like make not finish say

1 Auguste Rodin ··· born in Paris, France.
2 He ··· works of art like *The Thinker* and *The Kiss*.
3 *The Cathedral* is a sculpture of two hands. It is ··· of stone.
4 He ··· his final work of art, *The Gates of Hell*.
5 Many people ··· his work, they ··· that it wasn't finished.

7 Use the prompts to write the questions. Listen and check.
1 Antonio Gaudí / have a nickname / ?
Yes, it was 'God's Architect'.
2 he / finish the Sagrada Familia / ?
No, he didn't.
3 where / he find inspiration / ?
He found inspiration in nature.
4 he / like drawing plans / ?
No, he preferred to make 3D models.
5 when / he die / ?
He died in 1926.

8 NOW YOU! Close your books. In pairs, try to remember information about the works of art on these pages.

Dorothea Lange took photographs in America.

PROJECT TASK 1 Biography
- In pairs, you are going to research information about a famous person from the past. You will present the information to your class in the final task. First, choose an artist, writer or entertainer you would like to research.
- Together, find out some basic facts about your chosen person and their talent. Choose images that show the person and what they are famous for.

→ Workbook page 38

Do all exercises in your notebook

Workbook pages 22 and 23 29

ANSWER KEY

Pages 28-29

1 1 **Painter:** Raphael
Style: Renaissance
Inspired by: Beauty and harmony
Created: 1506

2 **Painter:** Mary Cassatt
Style: Impressionist
Inspired by: Women's social and private lives
Created: 1880

3 **Painter:** Juan Gris
Style: Cubist
Inspired by: Mathematics
Created: 1916

2

become	became
die	died
fall	fell
fight	fought
have	had
sit	sat

3 1 sat
2 fell
3 fought
4 died; became
5 had

4 *Student's own answers*

5 1 developed
2 did not have/didn't have
3 met; photographed
4 gave; created
5 took

6 1 was
2 created
3 made
4 didn't finish
5 don't like; say

7 1 Did Antoni Gaudí have a nickname?
2 Did he finish the Sagrada Familia?
3 Where did he find inspiration?
4 Did he like drawing plans?
5 When did he die?

8 *Student's own answers*

Remind students to do all the exercises in their notebook

LESSON FOCUS

Grammar Past simple
Vocabulary Irregular verbs
Listening Artist fact files
Speaking Evaluation of various art works
Project task 1 Choose a famous person from the past to research

Resources
Teacher's i-solutions, Student's Book audio, Vlog and worksheet

Flipped Learning

EMMA'S VLOG: An artistic crisis

- Make sure to set up the **Flipped Learning** work with the students beforehand. **See page 20-23 for complete Flipped Learning guidelines.**
- Ask students to put the **Flipped Learning worksheets** on their desks and walk around to check how many have completed the Flipped task.
- In pairs or small groups, ask students to compare and check the *Before you watch…* and *While you watch…* exercises on the worksheet.
- Show students **Emma's Vlog** and ask volunteers to provide correct answers and clarify any doubts other students may have.
- Choose three or four students to read aloud their answers to the *After you watch…* exercises on the worksheet and encourage some class discussion.
- Move straight to exercise 1 on page 28.

Warmer

Watch Emma's Vlog and discuss the questions with the whole class. If you don't have video facilities, simply discuss the questions.

LISTENING TOOLS

Get students to read the **Listening tool** and encourage them to put it into practice in exercise 1. You could ask volunteers to tell you words whose pronunciation surprised them after the exercise.

1 1.21 (See page 170 for transcripts) Before starting the exercise, ask students if they recognise any of the paintings and if so, where they have seen them.

2 Write the table on the board and complete it as a class. Review the past simple where necessary.

3 After students have completed the exercise, tell them to check their answers with the person sitting next to them.

4 After students have discussed their ideas in pairs, open up a class debate. Ask students to compare the five famous painters from this exercise to the three painters in exercise one.

FAST FINISHERS Students can complete this exercise alone or in pairs.

Flipped Learning

PAST SIMPLE

Draw students' attention to the **Grammar table**. Remind students that they can use this as a quick reference while completing the exercises.

Show students the **Grammar animation** and/or refer students to the **Grammar reference** on page 109 for further information on form and use.

➔ See pages 23 for how to flip the **grammar lesson**

5 Students should work alone on this exercise and use the **Grammar table** and the **Grammar reference** on page 109 for further guidance.

6 Get students to cover up the wordpool and as a class ask what verbs they would use to fill the gaps. Review the past simple where necessary. Students can then complete the exercise alone or in pairs.

7 1.22 (See page 170 for transcripts) Remind students that they should use the **Grammar table** to assist with constructing these questions correctly. They will be able to listen and check their answers.

8 NOW YOU! Write the names of the artists on the board (Raphael; Mary Cassatt; Juan Gris; Dorothea Lange; Auguste Rodin; Antonio Gaudí) and complete this exercise as a class. Encourage students to use the past simple and vocabulary from the previous exercises.

PROJECT TASK 1 Biography

Organise students in pairs. Students should decide between them which famous person from the past they wish to research in order to write a biography of them. When they have decided, students should find images of the person and what they are famous for. Remind students that they need to keep their project notes together in their **Workbook** (page 38) or in their own notebook.

➔ See pages 24-27 **Projects**

FURTHER PRACTICE

Workbook pages 22-23
- **Grammar reference and practice** pages 86 and 94-95
- **Wordlist and exercises** pages 99 and 103

Remind students to do all the exercises in their notebook

CONTINUOUS ASSESSMENT Students can use the past simple with regular and irregular verbs.

3.2 Vocabulary and listening

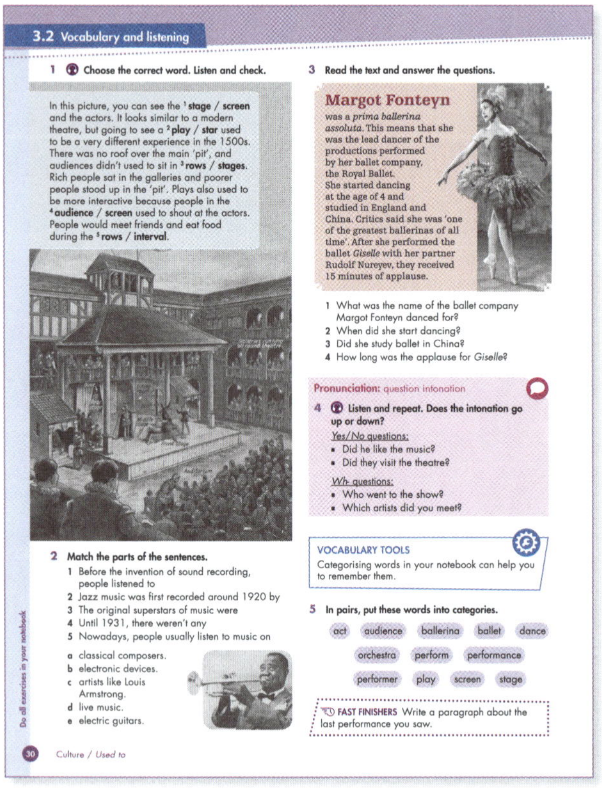

3.2 Vocabulary and listening

1 Choose the correct word. Listen and check.

In this picture, you can see the [1] **stage / screen** and the actors. It looks similar to a modern theatre, but going to see a [2] **play / star** used to be a very different experience in the 1500s. There was no roof over the main 'pit', and audiences didn't used to sit in [3] **rows / stages**. Rich people sat in the galleries and poorer people stood up in the 'pit'. Plays also used to be more interactive because people in the [4] **audience / screen** used to shout at the actors. People would meet friends and eat food during the [5] **rows / interval**.

2 Match the parts of the sentences.

1 Before the invention of sound recording, people listened to
2 Jazz music was first recorded around 1920 by
3 The original superstars of music were
4 Until 1931, there weren't any
5 Nowadays, people usually listen to music on

a classical composers.
b electronic devices.
c artists like Louis Armstrong.
d live music.
e electric guitars.

3 Read the text and answer the questions.

Margot Fonteyn was a *prima ballerina assoluta*. This means that she was the lead dancer of the productions performed by her ballet company, the Royal Ballet. She started dancing at the age of 4 and studied in England and China. Critics said she was 'one of the greatest ballerinas of all time'. After she performed the ballet *Giselle* with her partner Rudolf Nureyev, they received 15 minutes of applause.

1 What was the name of the ballet company Margot Fonteyn danced for?
2 When did she start dancing?
3 Did she study ballet in China?
4 How long was the applause for *Giselle*?

Pronunciation: question intonation

4 Listen and repeat. Does the intonation go up or down?

Yes/No questions:
- Did he like the music?
- Did they visit the theatre?

Wh- questions:
- Who went to the show?
- Which artists did you meet?

VOCABULARY TOOLS
Categorising words in your notebook can help you to remember them.

5 In pairs, put these words into categories.

act audience ballerina ballet dance orchestra perform performance performer play screen stage

FAST FINISHERS Write a paragraph about the last performance you saw.

Do all exercises in your notebook

30 Culture / *Used to*

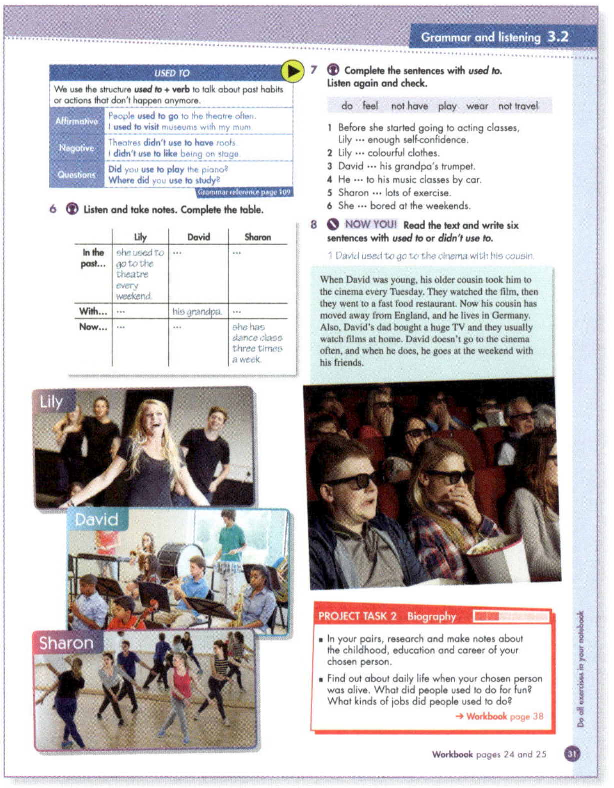

Grammar and listening 3.2

USED TO

We use the structure ***used to* + verb** to talk about past habits or actions that don't happen anymore.

Affirmative	People **used to go** to the theatre often. I **used to visit** museums with my mum.
Negative	Theatres **didn't use to have** roofs. I **didn't use to like** being on stage.
Questions	**Did** you **use to play** the piano? **Where did** you **use to study**?

Grammar reference page 109

6 Listen and take notes. Complete the table.

	Lily	David	Sharon
In the past...	she used to go to the theatre every weekend.	...	...
With...	...	his grandpa.	...
Now...	...	...	she has dance class three times a week.

Lily

David

Sharon

7 Complete the sentences with *used to*. Listen again and check.

do feel not have play wear not travel

1 Before she started going to acting classes, Lily ··· enough self-confidence.
2 Lily ··· colourful clothes.
3 David ··· his grandpa's trumpet.
4 He ··· to his music classes by car.
5 Sharon ··· lots of exercise.
6 She ··· bored at the weekends.

8 NOW YOU! Read the text and write six sentences with *used to* or *didn't use to*.

1 David used to go to the cinema with his cousin.

When David was young, his older cousin took him to the cinema every Tuesday. They watched the film, then they went to a fast food restaurant. Now his cousin has moved away from England, and he lives in Germany. Also, David's dad bought a huge TV and they usually watch films at home. David doesn't go to the cinema often, and when he does, he goes at the weekend with his friends.

PROJECT TASK 2 Biography
- In your pairs, research and make notes about the childhood, education and career of your chosen person.
- Find out about daily life when your chosen person was alive. What did people used to do for fun? What kinds of jobs did people used to do?

→ Workbook page 38

Do all exercises in your notebook

Workbook pages 24 and 25 31

ANSWER KEY

Pages 30-31

1 **1** stage **2** play **3** rows **4** audience **5** interval

2 **1** d **2** c **3** a **4** e **5** b

3 **1** the Royal Ballet
2 at the age of 4
3 Yes, and also in England
4 15 minutes

4 *Student's own answers*

5 *Suggested answer:*
Verbs: perform, dance
Nouns: audience, ballerina, ballet, orchestra, performance, performer, screen, stage
Both: play, act

6

	Lily	David	Sharon
In the past…	she used to go to the theatre every weekend.	he used to go to see concerts.	she used to watch a lot of TV.
With…	her aunt.	his grandpa.	her sister.
Now…	she is the star of the school show.	he plays in the school orchestra.	she has dance class three times a week.

7 **1** didn't use to have
2 used to wear
3 used to play
4 didn't use to travel
5 didn't use to do
6 used to feel

8 *Suggested answers:*
1 David used to go to the cinema with his cousin.
2 David and his cousin used to eat in a fast food restaurant.
3 David's cousin used to live in England.
4 David didn't use to watch films at home.
5 David used to go to the cinema every Tuesday.
6 David didn't use to go to the cinema with his friends.

Remind students to do all the exercises in their notebook

LESSON FOCUS

Grammar *Used to*
Vocabulary Culture
Listening Descriptions of past habitual actions; description of the theatre
Speaking Categorising words related to the stage
Project task 2 Make notes about the childhood and daily life of the famous person students have chosen

Resources
Teacher's i-solutions, Student's Book audio
Preparation Photographs of different kinds of stage performances (a play, ballet, opera, standup, concert, etc.)

Warmer

Show the students some photographs of different stage performances. Ask them to tell you what they think is happening in each photograph. Then ask them to say which performance they would most like to attend and why.

1 1.23 (See page 171 for transcripts) After students have completed the exercise, tell them to cover the text and ask them what they can see in the image. Try to elicit key vocabulary from the exercise (stage, audience, actors, etc.)

2 Students can complete the exercise alone, or in pairs.

3 Ask students what they know about ballet and if they have ever seen a ballet performance. Ask one student to read the text aloud, then answer the questions as a class.

Pronunciation

4 1.24 (See page 171 for transcripts) After the students complete the pronunciation exercise, tell them to write two more *yes/no* questions and two more *wh-* questions, and say them out loud making sure to use the correct intonation.

VOCABULARY TOOLS

Draw students' attention to the **Vocabulary tool** and encourage them to apply it to the next exercise.

5 In their pairs, students should discuss what kind of words these are (nouns and verbs) and what kind of art forms they belong to. Remind students that categorising the words in this way – both by the kind of vocabulary they are and what they describe – will help them to remember the words when they want to use them in speech and writing.

FAST FINISHERS Students can complete this exercise alone or in pairs.

USED TO

Flipped Learning

Draw students' attention to the **Grammar table**. Remind students that they can use this as a quick reference while completing the exercises.
Show students the **Grammar animation** and/or refer students to the **Grammar reference** on page 109 for further information on form and use.

→ See page 23 for how to flip the **grammar lesson**

6 1.25 (See page 171 for transcripts) Before starting this exercise, ask students what kind of activities they can see in the photos. Test their knowledge from the previous exercises by asking questions like:
- How are theatres today different to theatres in the 1500s?
- What style of music do you think David is playing? Do you think he uses any electronic devices? When was Jazz music first recorded?
- Is Sharon a ballerina? What can you remember about Margot Fonteyn?

7 1.26 (See page 171 for transcripts) Remind students that taking notes during a listening exercise improves their understanding and is good practice for exams. Tell them to refer to their notes from exercise 6 to help complete this exercise.

8 NOW YOU! Tell students to make use of the **Grammar table** and the **Grammar references** to help them complete this exercise. Once they have finished, ask them to write two extra sentences related to themselves and something they *used to* or *didn't used to* do.

PROJECT TASK 2 Biography

Ask students to research the famous person they have chosen in order to find out more about their early life and how and why they became famous, as well as to learn about daily life during the person's lifetime. Remind students that they need to keep their project notes together in their **Workbook** (page 38) or in their own notebook.

→ See pages 24-27 **Projects**

FURTHER PRACTICE

Workbook pages 24-25
- **Grammar reference and practice** pages 86 and 94-95
- **Wordlist and exercises** pages 99 and 103

Vocabulary and Grammar worksheets available to download and edit from the
Richmond*Learning***Platform**

→ See pages 38-39 **Mixed-ability classes**

Remind students to do all the exercises in their notebook

CONTINUOUS ASSESSMENT Students can talk about culture and use *used to*.

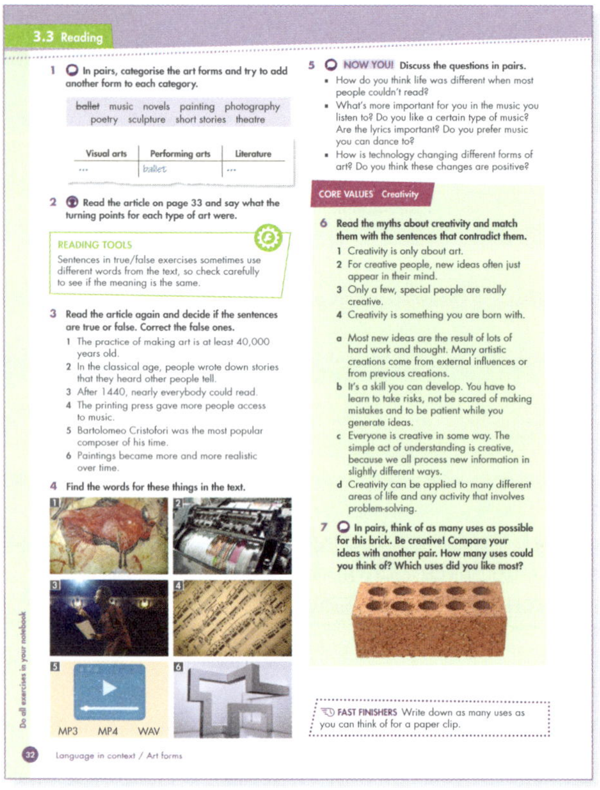

3.3 Reading

1 In pairs, categorise the art forms and try to add another form to each category.

~~ballet~~ music novels painting photography poetry sculpture short stories theatre

Visual arts	Performing arts	Literature
...	ballet	...

2 Read the article on page 33 and say what the turning points for each type of art were.

READING TOOLS
Sentences in true/false exercises sometimes use different words from the text, so check carefully to see if the meaning is the same.

3 Read the article again and decide if the sentences are true or false. Correct the false ones.

1 The practice of making art is at least 40,000 years old.
2 In the classical age, people wrote down stories that they heard other people tell.
3 After 1440, nearly everybody could read.
4 The printing press gave more people access to music.
5 Bartolomeo Cristofori was the most popular composer of his time.
6 Paintings became more and more realistic over time.

4 Find the words for these things in the text.

1 2 3 4 5 MP3 MP4 WAV 6

5 NOW YOU! Discuss the questions in pairs.

- How do you think life was different when most people couldn't read?
- What's more important for you in the music you listen to? Do you like a certain type of music? Are the lyrics important? Do you prefer music you can dance to?
- How is technology changing different forms of art? Do you think these changes are positive?

CORE VALUES Creativity

6 Read the myths about creativity and match them with the sentences that contradict them.

1 Creativity is only about art.
2 For creative people, new ideas often just appear in their mind.
3 Only a few, special people are really creative.
4 Creativity is something you are born with.

a Most new ideas are the result of lots of hard work and thought. Many artistic creations come from external influences or from previous creations.
b It's a skill you can develop. You have to learn to take risks, not be scared of making mistakes and to be patient while you generate ideas.
c Everyone is creative in some way. The simple act of understanding is creative, because we all process new information in slightly different ways.
d Creativity can be applied to many different areas of life and any activity that involves problem-solving.

7 In pairs, think of as many uses as possible for this brick. Be creative! Compare your ideas with another pair. How many uses could you think of? Which uses did you like most?

FAST FINISHERS Write down as many uses as you can think of for a paper clip.

Do all exercises in your notebook

32 Language in context / Art forms

Reading 3.3

TURNING POINTS IN THE ARTS

From the first cave paintings over 40,000 years ago to interactive multi-media artistic experiences today, art has a long and dynamic history. Let's take a look at some of the important moments in the history of the arts.

LITERATURE

The biggest change in the history of literature was the development of writing. People used to tell stories and perform plays from memory, and many famous classical texts come from stories passed down orally over generations. The invention of the printing press in 1440 meant that literature became available to nearly everybody, so many more people learnt to read (although literacy rates in Europe were still less than 50%). Interestingly, one form of literature that's becoming more popular now is performance poetry.

MUSIC

The printing press was also important for music, as it meant that we could print sheet music and distribute it for everyone to play. And in 1700, Bartolomeo Cristofori invented an instrument that quickly became the most popular to compose for, and is still the most popular to play: the piano. But probably the biggest change in music was digital audio files. Now we can listen to any piece of music whenever we want!

VISUAL ARTS

The visual arts used to refer mainly to drawing, painting, sculpture and architecture. One important development in painting was the discovery of linear perspective in the Renaissance period. This is the technique of creating the illusion of 3D space, and it led to more realistic and detailed paintings. Then came the Modern Art revolution of the 19th and 20th centuries, where visual art became more about experimentation and abstraction. The biggest modern changes have been the development of new art forms such as photography, cinema and computer art. Who knows what the future holds?

Do all exercises in your notebook

Workbook pages 26 and 27 33

ANSWER KEY

Pages 32-33

1

Visual arts	Performing arts	Literature
painting photography sculpture *Suggested added forms:* illustration, ceramics, architecture, cinema, etc	ballet music theatre *Suggested added forms:* opera, other types of dance, mime, etc	poetry novels short stories *Suggested added forms:* drama, essays, novellas, etc

2 **Literature:** The development of writing
Music: Digital audio files
Visual arts: The development of new art forms, such as photography, cinema and computer art

3 **1** True
2 True
3 False. Nearly everybody had access to books but less than 50% of Europeans could read.
4 True
5 False. He was the inventor of the piano, the most popular instrument to compose for at the time.
6 False. They became more realistic in the Renaissance with the discovery of perspective, and then more abstract in the 19th and 20th centuries.

4 **1** cave paintings
2 the printing press
3 performance poetry
4 sheet music
5 digital audio file
6 sculpture

5 *Student's own answers*

6 **1** d **2** a **3** c **4** b

7 *Student's own answers*

Remind students to do all the exercises in their notebook

LESSON FOCUS
Language in context Art forms
Core values Creativity

Resources
Teacher's i-solutions, Student's Book audio

Preparation Blank sheets of paper

➔ See pages 36-37 **Literature**

Warmer

Let students know that the lesson will be about creativity. To get them started, put the students in groups of five and play this quick game:

Make sure each student has a pen and a blank sheet of paper. Each student should write their name on the piece of paper. Students have 10 seconds to start drawing a picture. Once the time is up, each student passes their paper to the person on their right to continue the drawing. Repeat until each student has their original drawing back. In groups, ask students to share their pictures and discuss whether they consider them art.

1 Once students have completed the exercise in pairs, ask them why categorising new vocabulary is helpful. If they don't remember, remind them of the **Vocabulary tool** on page 30.

2 1.27 (See page 171 for transcripts) Before students begin reading the text on page 33, tell them to look at the title and the photographs and try to guess what the article is about.

READING TOOLS

Draw students' attention to the **Reading tool**. Reading comprehension questions often include synonyms so students should make sure they understand the question fully before answering it.

3 After completing the exercise, draw students' attention back to the **Reading tool** and ask students if they identified any synonyms. Write them on the board.

4 Complete the exercise as a class. Add the words to the board, to help students with the next exercise.

5 NOW YOU! After students have discussed the questions in pairs, open the discussion up to the class.

CORE VALUES Creativity

6 Before starting this exercise, ask students if they think that someone like Einstein, a physicist, would consider creativity to be an important skill. Let them know that Einstein said: "Imagination is more important than knowledge." Ask students what they think he meant by this. After students have completed the exercise, ask them to write a few sentences about their own beliefs about creativity and its value in society.

7 Once the pairs have come up with their different creations, ask them to pick their favourite one and share it with the class.

FAST FINISHERS Students can complete this exercise alone or in pairs.

FURTHER PRACTICE

Workbook pages 26-27

Remind students to do all the exercises in their notebook

CONTINUOUS ASSESSMENT Students can understand vocabulary for art forms in a text about historic moments in the history of the arts.

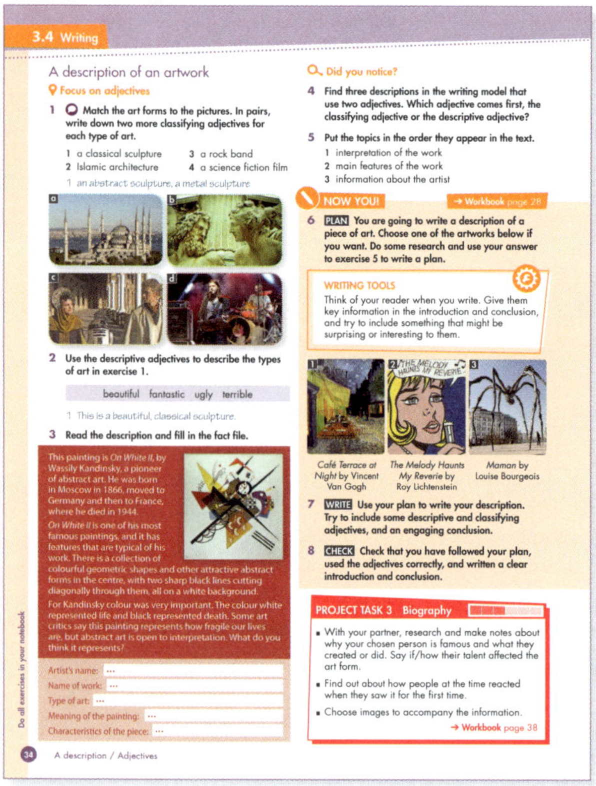
3.4 Writing

A description of an artwork

Focus on adjectives

1 Match the art forms to the pictures. In pairs, write down two more classifying adjectives for each type of art.

1 a classical sculpture
2 Islamic architecture
3 a rock band
4 a science fiction film

1 an abstract sculpture, a metal sculpture

2 Use the descriptive adjectives to describe the types of art in exercise 1.

beautiful fantastic ugly terrible

1 This is a beautiful, classical sculpture.

3 Read the description and fill in the fact file.

This painting is *On White II*, by Wassily Kandinsky, a pioneer of abstract art. He was born in Moscow in 1866, moved to Germany and then to France, where he died in 1944.

On White II is one of his most famous paintings, and it has features that are typical of his work. There is a collection of colourful geometric shapes and other attractive abstract forms in the centre, with two sharp black lines cutting diagonally through them, all on a white background.

For Kandinsky colour was very important. The colour white represented life and black represented death. Some art critics say this painting represents how fragile our lives are, but abstract art is open to interpretation. What do you think it represents?

Artist's name: ...
Name of work: ...
Type of art: ...
Meaning of the painting: ...
Characteristics of the piece: ...

Did you notice?

4 Find three descriptions in the writing model that use two adjectives. Which adjective comes first, the classifying adjective or the descriptive adjective?

5 Put the topics in the order they appear in the text.
1 interpretation of the work
2 main features of the work
3 information about the artist

NOW YOU! → Workbook page 28

6 PLAN You are going to write a description of a piece of art. Choose one of the artworks below if you want. Do some research and use your answer to exercise 5 to write a plan.

WRITING TOOLS
Think of your reader when you write. Give them key information in the introduction and conclusion, and try to include something that might be surprising or interesting to them.

Café Terrace at Night by Vincent Van Gogh
The Melody Haunts My Reverie by Roy Lichtenstein
Maman by Louise Bourgeois

7 WRITE Use your plan to write your description. Try to include some descriptive and classifying adjectives, and an engaging conclusion.

8 CHECK Check that you have followed your plan, used the adjectives correctly, and written a clear introduction and conclusion.

PROJECT TASK 3 Biography
- With your partner, research and make notes about why your chosen person is famous and what they created or did. Say if/how their talent affected the art form.
- Find out about how people at the time reacted when they saw it for the first time.
- Choose images to accompany the information.

→ Workbook page 38

Do all exercises in your notebook

34 A description / Adjectives

ANSWER KEY

Page 34

1 **1** b; *Student's own answers*
2 a; *Student's own answers*
3 d; *Student's own answers*
4 c; *Student's own answers*

2 *Student's own answers*

3 **Artist's name:** Wassily Kandinsky
Name of work: *On White II*
Type of art: abstract painting
Meaning of the painting: how fragile our lives are
Characteristics of the piece: colourful geometric shapes and abstract forms, two sharp black lines cutting diagonally through them, a white background

4 **1** colourful geometric shapes
2 attractive abstract forms
3 sharp black lines
the descriptive adjective comes before the classifying one.

5 3, 2, 1

6 *Student's own answers*

7 *Student's own answers*

8 *Student's own answers*

FURTHER PRACTICE

Workbook page 28

LESSON FOCUS

Focus on Adjectives

Writing A description of an artwork

Project task 3 Research what the chosen person became famous for

Resources

Teacher's i-solutions, Student's Book audio

Preparation Pictures of different artworks (buildings, paintings, films, books, sculpture)

Warmer

Put the pictures of the artworks up on one side of the board where the class can see them and get them to shout out adjectives that describe them. Write the words on the other side of the board.

Focus on adjectives

1 Ask students if they recognise any of the four pictures and which art form they prefer.

2 Do this exercise as a class and discuss differences in answers. For example, one student may answer: 'A terrible science fiction film' whereas another may answer: 'A fantastic science fiction film'.

3 Draw the fact file on the board. Once students have completed the exercise, ask them what they have written and fill in the fact file.

Did you notice?

4 Let students know that they can look back at exercises 1 and 2 to help them with this exercise.

5 Tell students that this exercise and the previous exercise will help them with the upcoming writing exercise.

6 **PLAN** Students will decide on the artwork they want to write about and use exercise 5 to write a plan.

WRITING TOOLS

Draw students' attention to the **Writing tool**. Remind them that it is important to remember that a reader might not know everything that the writer knows. If they bear this is mind, their writing will be easier to understand and more entertaining to read.

7 **WRITE** Encourage students to use descriptive and classifying adjectives in their writing.

8 **CHECK** Once students have checked their own work, they can swap with a partner and check theirs.

PROJECT TASK 3 Biography

Students will use the research they have done on their chosen artist to select one of their artworks to analyse. They will investigate whether the artist was popular during their lifetime or only after their death, and select an image to accompany the biography. Tell students that they need to keep their projects notes together in their **Workbook** (page 38) or in their own notebook.

→ See pages 24-27 **Projects**

Remind students to do all the exercises in their notebook

 CONTINUOUS ASSESSMENT Students can use adjectives to write a description of an artwork.

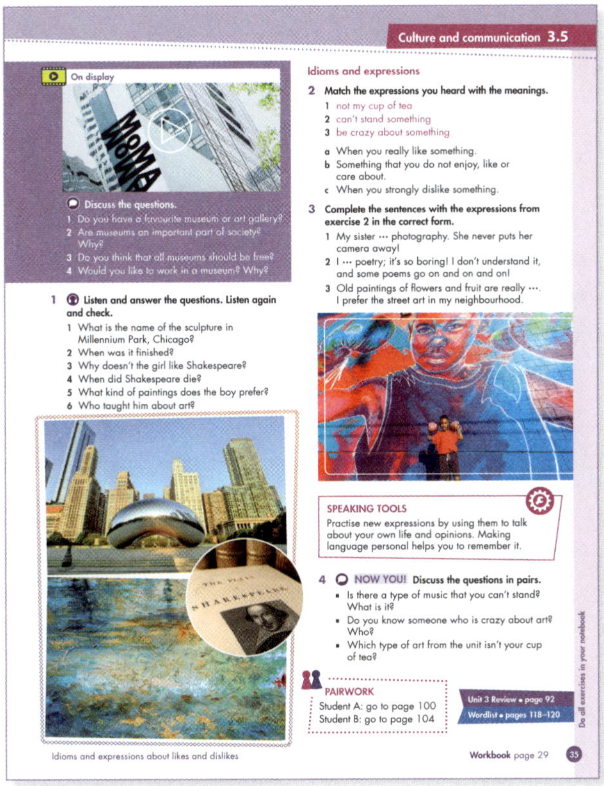
Culture and communication 3.5

On display

Discuss the questions.
1 Do you have a favourite museum or art gallery?
2 Are museums an important part of society? Why?
3 Do you think that all museums should be free?
4 Would you like to work in a museum? Why?

1 Listen and answer the questions. Listen again and check.
1 What is the name of the sculpture in Millennium Park, Chicago?
2 When was it finished?
3 Why doesn't the girl like Shakespeare?
4 When did Shakespeare die?
5 What kind of paintings does the boy prefer?
6 Who taught him about art?

Idioms and expressions

2 Match the expressions you heard with the meanings.
1 not my cup of tea
2 can't stand something
3 be crazy about something
a When you really like something.
b Something that you do not enjoy, like or care about.
c When you strongly dislike something.

3 Complete the sentences with the expressions from exercise 2 in the correct form.
1 My sister ··· photography. She never puts her camera away!
2 I ··· poetry; it's so boring! I don't understand it, and some poems go on and on and on!
3 Old paintings of flowers and fruit are really ···. I prefer the street art in my neighbourhood.

SPEAKING TOOLS
Practise new expressions by using them to talk about your own life and opinions. Making language personal helps you to remember it.

4 NOW YOU! Discuss the questions in pairs.
- Is there a type of music that you can't stand? What is it?
- Do you know someone who is crazy about art? Who?
- Which type of art from the unit isn't your cup of tea?

PAIRWORK
Student A: go to page 100
Student B: go to page 104

Unit 3 Review • page 92
Wordlist • pages 118–120

Do all exercises in your notebook

Idioms and expressions about likes and dislikes

Workbook page 29 35

LESSON FOCUS

Idioms and expressions Likes and dislikes
Listening Descriptions of artworks from around the world
Speaking Discussion of artworks and artistic preferences
Resources
Teacher's i-solutions, Student's Book audio, Culture video and worksheet

On display

Video and worksheet available on the
Richmond*Learning***Platform**

- In pairs, ask students to complete the *What I know...* exercises on the **Culture video worksheet**.
- Show students the **Culture video** and ask them to complete the *What I learned...* exercises on the worksheet.
- In pairs, students compare answers.
- In small groups, tell students to complete the *What I wonder...* exercises on the worksheet.

ANSWER KEY

Page 35

1 **1** Cloud Gate
2 2006
3 because she was forced to study Shakespeare at school
4 1616
5 paintings of people
6 his uncle

2 **1** b
2 c
3 a

3 **1** is crazy about
2 can't stand
3 not my cup of tea

4 *Student's own answers*

FURTHER PRACTICE AND UNIT ASSESSSMENT

Unit 3 Review Student's Book age 92
Workbook page 29
- **Reflect on your learning** page 29
- **Grammar reference and practice** pages 86 and 94-95
- **Wordlist and exercises** pages 99 and 103

Tests available to download and edit from the
Richmond*Learning***Platform**

➔ See pages 40-41 **Assessment**

Warmer

Watch the **Culture video** and discuss the questions with the whole class. If you don't have video facilities, simply discuss the questions.

1 1.28 (See page 171 for transcripts) Before listening to the audio, ask students which of the three pictures they prefer and why.

Idioms and expressions

2 Ask students if they are already familiar with any of the phrases and if they know any other words or phrases to express likes and dislikes.

3 Ask students to add one more sentence and apply it to a family member or a friend.

SPEAKING TOOLS

Draw students' attention to the **Speaking tool** and remind them that making words and phrases personal helps to remember them.

4 NOW YOU! Remind students to use the new phrases and idioms when talking about their preferences.

PAIRWORK Student's Book pages 100 and 104
See **Teacher's Book** page 88 for more information.
➔ See pages 30-33 **Mediation**

Remind students to do all the exercises in their notebook

CONTINUOUS ASSESSMENT Students can use idioms and expressions about likes and dislikes.

Unit 3 Review

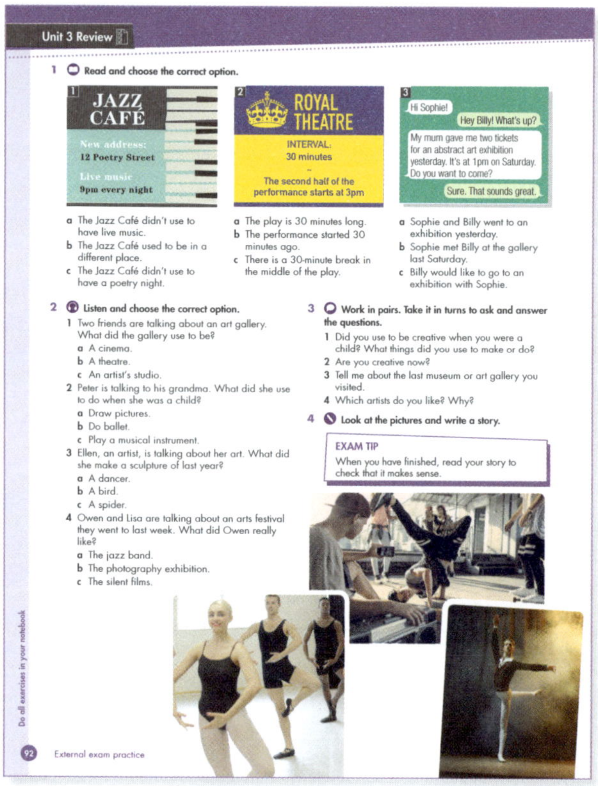
Unit 3 Review

1 Read and choose the correct option.

1
a The Jazz Café didn't use to have live music.
b The Jazz Café used to be in a different place.
c The Jazz Café didn't use to have a poetry night.

2
a The play is 30 minutes long.
b The performance started 30 minutes ago.
c There is a 30-minute break in the middle of the play.

3
a Sophie and Billy went to an exhibition yesterday.
b Sophie met Billy at the gallery last Saturday.
c Billy would like to go to an exhibition with Sophie.

2 Listen and choose the correct option.
1 Two friends are talking about an art gallery. What did the gallery use to be?
a A cinema.
b A theatre.
c An artist's studio.
2 Peter is talking to his grandma. What did she use to do when she was a child?
a Draw pictures.
b Do ballet.
c Play a musical instrument.
3 Ellen, an artist, is talking about her art. What did she make a sculpture of last year?
a A dancer.
b A bird.
c A spider.
4 Owen and Lisa are talking about an arts festival they went to last week. What did Owen really like?
a The jazz band.
b The photography exhibition.
c The silent films.

3 Work in pairs. Take it in turns to ask and answer the questions.
1 Did you use to be creative when you were a child? What things did you use to make or do?
2 Are you creative now?
3 Tell me about the last museum or art gallery you visited.
4 Which artists do you like? Why?

4 Look at the pictures and write a story.

EXAM TIP
When you have finished, read your story to check that it makes sense.

Do all exercises in your notebook

92 External exam practice

Student's Book page 92

ANSWER KEY

See page 180 for transcripts

1
1 b
2 c
3 c

2 2.39
1 b
2 c
3 a
4 b

3 *Student's own answers*

4 *Student's own answers*

Pairwork

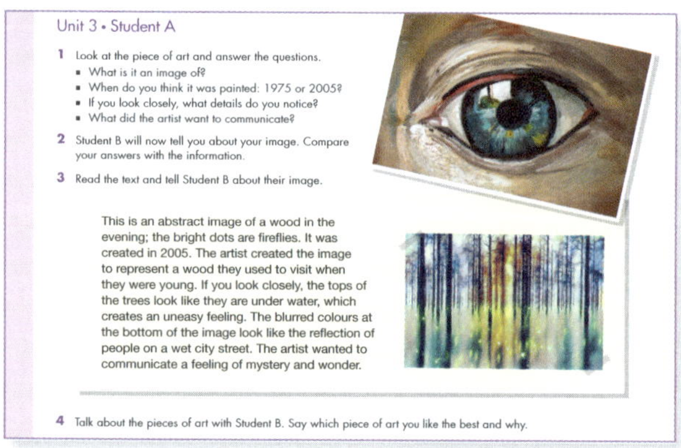
Unit 3 • Student A

1 Look at the piece of art and answer the questions.
- What is it an image of?
- When do you think it was painted: 1975 or 2005?
- If you look closely, what details do you notice?
- What did the artist want to communicate?

2 Student B will now tell you about your image. Compare your answers with the information.

3 Read the text and tell Student B about their image.

This is an abstract image of a wood in the evening; the bright dots are fireflies. It was created in 2005. The artist created the image to represent a wood they used to visit when they were young. If you look closely, the tops of the trees look like they are under water, which creates an uneasy feeling. The blurred colours at the bottom of the image look like the reflection of people on a wet city street. The artist wanted to communicate a feeling of mystery and wonder.

4 Talk about the pieces of art with Student B. Say which piece of art you like the best and why.

Student's Book page 100

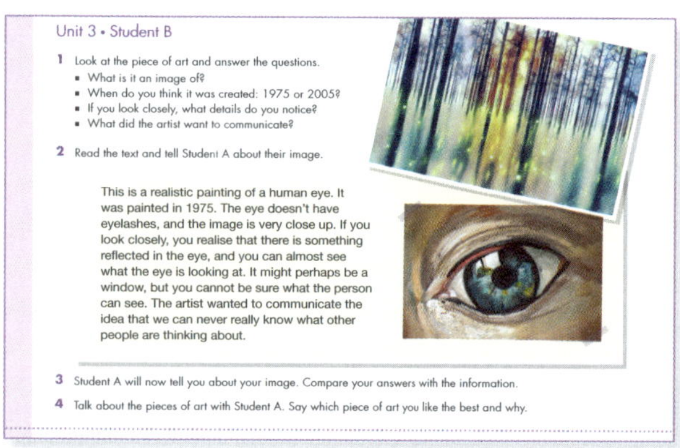
Unit 3 • Student B

1 Look at the piece of art and answer the questions.
- What is it an image of?
- When do you think it was created: 1975 or 2005?
- If you look closely, what details do you notice?
- What did the artist want to communicate?

2 Read the text and tell Student A about their image.

This is a realistic painting of a human eye. It was painted in 1975. The eye doesn't have eyelashes, and the image is very close up. If you look closely, you realise that there is something reflected in the eye, and you can almost see what the eye is looking at. It might perhaps be a window, but you cannot be sure what the person can see. The artist wanted to communicate the idea that we can never really know what other people are thinking about.

3 Student A will now tell you about your image. Compare your answers with the information.

4 Talk about the pieces of art with Student A. Say which piece of art you like the best and why.

Student's Book page 104

CEFR MEDIATION DESCRIPTOR

- **Adapting language**
  Students can paraphrase short written passages in a simple fashion, using the original order of the text.

- **Comparing information**
  Put the students in pairs, decide who is A and who is B and get them to turn to their corresponding page. Tell them they have the same instructions but different images and that they can't show each other their page. They will ask each other questions about two different paintings in order to find out more information. When they've finished, ask what they learnt about each other's artwork.

Remind students to do all the exercises in their notebook

Grammar reference

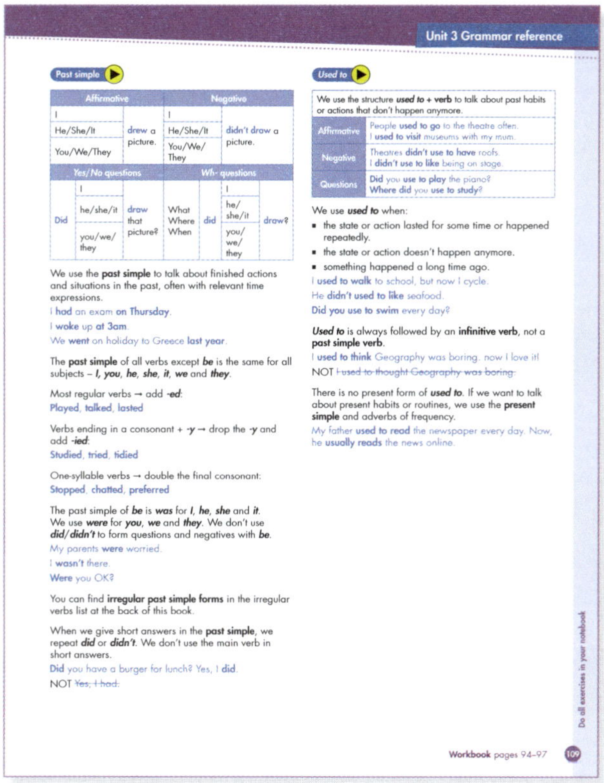

Past simple

Affirmative		Negative	
I	drew a picture.	I	didn't draw a picture.
He/She/It		He/She/It	
You/We/They		You/We/They	

Yes/No questions			Wh- questions			
Did	I	draw that picture?	What Where When	did	I	draw?
	he/she/it				he/she/it	
	you/we/they				you/we/they	

We use the **past simple** to talk about finished actions and situations in the past, often with relevant time expressions.

I **had** an exam **on Thursday**.

I **woke** up **at 3am**.

We **went** on holiday to Greece **last year**.

The **past simple** of all verbs except ***be*** is the same for all subjects – ***I, you, he, she, it, we*** and ***they***.

Most regular verbs → add ***-ed***:

Played, talked, lasted

Verbs ending in a consonant + ***-y*** → drop the ***-y*** and add ***-ied***:

Studied, tried, tidied

One-syllable verbs → double the final consonant:

Stopped, chatted, preferred

The past simple of ***be*** is ***was*** for ***I, he, she*** and ***it***. We use ***were*** for ***you, we*** and ***they***. We don't use ***did/didn't*** to form questions and negatives with ***be***.

My parents **were** worried.

I **wasn't** there.

Were you OK?

You can find **irregular past simple forms** in the irregular verbs list at the back of this book.

When we give short answers in the **past simple**, we repeat ***did*** or ***didn't***. We don't use the main verb in short answers.

Did you have a burger for lunch? Yes, I **did**.

NOT ~~Yes, I had.~~

Used to

We use the structure ***used to* + verb** to talk about past habits or actions that don't happen anymore.

Affirmative	People **used to go** to the theatre often. I **used to visit** museums with my mum.
Negative	Theatres **didn't use to have** roofs. I **didn't use to like** being on stage.
Questions	**Did** you **use to play** the piano? **Where did** you **use to study**?

We use ***used to*** when:

- the state or action lasted for some time or happened repeatedly.
- the state or action doesn't happen anymore.
- something happened a long time ago.

I **used to walk** to school, but now I cycle.

He **didn't used to like** seafood.

Did you use to swim every day?

Used to is always followed by an **infinitive verb**, not a **past simple verb**.

I **used to think** Geography was boring. now I love it!

NOT ~~I used to thought Geography was boring.~~

There is no present form of ***used to***. If we want to talk about present habits or routines, we use the **present simple** and adverbs of frequency.

My father **used to read** the newspaper every day. Now, he **usually reads** the news online.

Do all exercises in your notebook

Student's Book page 109

Wordlist

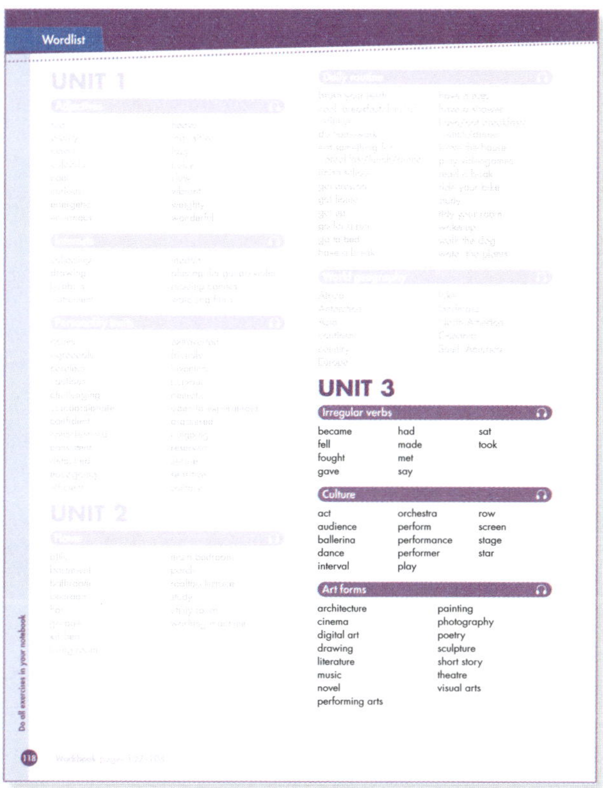

UNIT 3

Irregular verbs

became, fell, fought, gave, had, made, met, say, sat, took

Culture

act, audience, ballerina, dance, interval, orchestra, perform, performance, performer, play, row, screen, stage, star

Art forms

architecture, cinema, digital art, drawing, literature, music, novel, performing arts, painting, photography, poetry, sculpture, short story, theatre, visual arts

Do all exercises in your notebook

Student's Book page 118

2.52 2.53 2.54

Remind students to do all the exercises in their notebook

4 A SPECIAL DAY

At the start of each unit and lesson, explain to the students what the objectives are.

Language objectives

Grammar

There was* and *There were

- Students practise using *There was* and *There were* in the affirmative and the negative, and with questions.

Past continuous

- Students practise using the past continuous to talk about actions in progress in the past.

Vocabulary

Parties: *balloons, barbecue, birthday, biscuits, blow out, burgers, cake, candles, gift, gift tags, cupcakes, decorations, presents, sausages*

- Students use vocabulary related to parties.

Entertainment: *adventure, amusement park, backstage, camp, competition, concert, fancy restaurant, live music, rollercoaster, snorkelling, ticket, zip wire*

- Students use vocabulary to talk about entertainment.

Festivals and celebrations: *Easter, fireworks, gathering, graves, Halloween, make wishes, New Year, New Year's Eve, offerings, pagan, pole, powder, ritual, The Easter Bunny, water fights*

- Students learn new vocabulary related to festivals and celebrations.

Idioms and expressions

Feeling surprised: *someone's jaw drops, come out of the blue, take someone's breath away*

- Students look at idioms and expressions related to feeling surprised in the context of three short monologues.

Recycled language

Adverbs, Past simple

Skills objectives

Speaking

- Students talk about birthdays and celebrations.
- Students talk about special events and favourite memories.
- Students use their imagination to invent activities and discuss with a partner.
- Students talk about different festivals and celebrations from around the world and compare and contrast them.

Pronunciation: Students practise words with the /a:/ sound.

Pairwork: Students use various mediation techniques in order to answer questions about different types of parties.

Listening

- Students listen to complete a description of a birthday party.
- Students listen to complete information about different types of entertainment.
- Students listen to complete a diary entry about life at adventure camp.
- Students listen for information about achievements.

Reading

- Students read to answer multiple-choice questions about festivals and celebrations.
- Students read to find definitions of new words.
- Students read a story and make predictions about what happens next.

Core values: Students discuss **community** and the benefits of belonging to different community groups.

Writing

- Students write about their last birthday using *there was* and *there were*.
- Students plan, write and check a short story.

Focus on adverbs: *suddenly; every year; finally; last weekend*

Remind students to do all the exercises in their notebook

Learning to learn tools

SPEAKING TOOLS Students practise using new grammar and vocabulary in speech.	**LISTENING TOOLS** Students practise listening to the correct pronunciation of new words.
READING TOOLS Students practise making sure that they understand questions before completing a reading comprehension exercise.	**WRITING TOOLS** Students practise writing using pictures as prompts.

VOCABULARY TOOLS Students take care when learning new words in English that are similar in their language.

Project objectives: Biography

Task 4 Students investigate an important event in their chosen artist's life.

Task 5 Students invent a story about their chosen artist's life.

Task 6 Students evaluate the process of creating a biography.

Audiovisual objectives

Vlog: Students watch and listen to Sarah talk about a surprise birthday party.

Culture: Students watch and listen to Sarah talk about Saint Patrick's Day.

Grammar animations: Students are presented with visual presentations of the unit grammar.

Key competences

LC **Linguistic**
pages 36-45

MST **Mathematical and Science and Technology**
pages 36-37, 39, 41-42

DC **Digital**
pages 36-37, 39, 43

SCC **Social and Civic**
pages 40-41

CAE **Cultural awareness and expression**
pages 40-41, 43

LL **Learning to learn**
pages 36, 38, 40, 42-43

IE **Sense of initiative and entrepreneurship**
pages 37, 39, 42

→ See pages 43-43 **Key competences**

CEFR Mediation

4.1 Processing text in writing
Can pick out and reproduce key words and phrases from a short, spoken text.

4.2 Collaborating to construct meaning
Can ask someone to give reasons for their views.

4.3 Relaying specific information in writing
Can relay specific information in texts on familiar subjects.

4.4 Processing text in writing
Can pick out and reproduce key words and phrases from a short written text.

4.5 Facilitating pluricultural space
Can help develop shared communication by exchanging information about cultural values.

Project Processing text in speech
Can collate short pieces of information from several sources and summarise them.

Unit review Facilitating collaborative interaction with peers
Can collaborate in simple tasks, asking what others think and understanding responses.

Pairwork Relaying specific information in speech
Can relay specific information in short, simple texts on familiar subjects.

→ See pages 30-33 **Mediation**

Remind students to do all the exercises in their notebook

4 A SPECIAL DAY

In unit 4 you will:
- talk about parties and surprises.
- practise using *there was* and *there were*.
- use the past continuous.
- write a story.

4.1 Vocabulary and listening

SARAH'S VLOG: Surprise!

Discuss the questions.
1 Do you like surprise parties? Why?
2 What is the best present you have ever received?
3 How do you usually celebrate your birthday?

Flipped Learning

1 Listen and complete.

barbecue biscuits blow out burgers candles gift tags presents sausages

It was my brother's birthday this weekend, we had a [1]··· in the garden. There were [2]··· and [3]··· but my aunt is vegetarian, so there was a big pasta salad, too. For dessert there were [4]··· and a big birthday cake with seventeen [5]···. He couldn't [6]··· the candles because there were so many! After we ate, my brother opened his [7]···. There weren't [8]··· on some of the presents, and we still don't know who they were from!

VOCABULARY TOOLS
Take care when spelling words that are very similar in your language. Sometimes they are the easiest to misspell!

2 Match the words from exercise 1 to the definitions below.
1 An object you give to someone as a gift.
2 A flat, circular piece of meat.
3 A long, cylindrical piece of meat.
4 To extinguish the light of a candle.
5 A wax object that burns and produces light.
6 A meal (usually meat) cooked over fire.
7 A label attached to a present.
8 A small, sweet snack that is usually flat and circular.

Pronunciation: /a:/

3 Listen and repeat.
/a:/ barbecue, card, garden, guitar, party, start

4 NOW YOU! Answer the questions in pairs.
- When is your birthday?
- What is your best birthday memory?
- Have you ever been to a surprise party? What happened?
- Do you prefer parties with a lot of people or only a few people?
- How would you like to celebrate your next birthday?

FAST FINISHERS Write a paragraph about the perfect birthday party.

Do all exercises in your notebook

36 Parties / *There was* and *There were*

Grammar and vocabulary 4.1

THERE WAS AND THERE WERE	Affirmative	Negative	*Yes/No* questions	*Wh-* questions
Singular	There was a massive cake.	There was not (wasn't) a clown at the party.	Was there a DJ? Yes, there was. No, there was not (wasn't).	What kind of music was there?
Plural	There were burgers and sausages.	There were not (weren't) any gift tags on the presents.	Were there any balloons? Yes, there were. No, there were not (weren't).	What decorations were there?

Grammar reference page 110

5 Complete the conversation with *there was* and *there were* in the correct form. Listen and check.

Chloe: Hi, Jenny. How was your birthday party?
Jenny: Hey, it was great! It's sad you couldn't be there.
Chloe: I know! Tell me all about it.
Jenny: [1]··· a big table under the trees. My little cousins helped with the decorations. [2]··· colourful balloons and tiny flags all over the garden!
Chloe: It sounds lovely. Who was at the party? Anyone from our class?
Jenny: No, [3]··· any friends from school at the party, it was just for family.
Chloe: Ahh. So, what kinds of food [4]···?
Jenny: [5]··· a huge salad and a big cheese and mushroom pizza. [6]··· mini-sandwiches, too.
Chloe: [7]··· anything for dessert?
Jenny: Of course! [8]··· tiny cupcakes and biscuits on the table. [9]··· also a massive cake with cream and fruit on top, but there [10]··· any ice cream this year.
Chloe: That all sounds lovely! I hope I can come next year!

6 Correct the sentences.
1 There weren't any decorations.
2 There were lots of people from Jenny's class.
3 There were two pizzas.
4 There was a small birthday cake.
5 There was lots of ice cream.

7 Answer the questions with full sentences.
1 What was there under the trees?
2 What was there all over the garden?
3 What kind of pizza was there?
4 Were there any cupcakes or biscuits?
5 Was there chocolate on top of the cake?

8 NOW YOU! Describe your last birthday party. Use *there was* and *there were*.

PROJECT TASK 4 Biography
- In your pair, find out about an important event in your chosen person's life. Say what happened and how it affected their work.
- Find a picture of this event, or an image to accompany the story. Make notes about what you can see in the image.

→ Workbook page 39

Do all exercises in your notebook

Workbook pages 30 and 31 37

ANSWER KEY

Pages 36-37

1
1 barbecue
2 burgers
3 sausages
4 biscuits
5 candles
6 blow out
7 presents
8 gift tags

2
1 present
2 burger
3 sausage
4 blow out
5 candle
6 barbecue
7 gift tag
8 biscuit

3 *Student's own answers*

4 *Student's own answers*

5
1 There was
2 There were
3 There weren't
4 Was there
5 There was
6 There were
7 Was there
8 There were
9 There was
10 Wasn't

6
1 There were decorations.
2 There weren't any people from her class.
3 There was one pizza.
4 There was a massive birthday cake.
5 There wasn't any ice cream.

7
1 There was a big table under the trees.
2 There were colourful balloons and tiny flags all over the garden.
3 There was a cheese and mushroom pizza.
4 Yes, there were cupcakes and biscuits.
5 No, there was not chocolate on top of the cake.

8 *Student's own answers*

Remind students to do all the exercises in their notebook

LESSON FOCUS

Grammar *There was* and *There were*
Vocabulary Parties
Listening Descriptions of birthday parties
Speaking Discussion of birthday memories
Project task 4 Investigate an important life event for the biography

Resources
Teacher's i-solutions, Student's Book audio, Vlog video and worksheet

Flipped Learning

SARAH'S VLOG: Surprise!

- Make sure to set up the **Flipped Learning** work with the students beforehand. **See pages 20-23 for complete Flipped Learning guidelines.**
- Ask students to put the **Flipped Learning worksheets** on their desks and walk around to check how many have completed the Flipped task.
- In pairs or small groups, ask students to compare and check the *Before you watch…* and *While you watch…* exercises on the worksheet.
- Show students **Sarah's Vlog** and ask volunteers to provide correct answers and clarify any doubts other students may have.
- Choose three or four students to read aloud their answers to the *After you watch…* exercises on the worksheet and encourage some class discussion.
- Move straight to exercise 1 on page 36.

Warmer

Watch Sarah's Vlog and discuss the questions with the whole class. If you don't have video facilities, simply discuss the questions.

1 1.29 (See page 171 for transcripts) Check students' understanding of the vocabulary before starting the exercise. Ask them if they know any other words related to parties and birthdays.

VOCABULARY TOOLS

Ask students to read the **Vocabulary tool** and to remember that some words in English look similar to words in their language, and to always pay close attention to spelling.

2 Students should visualise the descriptions to help them find the correct word. They can also use the text from exercise 1 to guide them.

Pronunciation

3 1.30 (See page 172 for transcripts) Students can complete this task in pairs and respectfully correct each other's pronunciation where necessary.

4 NOW YOU! Write some of the vocabulary from the previous exercises, as well as one or two sentences with *There was* and *There were*, on the board to help students with this exercise.

FAST FINISHERS Students can complete this exercise alone or in pairs.

Flipped Learning

THERE WAS AND *THERE WERE*

Draw students' attention to the **Grammar table**. Remind students that they can use this as a quick reference while completing the exercises.

Show students the **Grammar animation** and/or refer students to the **Grammar reference** on page 110 for further information on form and use.

→ See page 23 for how to flip the **grammar lesson**

5 1.31 (See page 172 for transcripts) Ask students if there were any phrases or words they didn't understand from this exercise. Discuss them and write them and their definitions on the board.

6 Check that students understand when to use *There was* and *There were* (with the singular and the plural respectively).

7 See if students can add one more question and answer using the text from exercise 1 or 5.

8 NOW YOU! Students should use as much of the new vocabulary and grammar in this exercise as possible. Encourage students to share their descriptions with the class.

PROJECT TASK 4 Biography

Students need to investigate and select an important event from the life of the artist they are writing about and source an image to accompany it. Students will analyse how this important event affected the work of the artist. Remind students that they need to keep their project notes together in their **Workbook** (page 39) or in their own notebook.

→ See pages 24-27 **Projects**

FURTHER PRACTICE

Workbook pages 30-31
- Grammar reference and practice pages 87 and 95
- Wordlist and exercises pages 100 and 103

Remind students to do all the exercises in their notebook

CONTINUOUS ASSESSMENT Students can talk about parties and use *There was* and *There were.*

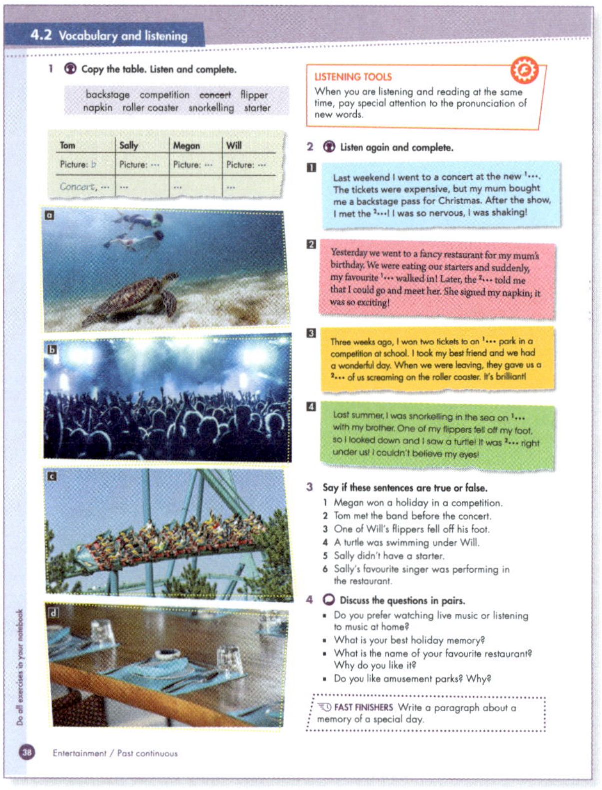

4.2 Vocabulary and listening

1 Copy the table. Listen and complete.

backstage competition concert flipper napkin roller coaster snorkelling starter

Tom	Sally	Megan	Will
Picture: b	Picture: ···	Picture: ···	Picture: ···
Concert, ···	···	···	···

LISTENING TOOLS
When you are listening and reading at the same time, pay special attention to the pronunciation of new words.

2 Listen again and complete.

1 Last weekend I went to a concert at the new ¹···. The tickets were expensive, but my mum bought me a backstage pass for Christmas. After the show, I met the ²···! I was so nervous, I was shaking!

2 Yesterday we went to a fancy restaurant for my mum's birthday. We were eating our starters and suddenly, my favourite ¹··· walked in! Later, the ²··· told me that I could go and meet her. She signed my napkin; it was so exciting!

3 Three weeks ago, I won two tickets to an ¹··· park in a competition at school. I took my best friend and we had a wonderful day. When we were leaving, they gave us a ²··· of us screaming on the roller coaster. It's brilliant!

4 Last summer, I was snorkelling in the sea on ¹··· with my brother. One of my flippers fell off my foot, so I looked down and I saw a turtle! It was ²··· right under us! I couldn't believe my eyes!

3 Say if these sentences are true or false.
1 Megan won a holiday in a competition.
2 Tom met the band before the concert.
3 One of Will's flippers fell off his foot.
4 A turtle was swimming under Will.
5 Sally didn't have a starter.
6 Sally's favourite singer was performing in the restaurant.

4 Discuss the questions in pairs.
- Do you prefer watching live music or listening to music at home?
- What is your best holiday memory?
- What is the name of your favourite restaurant? Why do you like it?
- Do you like amusement parks? Why?

FAST FINISHERS Write a paragraph about a memory of a special day.

Do all exercises in your notebook

38 Entertainment / Past continuous

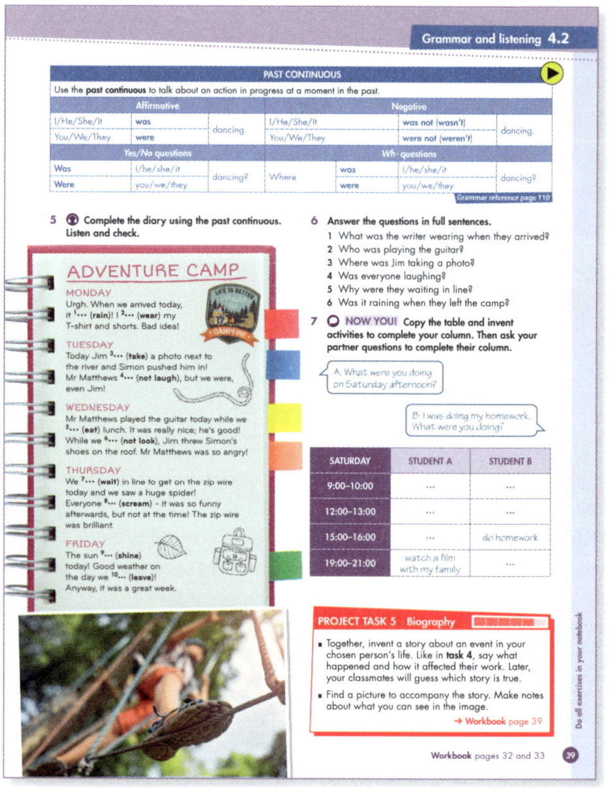

Grammar and listening 4.2

PAST CONTINUOUS
Use the past continuous to talk about an action in progress at a moment in the past.

Affirmative			Negative		
I/He/She/It	was	dancing.	I/He/She/It	was not (wasn't)	dancing.
You/We/They	were		You/We/They	were not (weren't)	
Yes/No questions			Wh- questions		
Was	I/he/she/it	dancing?	Where	was I/he/she/it	dancing?
Were	you/we/they			were you/we/they	

Grammar reference page 110

5 Complete the diary using the past continuous. Listen and check.

ADVENTURE CAMP
MONDAY
Urgh. When we arrived today, it ¹··· (rain)! I ²··· (wear) my T-shirt and shorts. Bad idea!
TUESDAY
Today Jim ³··· (take) a photo next to the river and Simon pushed him in! Mr Matthews ⁴··· (not laugh), but we were, even Jim!
WEDNESDAY
Mr Matthews played the guitar today while we ⁵··· (eat) lunch. It was really nice; he's good! While we ⁶··· (not look), Jim threw Simon's shoes on the roof. Mr Matthews was so angry!
THURSDAY
We ⁷··· (wait) in line to get on the zip wire today and we saw a huge spider! Everyone ⁸··· (scream) - it was so funny afterwards, but not at the time! The zip wire was brilliant.
FRIDAY
The sun ⁹··· (shine) today! Good weather on the day we ¹⁰··· (leave)! Anyway, it was a great week.

6 Answer the questions in full sentences.
1 What was the writer wearing when they arrived?
2 Who was playing the guitar?
3 Where was Jim taking a photo?
4 Was everyone laughing?
5 Why were they waiting in line?
6 Was it raining when they left the camp?

7 NOW YOU! Copy the table and invent activities to complete your column. Then ask your partner questions to complete their column.

A: What were you doing on Saturday afternoon?
B: I was doing my homework. What were you doing?

SATURDAY	STUDENT A	STUDENT B
9:00-10:00	···	···
12:00-13:00	···	···
15:00-16:00	···	do homework
19:00-21:00	watch a film with my family	···

PROJECT TASK 5 Biography
- Together, invent a story about an event in your chosen person's life. Like in task 4, say what happened and how it affected their work. Later, your classmates will guess which story is true.
- Find a picture to accompany the story. Make notes about what you can see in the image.

→ Workbook page 39

Workbook pages 32 and 33 39

Do all exercises in your notebook

ANSWER KEY

Pages 38-39

1

Tom	Sally	Megan	Will
Picture: b	Picture: d	Picture: c	Picture: a
Concert, backstage	Starter, napkin	Competition, roller coaster	Snorkelling, flipper

2
1 1 stadium, 2 band
2 1 singer, 2 waiter
3 1 amusement, 2 photo
4 1 holiday, 2 swimming

3 **1** False **2** False **3** True **4** True **5** False **6** False

4 *Student's own answers*

5 **1** was raining **2** was wearing **3** was taking **4** wasn't laughing **5** were eating **6** weren't looking **7** were waiting **8** was screaming **9** was shining **10** were leaving

6
1 He was wearing a T-shirt and shorts.
2 Mr Matthews was playing the guitar.
3 Jim was taking a photo next to the river.
4 Everyone was laughing because Simon pushed Jim into the river.
5 They were waiting in line to get on the zip wire.
6 No, it was sunny when they left the camp.

7 *Student's own answers*

Remind students to do all the exercises in their notebook

LESSON FOCUS

Grammar Past continuous
Vocabulary Entertainment
Listening Descriptions of events and entertainment
Speaking Discussion of favourite memories
Project task 5 Invent a story about the artist's life

Resources
Teacher's i-solutions, Student's Book audio
Preparation A story about the weekend, or a past event

Warmer

Tell students about something you did last weekend using the past continuous. Write some days and times on the board. For example: *Friday 9pm; Saturday 2 o'clock; Sunday 11am*. Ask students what they were doing at these times. They should answer using full sentences in the past continuous.

1 1.32 (See page 172 for transcripts) Before listening, ask students what they think is happening in these pictures. They can use the vocabulary from the wordpool to help them.

LISTENING TOOLS

Get students to read the **Listening tool** and remind them that English words are not always pronounced phonetically.

2 1.33 (See page 172 for transcripts) Remind students to listen carefully to all the information given and not just listen in order to fill in the gaps. They should take notes to help them with exercise 3.

3 Students should pay attention to the wording in the questions and look out for distractors. They can also use their notes from the previous exercise to help them answer the questions correctly.

4 Round this up with a class discussion. Ask students if they have experienced any of the events described in exercises 1 and 2.

FAST FINISHERS Students can complete this exercise alone or in pairs.

PAST CONTINUOUS

Flipped Learning

Draw students' attention to the **Grammar table**. Remind students that they can use this as a quick reference while completing the exercises.
Show students the **Grammar animation** and/or refer students to the **Grammar reference** on page 110 for further information on form and use.

→ See page 23 for how to flip the **grammar lesson**

5 1.34 (See page 172 for transcripts) After completing the diary and before listening to the audio, get students to check their answers against the **Grammar table**.

6 After finishing, students can check their answers in pairs.

7 NOW YOU! Students can use ideas from the previous exercises to complete this task, but also encourage them to come up with new ones related to their own interests.

PROJECT TASK 5 Biography

Students are going to invent a story about their chosen artist's life and how this event affected their work. Students should make the story as convincing as possible because at the end of the project their classmates will guess whether the story is true or not. Remind students that they need to keep their project notes together in their **Workbook** (page 39) or in their own notebook.

→ See pages 24-27 **Projects**

FURTHER PRACTICE

Workbook pages 32-33
- **Grammar reference and practice** pages 87 and 95
- **Wordlist and exercises** pages 100 and 103

Vocabulary and Grammar worksheets available to download from the **Richmond***Learning***Platform**

→ See pages 38-39 **Mixed-ability classes**

Remind students to do all the exercises in their notebook

CONTINUOUS ASSESSMENT Students can talk about entertainment and use the past continuous.

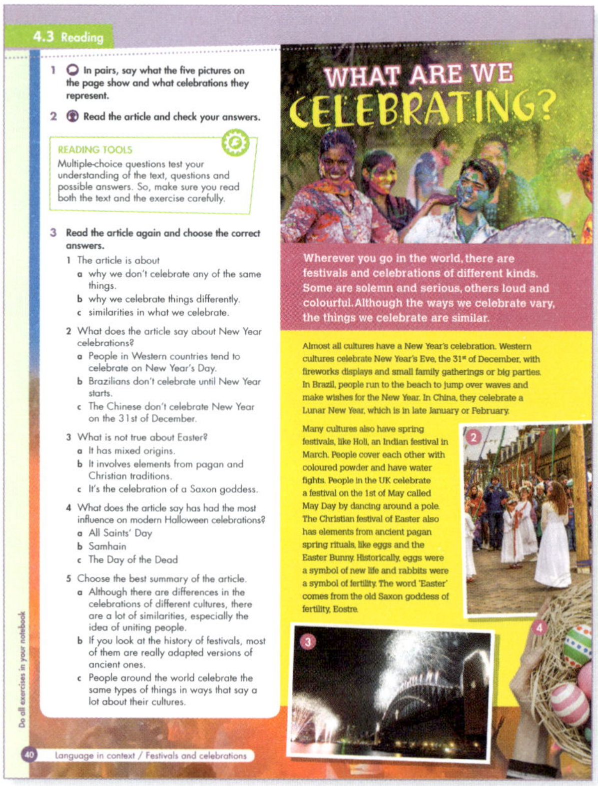

4.3 Reading

1 In pairs, say what the five pictures on the page show and what celebrations they represent.

2 Read the article and check your answers.

READING TOOLS
Multiple-choice questions test your understanding of the text, questions and possible answers. So, make sure you read both the text and the exercise carefully.

3 Read the article again and choose the correct answers.
1 The article is about
a why we don't celebrate any of the same things.
b why we celebrate things differently.
c similarities in what we celebrate.
2 What does the article say about New Year celebrations?
a People in Western countries tend to celebrate on New Year's Day.
b Brazilians don't celebrate until New Year starts.
c The Chinese don't celebrate New Year on the 31st of December.
3 What is not true about Easter?
a It has mixed origins.
b It involves elements from pagan and Christian traditions.
c It's the celebration of a Saxon goddess.
4 What does the article say has had the most influence on modern Halloween celebrations?
a All Saints' Day
b Samhain
c The Day of the Dead
5 Choose the best summary of the article.
a Although there are differences in the celebrations of different cultures, there are a lot of similarities, especially the idea of uniting people.
b If you look at the history of festivals, most of them are really adapted versions of ancient ones.
c People around the world celebrate the same types of things in ways that say a lot about their cultures.

WHAT ARE WE CELEBRATING?

Wherever you go in the world, there are festivals and celebrations of different kinds. Some are solemn and serious, others loud and colourful. Although the ways we celebrate vary, the things we celebrate are similar.

Almost all cultures have a New Year's celebration. Western cultures celebrate New Year's Eve, the 31st of December, with fireworks displays and small family gatherings or big parties. In Brazil, people run to the beach to jump over waves and make wishes for the New Year. In China, they celebrate a Lunar New Year, which is in late January or February.

Many cultures also have spring festivals, like Holi, an Indian festival in March. People cover each other with coloured powder and have water fights. People in the UK celebrate a festival on the 1st of May called May Day by dancing around a pole. The Christian festival of Easter also has elements from ancient pagan spring rituals, like eggs and the Easter Bunny. Historically, eggs were a symbol of new life and rabbits were a symbol of fertility. The word 'Easter' comes from the old Saxon goddess of fertility, Eostre.

Do all exercises in your notebook

40 Language in context / Festivals and celebrations

Reading 4.3

There are also many autumn celebrations to honour the dead. The most famous is Halloween, on the 31st of October. Like Easter, it's a mixture of Christian and pagan festivals. It coincides with the night before All Saints' Day, but now it has more in common with the ancient Celtic festival of Samhain, in which people used to dress up as pagan gods or fairies and visit houses asking for offerings. Sound familiar? Mexicans celebrate it as the Day of the Dead by visiting the graves of departed loved ones and leaving gifts.

A lot of celebrations are more local and less universal, but they all have one important thing in common: the idea of bringing communities together.

4 Find these words in the text and match them to their definitions.
1 gathering
2 make wishes
3 powder
4 water fights
5 pole
6 pagan
7 offerings
8 graves
a Of a religion with many gods.
b Holes where dead people are buried.
c Things you give to a god.
d Very small, dry particles of something, e.g. talc.
e A small, informal party or meeting.
f Play combat where people wet each other.
g A long, thin, round stick standing in the ground.
h To vocalise a hope for things to come true.

5 NOW YOU! In groups, compare how you celebrate the events mentioned in the text.

CORE VALUES Community

6 In pairs, look at the examples of community below and write a way in which each can benefit its members. What general benefits are there of belonging to a community?

A historical re-enactment group · A music group · A sports team · An environmental action group · An online community · Your neighbourhood

FAST FINISHERS Think of another type of community and say how it benefits its members.

Do all exercises in your notebook

Workbook pages 34 and 35 41

ANSWER KEY

Pages 40-41

1 **1** People covering each other with coloured powder in India; Holi
2 People dancing around a maypole; May Day
3 Fireworks; New Year's Eve
4 Painted eggs; Easter
5 People visiting the graves of departed loved ones and leaving gifts; the Day of the Dead

2 *Student's own answers*

3 **1** c
2 c
3 c
4 b
5 a

4 **1** e
2 h
3 d
4 f
5 g
6 a
7 c
8 b

5 *Student's own answers*

6 *Suggested answers:*
A historical re-enactment group: encourages the learning of history, encourages imagination and empathy
A music group: you can work together to make something that is very beautiful and inspiring
A sports team: you push each other to play better and learn from each other; you help each other get and stay fit
An environmental action group: you can achieve more by working together and have a stronger sense that what you're fighting for is worthwhile, and that you're getting somewhere
An online community: you meet people from very different backgrounds with similar interests; it can make people who don't fit into their immediate physical environments feel less alone
Your neighbourhood: you can meet people regularly in person and you can help each other more easily
General benefits: make us feel less alone, help us grow and learn, make us feel better about ourselves

Remind students to do all the exercises in their notebook

LESSON FOCUS

Language in context Festivals and celebrations

Core values Community

Resources

Teacher's i-solutions, Student's Book audio

Preparation Countries and their celebrations

→ See pages 36-37 **Literature**

Warmer

Draw three columns on the board. Write four or five countries in the first column and four or five celebrations in the second column. The matching country and celebration should be on different lines. Suggestions: *Ireland/Saint Patrick's Day; Spain/Las Fallas; USA/Martin Luther King Day; France/Bastille Day.* Ask students to match the country to the celebration. Next, ask students what they think the purpose of each celebration is and write that in the third column. They should see that although there are some specific purposes to each celebration, in general they are all similar and are mainly about bringing people and communities together.

1 If students are not familiar with the celebrations represented, encourage them to use their imagination to guess what they might be about.

2 1.35 (See page 172 for transcripts) Round up with a class discussion and ask students if they already knew about these celebrations and if any of the students have celebrated these events before, at home or abroad.

READING TOOLS

Ask students to study the **Reading tool** and remind them that it is just as important to understand the question as it is to understand the text in order to select the correct answer.

3 Tell students to read the questions before reading the text and draw their attention back to the advice in the **Reading tool** before completing the exercise.

4 Ask students to look at the words and guess their definitions before completing the exercise. Ask students if there were any other new words in the text that they weren't familiar with and provide definitions.

5 NOW YOU! Round up with a class discussion. Ask students if they have any special celebrations or traditions within their family.

CORE VALUES Community

6 Encourage students to add one or two further examples to the ones already given and discuss what benefits they have.

FAST FINISHERS Students can complete this exercise alone or in pairs.

FURTHER PRACTICE

Workbook pages 34-35

Remind students to do all the exercises in their notebook

CONTINUOUS ASSESSMENT Students can understand a text about festivals and celebrations around the world.

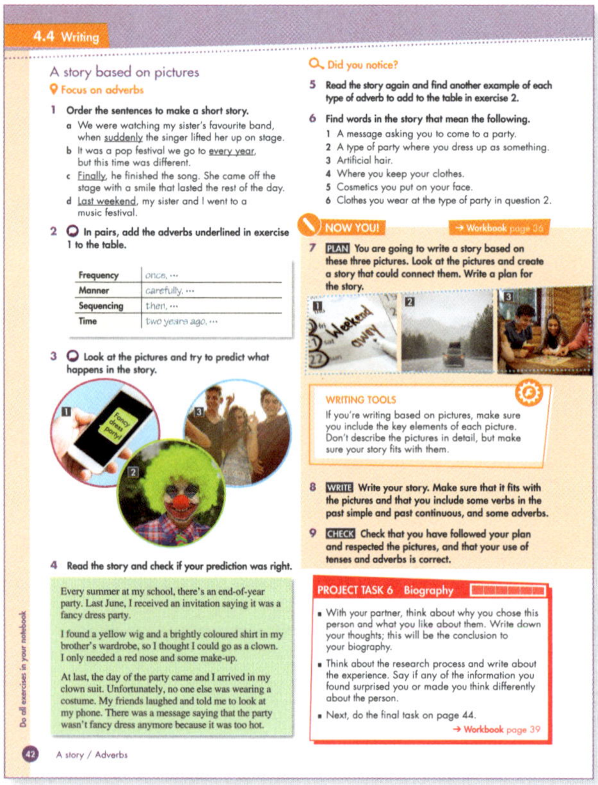

4.4 Writing

A story based on pictures

Focus on adverbs

1 Order the sentences to make a short story.

a We were watching my sister's favourite band, when suddenly the singer lifted her up on stage.
b It was a pop festival we go to every year, but this time was different.
c Finally, he finished the song. She came off the stage with a smile that lasted the rest of the day.
d Last weekend, my sister and I went to a music festival.

2 In pairs, add the adverbs underlined in exercise 1 to the table.

Frequency	once, …
Manner	carefully, …
Sequencing	then, …
Time	two years ago, …

3 Look at the pictures and try to predict what happens in the story.

4 Read the story and check if your prediction was right.

Every summer at my school, there's an end-of-year party. Last June, I received an invitation saying it was a fancy dress party.

I found a yellow wig and a brightly coloured shirt in my brother's wardrobe, so I thought I could go as a clown. I only needed a red nose and some make-up.

At last, the day of the party came and I arrived in my clown suit. Unfortunately, no one else was wearing a costume. My friends laughed and told me to look at my phone. There was a message saying that the party wasn't fancy dress anymore because it was too hot.

Did you notice?

5 Read the story again and find another example of each type of adverb to add to the table in exercise 2.

6 Find words in the story that mean the following.

1 A message asking you to come to a party.
2 A type of party where you dress up as something.
3 Artificial hair.
4 Where you keep your clothes.
5 Cosmetics you put on your face.
6 Clothes you wear at the type of party in question 2.

NOW YOU! → Workbook page 36

7 PLAN You are going to write a story based on these three pictures. Look at the pictures and create a story that could connect them. Write a plan for the story.

WRITING TOOLS

If you're writing based on pictures, make sure you include the key elements of each picture. Don't describe the pictures in detail, but make sure your story fits with them.

8 WRITE Write your story. Make sure that it fits with the pictures and that you include some verbs in the past simple and past continuous, and some adverbs.

9 CHECK Check that you have followed your plan and respected the pictures, and that your use of tenses and adverbs is correct.

PROJECT TASK 6 Biography

- With your partner, think about why you chose this person and what you like about them. Write down your thoughts; this will be the conclusion to your biography.
- Think about the research process and write about the experience. Say if any of the information you found surprised you or made you think differently about the person.
- Next, do the final task on page 44.

→ Workbook page 39

Do all exercises in your notebook

42 A story / Adverbs

ANSWER KEY

Page 42

1 d, b, a, c

2

Frequency	once; every year
Manner	carefully; suddenly
Sequencing	then; finally
Time	two years ago; last weekend

3 *Student's own answers*

4 *Student's own answers*

5 **Frequency**: every summer
Manner: brightly
Sequencing: at last
Time: last June

6 **1** invitation
2 fancy dress
3 wig
4 wardrobe
5 make-up
6 costume

7 *Student's own answers*

8 *Student's own answers*

9 *Student's own answers*

FURTHER PRACTICE

Workbook page 36

LESSON FOCUS

Focus on Adverbs

Writing A short story

Project task 6 Evaluate the process of creating a biography.

Resources

Teacher's i-solutions

Preparation Prepare a summary of the plot of a story or film

Warmer

Tell the class a short story with a clear beginning, middle and end, utilising some of the adverbs in exercise 1. Tell students that adverbs help the reader to identify the timeline of a story.

Focus on adverbs

1 Complete this exercise as a class and discuss how adverbs help us to understand stories.

2 Ask the class if they can think of any more adverbs for the list (*next; first; last; quickly; thoughtfully; accidentally; one month ago; last summer*). Remind them of the adverbs of frequency they studied in Unit 2.

3 Students can do this exercise in groups of three.

4 Ask three students to read out one paragraph each. Correct pronunciation where necessary.

Did you notice?

5 Complete this exercise as a class and write the new adverbs on the board.

6 Students can complete this exercise alone or in pairs. Check if there is extra vocabulary the students weren't already familiar with and help them to understand it.

7 PLAN Once students have finished their plan, encourage them to compare it in pairs.

WRITING TOOLS

Ensure that students have read the **Writing tool**. The pictures should be used as prompts; the story should not just be a description of the pictures.

8 WRITE Before students start writing, make a checklist on the board of any elements related to content, structure, language and style that they should bear in mind.

9 CHECK Once students have checked their own stories, they can swap with a partner and check theirs and see how well they've followed the tips.

PROJECT TASK 6 Biography

Students will evaluate the biography they have written; thinking about the artist they chose and why, any surprising information that they found and whether their opinion about the person changed over the course of researching and writing the biography. Remind students that they need to keep their project notes together in their **Workbook** (page 39) or in their own notebook.

→ See pages 24-27 **Projects**

Remind students to do all the exercises in their notebook

CONTINUOUS ASSESSMENT Students can use adverbs appropriately to write a story based on pictures.

Culture and communication 4.5

Saint Patrick's Day

Discuss the questions.
1 Which special national days are there in your country?
2 How do you celebrate them?
3 What famous parades are there in your country?
4 Does your country have a national plant or flower?

1 Listen, match the pictures and take notes. In pairs, say why they won the prizes.

1 Tracy
2 Adam
3 Ross

2 Answer the questions. Listen again and check.
1 Who was at the ceremony with Tracy?
2 Did Tracy expect to win best young writer of the year?
3 Who did Adam help raise money for?
4 What does Adam's group sell to raise money?
5 Why didn't Ross run in the last race?
6 How did he feel about his friend winning a silver medal?

GOLD SILVER BRONZE

Idioms and expressions

3 Match the expressions you heard with the meanings.
1 someone's jaw drops
2 come out of the blue
3 take someone's breath away

a When someone is amazed.
b When something is surprising or beautiful.
c When something is completely unexpected.

SPEAKING TOOLS
To make the most of speaking tasks, think about the grammar and vocabulary you learnt in the unit and try to use it in your answer.

4 NOW YOU! Use the expressions and tell a story about a special day. Talk about...
- when and where it happened.
- what happened.
- who was with you.
- how you felt.

PAIRWORK
Student A: go to page 100
Student B: go to page 104

Unit 4 Review • page 93
Wordlist • pages 118–120

Do all exercises in your notebook

Idioms and expressions about feeling surprised

Workbook page 37 43

LESSON FOCUS

Idioms and expressions Feeling surprised
Listening Short monologues about winning
Speaking Discussing surprising events

Resources

Teacher's i-solutions, Student's Book audio, Culture video and worksheet

Saint Patrick's Day

Video and worksheet available on the Richmond *Learning* Platform

- In pairs, ask students to complete the *What I know...* exercises on the **Culture video worksheet**.
- Show students the **Culture video** and ask them to complete the *What I learned...* exercises on the worksheet.
- In pairs, students compare answers.
- In small groups, tell students to complete the *What I wonder...* exercises on the worksheet.

Warmer

Watch the **Culture video** and discuss the questions with the whole class. If you don't have video facilities, simply discuss the questions.

1 1.36 (See page 172 for transcripts) Remind students to take notes as they are listening and then complete the exercise in pairs.

2 1.37 (See page 173 for transcripts) Students should use their notes to try and answer all the questions. Tell the class they will be able to listen again to the audio to check their answers.

Idioms and expressions

3 Ask students if they could guess the meaning of the expressions from the words used to describe the feeling of surprise.

SPEAKING TOOLS

Draw students' attention to the **Speaking tool** and remind them that using what they have learnt in speech will help to consolidate learning.

4 NOW YOU! Students can work in pairs and then students that would like to can share their stories with the class.

PAIRWORK Student's Book pages 100 and 104
See **Teacher's Book** page 100 for more information.
→ See pages 30-33 **Mediation**

ANSWER KEY

Page 43

1
1 b; She won the prize for best young writer of the year.
2 c; They won the prize for the money they raised for the hospital.
3 a; He won the medal in a race.

2
1 Her brother
2 No
3 The local hospital
4 Make and sell bags and hats, and organise events
5 He had a bad knee
6 He was happy and amazed

3
1 a
2 c
3 b

4 *Student's own answers*

FURTHER PRACTICE AND UNIT ASSESSSMENT

Unit 4 Review Student's Book page 93
Workbook page 37
- **Reflect on your learning** page 37
- **Grammar reference and practice** pages 87 and 95
- **Wordlist and exercises** pages 100 and 103

Tests available to download and edit from the **Richmond *Learning* Platform**

→ See pages 40-41 **Assessment**

Remind students to do all the exercises in their notebook

Unit 4 Review

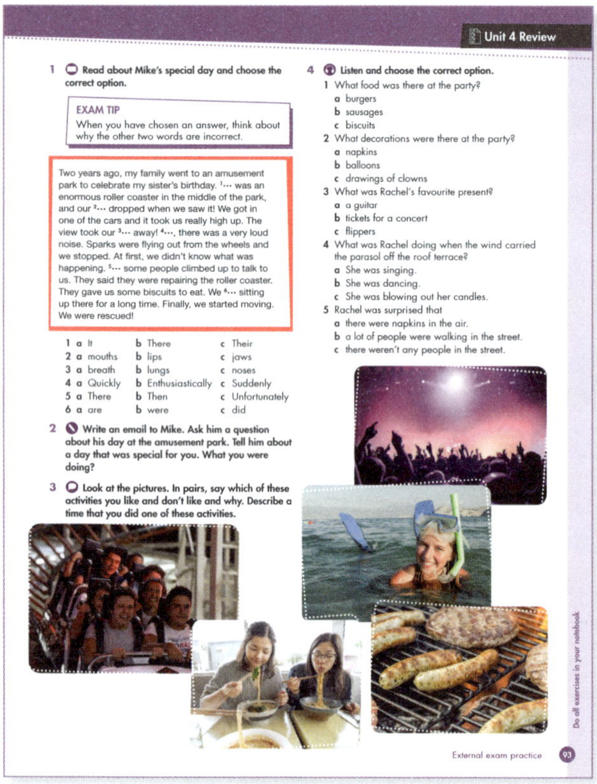

Unit 4 Review

1 Read about Mike's special day and choose the correct option.

EXAM TIP
When you have chosen an answer, think about why the other two words are incorrect.

Two years ago, my family went to an amusement park to celebrate my sister's birthday. [1]··· was an enormous roller coaster in the middle of the park, and our [2]··· dropped when we saw it! We got in one of the cars and it took us really high up. The view took our [3]··· away! [4]···, there was a very loud noise. Sparks were flying out from the wheels and we stopped. At first, we didn't know what was happening. [5]··· some people climbed up to talk to us. They said they were repairing the roller coaster. They gave us some biscuits to eat. We [6]··· sitting up there for a long time. Finally, we started moving. We were rescued!

	a	b	c
1	It	There	Their
2	mouths	lips	jaws
3	breath	lungs	noses
4	Quickly	Enthusiastically	Suddenly
5	There	Then	Unfortunately
6	are	were	did

2 Write an email to Mike. Ask him a question about his day at the amusement park. Tell him about a day that was special for you. What you were doing?

3 Look at the pictures. In pairs, say which of these activities you like and don't like and why. Describe a time that you did one of these activities.

4 Listen and choose the correct option.

1 What food was there at the party?
a burgers
b sausages
c biscuits

2 What decorations were there at the party?
a napkins
b balloons
c drawings of clowns

3 What was Rachel's favourite present?
a a guitar
b tickets for a concert
c flippers

4 What was Rachel doing when the wind carried the parasol off the roof terrace?
a She was singing.
b She was dancing.
c She was blowing out her candles.

5 Rachel was surprised that
a there were napkins in the air.
b a lot of people were walking in the street.
c there weren't any people in the street.

Do all exercises in your notebook

External exam practice 93

Student's Book page 93

ANSWER KEY

See page 180 for transcripts

1

1 b	**3** a	**5** b
2 c	**4** c	**6** b

2 *Student's own answers*

3 *Student's own answers*

4 2.40

1 b	**2** a	**3** b	**4** c	**5** c

Pairwork

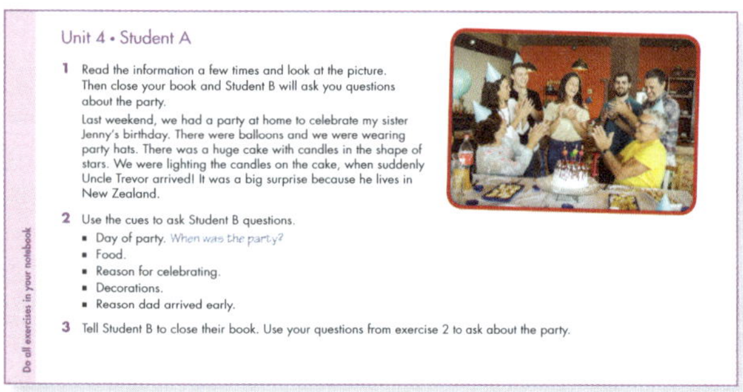

Unit 4 • Student A

1 Read the information a few times and look at the picture. Then close your book and Student B will ask you questions about the party.

Last weekend, we had a party at home to celebrate my sister Jenny's birthday. There were balloons and we were wearing party hats. There was a huge cake with candles in the shape of stars. We were lighting the candles on the cake, when suddenly Uncle Trevor arrived! It was a big surprise because he lives in New Zealand.

2 Use the cues to ask Student B questions.
- Day of party. *When was the party?*
- Food.
- Reason for celebrating.
- Decorations.
- Reason dad arrived early.

3 Tell Student B to close their book. Use your questions from exercise 2 to ask about the party.

Do all exercises in your notebook

Student's Book page 100

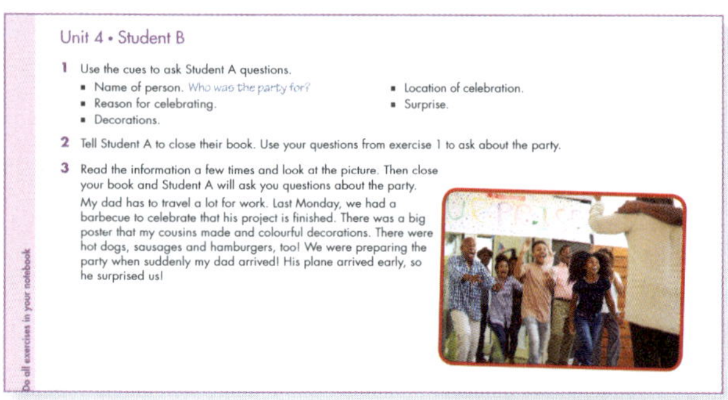

Unit 4 • Student B

1 Use the cues to ask Student A questions.
- Name of person. *Who was the party for?*
- Reason for celebrating.
- Decorations.
- Location of celebration.
- Surprise.

2 Tell Student A to close their book. Use your questions from exercise 1 to ask about the party.

3 Read the information a few times and look at the picture. Then close your book and Student A will ask you questions about the party.

My dad has to travel a lot for work. Last Monday, we had a barbecue to celebrate that his project is finished. There was a big poster that my cousins made and colourful decorations. There were hot dogs, sausages and hamburgers, too! We were preparing the party when suddenly my dad arrived! His plane arrived early, so he surprised us!

Do all exercises in your notebook

Student's Book page 104

CEFR MEDIATION DESCRIPTOR

- **Processing text in speech**
  Students can convey the main point(s) contained in clearly-structured, short, simple spoken and written texts.

- **Summarising information**
  Tell Student A and B that they each have information about a party. They have to read and memorise the information and take it in turns to ask and answer questions about the parties.

Grammar reference

Unit 4 Grammar reference

There was and there were

	Affirmative	Negative	Yes/No questions	Wh- questions
Singular	There was a massive cake.	There was not (wasn't) a clown at the party.	Was there a DJ? Yes, there was. No, there was not (wasn't).	What kind of music was there?
Plural	There were burgers and sausages.	There were not (weren't) any gift tags on the presents.	Were there any balloons? Yes, there were. No, there were not (weren't).	What decorations were there?

We use ***there was*** and ***there were*** to describe scenes in the past.

There was a very tall man at the door.

There was some water on the floor.

There were four hotels in the square.

Time and location expressions come at the end of sentences with ***there was/were***.

There was some milk **in the fridge.**

NOT ~~There was in the fridge some milk.~~

We usually use the contracted forms of the negative. ***There wasn't*** is used with singular and uncountable nouns. ***There weren't*** goes with plural and countable nouns.

There wasn't a cloud in the sky.

There wasn't any bread in the shop.

There weren't any internet cafés in those days.

In questions, ***was/were*** is located at the start of the sentence.

Was there a big queue at the cinema?

NOT ~~There was a big queue at the cinema?~~

Past continuous

Use the **past continuous** to talk about an action in progress at a moment in the past.

Affirmative			Negative		
I/He/She/It	was	dancing.	I/He/She/It	was not (wasn't)	dancing.
You/We/They	were		You/We/They	were not (weren't)	

Yes/No questions			Wh- questions			
Was	I/he/she/it	dancing?	Where	was	I/he/she/it	dancing?
Were	you/we/they			were	you/we/they	

The ***past continuous*** is made up of the **past simple** of ***be*** + the ***-ing*** form of the main verb.

I **was running**, you **were walking**, he **wasn't looking**, etc.

We use the **past continuous**:

- to talk about something that happened at a certain moment in the past.

At two o'clock yesterday we **were having** lunch in Rome.

- To talk about an action that took place while something else was happening.

It **was raining** very heavily **when** we **arrived** at the campsite.

- To talk about two things that happened at the same time in the past. In this type of sentence, we often use ***while*** or ***when*** + **past continuous**.

The dog **was running** around the kitchen **while** I **was cleaning** the floor.

It is very common to use the contracted forms in the negative and interrogative.

The students **weren't talking** when the teacher came in.

Wasn't it **raining** when you arrived?

I **wasn't shopping** in Manchester yesterday afternoon. I **was shopping** in Liverpool.

In short answers with the **past continuous**, we do not repeat the ***-ing*** verb.

Were you **looking** for a particular book?

Yes, **I was.**

NOT ~~Yes, I was looking.~~

Do all exercises in your notebook

110 **Workbook** pages 94–97

Student's Book page 110

Wordlist

UNIT 4

Parties

balloons
barbecue
birthday
biscuits
blow out
burgers
cake
candles
gift
gift tags
cupcakes
decorations
presents
sausages

Entertainment

adventure
amusement park
backstage
camp
competition
concert
fancy restaurant
live music
roller coaster
snorkelling
ticket
zip wire

Festivals and celebrations

Easter
fireworks
gathering
graves
Halloween
make wishes
New Year
New Year's Eve
offerings
pagan
pole
powder
ritual
The Easter Bunny
water fights

Do all exercises in your notebook

Workbook pages 102–104 119

Student's Book page 119

2.55 2.56 2.57

Remind students to do all the exercises in their notebook

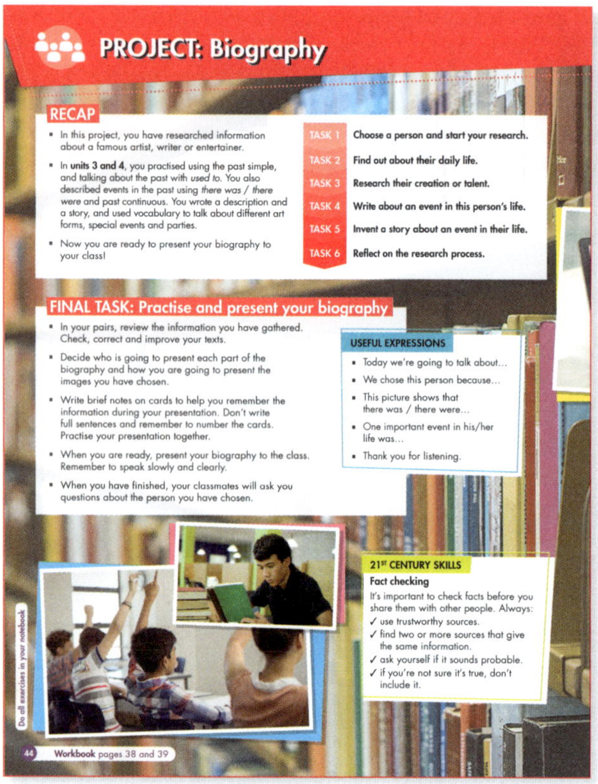

PROJECT: Biography

RECAP

- In this project, you have researched information about a famous artist, writer or entertainer.
- In **units 3 and 4**, you practised using the past simple, and talking about the past with *used to*. You also described events in the past using *there was / there were* and past continuous. You wrote a description and a story, and used vocabulary to talk about different art forms, special events and parties.
- Now you are ready to present your biography to your class!

TASK 1 Choose a person and start your research.
TASK 2 Find out about their daily life.
TASK 3 Research their creation or talent.
TASK 4 Write about an event in this person's life.
TASK 5 Invent a story about an event in their life.
TASK 6 Reflect on the research process.

FINAL TASK: Practise and present your biography

- In your pairs, review the information you have gathered. Check, correct and improve your texts.
- Decide who is going to present each part of the biography and how you are going to present the images you have chosen.
- Write brief notes on cards to help you remember the information during your presentation. Don't write full sentences and remember to number the cards. Practise your presentation together.
- When you are ready, present your biography to the class. Remember to speak slowly and clearly.
- When you have finished, your classmates will ask you questions about the person you have chosen.

USEFUL EXPRESSIONS

- Today we're going to talk about…
- We chose this person because…
- This picture shows that there was / there were…
- One important event in his/her life was…
- Thank you for listening.

21ST CENTURY SKILLS

Fact checking

It's important to check facts before you share them with other people. Always:
✓ use trustworthy sources.
✓ find two or more sources that give the same information.
✓ ask yourself if it sounds probable.
✓ if you're not sure it's true, don't include it.

Do all exercises in your notebook

44 **Workbook** pages 38 and 39

Project • Units 3 and 4

GO BEYOND

PAPARAZZI

Independent photographers who take photos of famous people are called 'Paparazzi'. They sell the images to newspapers, magazines, websites, etc. They often take the pictures secretly, while the celebrity goes about their daily life. Sometimes, they wait outside buildings to 'catch' them. These 'stolen images' can damage a celebrity's reputation, or make them even more famous!

There are some laws that control the sale of the photos, as famous people often express their anger at these photographers and the way that they invade their private lives. Celebrities sometimes use paparazzi to their own benefit however, by selling photographs of themselves to magazines for huge amounts of money. The most expensive photographs are usually the first picture of a celebrity's baby, or wedding photos.

The question is, who is to blame for this type of invasive culture? The paparazzi, the celebrities or the people who look at the photos?

Answer the questions in pairs.

1 Do you think famous people should have the right to a private life?
2 What are the negative ways that fame can affect people?
3 How would you feel if someone secretly took a photograph of you?
4 Do you think famous people have a responsibility to behave well in public?

EVALUATION

Answer the questions in groups of four.

1 What sources did you use?
2 How did you check the information that you found?
3 Did you enjoy the process of finding information?
4 Which pair's biography did you enjoy the most? Why?

Do all exercises in your notebook

45

Workbook project task notes

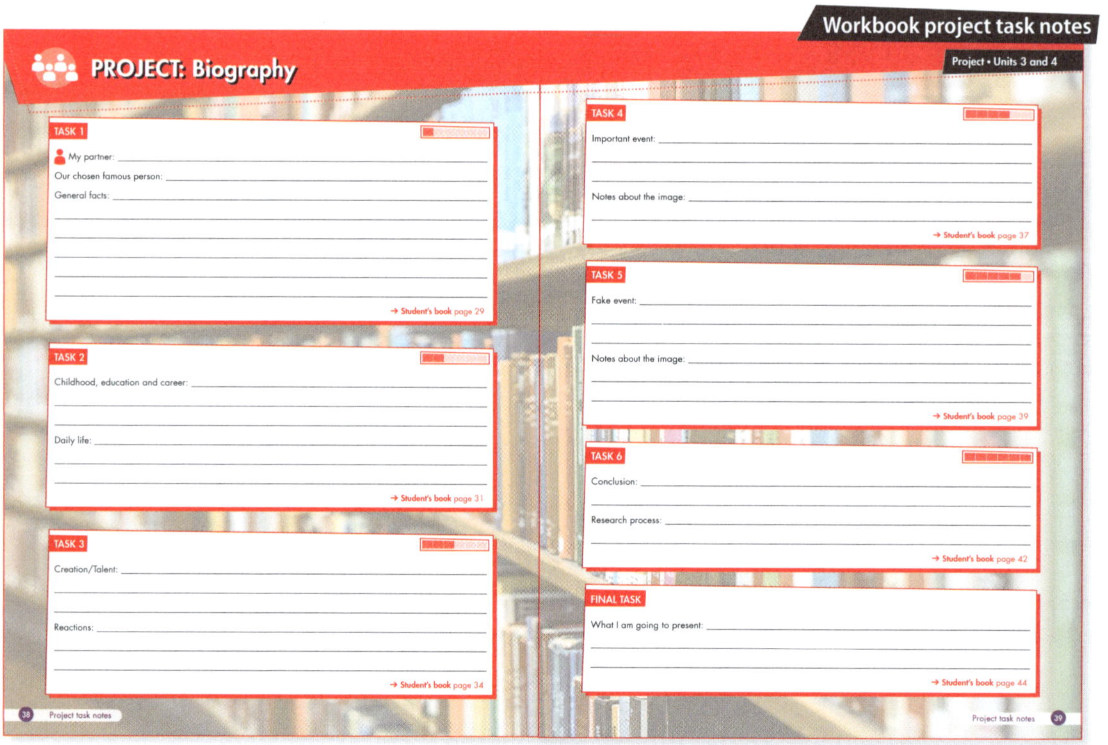

PROJECT: Biography

TASK 1
My partner: ___
Our chosen famous person: ___
General facts: ___
→ Student's book page 29

TASK 2
Childhood, education and career: ___
Daily life: ___
→ Student's book page 31

TASK 3
Creation/Talent: ___
Reactions: ___
→ Student's book page 34

38 Project task notes

Project • Units 3 and 4

TASK 4
Important event: ___
Notes about the image: ___
→ Student's book page 37

TASK 5
Fake event: ___
Notes about the image: ___
→ Student's book page 39

TASK 6
Conclusion: ___
Research process: ___
→ Student's book page 42

FINAL TASK
What I am going to present: ___
→ Student's book page 44

Project task notes 39

Remind students to do all the exercises in their notebook

PROJECT FOCUS

→ See pages 24-27 **Projects**

Skills

- Discuss and collaborate on a series of texts with images
- Research and write about a famous person from the past, including the reason for their fame, their childhood, education, career and influence
- Write one true story and one false story about events in the person's life
- Write a summary of why you chose the person
- Write a report on your personal experience of the research process
- Edit and correct texts
- Present a biography from cue cards
- Discuss evaluations of the project
- Read and discuss a text related to the project

CEFR mediation

Processing text in speech

Can collate short pieces of information from several sources and summarise them for somebody else.

→ See pages 30-33 **Mediation**

Preparation Remind students to bring the elements they created in tasks 1-6 and their notes from **Workbook** project task notes pages 38-39. Prepare cue cards for all students. Get them to bring in their self-assessment diaries if they are writing them.

Recap

Put students in their pairs and read through the **Recap** as a class. Draw their attention to the project tasks and the unit objectives and ask which task helped achieve which objectives. Make sure they have all the materials and notes that they need (see **Preparation**) for the **Final task**.

Final Task: Practise and present your biography

Tell students they are now going to present their biographies. Read through the steps of the **Final task** and make sure students have cue cards. Agree on a time limit to prepare their presentations that will allow the class to complete the presentations and **Evaluation**. Students waiting for others to finish can choose useful expressions to include in their presentations and practise them. Make sure that they decide who is presenting which part and who is speaking when before they begin. As they prepare their cards, make sure they are writing in note form and be prepared to help them do this. Tell them to focus on speaking clearly and using eye contact, intonation and gestures to engage the audience.

Start and finish each presentation with a round of applause to help generate confidence and enthusiasm, and make sure there is an opportunity for students to decide which story was false and why. Lead the discussion with a question of your own after each group has finished.

After everyone has finished, ask students how they knew which stories were false. Ask them how they can tell if stories they read and hear in the different media are true or not, and direct their attention to the **21st century skill** (see below).

21ST CENTURY SKILLS

Read through the text with the students. Ask them what they think trustworthy and untrustworthy sources are. Ask them if they generally follow the advice and if they followed it during the project.

→ See pages 28-29 **21st century skills**

Evaluation

Make groups of four by putting project pairs together. Before they discuss the questions in their groups, give them time either alone or in their pairs to prepare notes about their experience in the project. Remind students to be supportive and give constructive criticism if necessary, with ideas on how to do things better next time. Monitor discussions, adding your own feedback where appropriate and noting common observations to then convey to the class as a whole. Have a class discussion about what students have learnt from the project, reminding them of the unit objectives, the **Core values** and the **Learning to learn tools** of units 3 and 4, as well as the **21st century skills** section of the Project pages.

If you have decided to use the evaluation exercise as a springboard for a student self-assessment diary (see **Evaluation** notes page 77), give them time to do this now and remind them to refer to the **Reflect on your learning** section of the **Workbook** if they have one.

→ See pages 40-41 **Assessment**

Go beyond

Draw students' attention to the title of the text and ask what paparazzi are and what they do. Get them to read the text to check their understanding and then discuss the questions in pairs or in their **Evaluation** groups.

Remind students to do all the exercises in their notebook

CONTINUOUS ASSESSMENT Students can prepare and present a biography of a famous person.

5 GET CONNECTED

At the start of each unit and lesson, explain to the students what the objectives are.

Language objectives

Grammar

Imperatives

- Students use the imperative to give instructions, warnings and advice.

Future with *will*

- Students use *will* to talk about the future and to make requests and predictions.

Vocabulary

Technology I: *alarm clock, attach, charge, click, connection, digital platform, download, drag, homepage, laptop, machine, main menu, password, printer, right-click, track, type, video clip*

Technology II: *camera, computer programme, circuit, connection, data, electronics, hardware, insert, memory card, mobile phone, robot, software, update, wire*

Phrasal verbs: *log in/out, plug in* (opposite: *unplug*), *sign in/out, switch on/off, turn on/off, turn up/down*

Future technologies: *artificial intelligence (AI), driverless cars, electric cars, futurologist, genetic research, nanobot, nanotechnology, robotics in medicine, self-driving vehicle, smart factory, smart home*

Idioms and expressions

Understanding: *not have a clue, know something like the back of your hand, not be rocket science*

- Students look at idioms and expressions in the context of two short conversations and a monologue.

Recycled language

Modal verbs, Past participles, Past perfect

Skills objectives

Speaking

- Students guess the definitions of new words related to technology.
- Students discuss the future of new technology.
- Students make predictions about the future.
- Students give technical advice.

Pronunciation: Students practise words with the /dʒ/ and /ʒ/ sounds.

Pairwork: Students use various mediation techniques to give advice.

Listening

- Students listen in order to complete conversations about technology.
- Students listen to answer questions about a science fair.
- Students listen to put instructions in the correct order.
- Students listen to complete sentences with *will*.
- Students listen and answer questions about projects and inventions.

Reading

- Students read and complete a conversation about using a new internet platform.
- Students read and match parts of a sentence.
- Students read and complete a text about the future and predictions.
- Students read a review and identify compound nouns and verbs.

Core values: Students discuss **being prepared** in the context of new technology.

Writing

- Students write tips for good digital habits.
- Students write sentences with *will* or *won't*.
- Students write a review of a tech product.

Focus on Compound nouns and verbs: *computer programme, headphones, homepage, laptop, left-click, main menu, mobile phone, phone call, playlist, upload*

Remind students to do all the exercises in their notebook

Learning to learn tools

SPEAKING TOOLS Students practise committing new phrases to memory while they are still fresh in their minds.	LISTENING TOOLS Students practise listening for *will* in the contracted form.
READING TOOLS Students pay special attention to the key words in a sentence.	WRITING TOOLS Students practise using a clear structure when writing.

VOCABULARY TOOLS Students look at irregular phrasal verbs.

Project objectives: Invention

Task 1 Students form groups of four and create an idea for a new invention.

Task 2 Students create a prototype and/or a poster for their new invention.

Task 3 Students put together a presentation for their new invention.

Audiovisual objectives

Vlog: Students watch and listen to George talk about cassette tapes.

Culture: Students watch and listen to George talk about Scotland.

Grammar animations: Students are presented with visual presentations of the unit grammar.

Key competences

LC **Linguistic**
pages 46-55

MST **Mathematical and Science and Technology**
pages 46-55

DC **Digital**
pages 46-47, 49, 53

SCC **Social and Civic**
pages 50-53

CAE **Cultural awareness and expression**
pages 51, 53

LL **Learning to learn**
pages 46, 49-50, 52-53

IE **Sense of initiative and entrepreneurship**
pages 47, 49, 52

→ See pages 42-43 Key competences

CEFR Mediation

5.1 Relaying specific information in writing
Can write specific information in spoken texts on familiar subjects.

5.2 Processing text in writing
Can pick out and reproduce key words or phrases from a text.

5.3 Processing text in writing
Can summarise in writing information in texts of general interest.

5.4 Relaying specific information in speech
Can relay specific information in short written texts on familiar subjects.

5.5 Collaborating to construct meaning
Can ask someone to give reasons for their views and check mutual understanding.

Project Encouraging conceptual talk
Can ask questions to clarify understanding, including about how someone thinks something would work.

Unit review Relaying specific information in writing
Can list numbers and other information given clearly.

Pairwork Collaborating to construct meaning
Can make suggestions to move a discussion forward..

→ See pages 30-33 Mediation

Remind students to do all the exercises in their notebook

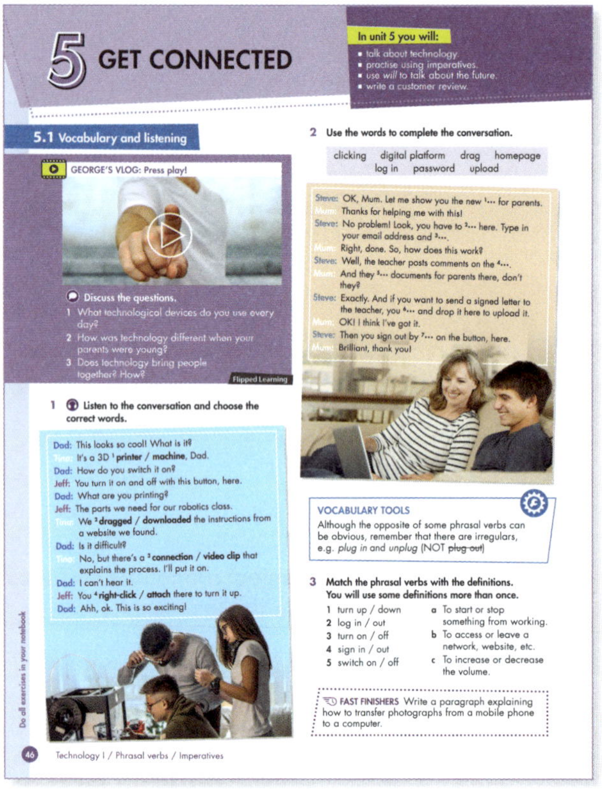

5 GET CONNECTED

In unit 5 you will:
- talk about technology.
- practise using imperatives.
- use will to talk about the future.
- write a customer review.

5.1 Vocabulary and listening

GEORGE'S VLOG: Press play!

Discuss the questions.
1 What technological devices do you use every day?
2 How was technology different when your parents were young?
3 Does technology bring people together? How?

Flipped Learning

1 Listen to the conversation and choose the correct words.

Dad: This looks so cool! What is it?
Tina: It's a 3D [1] printer / machine, Dad.
Dad: How do you switch it on?
Jeff: You turn it on and off with this button, here.
Dad: What are you printing?
Jeff: The parts we need for our robotics class.
Tina: We [2] dragged / downloaded the instructions from a website we found.
Dad: Is it difficult?
Tina: No, but there's a [3] connection / video clip that explains the process. I'll put it on.
Dad: I can't hear it.
Jeff: You [4] right-click / attach there to turn it up.
Dad: Ahh, ok. This is so exciting!

2 Use the words to complete the conversation.

clicking digital platform drag homepage log in password upload

Steve: OK, Mum. Let me show you the new [1]... for parents.
Mum: Thanks for helping me with this!
Steve: No problem! Look, you have to [2]... here. Type in your email address and [3]....
Mum: Right, done. So, how does this work?
Steve: Well, the teacher posts comments on the [4]....
Mum: And they [5]... documents for parents there, don't they?
Steve: Exactly. And if you want to send a signed letter to the teacher, you [6]... and drop it here to upload it.
Mum: OK! I think I've got it.
Steve: Then you sign out by [7]... on the button, here.
Mum: Brilliant, thank you!

VOCABULARY TOOLS
Although the opposite of some phrasal verbs can be obvious, remember that there are irregulars, e.g. *plug in* and *unplug* (NOT ~~plug out~~)

3 Match the phrasal verbs with the definitions. You will use some definitions more than once.
1 turn up / down
2 log in / out
3 turn on / off
4 sign in / out
5 switch on / off

a To start or stop something from working.
b To access or leave a network, website, etc.
c To increase or decrease the volume.

FAST FINISHERS Write a paragraph explaining how to transfer photographs from a mobile phone to a computer.

Do all exercises in your notebook

46 Technology I / Phrasal verbs / Imperatives

Grammar and listening 5.1

IMPERATIVES
Use **imperatives** to give instructions, advice and warnings.

Affirmative	Right-click on the icon Push the big button
Negative	Don't touch that! Never give your personal details.
Expressions	Be careful! Watch out!

Grammar reference page 111

4 Listen and answer the questions.
1 What has Rachel's grandma got?
2 What does she want to do?
3 What is the problem?
4 Which button turns it off?
5 What advice does Rachel give her?

5 Put the sentences in the correct order. Listen and check.
a Open the message and click on the link I sent you.
b Use the + and – buttons to turn the volume up or down.
c First, turn the phone on.
d Choose the track that you want to hear.
e Click on the 'play' symbol.
f Turn it off when you're finished.
g Remember to plug in the headphones.

6 Match the parts of the sentences. Check your answers in pairs.
1 To turn on the phone,
2 To add a new contact,
3 To make a phone call,
4 To keep your details safe,
5 To charge your laptop,

a don't tell anyone your password.
b push the button on the side.
c plug it into the wall.
d go to the main menu.
e press the green button.

7 Say what to do in these situations.
1 The battery on your phone is low.
1 Plug it into the wall.
2 The music is too loud.
3 Your alarm clock is ringing.
4 You finish checking your emails.
5 You want to download a document.
6 You finish using your laptop.

8 NOW YOU! With your partner, write five tips for good digital habits.
1 Keep your passwords secret.

PROJECT TASK 1 Invention
- Get into a group of four. You are going to create an idea for an invention and present a poster or prototype at a science fair.
- Together, write a general description of your invention. Talk about the basic characteristics, parts and the materials that it could be made from.

→ Workbook page 56

Do all exercises in your notebook

Workbook pages 40 and 41 47

ANSWER KEY

Pages 46-47

1 **1** printer
2 downloaded
3 video clip
4 right-click

2 **1** homepage
2 log in
3 password
4 digital platform
5 upload
6 drag
7 clicking

3 **1** c
2 b
3 a
4 b
5 a

4 **1** a smartphone
2 take a selfie
3 she doesn't know how to do it
4 the button on the side of the phone
5 push the button on the selfie stick

5 c, a, d, e, g, b, f

6 **1** b
2 d
3 e
4 a
5 c

7 *Suggested answers:*
1 Plug it into the wall
2 Turn the volume down
3 Turn it off
4 Log out
5 Drag and drop it
6 Switch it off

8 *Student's own answers*

Remind students to do all the exercises in their notebook

LESSON FOCUS

Grammar Imperatives
Vocabulary Technology I; Phrasal verbs
Listening Conversations about new technology
Speaking Giving advice
Project task 1 Create an idea for a new invention

Resources
Teacher's i-solutions, Student's Book audio, Vlog and worksheet

Flipped Learning

GEORGE'S VLOG: Press play!

- Make sure to set up the **Flipped Learning** work with the students beforehand. **See pages 20-23 for complete Flipped Learning guidelines.**
- Ask students to put the **Flipped Learning worksheets** on their desks and walk around to check how many have completed the Flipped task.
- In pairs or small groups, ask students to compare and check the *Before you watch…* and *While you watch…* exercises on the worksheet.
- Show students **George's Vlog** and ask volunteers to provide correct answers and clarify any doubts other students may have.
- Choose three or four students to read aloud their answers to the *After you watch…* exercises on the worksheet and encourage some class discussion.
- Move straight to exercise 1 on page 46.

Warmer

Watch George's Vlog and discuss the questions with the whole class. If you don't have video facilities, simply discuss the questions.

1 1.38 (See page 173 for transcripts) Let students read the conversation and try to choose the correct words before playing the audio. Play the audio to check the answers and help to correct where necessary.

2 Ask students if they know the definitions of the words in the wordpool. After they complete the exercise, see if any of the words they did not know before are now clearer after reading them in context.

VOCABULARY TOOLS

Get students to read the **Vocabulary tool**. Ask if they can think of any other examples where phrasal verbs are irregular (*tie up/untie; cover up/uncover; wind up/unwind*).

3 Ask students if they know any other phrasal verbs related to technology (*print out; back up; go online/offline; set up; drop down*) and write them on the board.

FAST FINISHERS Students can complete this exercise alone or in pairs.

Flipped Learning

IMPERATIVES

Draw students' attention to the **Grammar table**. Remind students that they can use this as a quick reference while completing the exercises.

Show students the **Grammar animation** and/or refer students to the **Grammar reference** on page 111 for further information on form and use.

→ See page 23 to flip the **grammar lesson**

4 1.39 (See page 173 for transcripts) Encourage students to answer the questions in full sentences. After listening ask if students think that Rachel's grandma is good with new technology. Is it harder for older generations to understand new technology?

5 1.40 (See page 173 for transcripts) Ask students if they noticed anything unusual about the sentences (most of them don't have subject pronouns) and what they call this kind of speech (the imperative).

6 After completing the exercise, students should check their answers in pairs.

7 Remind students to make use of the **Grammar table** and **Grammar reference** for guidance.

8 NOW YOU! Round up with a class discussion. Were there any tips that students came up with that they weren't doing before, but which they think are a good idea to follow in the future?

PROJECT TASK 1 Invention

Organise students into teams of four. They are going to come up with an idea for a new invention. They need to think about the materials needed to make it and the functionality of their invention and/or its use for society. Remind students that they need to keep their project notes together in their **Workbook** (page 56) or in their own notebook.

→ See pages 24-27 **Projects**

FURTHER PRACTICE

Workbook pages 40-41
- **Grammar reference and practice** pages 88 and 95
- **Wordlist and exercises** pages 100 and 103

Remind students to do all the exercises in their notebook

CONTINUOUS ASSESSMENT Students can talk about technology and use phrasal verbs and imperatives.

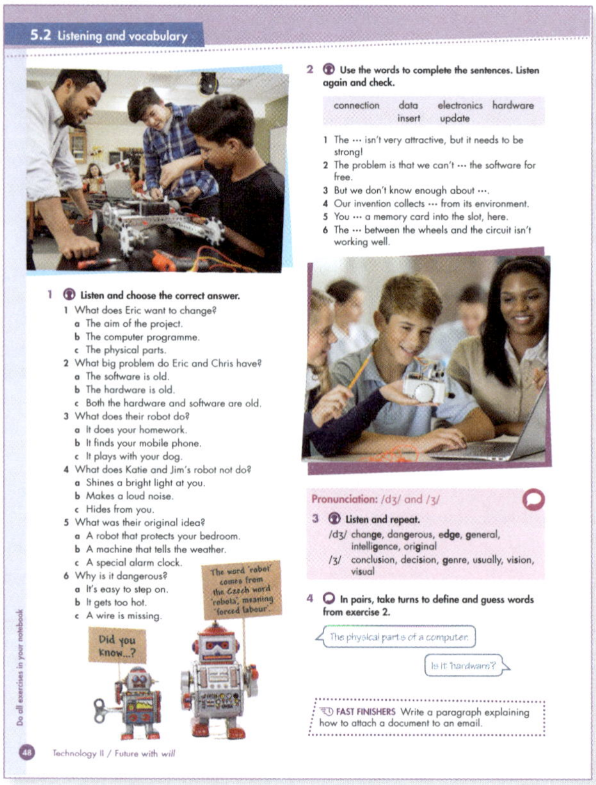

5.2 Listening and vocabulary

1 Listen and choose the correct answer.

1 What does Eric want to change?
a The aim of the project.
b The computer programme.
c The physical parts.

2 What big problem do Eric and Chris have?
a The software is old.
b The hardware is old.
c Both the hardware and software are old.

3 What does their robot do?
a It does your homework.
b It finds your mobile phone.
c It plays with your dog.

4 What does Katie and Jim's robot not do?
a Shines a bright light at you.
b Makes a loud noise.
c Hides from you.

5 What was their original idea?
a A robot that protects your bedroom.
b A machine that tells the weather.
c A special alarm clock.

6 Why is it dangerous?
a It's easy to step on.
b It gets too hot.
c A wire is missing.

2 Use the words to complete the sentences. Listen again and check.

connection data electronics hardware insert update

1 The ··· isn't very attractive, but it needs to be strong!
2 The problem is that we can't ··· the software for free.
3 But we don't know enough about ···.
4 Our invention collects ··· from its environment.
5 You ··· a memory card into the slot, here.
6 The ··· between the wheels and the circuit isn't working well.

Pronunciation: /dʒ/ and /ʒ/

3 Listen and repeat.
/dʒ/ change, dangerous, edge, general, intelligence, original
/ʒ/ conclusion, decision, genre, usually, vision, visual

4 In pairs, take turns to define and guess words from exercise 2.

FAST FINISHERS Write a paragraph explaining how to attach a document to an email.

Do all exercises in your notebook

48 Technology II / Future with *will*

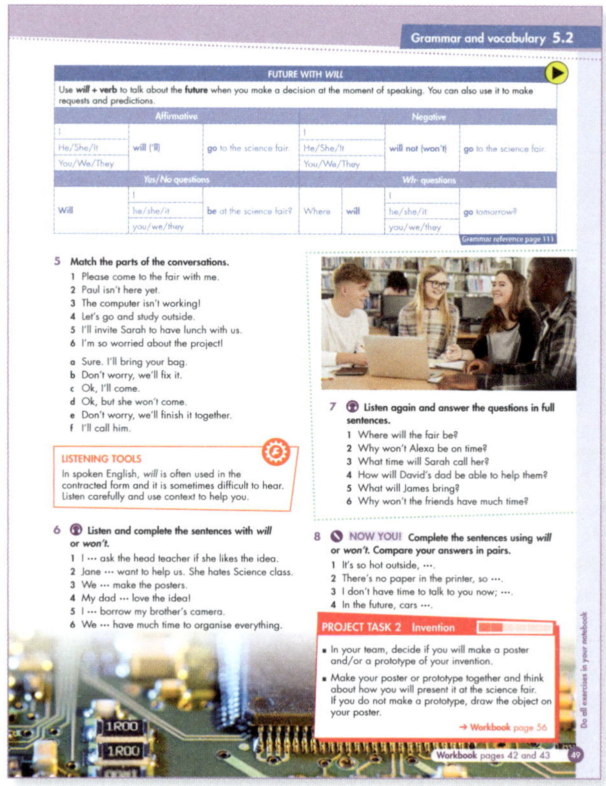

Grammar and vocabulary 5.2

FUTURE WITH *WILL*						
Use **will + verb** to talk about the **future** when you make a decision at the moment of speaking. You can also use it to make requests and predictions.						
Affirmative			**Negative**			
I / He/She/It / You/We/They	**will ('ll)**	**go** to the science fair.	I / He/She/It / You/We/They	**will not (won't)**	**go** to the science fair.	
***Yes/No* questions**			***Wh-* questions**			
Will	I / he/she/it / you/we/they	**be** at the science fair?	Where	**will**	I / he/she/it / you/we/they	**go** tomorrow?

Grammar reference page 111

5 Match the parts of the conversations.

1 Please come to the fair with me.
2 Paul isn't here yet.
3 The computer isn't working!
4 Let's go and study outside.
5 I'll invite Sarah to have lunch with us.
6 I'm so worried about the project!

a Sure. I'll bring your bag.
b Don't worry, we'll fix it.
c Ok, I'll come.
d Ok, but she won't come.
e Don't worry, we'll finish it together.
f I'll call him.

LISTENING TOOLS
In spoken English, *will* is often used in the contracted form and it is sometimes difficult to hear. Listen carefully and use context to help you.

6 Listen and complete the sentences with *will* or *won't*.

1 I ··· ask the head teacher if she likes the idea.
2 Jane ··· want to help us. She hates Science class.
3 We ··· make the posters.
4 My dad ··· love the idea!
5 I ··· borrow my brother's camera.
6 We ··· have much time to organise everything.

7 Listen again and answer the questions in full sentences.

1 Where will the fair be?
2 Why won't Alexa be on time?
3 What time will Sarah call her?
4 How will David's dad be able to help them?
5 What will James bring?
6 Why won't the friends have much time?

8 NOW YOU! Complete the sentences using *will* or *won't*. Compare your answers in pairs.

1 It's so hot outside, ···.
2 There's no paper in the printer, so ···.
3 I don't have time to talk to you now; ···.
4 In the future, cars ···.

PROJECT TASK 2 Invention
- In your team, decide if you will make a poster and/or a prototype of your invention.
- Make your poster or prototype together and think about how you will present it at the science fair. If you do not make a prototype, draw the object on your poster.

→ Workbook page 56

Workbook pages 42 and 43 49

Do all exercises in your notebook

ANSWER KEY

Pages 48-49

1
1 c
2 a
3 c
4 a
5 a
6 b

2
1 hardware
2 update
3 electronics
4 data
5 insert
6 connection

3 *Student's own answers*

4 *Student's own answers*

5
1 c
2 f
3 b
4 a
5 d
6 e

6
1 will
2 won't
3 will
4 will
5 will
6 won't

7
1 In the school cafeteria
2 She has extra classes
3 At 1:30pm
4 He will help with setting up the tables.
5 His brother's camera
6 The school cafeteria will closed for repairs soon.

8 *Student's own answers*

Remind students to do all the exercises in their notebook

LESSON FOCUS

Grammar Future with *will*
Vocabulary Technology II
Listening Trouble shooting new inventions; a science fair
Speaking Defining new words
Project task 2 Create a prototype and/or a poster of the new invention.

Resources
Teacher's i-solutions, Student's Book audio

Warmer

Ask students if there is one invention they cannot imagine living without. It could be something they have used their whole life, or something they have discovered recently. Ask them if they know the phrase 'necessity is the mother of invention', and if they know what the phrase refers to.

1 1.41 (See page 173 for transcripts) Write some key vocabulary from the exercise on the board for students to use in later exercises (*programme; parts; software; hardware; robot; machine; mobile*). Check students' understanding of the vocabulary.

2 1.42 (See page 173 for transcripts) Ask students if they know the definitions of the words in the wordpool. After they complete the exercise see if any of the words they didn't know before are now clearer after reading them in context. Write the words on the board, along with the other words from exercise 1, so that the students can use them all in exercise 4.

Pronunciation

3 1.43 (See page 173 for transcripts) Get students to practise the sounds before drilling the words. Contrast the /dʒ/ sound with the /ʒ/ sound to make sure they can hear and make the distinctions.

4 Students can mime the words to their partner and get them to guess the word.

FAST FINISHERS Students can complete this exercise alone or in pairs.

FUTURE WITH *WILL*

Flipped Learning

Draw students' attention to the **Grammar table**. Remind students that they can use this as a quick reference while completing the exercises.
Show students the **Grammar animation** and/or refer students to the **Grammar reference** on page 111 for further information on form and use.

→ See page 23 for how to flip the **grammar lesson**

5 After students have completed the exercise, ask them if they noticed anything unusual about the verbs (*will* is in the contracted form). This leads into the **Listening tool.**

LISTENING TOOLS

Draw students' attention to the **Listening tool** and work on some examples of *will* in the contracted form so that the class can identify them more easily when listening.

6 1.44 (See page 173 for transcripts) After listening remind students to always utilise the **Grammar table** and the **Grammar reference** to help them.

7 1.45 (See page 174 for transcripts) Students should take notes as they listen again to make sure they have all the information they need to complete the exercise.

8 NOW YOU! Students can use the vocabulary on the board to help them complete the sentences. Students should add one sentence of their own before checking in pairs.

PROJECT TASK 2 Invention

Students will decide whether to make a prototype of their invention, or a poster demonstrating the functions of the invention, or both. Remind students that they need to keep their project notes together in their **Workbook** (page 56) or in their own notebook.

→ See pages 24-27 **Projects**

FURTHER PRACTICE

Workbook pages 42-43
- **Grammar reference and practice** pages 88 and 95
- **Wordlist and exercises** pages 100 and 103

Vocabulary and Grammar worksheets available to download from the **Richmond***Learning***Platform**

→ See pages 38-39 **Mixed-ability classes**

CONTINUOUS ASSESSMENT Students can talk about technology and use *will* for the future.

Remind students to do all the exercises in their notebook

5.3 Reading

5.3 Reading

1 Match the technologies to the pictures. In pairs, make predictions about the future of each type of technology.

artificial intelligence | robotics in medicine | driverless cars | smart homes

READING TOOLS
The first sentence of a paragraph often contains a key word or phrase that tells you what the rest of the paragraph is about.

2 Read the article and complete it with the sentences.
a Most of these predictions involve humans trusting technology and giving up a lot of our control.
b There are also some exciting predictions for medicine.
c A prediction everyone agrees on is the increased connectivity of everything.
d The future of transport will be interesting.
e Here are some of their predictions.

3 Complete the sentences with information from the article.
1 The article mentions H.G. Wells' book *Anticipations* because it ···.
2 The writer says that there will be more cars that ···.
3 It's possible that genetic research will help us find ways to ···.
4 Experts think that smart technology will ···.
5 Sam Altman thinks that human beings will ···.

A WHOLE NEW WORLD

In 1901, English science fiction writer H.G. Wells made a series of predictions for the next one hundred years in a book called *Anticipations*. He predicted the success of cars and trains and their effects on cities, the industrialisation of war and the establishment of a European Union. Now you can find the theories of 'futurologists' all over the internet. [1]...

[2]... Many big car companies are developing self-driving and electric vehicles, so they will probably become more common. In fact, we are already seeing privately owned and shared electric cars on our city streets. Several countries are also experimenting with 'hyperloops', capsules that carry passengers along magnetised tubes with very little friction. They say hyperloops will reach speeds of over 1,000 km/h.

[3]... Researchers are studying ways to locate and edit defective genes, and that could lead to the eradication of some of the world's most lethal diseases. Advances in nanotechnology could also give us nanobots that patrol our bodies and destroy diseased cells. Some experts even predict that we will have brain-computer interfaces so we can artificially increase our mental capacity.

[4]... We already have smart houses, where security, heating, and entertainment systems connect to create more comfortable living spaces. Experts also talk of smart factories and even smart cities, with different technologies all working together to make everything run efficiently.

[5]... Fans of science fiction know that this could end badly. Some technology experts suggest that governments dedicate more resources to investigating the dangers of new technologies, especially artificial intelligence (AI). As tech entrepreneur Sam Altman says, 'In the next few decades we are either going to head toward self-destruction or toward humans colonising the universe.'

Do all exercises in your notebook

50 Language in context / Future technologies

Reading 5.3

4 Identify these objects using words or expressions from the text on page 50.

5 NOW YOU! Discuss the questions in groups.
- Which of the predictions in the text on page 50 do you think will come true and when?
- What other predictions do you have?
- Do you feel optimistic or pessimistic about the future? Why?

CORE VALUES Being prepared

6 Say what preparations the people in these situations need to make and what will happen if they don't.
- Sarah has a new laptop and wants to start using it immediately.
- John wants to buy a new mobile phone.
- Maria is going to write a blog about her family holiday.
- David wants to make a video and put it online.

Sarah should download some anti-virus software or she'll get a virus.

7 Discuss how you think we can prepare ourselves for the future. Use the prompts to help you.

Energy and resources | Health and medicine | Jobs | Population | Technology | The environment

FAST FINISHERS Write about one of your predictions from exercise 1.

Workbook pages 44 and 45

Do all exercises in your notebook

51

ANSWER KEY

Pages 50-51

1 **1** smart homes; *Student's own answers*
2 driverless cars; *Student's own answers*
3 robotics in medicine; *Student's own answers*
4 artificial intelligence; *Student's own answers*

2 **1** e
2 d
3 b
4 c
5 a

3 **1** is an early example of successful 'futurology'
2 use electricity and don't need human drivers
3 eradicate lethal diseases
4 connect everything and make it run efficiently
5 either destroy themselves or colonise the universe

4 **1** smart factory
2 nanobot
3 hyperloop

5 *Student's own answers*

6 *Student's own answers*

7 *Student's own answers*

Remind students to do all the exercises in their notebook

LESSON FOCUS

Language in context Future technologies

Core values Being prepared

Resources

Teacher's i-solutions, Student's Book audio

Preparation Research books and films that predicted the future. If possible show clips from the films or extracts from the books.

➔ See pages 36-37 **Literature**

Warmer

Ask students what films and books they know that have predicted the future. Examples:

- Jules Verne, *Twenty Thousand Leagues Under the Sea* – predicted the electric submarine.
- Mary Shelley, *Frankenstein* – predicted modern transplants.
- The Truman Show – predicted reality TV

Ask students why they think that these authors were able to predict future technologies and inventions. Ask them if they think that the inventions would have happened without the stories.

1 After students have discussed their ideas in pairs, open the discussion up to the class. Ask them which new technologies they would like to use in their own lives, and which they think would be of the greatest benefit to society as a whole.

READING TOOLS

Get students to look at the **Reading tool** and apply this method to the next exercise.

2 1.46 (See page 174 for transcripts) Remind students of the **Reading tool** and to pay special attention to the beginnings of the sentences that they are inserting, as well as the sentence that follows on from it in the paragraph.

3 Ask students why they think the writer of the article used *will* to talk about the future (because it is used to make predictions). Ask students to add one more sentence, using a prediction of their own about the future.

4 Before the students looks for the words in the text, ask them to describe what they think is happening in the pictures.

5 NOW YOU! After the students have discussed their ideas in groups, ask each group for one prediction. Have a class discussion about which prediction they think is most likely to come true.

CORE VALUES Being prepared

6 Ask students if they feel it is important to be prepared? Is life easier that way, or do they prefer not to plan ahead.

7 Open this up to a class discussion. Write any other new prompts on the board that could help with the discussion.

FAST FINISHERS Students can complete this exercise alone or in pairs.

FURTHER PRACTICE

Workbook pages 44-45

Remind students to do all the exercises in their notebook

CONTINUOUS ASSESSMENT Students can understand a text about future technologies.

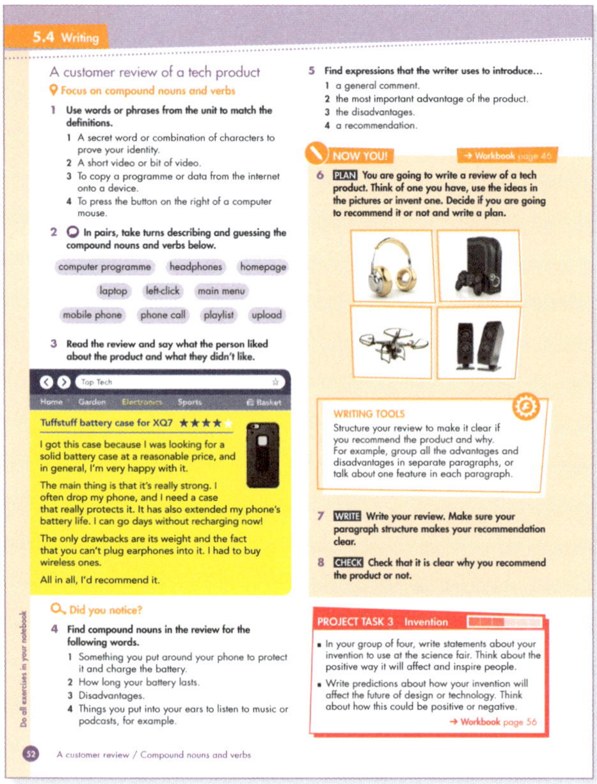

5.4 Writing

A customer review of a tech product

Focus on compound nouns and verbs

1 **Use words or phrases from the unit to match the definitions.**
1 A secret word or combination of characters to prove your identity.
2 A short video or bit of video.
3 To copy a programme or data from the internet onto a device.
4 To press the button on the right of a computer mouse.

2 **In pairs, take turns describing and guessing the compound nouns and verbs below.**

computer programme | headphones | homepage | laptop | left-click | main menu | mobile phone | phone call | playlist | upload

3 **Read the review and say what the person liked about the product and what they didn't like.**

Top Tech
Home Garden Electronics Sports Basket

Tuffstuff battery case for XQ7 ★★★★

I got this case because I was looking for a solid battery case at a reasonable price, and in general, I'm very happy with it.

The main thing is that it's really strong. I often drop my phone, and I need a case that really protects it. It has also extended my phone's battery life. I can go days without recharging now!

The only drawbacks are its weight and the fact that you can't plug earphones into it. I had to buy wireless ones.

All in all, I'd recommend it.

Did you notice?

4 **Find compound nouns in the review for the following words.**
1 Something you put around your phone to protect it and charge the battery.
2 How long your battery lasts.
3 Disadvantages.
4 Things you put into your ears to listen to music or podcasts, for example.

5 **Find expressions that the writer uses to introduce…**
1 a general comment.
2 the most important advantage of the product.
3 the disadvantages.
4 a recommendation.

NOW YOU! → Workbook page 46

6 PLAN **You are going to write a review of a tech product. Think of one you have, use the ideas in the pictures or invent one. Decide if you are going to recommend it or not and write a plan.**

WRITING TOOLS
Structure your review to make it clear if you recommend the product and why. For example, group all the advantages and disadvantages in separate paragraphs, or talk about one feature in each paragraph.

7 WRITE **Write your review. Make sure your paragraph structure makes your recommendation clear.**

8 CHECK **Check that it is clear why you recommend the product or not.**

PROJECT TASK 3 Invention
- In your group of four, write statements about your invention to use at the science fair. Think about the positive way it will affect and inspire people.
- Write predictions about how your invention will affect the future of design or technology. Think about how this could be positive or negative.

→ Workbook page 56

Do all exercises in your notebook

52 A customer review / Compound nouns and verbs

ANSWER KEY

Page 52

1 **1** password **2** video clip **3** download **4** right-click

2 *Student's own answers*

3 **Liked:** strength, added battery life
Didn't like: weight, you can't plug earphones into it

4 **1** battery case **2** battery life **3** drawbacks **4** earphones

5 **1** In general, all in all
2 The main thing is
3 The only drawbacks are
4 I'd recommend it

6 *Student's own answers*

7 *Student's own answers*

8 *Student's own answers*

FURTHER PRACTICE

Workbook page 46

LESSON FOCUS

Focus on Compound nouns and verbs
Writing A customer review of a tech product
Project task 3 Put together a presentation of the invention.

Resources
Teacher's i-solutions
Preparation Two tech devices as props

Warmer

Show the class two different tech devices – for example, a smart phone and bluetooth headphones – and ask students which one they prefer and why.

Focus on compound nouns and verbs

1 Check that students understand what a compound noun and a verb are. They can look back through the unit to help them to remember.

2 Students can mime the words for their partner to guess.

3 Students can stay in their pairs to do this exercise. They should decide whether after reading the review they would buy the product or not.

Did you notice?

4 Answer the questions as a class and check if there is any new vocabulary that students did not understand.

5 Students can complete this exercise in pairs and then add any other phrases or words that they know. Once they have finished, write some examples on the board to assist students with the writing task.

6 PLAN Tell students that they are going to write a review of a tech product. They must decide if they are going to recommend it to readers or not, and plan accordingly.

WRITING TOOLS

Get students to read the **Writing tool**. They should follow this structure when planning and writing their reviews, so that their purpose is clear to readers.

7 WRITE Before students start writing, make a checklist on the board of any elements related to content, structure, language and style that they should bear in mind.

8 CHECK Once students have checked their own reviews, they can swap with a partner and check each other's.

PROJECT TASK 3 Invention

Students are going to present their new invention at a science fair and must prepare some statements about it. These should include the advantages of the product and also what impact the product may have on society in the future. Remind students that they need to keep their project notes together in their **Workbook** (page 56) or in their own notebook.

→ See pages 24-27 **Projects**

Remind students to do all the exercises in their notebook

 CONTINUOUS ASSESSMENT Students can use compound nouns and verbs to write a customer review of a tech product.

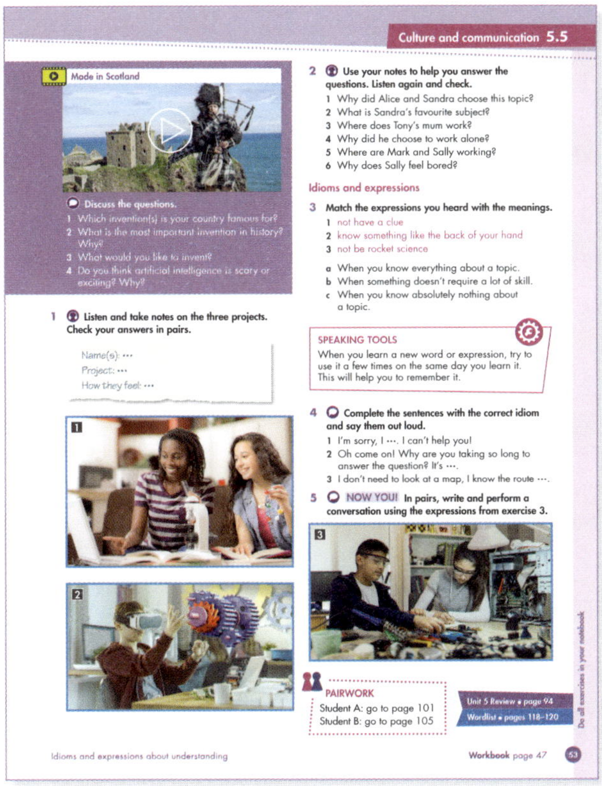
Culture and communication 5.5

Made in Scotland

Discuss the questions.
1 Which invention(s) is your country famous for?
2 What is the most important invention in history? Why?
3 What would you like to invent?
4 Do you think artificial intelligence is scary or exciting? Why?

1 Listen and take notes on the three projects. Check your answers in pairs.

Name(s): ···
Project: ···
How they feel: ···

2 Use your notes to help you answer the questions. Listen again and check.
1 Why did Alice and Sandra choose this topic?
2 What is Sandra's favourite subject?
3 Where does Tony's mum work?
4 Why did he choose to work alone?
5 Where are Mark and Sally working?
6 Why does Sally feel bored?

Idioms and expressions

3 Match the expressions you heard with the meanings.
1 not have a clue
2 know something like the back of your hand
3 not be rocket science

a When you know everything about a topic.
b When something doesn't require a lot of skill.
c When you know absolutely nothing about a topic.

SPEAKING TOOLS
When you learn a new word or expression, try to use it a few times on the same day you learn it. This will help you to remember it.

4 Complete the sentences with the correct idiom and say them out loud.
1 I'm sorry, I ···. I can't help you!
2 Oh come on! Why are you taking so long to answer the question? It's ···.
3 I don't need to look at a map, I know the route ···.

5 NOW YOU! In pairs, write and perform a conversation using the expressions from exercise 3.

PAIRWORK
Student A: go to page 101
Student B: go to page 105

Unit 5 Review • page 94
Wordlist • pages 118–120

Do all exercises in your notebook

Idioms and expressions about understanding

Workbook page 47

53

ANSWER KEY

Page 53

1
1 **Name(s):** Sandra
Project: Investigating chemical structures
How they feel: Confused

2 **Name(s):** Tony
Project: Developing an interactive guide about how machines work
How they feel: Excited

3 **Name(s):** Mark and Sally
Project: Creating a computer from parts
How they feel: Bored

2
1 They didn't know anything about it and they thought it would be interesting.
2 Biology
3 In a factory
4 He thinks he will get better marks that way.
5 At Mark´s house
6 She thought the project would be more difficult.

3 1 c 2 a 3 b

4
1 don't have a clue
2 not rocket science
3 like the back of my hand

5 *Student's own answers*

PAIRWORK Student's Book pages 101 and 105
See **Teacher's Book** page 114 for more information.

➔ See pages 30-33 **Mediation**

LESSON FOCUS

Idioms and expressions Understanding
Listening Conversations and a monologue about projects
Speaking Using expressions about understanding

Resources
Teacher's i-solutions, Student's Book audio, Culture video and worksheet

Made in Scotland

Video and worksheet available on the RichmondLearningPlatform

- In pairs, ask students to complete the *What I know...* exercises on the **Culture video worksheet**.
- Show students the **Culture video** and ask them to complete the *What I learned...* exercises on the worksheet.
- In pairs, students compare answers.
- In small groups, tell students to complete the *What I wonder...* exercises on the worksheet.

Warmer

Watch the **Culture video** and discuss the questions with the whole class. If you don't have video facilities, simply discuss the questions.

1 1.47 (See page 174 for transcripts) Before completing the exercise, ask students what projects they think are being worked on in the photographs.

2 1.48 (See page 174 for transcripts) Students should use their notes to answer the questions where possible.

Idioms and expressions

3 Before looking at the definitions, ask students which expressions they think are positive and which are negative.

SPEAKING TOOLS

Draw students' attention to the **Speaking tool**. As a class repeat the new idioms.

4 After finishing the exercise, repeat the new expressions in the completed sentences.

5 NOW YOU! Students can use the pictures from exercise 1 for inspiration.

FURTHER PRACTICE AND UNIT ASSESSMENT

Unit 5 Review Student's Book page 94
Workbook page 47
- **Reflect on your learning** page 47
- **Grammar reference and practice** pages 88 and 95
- **Wordlist and exercises** pages 100 and 103

Tests available to download and edit from the **RichmondLearningPlatform**

➔ See pages 40-41 **Assessment**

Remind students to do all the exercises in their notebook

CONTINUOUS ASSESSMENT Students can use idioms and expressions about understanding.

Unit 5 Review

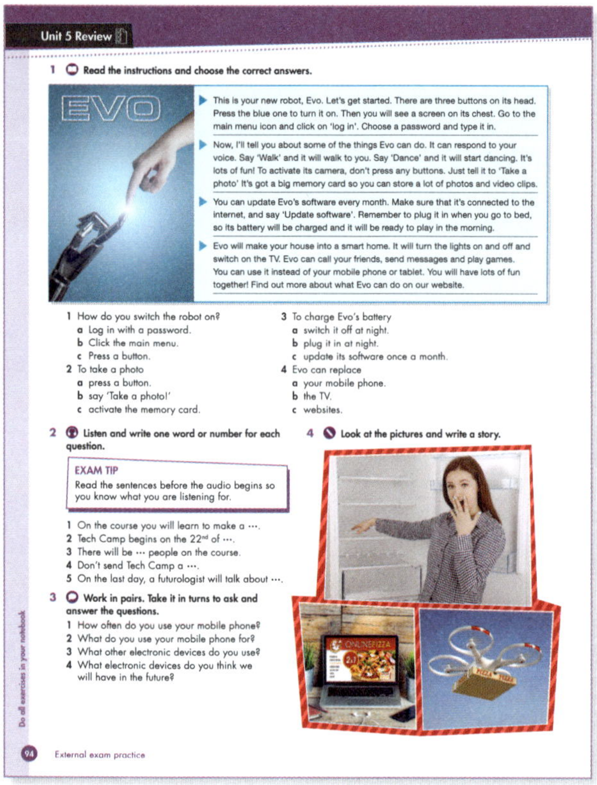

Unit 5 Review

1 Read the instructions and choose the correct answers.

EVO

- This is your new robot, Evo. Let's get started. There are three buttons on its head. Press the blue one to turn it on. Then you will see a screen on its chest. Go to the main menu icon and click on 'log in'. Choose a password and type it in.
- Now, I'll tell you about some of the things Evo can do. It can respond to your voice. Say 'Walk' and it will walk to you. Say 'Dance' and it will start dancing. It's lots of fun! To activate its camera, don't press any buttons. Just tell it to 'Take a photo' It's got a big memory card so you can store a lot of photos and video clips.
- You can update Evo's software every month. Make sure that it's connected to the internet, and say 'Update software'. Remember to plug it in when you go to bed, so its battery will be charged and it will be ready to play in the morning.
- Evo will make your house into a smart home. It will turn the lights on and off and switch on the TV. Evo can call your friends, send messages and play games. You can use it instead of your mobile phone or tablet. You will have lots of fun together! Find out more about what Evo can do on our website.

1 How do you switch the robot on?
  a Log in with a password.
  b Click the main menu.
  c Press a button.
2 To take a photo
  a press a button.
  b say 'Take a photo!'
  c activate the memory card.
3 To charge Evo's battery
  a switch it off at night.
  b plug it in at night.
  c update its software once a month.
4 Evo can replace
  a your mobile phone.
  b the TV.
  c websites.

2 Listen and write one word or number for each question.

EXAM TIP
Read the sentences before the audio begins so you know what you are listening for.

1 On the course you will learn to make a ···.
2 Tech Camp begins on the 22nd of ···.
3 There will be ··· people on the course.
4 Don't send Tech Camp a ···.
5 On the last day, a futurologist will talk about ···.

3 Work in pairs. Take it in turns to ask and answer the questions.
1 How often do you use your mobile phone?
2 What do you use your mobile phone for?
3 What other electronic devices do you use?
4 What electronic devices do you think we will have in the future?

4 Look at the pictures and write a story.

Do all exercises in your notebook

94 External exam practice

Student's Book page 94

ANSWER KEY

See page 180 for transcripts

1 **1** c **2** b **3** b **4** a

2 2.41
1 robot
2 June
3 30
4 photo
5 nanobots

3 *Student's own answers*

4 *Student's own answers*

Pairwork

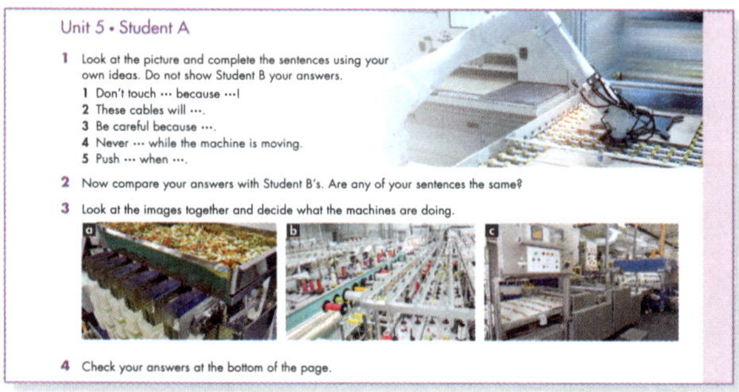

Unit 5 • Student A

1 Look at the picture and complete the sentences using your own ideas. Do not show Student B your answers.
1 Don't touch ··· because ···!
2 These cables will ···.
3 Be careful because ···.
4 Never ··· while the machine is moving.
5 Push ··· when ···.

2 Now compare your answers with Student B's. Are any of your sentences the same?

3 Look at the images together and decide what the machines are doing.

a b c

4 Check your answers at the bottom of the page.

Student's Book page 101

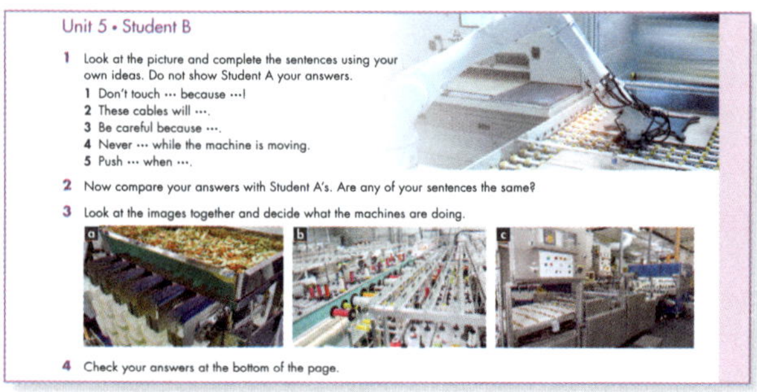

Unit 5 • Student B

1 Look at the picture and complete the sentences using your own ideas. Do not show Student A your answers.
1 Don't touch ··· because ···!
2 These cables will ···.
3 Be careful because ···.
4 Never ··· while the machine is moving.
5 Push ··· when ···.

2 Now compare your answers with Student A's. Are any of your sentences the same?

3 Look at the images together and decide what the machines are doing.

a b c

4 Check your answers at the bottom of the page.

Student's Book page 105

CEFR MEDIATION DESCRIPTOR

- **Encouraging conceptual talk**
  Students can ask what somebody thinks of a certain idea.

- **Comparing ideas**
  Tell students that they have the same set of instructions and warnings, but that they must complete them separately. After they are complete, tell students to compare answers to see how similar they are. Then ask them to work together to decide what is happening in the pictures in exercise 3.

Remind students to do all the exercises in their notebook

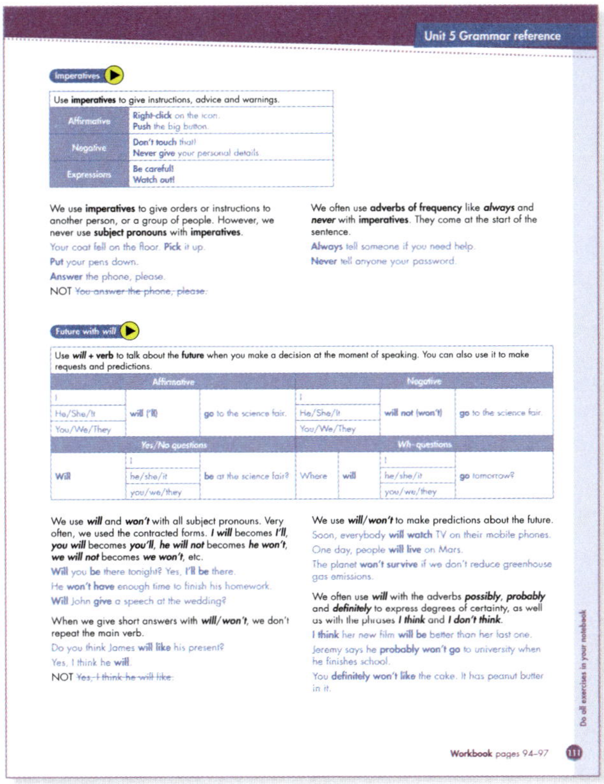

Imperatives

Use **imperatives** to give instructions, advice and warnings.	
Affirmative	**Right-click** on the icon. **Push** the big button.
Negative	**Don't touch** that! **Never give** your personal details
Expressions	**Be careful!** **Watch out!**

We use **imperatives** to give orders or instructions to another person, or a group of people. However, we never use **subject pronouns** with **imperatives**.

Your coat fell on the floor. **Pick** it up.

Put your pens down.

Answer the phone, please.

NOT ~~You answer the phone, please.~~

We often use **adverbs of frequency** like ***always*** and ***never*** with **imperatives**. They come at the start of the sentence.

Always tell someone if you need help.

Never tell anyone your password.

Future with *will*

Use ***will* + verb** to talk about the **future** when you make a decision at the moment of speaking. You can also use it to make requests and predictions.

Affirmative			Negative		
I He/She/It You/We/They	**will ('ll)**	**go** to the science fair.	I He/She/It You/We/They	**will not (won't)**	**go** to the science fair.

Yes/No questions			Wh- questions			
Will	I he/she/it you/we/they	**be** at the science fair?	Where	**will**	I he/she/it you/we/they	**go** tomorrow?

We use ***will*** and ***won't*** with all subject pronouns. Very often, we used the contracted forms. ***I will*** becomes ***I'll***, ***you will*** becomes ***you'll***, ***he will not*** becomes ***he won't***, ***we will not*** becomes ***we won't***, etc.

Will you **be** there tonight? Yes, **I'll be** there.

He **won't have** enough time to finish his homework.

Will John **give** a speech at the wedding?

When we give short answers with ***will/won't***, we don't repeat the main verb.

Do you think James **will like** his present?

Yes, I think he **will**.

NOT ~~Yes, I think he will like.~~

We use ***will/won't*** to make predictions about the future.

Soon, everybody **will watch** TV on their mobile phones.

One day, people **will live** on Mars.

The planet **won't survive** if we don't reduce greenhouse gas emissions.

We often use ***will*** with the adverbs ***possibly***, ***probably*** and ***definitely*** to express degrees of certainty, as well as with the phrases ***I think*** and ***I don't think***.

I think her new film **will be** better than her last one.

Jeremy says he **probably won't go** to university when he finishes school.

You **definitely won't like** the cake. It has peanut butter in it.

Do all exercises in your notebook

Workbook pages 94–97

Student's Book page 111

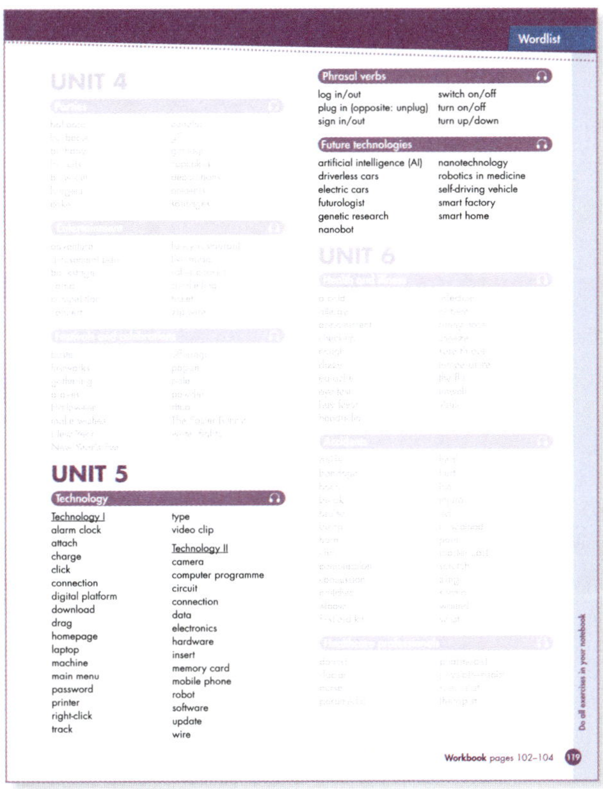

UNIT 5

Technology

Technology I
alarm clock
attach
charge
click
connection
digital platform
download
drag
homepage
laptop
machine
main menu
password
printer
right-click
track
type
video clip

Technology II
camera
computer programme
circuit
connection
data
electronics
hardware
insert
memory card
mobile phone
robot
software
update
wire

Phrasal verbs

log in/out
plug in (opposite: unplug)
sign in/out
switch on/off
turn on/off
turn up/down

Future technologies

artificial intelligence (AI)
driverless cars
electric cars
futurologist
genetic research
nanobot
nanotechnology
robotics in medicine
self-driving vehicle
smart factory
smart home

Do all exercises in your notebook

Workbook pages 102–104

Student's Book page 119

2.58 2.59 2.60

Remind students to do all the exercises in their notebook

6 STAYING HEALTHY

At the start of each unit and lesson, explain to the students what the objectives are.

Language objectives

Grammar

Modal verbs: advice and permission

- Students practise using *should* to give advice and *can* to ask for permission.

Modal verbs: rules and necessity

- Students practise using *have to* and *mustn't* in the context of rules and using *don't have to* and *must* to talk about things that are important or necessary.

Vocabulary

Health and illness: *a cold, allergy, appointment, check-up, cough dizzy, earache, eye test, hay fever, headache, infection, patient, runny nose, sneeze, sore throat, temperature, the flu, unwell, virus*

- Students use vocabulary about illness in a variety of contexts.

Accidents: *ankle, bandage, bone, break, bruise, bump, burn, chin, compression, concussion, crutches, elbow, first aid kit, heal, hurt, ice, injure, itch, nosebleed, pain, plaster cast, scratch, sling, sprain, wound, wrist*

- Students use vocabulary to talk about different kinds of accidents and injuries.

Healthcare professionals: *dentist, doctor, nurse, paramedic, pharmacist, physiotherapist, specialist, therapist*

- Students learn the names of common jobs in healthcare.

Idioms and expressions

Feeling unwell: *be sick as a dog, feel under the weather, have a frog in your throat*

- Students look at idioms and expressions related to illness in the context of a story.

Recycled language

Present simple

Skills objectives

Speaking

- Students guess new vocabulary about body parts and injuries.
- Students perform a conversation between a patient and a doctor.
- Students discuss different professions in healthcare.
- Students discuss their own experiences of being ill.

Pronunciation: Students practise the /m/ and /n/ sounds in a range of words.

Pairwork: Students use various mediation techniques to arrange a trip to see a friend who is injured.

Listening

- Students listen to match words about illness.
- Students listen to modal verbs of permission in the context of a conversation.
- Students listen to complete a monologue about injuries.
- Students listen to complete a text about rules.
- Students listen to put photographs in the correct order.

Reading

- Students read and complete sentences giving advice in response to descriptions of symptoms.
- Students read about jobs in healthcare and complete the text with headings.
- Students read and answer questions about healthcare professions.
- Students read an article to find definitions of new vocabulary.
- Students read about healthy eating and identify eight foods everyone should include in their diet.

Core values: Students think about advice around **health** and discuss their own opinions on how to stay well.

Writing

- Students write a conversation between a doctor and a patient.
- Students plan, write and check a list of tips about exercise.

Focus on Language of obligation and advice: *have to, should, make sure, could, try* + gerund

Remind students to do all the exercises in their notebook

Learning to learn tools

SPEAKING TOOLS Students practise describing and defining new words.	**LISTENING TOOLS** Students practise listening to tone and intonation to help with understanding of new expressions.
READING TOOLS Students practise both skimming a text and reading for detail.	**WRITING TOOLS** Students practise backing up arguments in order to make their points stronger.

Project objectives: Invention

Task 4 Students write safety advice for their invention and instructions on what it can and can't do.

Task 5 Students write rules for using their invention.

Task 6 Students look back at tasks 4 and 5, correct any errors and make improvements.

Audiovisual objectives

Vlog: Students watch and listen to Emma talk about doctors and dentists.

Culture: Students watch and listen to Emma talk about Australia's flying doctors.

Grammar animations: Students are presented with visual presentations of the unit grammar.

Key competences

LC **Linguistic**
pages 54-61

MST **Mathematical and Science and Technology**
pages 57, 60

DC **Digital**
pages 54-55, 57, 61

SCC **Social and Civic**
pages 57-60

CAE **Cultural awareness and expression**
pages 59, 61

LL **Learning to learn**
pages 56-58, 60-61

IE **Sense of initiative and entrepreneurship**
pages 55, 57, 60

→ See pages 42-43 **Key competences**

CEFR Mediation

6.1 Relay specific information in writing
Can write specific information from spoken texts on familiar subjects.

6.2 Note-taking
Can make simple notes on a simple spoken text.

6.3 Adapting language
Can repeat the main point of a simple message using different words.

6.4 Processing text in writing
Can pick out and reproduce key words and phrases from a short text.

6.5 Collaborating to construct meaning
Can ask someone for reasons for their views and check mutual understanding.

Project Encouraging conceptual talk
Can ask questions to clarify understanding, including about how someone thinks something would work.

Unit review Facilitating collaborative interaction with peers
Can ask what others think, make suggestions and understand responses.

Pairwork Relaying specific information in speech
Can relay specific information in short, simple texts on familiar subjects.

→ See pages 30-33 **Mediation**

Remind students to do all the exercises in their notebook

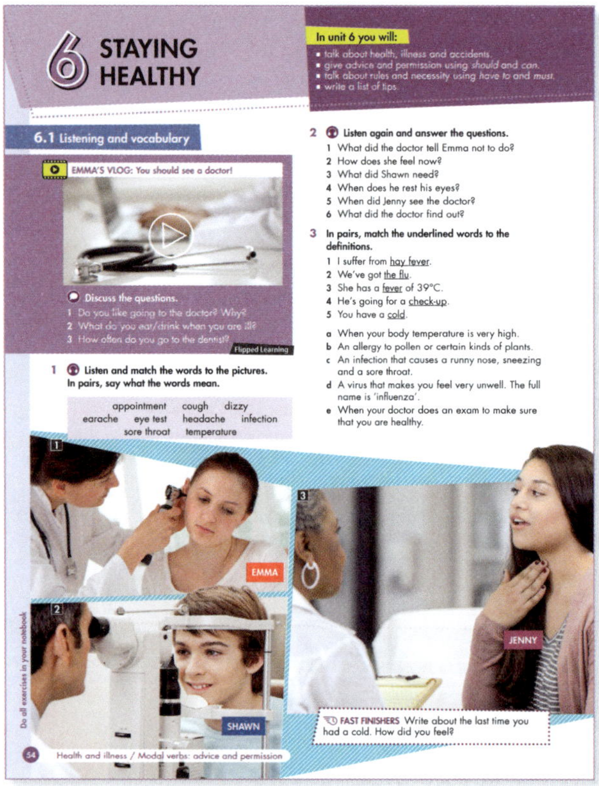

6 STAYING HEALTHY

In unit 6 you will:
- talk about health, illness and accidents.
- give advice and permission using *should* and *can*.
- talk about rules and necessity using *have to* and *must*.
- write a list of tips.

6.1 Listening and vocabulary

EMMA'S VLOG: You should see a doctor!

Discuss the questions.
1 Do you like going to the doctor? Why?
2 What do you eat/drink when you are ill?
3 How often do you go to the dentist?

Flipped Learning

1 Listen and match the words to the pictures. In pairs, say what the words mean.

appointment cough dizzy earache eye test headache infection sore throat temperature

1 EMMA
2 SHAWN
3 JENNY

2 Listen again and answer the questions.
1 What did the doctor tell Emma not to do?
2 How does she feel now?
3 What did Shawn need?
4 When does he rest his eyes?
5 When did Jenny see the doctor?
6 What did the doctor find out?

3 In pairs, match the underlined words to the definitions.
1 I suffer from hay fever.
2 We've got the flu.
3 She has a fever of 39°C.
4 He's going for a check-up.
5 You have a cold.

a When your body temperature is very high.
b An allergy to pollen or certain kinds of plants.
c An infection that causes a runny nose, sneezing and a sore throat.
d A virus that makes you feel very unwell. The full name is 'influenza'.
e When your doctor does an exam to make sure that you are healthy.

FAST FINISHERS Write about the last time you had a cold. How did you feel?

Do all exercises in your notebook

54 Health and illness / Modal verbs: advice and permission

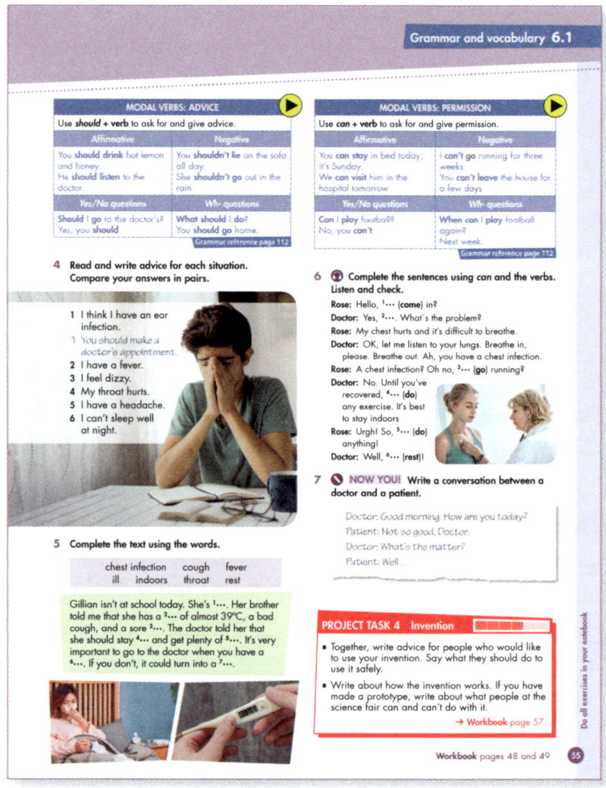

Grammar and vocabulary 6.1

MODAL VERBS: ADVICE	
Use *should* + verb to ask for and give advice.	
Affirmative	Negative
You should drink hot lemon and honey. He should listen to the doctor.	You shouldn't lie on the sofa all day. She shouldn't go out in the rain.
Yes/No questions	Wh- questions
Should I go to the doctor's? Yes, you should.	What should I do? You should go home.

Grammar reference page 112

MODAL VERBS: PERMISSION	
Use *can* + verb to ask for and give permission.	
Affirmative	Negative
You can stay in bed today; it's Sunday. We can visit him in the hospital tomorrow.	I can't go running for three weeks. You can't leave the house for a few days.
Yes/No questions	Wh- questions
Can I play football? No, you can't.	When can I play football again? Next week.

Grammar reference page 112

4 Read and write advice for each situation. Compare your answers in pairs.
1 I think I have an ear infection.
1 You should make a doctor's appointment.
2 I have a fever.
3 I feel dizzy.
4 My throat hurts.
5 I have a headache.
6 I can't sleep well at night.

5 Complete the text using the words.

chest infection cough fever ill indoors throat rest

Gillian isn't at school today. She's [1]···. Her brother told me that she has a [2]··· of almost 39°C, a bad cough, and a sore [3]···. The doctor told her that she should stay [4]··· and get plenty of [5]···. It's very important to go to the doctor when you have a [6]···. If you don't, it could turn into a [7]···.

6 Complete the sentences using *can* and the verbs. Listen and check.

Rose: Hello, [1]··· **(come)** in?
Doctor: Yes, [2]···. What's the problem?
Rose: My chest hurts and it's difficult to breathe.
Doctor: OK, let me listen to your lungs. Breathe in, please. Breathe out. Ah, you have a chest infection.
Rose: A chest infection? Oh no, [3]··· **(go)** running?
Doctor: No. Until you've recovered, [4]··· **(do)** any exercise. It's best to stay indoors
Rose: Urgh! So, [5]··· **(do)** anything!
Doctor: Well, [6]··· **(rest)**!

7 NOW YOU! Write a conversation between a doctor and a patient.

Doctor: Good morning. How are you today?
Patient: Not so good, Doctor.
Doctor: What's the matter?
Patient: Well...

PROJECT TASK 4 Invention
- Together, write advice for people who would like to use your invention. Say what they should do to use it safely.
- Write about how the invention works. If you have made a prototype, write about what people at the science fair can and can't do with it.

→ Workbook page 57

Do all exercises in your notebook

Workbook pages 48 and 49 55

ANSWER KEY

Pages 54-55

1
1 dizzy, earache, infection
2 appointment, eye test, headache
3 cough, sore throat, temperature

2
1 go swimming
2 a lot better, almost recovered
3 glasses
4 after using the computer
5 yesterday
6 that she had a temperature

3 **1** b **2** d **3** a **4** e **5** c

4 *Suggested answers:*
1 You should make a doctor's appointment.
2 You should take your temperature.
3 You should sit down.
4 You should drink hot lemon and honey.
5 You should take a nap.
6 You should try and do exercise every day.

5
1 ill
2 fever
3 throat
4 indoors
5 rest
6 cough
7 chest infection

6
1 can I come
2 you can
3 can I go
4 you can't do
5 I can't do
6 you can rest

7 *Student's own answers*

Remind students to do all the exercises in their notebook

LESSON FOCUS

Grammar Modal verbs: advice and permission
Vocabulary Health and illness
Listening Being ill; A conversation with a doctor
Project task 4 Write safety advice for the invention and instructions on what it can and can't do.

Resources

Teacher's i-solutions, Student's Book audio, Vlog and worksheet

Flipped Learning

EMMA'S VLOG: You should see a doctor!

- Make sure to set up the **Flipped Learning** work with the students beforehand. **See pages 20-23 for complete Flipped Learning guidelines.**
- Ask students to put the **Flipped Learning worksheets** on their desks and walk around to check how many have completed the Flipped task.
- In pairs or small groups, ask students to compare and check the *Before you watch...* and *While you watch...* exercises on the worksheet.
- Show students **Emma's Vlog** and ask volunteers to provide correct answers and clarify any doubts other students may have.
- Choose three or four students to read aloud their answers to the *After you watch...* exercises on the worksheet and encourage some class discussion.
- Move straight to exercise 1 on page 54.

Warmer

Watch Emma´s Vlog and discuss the questions with the whole class. If you don't have video facilities, simply discuss the questions.

1 2.1 (See page 174 for transcripts) Tell students to cover up the wordpool and ask them to describe what is happening in each photograph. Remind students to take notes as they listen. After completing the exercise, see if the students' guesses were correct.

2 2.2 (See page 174 for transcripts) Encourage students to answer the questions with full sentences using the present simple.

3 After completing the exercises, students should discuss in pairs if they have ever experienced any of the illnesses described.

FAST FINISHERS Students can complete this exercise alone or in pairs.

Flipped Learning

MODAL VERBS: ADVICE AND PERMISSION

Draw students' attention to both **Grammar tables**. Remind students that they can use them as quick references while completing the exercises.

Show students the **Grammar animations** and/or refer students to the **Grammar reference** on page 112 for further information on form and use.

→ See page 23 for how to flip the **grammar lesson**

4 Remind students that they can use their notes from exercises 1 and 2 to help with this task.

5 Complete the exercise as a class. Check students' understanding of the new vocabulary as you go through the exercise and provide explanations and definitions where necessary.

6 2.3 (See page 174 for transcripts) Before completing the exercise, draw students' attention to the **Grammar tables** and modal verbs for permission, in particular. Give them a few minutes to go over them and check they understand.

7 NOW YOU! Once students have finished writing the conversation, they should perform them in pairs.

PROJECT TASK 4 Invention

Organise students into teams of three. Students will write safety advice for the people who will use their invention. They should also prepare information about the functionality of the invention for the audience at the science fair.
Remind students that they need to keep their project notes together in their **Workbook** (page 57) or in their own notebook.

→ See pages 24-25 **Projects**

FURTHER PRACTICE

Workbook pages 48-49
- **Grammar reference and practice** pages 89-90 and 96
- **Wordlist and exercises** pages 100 and 103-104

Remind students to do all the exercises in their notebook

CONTINUOUS ASSESSMENT Students can talk about health and illness, and use modal verbs for advice and permission.

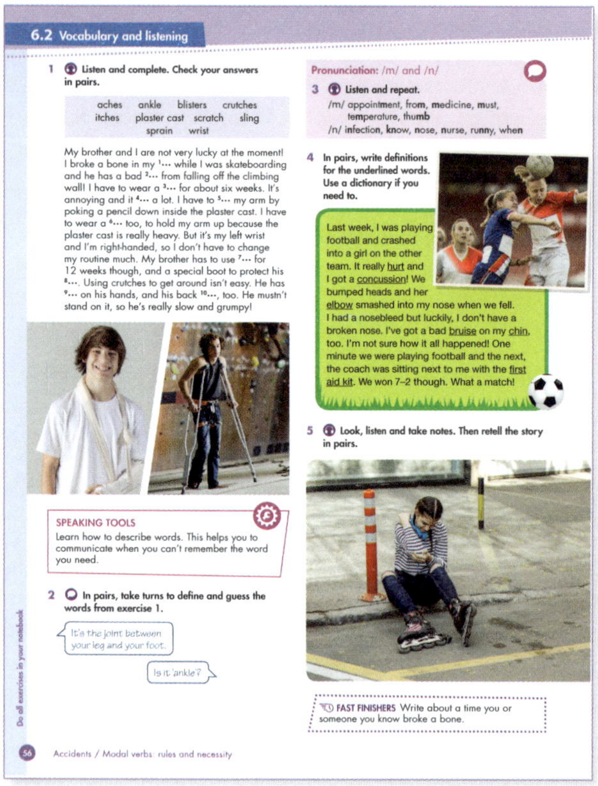

1 **Listen and complete. Check your answers in pairs.**

aches ankle blisters crutches itches plaster cast scratch sling sprain wrist

My brother and I are not very lucky at the moment! I broke a bone in my [1]··· while I was skateboarding and he has a bad [2]··· from falling off the climbing wall! I have to wear a [3]··· for about six weeks. It's annoying and it [4]··· a lot. I have to [5]··· my arm by poking a pencil down inside the plaster cast. I have to wear a [6]··· too, to hold my arm up because the plaster cast is really heavy. But it's my left wrist and I'm right-handed, so I don't have to change my routine much. My brother has to use [7]··· for 12 weeks though, and a special boot to protect his [8]···. Using crutches to get around isn't easy. He has [9]··· on his hands, and his back [10]···, too. He mustn't stand on it, so he's really slow and grumpy!

SPEAKING TOOLS
Learn how to describe words. This helps you to communicate when you can't remember the word you need.

2 **In pairs, take turns to define and guess the words from exercise 1.**

It's the joint between your leg and your foot.

Is it 'ankle'?

Pronunciation: /m/ and /n/

3 **Listen and repeat.**
/m/ appointment, from, medicine, must, temperature, thumb
/n/ infection, know, nose, nurse, runny, when

4 **In pairs, write definitions for the underlined words. Use a dictionary if you need to.**

Last week, I was playing football and crashed into a girl on the other team. It really hurt and I got a concussion! We bumped heads and her elbow smashed into my nose when we fell. I had a nosebleed but luckily, I don't have a broken nose. I've got a bad bruise on my chin, too. I'm not sure how it all happened! One minute we were playing football and the next, the coach was sitting next to me with the first aid kit. We won 7–2 though. What a match!

5 **Look, listen and take notes. Then retell the story in pairs.**

FAST FINISHERS Write about a time you or someone you know broke a bone.

Do all exercises in your notebook

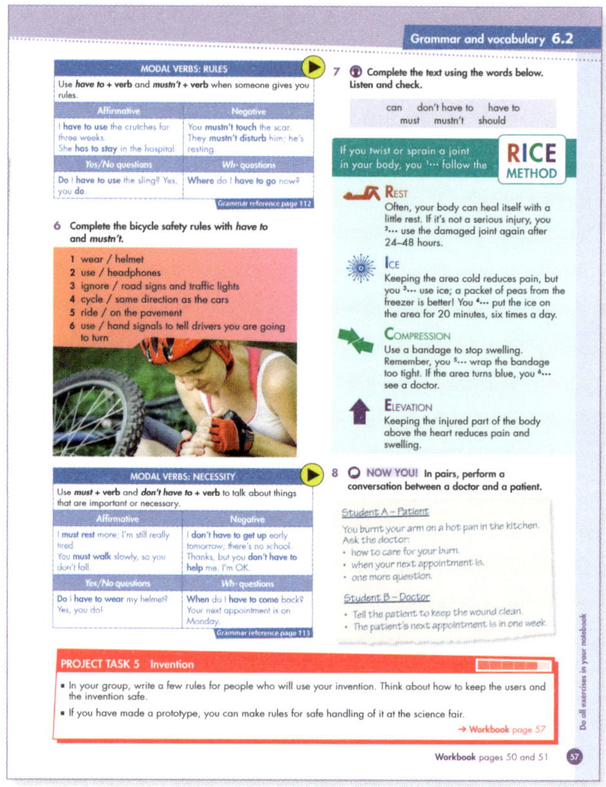

MODAL VERBS: RULES	
Use *have to* + verb and *mustn't* + verb when someone gives you rules.	
Affirmative	**Negative**
I **have to use** the crutches for three weeks. She **has to stay** in the hospital.	You **mustn't touch** the scar. They **mustn't disturb** him; he's resting.
Yes/No questions	**Wh- questions**
Do I **have to use** the sling? Yes, you **do**.	**Where** do I **have to go** now?

Grammar reference page 112

6 **Complete the bicycle safety rules with *have to* and *mustn't*.**

1 wear / helmet
2 use / headphones
3 ignore / road signs and traffic lights
4 cycle / same direction as the cars
5 ride / on the pavement
6 use / hand signals to tell drivers you are going to turn

MODAL VERBS: NECESSITY	
Use *must* + verb and *don't have to* + verb to talk about things that are important or necessary.	
Affirmative	**Negative**
I **must rest** more; I'm still really tired. You **must walk** slowly, so you don't fall.	I **don't have to get up** early tomorrow; there's no school. Thanks, but you **don't have to help** me. I'm OK.
Yes/No questions	**Wh- questions**
Do I **have to wear** my helmet? Yes, you do!	**When** do I **have to come** back? Your next appointment is on Monday.

Grammar reference page 113

7 **Complete the text using the words below. Listen and check.**

can don't have to have to must mustn't should

If you twist or sprain a joint in your body, you [1]··· follow the RICE METHOD

REST
Often, your body can heal itself with a little rest. If it's not a serious injury, you [2]··· use the damaged joint again after 24–48 hours.

ICE
Keeping the area cold reduces pain, but you [3]··· use ice; a packet of peas from the freezer is better! You [4]··· put the ice on the area for 20 minutes, six times a day.

COMPRESSION
Use a bandage to stop swelling. Remember, you [5]··· wrap the bandage too tight. If the area turns blue, you [6]··· see a doctor.

ELEVATION
Keeping the injured part of the body above the heart reduces pain and swelling.

8 **NOW YOU! In pairs, perform a conversation between a doctor and a patient.**

Student A – Patient
You burnt your arm on a hot pan in the kitchen. Ask the doctor:
- how to care for your burn.
- when your next appointment is.
- one more question.

Student B – Doctor
- Tell the patient to keep the wound clean.
- The patient's next appointment is in one week.

PROJECT TASK 5 Invention
- In your group, write a few rules for people who will use your invention. Think about how to keep the users and the invention safe.
- If you have made a prototype, you can make rules for safe handling of it at the science fair.

→ Workbook page 57

Do all exercises in your notebook

ANSWER KEY

Pages 56-57

1
1 wrist
2 sprain
3 plaster cast
4 itches
5 scratch
6 sling
7 crutches
8 ankle
9 blisters
10 aches

2 *Student's own answers*

3 *Student's own answers*

4 *Student's own answers*

5 *Student's own answers*

6
1 You have to wear a helmet.
2 You musn't use headphones.
3 You musn't ignore road signs and traffic lights.
4 You have to cycle in the same direction as the cars.
5 You musn't cycle on the pavement.
6 You have to use hand signals to tell drivers you are going to turn.

7
1 should
2 can
3 don't have to
4 must
5 mustn't
6 have to

8 *Student's own answers*

Remind students to do all the exercises in their notebook

LESSON FOCUS

Grammar Modal verbs: rules and necessity
Vocabulary Accidents
Listening Short monologues about suffering an injury; Advice on how to treat an injury
Speaking Defining and guessing new words; perform a conversation
Project task 5 Write rules for using the invention

Resources
Teacher's i-solutions, Student's Book audio

Warmer

Ask students what the difference is between an illness and an injury. Get them to give examples of each. Tell them that, in the UK, the emergency department of a hospital is called A&E (Accident and Emergency). People often go there instead of going to see their GP (General Practitioner). Ask students when they think that someone should go to A&E and when they should see their GP instead.

1 2.4 (See page 174 for transcripts) Give students time to do the exercise and use the images to clarify the meaning of the vocabulary in the descriptions. Extend the exercise by getting them to describe to each other a time when they were injured.

SPEAKING TOOLS

Give students some examples of how the **Speaking tool** can be employed. Tell students you are going to choose a prominent word from exercise 7 on page 57; *ice*, for example. Then tell them that this is achieved when water freezes, and see if they can guess the word.

2 Write the words from the wordpool in exercise 1 on the board. Building on what has just been learnt in the **Speaking tool**, students should complete this task in pairs.

Pronunciation

3 2.5 (See page 175 for transcripts) Tell students that these two sounds can be easy to confuse. Check that they can make the sounds in isolation. Say words from the rest of the page and see if they can hear where the /n/ and /m/ sounds are.

4 After students have completed the task in pairs, ask the class what definitions they came up with and correct any errors.

5 2.6 (See page 175 for transcripts) Before listening to the audio, students can tell a partner what they think has happened to the girl in the picture. After listening, see who in the class was closest.

FAST FINISHERS Students can complete this exercise alone or in pairs.

MODAL VERBS: RULES

Flipped Learning

Draw students' attention to the **Grammar table**. Remind students that they can use this as a quick reference while completing the exercises.

Show students the **Grammar animation** and/or refer students to the **Grammar reference** on page 112 for further information on form and use.

→ See page 23 for how to flip the **grammar lesson**

6 Make sure that students have read and understood the two **Grammar tables** before completing the exercise. They can use the **Grammar reference** on pages 112 and 113 of the **Student's Book** for further guidance.

MODAL VERBS: NECESSITY

Flipped Learning

Draw students' attention to the **Grammar table**. Remind students that they can use this as a quick reference while completing the exercises.

Show students the **Grammar animation** and/or refer students to the **Grammar reference** on page 113 for further information on form and use.

→ See page 23 for how to flip the **grammar lesson**

7 2.7 (See page 175 for transcripts) Before or after the exercise, ask students if they know what an acronym is and if they know any other examples. Explain that these are often used in medical or military situations to remember important information quickly. They can also be used to aid learning in general.

8 NOW YOU! Students should try and perform this task as spontaneously as possible using their new knowledge from the class. They shouldn't take notes beforehand or revise the notes they have already taken.

PROJECT TASK 5 Invention

Students will need to think about the functionality of their invention and whether there are any potential risks they should make their users aware of. If the students have made a prototype they could also create a set of rules for using the invention safely. Remind students that they need to keep their project notes together in their **Workbook** (page 57) or in their own notebook.

→ See pages 24-27 **Projects**

FURTHER PRACTICE

Workbook pages 50-51
- **Grammar reference and practice** pages 89-90 and 96
- **Wordlist and exercises** pages 100 and 103-104

Vocabulary and Grammar worksheets available to download from the **Richmond***Learning***Platform**

→ See pages 38-39 **Mixed-ability classes**

Remind students to do all the exercises in their notebook

CONTINUOUS ASSESSMENT Students can talk about accidents, and use modal verbs for rules and necessity.

1 Match the healthcare professions to the photos. Say what the people are doing and what you think their job involves.

dentist doctor nurse paramedic pharmacist therapist

1 2 3 4 5 6

READING TOOLS
Reading quickly for general meaning is a different skill to reading for detail. Practise all your reading skills to make sure you are ready for exams.

2 Read the article and complete it using the professions from exercise 1 as headings.

Jobs in healthcare

When we think of healthcare, we think of doctors. But there are many different types of healthcare professionals. Let's take a look at some of them and what they do.

[1]... You and your family should have a doctor you go to regularly. They're called a general practitioner, or GP, and they know you and your medical history best. They can diagnose and treat you themselves, or refer to you a specialist.

[2]... These people work very closely with patients, especially in hospitals. They test and monitor them, and they follow doctors' instructions to help patients recover effectively.

[3]... When your doctor prescribes you medication, these are the people you have to take the prescription to. They can answer questions about prescribed medications, and give you advice on medicine that you don't need a prescription for.

[4]... These healthcare specialists don't have to have the same full medical training as doctors, and there are lots of different types. One of the best known are physiotherapists. They can help you recover from injuries or manage back pain, for example. You don't have to have a referral from your GP to see a physiotherapist.

Do all exercises in your notebook

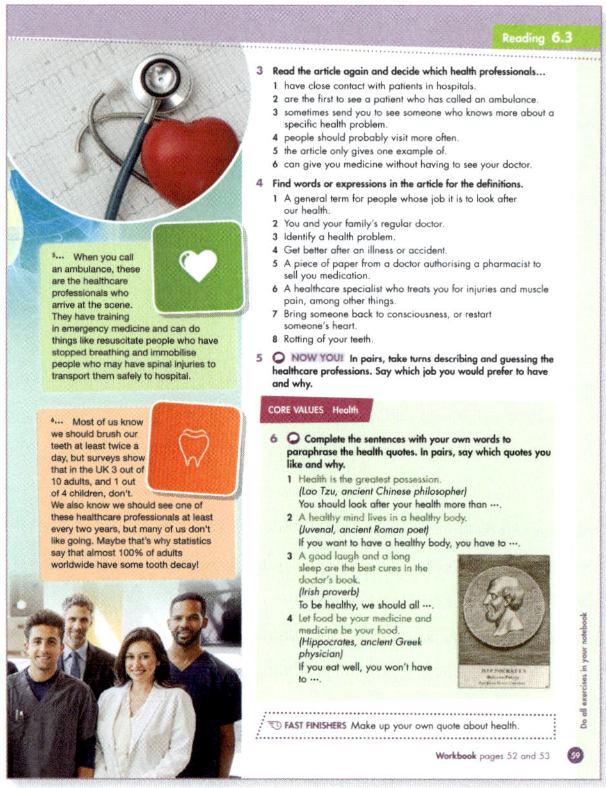

[5]... When you call an ambulance, these are the healthcare professionals who arrive at the scene. They have training in emergency medicine and can do things like resuscitate people who have stopped breathing and immobilise people who may have spinal injuries to transport them safely to hospital.

[6]... Most of us know we should brush our teeth at least twice a day, but surveys show that in the UK 3 out of 10 adults, and 1 out of 4 children, don't. We also know we should see one of these healthcare professionals at least every two years, but many of us don't like going. Maybe that's why statistics say that almost 100% of adults worldwide have some tooth decay!

3 Read the article again and decide which health professionals…
1 have close contact with patients in hospitals.
2 are the first to see a patient who has called an ambulance.
3 sometimes send you to see someone who knows more about a specific health problem.
4 people should probably visit more often.
5 the article only gives one example of.
6 can give you medicine without having to see your doctor.

4 Find words or expressions in the article for the definitions.
1 A general term for people whose job it is to look after our health.
2 You and your family's regular doctor.
3 Identify a health problem.
4 Get better after an illness or accident.
5 A piece of paper from a doctor authorising a pharmacist to sell you medication.
6 A healthcare specialist who treats you for injuries and muscle pain, among other things.
7 Bring someone back to consciousness, or restart someone's heart.
8 Rotting of your teeth.

5 NOW YOU! In pairs, take turns describing and guessing the healthcare professions. Say which job you would prefer to have and why.

CORE VALUES Health

6 Complete the sentences with your own words to paraphrase the health quotes. In pairs, say which quotes you like and why.
1 Health is the greatest possession.
(Lao Tzu, ancient Chinese philosopher)
You should look after your health more than ….
2 A healthy mind lives in a healthy body.
(Juvenal, ancient Roman poet)
If you want to have a healthy body, you have to ….
3 A good laugh and a long sleep are the best cures in the doctor's book.
(Irish proverb)
To be healthy, we should all ….
4 Let food be your medicine and medicine be your food.
(Hippocrates, ancient Greek physician)
If you eat well, you won't have to ….

FAST FINISHERS Make up your own quote about health.

Do all exercises in your notebook

ANSWER KEY

Pages 58-59

1
1 Doctor
2 Paramedic
3 Therapist
4 Nurse
5 Dentist
6 Pharmacist

2
1 Doctors
2 Nurses
3 Pharmacists
4 Therapists
5 Paramedics
6 Dentists

3
1 Nurses
2 Paramedics
3 Doctors
4 Dentists
5 Therapists
6 Pharmacists

4
1 healthcare professionals
2 general practitioner, or GP
3 diagnose
4 recover
5 prescription
6 physiotherapists
7 resuscitate
8 tooth decay

5 *Student's own answers*

6 *Suggested answers:*
1 your possessions
2 have a healthy mind
3 enjoy ourselves and get lots of rest
5 cure an illness after it after happens

Remind students to do all the exercises in their notebook

LESSON FOCUS

Language in context Healthcare professionals

Core values Health

Resources

Teacher's i-solutions, Student's Book audio

→ See pages 36-37 **Literature**

Warmer

Ask students to brainstorm the personality traits necessary for jobs in healthcare. Ask them to think about the different professions in the wordpool in exercise 1. Use revision of the **Core values** sections in previous units to do so (*Being prepared, Community, Altruism*)

1 Complete the exercise as a class and write the new vocabulary on the board. Ask students if they know anyone that works in any of these professions.

READING TOOLS

Draw students' attention to the **Reading tool** and ensure that they understand the importance of practising both reading skills for exams, as well as for better reading comprehension.

2 2.8 (See page 175 for transcripts) Tell students to read the article twice, once skimming for general meaning and to add the headings and a second time to find more details in order to move on to exercises 3 and 4.

3 Students can complete this exercise alone or in small groups.

4 Complete the exercise as a class and check students' understanding of the new vocabulary.

5 NOW YOU! In pairs, students can act out the roles of the different healthcare professionals, describing what their job involves, for each other to guess. Students should then pick one of the professions that they would most like to do and explain to their partner why they chose this profession.

CORE VALUES Health

6 Round up with a class discussion. Did students know any of these quotes already? Which one do they think offers the best advice? As a class, decide which quote is the most useful.

FAST FINISHERS Students can complete this exercise alone or in pairs.

FURTHER PRACTICE

Workbook pages 52-53

Remind students to do all the exercises in their notebook

CONTINUOUS ASSESSMENT Students can understand a text about healthcare professionals.

A list of health tips

Focus on language of obligation and advice

1 **Read the pieces of advice and, in pairs, decide which health problem they refer to.**
1 We'll put a plaster cast on it, and you'll have to use crutches for a couple of months.
2 Stay in bed and rest. If you can, you should buy a thermometer to monitor your temperature.
3 Make sure you drink plenty of water and eat only soup for a few days.
4 You could put an icepack on your head or give yourself a massage.
5 Try putting Vaseline on the bottom of your nose to trap the pollen. It might work!

2 **Rank the underlined expressions in exercise 1 from strongest obligation to gentlest suggestion.**

3 **Read the list of tips for healthy eating and find eight foods you should include in a healthy diet.**

Tips for healthy eating

There is a lot of different advice out there on healthy eating. Here are some tips everyone agrees on.

1 You should avoid fizzy drinks and processed foods. They contain a lot of sugar, and processed foods contain chemicals and unhealthy fats.
2 Eat lots of fruit and vegetables. Experts recommend five portions a day.
3 Try to eat foods with lots of fibre, like wholegrain bread, pasta and rice. They fill you up for longer and help digestion.
4 Protein is important, and it's a good idea to get it from fish. Fish has less bad fat, and oily fish like salmon and sardines have good fat.
5 Make sure you drink enough water. Your body needs it, and studies suggest that drinking more can help you burn calories.

Did you notice?

4 **Find the following structures for giving advice:**
1 Two structures in exercise 1.
2 Two uses of the imperative in exercise 2.
3 Two phrases for introducing evidence-based advice in exercise 2.
4 A phrase ending in an infinitive.

NOW YOU! → Workbook page 54

5 PLAN **You are going to write a list of tips about exercise. First, plan 4 or 5 tips and an introductory sentence.**

WRITING TOOLS
When you give advice, always give reasons. This helps to make your argument stronger.

6 WRITE **Write your list of tips. Use some of the structures for advice and obligation that you have learnt.**

7 CHECK **Check that your advice is clear and convincing and that you have used the language of advice and obligation correctly.**

PROJECT TASK 6 Invention
- In your group, read the information you have written in **tasks 4** and **5**. Correct any errors and improve it where you can.
- Next, do the final task on page 62.

→ **Workbook** page 57

Do all exercises in your notebook

LESSON FOCUS

Focus on Language of obligation and advice

Writing A list of tips about exercise

Project task 6 Look back at tasks 4 and 5, correct any errors and make improvements

Resources

Teacher's i-solutions

Preparation Prepare some parental advice and rules

Warmer

Give students examples of the kind of advice and rules your parents used to give you when you were their age. Ask students to write down three things their parents always say to them regarding advice and obligation. Share with the class and see which are most common.

Focus on language of obligation and advice

1 Write on the board a recap of vocabulary related to illness and injury from the unit to assist students with this task.

2 Remind students of the modal verbs for advice, rules, permission and necessity. They can revise the **Grammar tables** in the unit for guidance in completing this exercise.

3 Round up with a class discussion. What do students think of these tips? Are they well written and convincing? Will students adopt any of them in their lives in the future? How many do they already follow?

Did you notice?

4 Students should pay special attention to this exercise and use their answers to assist them with the writing task.

5 PLAN Once students have finished their plan, encourage them to talk it through with a partner.

WRITING TOOLS

Draw students' attention to the **Writing tool**. Remind them that giving reasons to back up your arguments always makes them more convincing, especially if you are writing to give advice.

6 WRITE Before students start writing, make a checklist on the board of any elements related to content, structure, language and style that they should bear in mind.

7 CHECK Once students have checked their own work, they can swap with classmates. Ask if students would like to share any of their tips with the class.

ANSWER KEY

Page 60

1 *Suggested answers:*
1 a broken leg
2 a fever
3 gastroenteritis
4 headache
5 hayfever

2 have to, make sure, should, try, could

3 fruit, vegetables, wholegrain bread, pasta, rice, salmon, sardines and other fish

4 **1** should, make sure
2 eat, try
3 experts recommend, studies suggest that
4 it's a good idea

5 *Student's own answers*

6 *Student's own answers*

7 *Student's own answers*

PROJECT TASK 6 Invention

Students should revise the work they have done for **Project tasks 4** and **5**, correct any errors and make any last-minute improvements. Tell students that they need to keep their project notes together in their **Workbook** (page 57) or in their own notebook.

→ See pages 24-27 **Projects**

FURTHER PRACTICE

Workbook page 55

Remind students to do all the exercises in their notebook

 CONTINUOUS ASSESSMENT Students can use language of obligation and advice to write a list of health tips.

Culture and communication 6.5

Discuss the questions.

1 Is the healthcare in your country good?
2 What are the hospitals like? Are they big? Are they busy?
3 Do most people in your country have a healthy lifestyle?
4 Which country do you think has the healthiest people? Why?

LISTENING TOOLS
Pay attention to the speaker's intonation and tone to help you understand the meaning of new expressions.

1 Listen and put the pictures in order.

a b c

2 Listen again and say if the sentences below are true or false.

1 Daniel woke up at a quarter to seven.
2 In the morning he felt very ill.
3 Around lunchtime, his throat started to hurt.
4 He drank tea with lemon and honey.
5 He felt better in the afternoon.
6 He went to bed very early that night.

Idioms and expressions

3 Match the expressions you heard with the meanings.

1 be sick as a dog
2 feel under the weather
3 have a frog in your throat

a When you don't feel good.
b When you can't talk or have a bad cough.
c When you feel very ill.

4 Complete the sentences with the expressions from exercise 2.

1 When Daniel woke up in the morning, he ···.
2 Around lunchtime, he ···.
3 In the evening, he ···.

5 In pairs, write six pieces of advice for Daniel.

1 You should stay in bed.

6 NOW YOU! Discuss the questions in pairs.

- What do you eat and drink when you have a frog in your throat?
- Have you ever been sick as a dog on holiday?
- Who takes care of you when you're feeling under the weather?

PAIRWORK
Student A: go to page 101
Student B: go to page 105

Unit 6 Review • page 95
Wordlist • pages 118–120

Do all exercises in your notebook

Idioms and expressions about feeling unwell

Workbook page 55 61

ANSWER KEY

Page 61

1 a, c, b

2
1 True
2 False
3 True
4 False
5 False
6 True

3 **1** c **2** a **3** b

4
1 was feeling under the weather
2 had a frog in his throat
3 was sick as a dog

5 *Student's own answers*

6 *Student's own answers*

FURTHER PRACTICE AND UNIT ASSESSMENT

Unit 6 Review **Student's Book** page 95
Workbook page 55
- Reflect on your learning page 55
- Grammar reference and practice pages 89-90 and 96
- Wordlist and exercises pages 100 and 103-104

Tests available to download and edit from the
RichmondLearning**Platform**

➔ See pages 40-41 **Assessment**

LESSON FOCUS

Idioms and expressions Feeling unwell
Listening Put a sequence of events in the correct order
Speaking Experiences of illnesses

Resources

Teacher's i-solutions, Student's Book audio, Culture video and worksheet

Australia's flying doctors

Video and worksheet available on the
RichmondLearning**Platform**

- In pairs, ask students to complete the *What I know...* exercises on the **Culture video worksheet**.
- Show students the **Culture video** and ask them to complete the *What I learned...* exercises on the worksheet.
- In pairs, students compare answers.
- In small groups, tell students to complete the *What I wonder...* exercises on the worksheet.

Warmer

Watch the **Culture video** and discuss the questions with the whole class. If you don't have video facilities, simply discuss the questions.

LISTENING TOOLS

Ask students to read the **Listening tool**. The way people speak and emphasise certain words will help to uncover meaning.

1 2.9 (See page 175 for transcripts) Before listening to the audio, ask students what kind of illness they think the boy in the photos has.

2 2.10 (See page 175 for transcripts) Students should take notes while listening and then do the exercise.

Idioms and expressions

3 Before completing the exercise, ask students what they think the expressions could mean and if the words used give any clue to the meaning.

4 Students should look back at their notes from exercise 2 in order to complete this task. Remind them of the importance of taking notes when listening to audios.

5 After writing the pieces of advice, students should compare with the pair next to them. Did they write the same pieces of advice or different ones?

6 NOW YOU! After discussing in pairs, open up the questions to class discussion.

PAIRWORK **Student's Book** pages 101 and 105
See **Teacher's Book** page 126 for more information.

➔ See pages 30-33 **Mediation**

Remind students to do all the exercises in their notebook

CONTINUOUS ASSESSMENT Students can use idioms and expressions about feeling unwell.

Unit 6 Review

Unit 6 Review

1 Listen and choose the correct option.

1 Harry is telling Amanda about a health problem. Who has he got an appointment with?
   a A GP.
   b A dentist.
   c A physiotherapist.

2 Jake has hurt his wrist. What does the paramedic say he has to wear now?
   a A plaster cast.
   b A bandage.
   c A sling.

3 Lucy tells her dad she's feeling unwell. What does her dad say Lucy should do?
   a Go to the doctor's.
   b Take her temperature.
   c Go to school.

4 Bella is talking to a friend about work. What job does she think she should do?
   a A paramedic.
   b A nurse.
   c A therapist.

2 Look at the pictures. In pairs, say which of these things you like and don't like and why. When do you do them? Which should you do to be healthy? Which shouldn't you do?

3 Read Frida's email to her friend Paul. Write one word in each space.

EXAM TIP
When you have decided your words, read the email again and make sure it makes sense.

To: Paul From: Frida

Hi Paul,

I hope you're well. I'm camping with my family in the countryside. I was climbing a tree and I fell and hurt my leg. There was a big purple [1]… and a lot of swelling. It was very painful. My mum took me to hospital and the specialist said it was broken! It will take two months to [2]… and I have [3]… wear a plaster cast and walk using [4]…. It doesn't hurt but it itches a lot. The specialist said I mustn't [5]… it because it could cause an infection.

See you next week. You [6]… sign my plaster cast!

Frida

4 Look at the pictures and write a story.

Do all exercises in your notebook

External exam practice 95

Student's Book page 95

ANSWER KEY

See page 180 for transcripts

1 2.41

1 a
2 c
3 a
4 b

2 *Student's own answers*

3
1 bruise
2 heal
3 to
4 crutches
5 scratch
6 can

4 *Student's own answers*

Pairwork

Unit 6 • Student A

1 Your friend Dave has got a broken leg. The doctor has told him to rest, but he is very bored at home. You and Student B want to cheer him up, so you are organising a visit to his house. Ask Student B questions to complete the missing parts of your table.

Can you come to Dave's house?

Yes, I can, but…

NAME	GOING?	MORE INFORMATION
Student A	✓	and I want to know if I should bring balloons.
Student B	…	…
Julie	✗	because she has to visit his grandma.
Frank	…	…
Amira	✓	and she wants to know if she can bring her sister.
Lynn	…	…
Duncan	✓	although he can only come later in the evening.
Jordan	…	…

2 Answer Student B's questions.

3 Compare your answers with Student B and say how many people are going to go to Dave's house.

Unit 5 answers
3 a: machine for cutting and sorting vegetables / b: machine for sewing patterns on clothes / c: machine for making biscuits

Do all exercises in your notebook

Student's Book page 101

Unit 6 • Student B

1 Your friend Dave has got a broken leg. The doctor has told him to rest, but he is very bored at home. You and Student A want to cheer him up, so you are organising a visit to his house. Student A will ask you questions to complete their table.

NAME	GOING?	MORE INFORMATION
Student A	…	…
Student B	✓	but I can only stay for one hour.
Julie	…	…
Frank	✗	because he must study for the exam next week.
Amira	…	…
Lynn	✓	and she says we should invite James and Sally from class too.
Duncan	…	…
Jordan	✗	because he has a cold and has to stay in bed.

2 Ask Student A questions to complete the missing parts of your table.

Can you come to Dave's house?

Yes, I can, and…

3 Compare your answers with Student A and say how many people are going to go to Dave's house.

Unit 5 answers
3 a: machine for cutting and sorting vegetables / b: machine for sewing patterns on clothes / c: machine for making biscuits

Do all exercises in your notebook

Student's Book page 105

CEFR MEDIATION DESCRIPTOR

- **Relaying specific information in writing**
  Students can list the main points of short, clear, simple messages and announcements.

- **Interpreting information**
  Students will be arranging to visit a friend who has broken his leg. They will exchange information in order to find a time and date that suits everyone, and decide who should bring which gift. At the end, they will summarise all the information they have shared and decide on the best course of action.

Remind students to do all the exercises in their notebook

Grammar reference

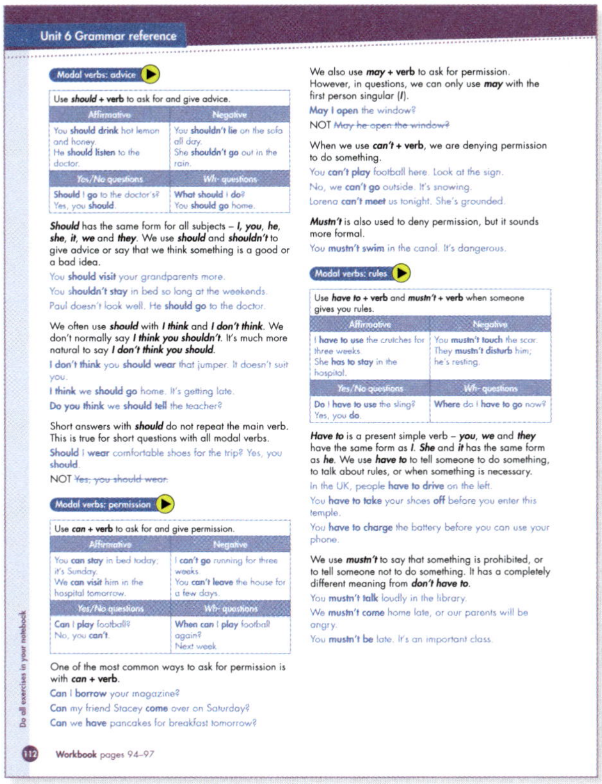

Unit 6 Grammar reference

Modal verbs: advice

Use *should* + verb to ask for and give advice.	
Affirmative	**Negative**
You **should drink** hot lemon and honey. He **should listen** to the doctor.	You **shouldn't lie** on the sofa all day. She **shouldn't go** out in the rain.
Yes/No questions	**Wh- questions**
Should I **go** to the doctor's? Yes, you **should**.	**What should** I **do**? You **should go** home.

Should has the same form for all subjects – ***I, you, he, she, it, we*** and ***they***. We use ***should*** and ***shouldn't*** to give advice or say that we think something is a good or a bad idea.

You **should visit** your grandparents more.

You **shouldn't stay** in bed so long at the weekends.

Paul doesn't look well. He **should go** to the doctor.

We often use ***should*** with ***I think*** and ***I don't think***. We don't normally say ***I think you shouldn't***. It's much more natural to say ***I don't think you should***.

I don't think you **should wear** that jumper. It doesn't suit you.

I think we **should go** home. It's getting late.

Do you think we **should tell** the teacher?

Short answers with ***should*** do not repeat the main verb. This is true for short questions with all modal verbs.

Should I **wear** comfortable shoes for the trip? Yes, you should.

NOT ~~Yes, you should wear.~~

Modal verbs: permission

Use *can* + verb to ask for and give permission.	
Affirmative	**Negative**
You **can stay** in bed today; it's Sunday. We **can visit** him in the hospital tomorrow.	I **can't go** running for three weeks. You **can't leave** the house for a few days.
Yes/No questions	**Wh- questions**
Can I **play** football? No, you **can't**.	**When can** I **play** football again? Next week.

One of the most common ways to ask for permission is with ***can*** + **verb**.

Can I **borrow** your magazine?

Can my friend Stacey **come** over on Saturday?

Can we **have** pancakes for breakfast tomorrow?

We also use ***may*** + **verb** to ask for permission. However, in questions, we can only use ***may*** with the first person singular (***I***).

May I open the window?

NOT ~~May he open the window?~~

When we use ***can't*** + **verb**, we are denying permission to do something.

You **can't play** football here. Look at the sign.

No, we **can't go** outside. It's snowing.

Lorena **can't meet** us tonight. She's grounded.

Mustn't is also used to deny permission, but it sounds more formal.

You **mustn't swim** in the canal. It's dangerous.

Modal verbs: rules

Use *have to* + verb and *mustn't* + verb when someone gives you rules.	
Affirmative	**Negative**
I **have to use** the crutches for three weeks. She **has to stay** in the hospital.	You **mustn't touch** the scar. They **mustn't disturb** him; he's resting.
Yes/No questions	**Wh- questions**
Do I **have to use** the sling? Yes, you **do**.	**Where** do I **have to go** now?

Have to is a present simple verb – ***you, we*** and ***they*** have the same form as ***I***. ***She*** and ***it*** has the same form as ***he***. We use ***have to*** to tell someone to do something, to talk about rules, or when something is necessary.

In the UK, people **have to drive** on the left.

You **have to take** your shoes **off** before you enter this temple.

You **have to charge** the battery before you can use your phone.

We use ***mustn't*** to say that something is prohibited, or to tell someone not to do something. It has a completely different meaning from ***don't have to***.

You **mustn't talk** loudly in the library.

We **mustn't come** home late, or our parents will be angry.

You **mustn't be** late. It's an important class.

Do all exercises in your notebook

112 **Workbook** pages 94–97

Student's Book page 112

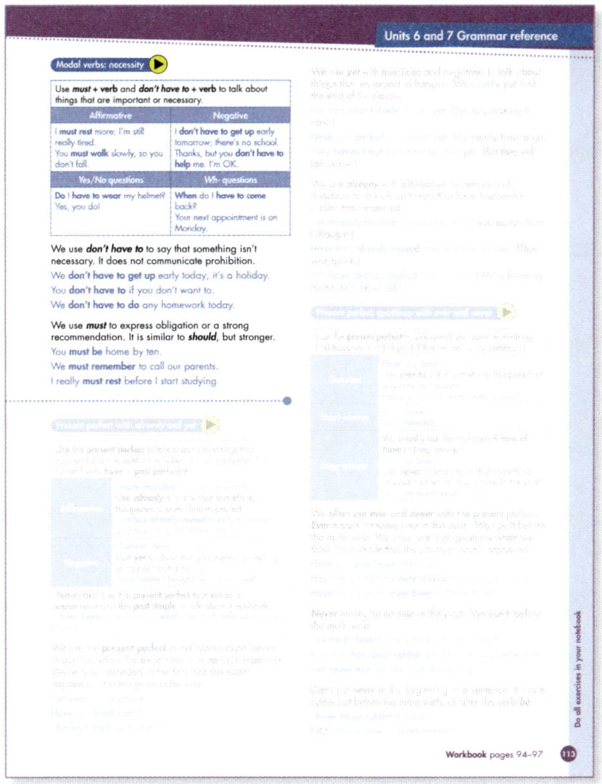

Units 6 and 7 Grammar reference

Modal verbs: necessity

Use *must* + verb and *don't have to* + verb to talk about things that are important or necessary.	
Affirmative	**Negative**
I **must rest** more; I'm still really tired. You **must walk** slowly, so you don't fall.	I **don't have to get up** early tomorrow; there's no school. Thanks, but you **don't have to help** me. I'm OK.
Yes/No questions	**Wh- questions**
Do I **have to wear** my helmet? Yes, you do!	**When** do I **have to come** back? Your next appointment is on Monday.

We use ***don't have to*** to say that something isn't necessary. It does not communicate prohibition.

We **don't have to get up** early today; it's a holiday.

You **don't have to** if you don't want to.

We **don't have to do** any homework today.

We use ***must*** to express obligation or a strong recommendation. It is similar to ***should***, but stronger.

You **must be** home by ten.

We **must remember** to call our parents.

I really **must rest** before I start studying.

Do all exercises in your notebook

Workbook pages 94–97 113

Student's Book page 113

Wordlist

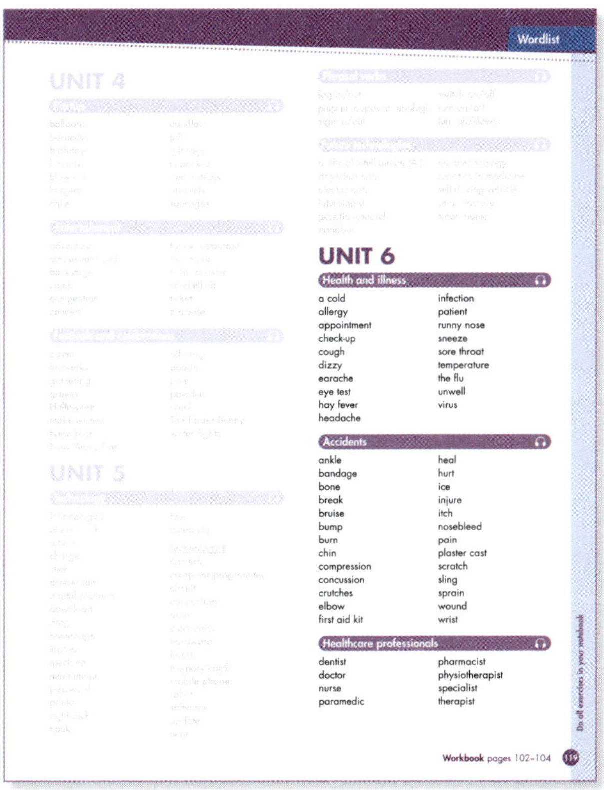

Wordlist

UNIT 4

UNIT 5

UNIT 6

Health and illness

a cold	infection
allergy	patient
appointment	runny nose
check-up	sneeze
cough	sore throat
dizzy	temperature
earache	the flu
eye test	unwell
hay fever	virus
headache	

Accidents

ankle	heal
bandage	hurt
bone	ice
break	injure
bruise	itch
bump	nosebleed
burn	pain
chin	plaster cast
compression	scratch
concussion	sling
crutches	sprain
elbow	wound
first aid kit	wrist

Healthcare professionals

dentist	pharmacist
doctor	physiotherapist
nurse	specialist
paramedic	therapist

Do all exercises in your notebook

Workbook pages 102–104 119

Student's Book page 119

2.61 2.62 2.63

Remind students to do all the exercises in their notebook

PROJECT: Invention

RECAP

- In this project, you have designed and developed an idea for an invention.
- In **unit 5**, you learnt vocabulary and phrasal verbs for discussing technology, used imperatives to give instructions and talked about the future with *will*. You also wrote a customer review.
- In **unit 6**, you learnt vocabulary for health and accidents. You practised using modal verbs to talk about advice, permission, rules and necessity and wrote a list of tips about exercise.
- Now, you are ready to present your invention in a class science fair!

TASK 1 Write a general description of your invention.
TASK 2 Make your poster or prototype and prepare your presentation.
TASK 3 Say how your design will affect the future.
TASK 4 Write about how people should use your invention.
TASK 5 Make rules to protect the invention and the users.
TASK 6 Write a list of tips about how to use the invention.

FINAL TASK: Have a science fair

As a class, decide:

- where you will have your science fair and who you will invite.
- how long everyone's presentation should be.
- if there will be any prizes given.

In your group:

- prepare the short speeches and statements you wrote in the tasks.
- review your prototype and/or poster and improve it if you can.
- decide who will give which part of the presentation.

USEFUL EXPRESSIONS

- Our invention will be made of…
- We believe that…
- The advantages/disadvantages are…
- We think that it will change the world because…
- These are important rules to take into account.
- Here are some useful 'how-to' tips.

21ST CENTURY SKILLS

Making connections

Humans can sort, group and categorise objects from a very early age. Understanding the relationships between objects and concepts is a very human quality.

Don't forget, a big part of modern development and innovation is about being able to make unusual connections.

Do all exercises in your notebook

EVALUATION

Complete the tasks in pairs.

1 Decide together which was the best invention. Say why.
2 Choose two of the inventions and think of a way to combine them.
3 Think of one of the inventions and develop the idea further.
4 List three ways you could improve your own invention.

GO BEYOND

YOUNG INVENTORS

Sometimes, an invention comes after decades of research. However, some inventions are created quickly and organically in response to real needs.

Louis Braille lost his eyesight when he was very young. At the time, there was no easy way for blind people to read and write. He invented the reading and writing code known as Braille in 1824 when he was only 15 years old.

George Nissen saw elastic nets at a circus when he was 16 years old and decided that they would be useful for his gymnastics training. He and his coach created the first trampoline together in 1934. Trampolining is now an Olympic sport.

In 2014, 11-year-old Kylie Simonds invented a chemotherapy backpack after she survived cancer. The backpack allows children to carry chemotheraphy equipment on their backs, and eliminates the need for annoying poles and wires.

As you can see, some great inventions have come from young people like you!

Answer the questions in pairs.

1 What's an invention you wish existed?
2 What inventions have really helped people or improved people's lives?
3 Which everyday object do you wish didn't exist?
4 Was the internet a positive or negative invention? Why?

Do all exercises in your notebook

Workbook project task notes

PROJECT: Invention

Team members

TASK 1

Our idea:
Basic characteristics:
Parts:
Materials:

→ Student's book page 47

TASK 2

Poster: ☐ Prototype: ☐
Presentation notes:

→ Student's book page 49

TASK 3

How our invention will affect the world:

→ Student's book page 52

TASK 4

Safety advice:
How to use it:

→ Student's book page 55

TASK 5

Rules:

→ Student's book page 57

TASK 6

Notes:

→ Student's book page 60

FINAL TASK

Where and who:
Length of presentations:
Prize(s):
My presentation task:

→ Student's book page 62

Remind students to do all the exercises in their notebook

PROJECT FOCUS

→ See pages 24-27 **Projects**

Skills

- Create an idea for an invention
- Discuss and collaborate on a poster or prototype
- Collaborate to write about the invention, including a description, its uses, predictions about its impact, advice on how to use it and safety guidelines
- Edit and correct texts
- Reach a class consensus on guidelines for a science fair
- Present the invention
- Discuss and evaluate the project
- Read and discuss a text related to the project

CEFR mediation

Encouraging conceptual talk

Can ask questions to clarify understanding, including about how someone thinks something would work.

→ See pages 30-33 **Mediation**

Preparation Remind students to bring their work from tasks 1-6 and their notes from the **Workbook** project task notes pages 56-57. Get them to bring in their self-assessment diaries if you decided you wanted them to keep one.

Recap

Put students in their teams and read through the **Recap** as a class. Draw their attention to the project tasks and the unit objectives and ask which tasks helped achieve which objectives. Make sure they have all the materials and notes that they need (see **Preparation**) for the **Final task**.

Final Task: Have a science fair

Tell students they are now going to have a class science fair at which they will present their inventions. Decide the guidelines for the fair as a class (make sure you have enough time to complete all parts of the project lesson) and then put them in their groups to prepare the presentation. Before they start, direct their attention the **21st century skill** (see next column). Give them as much preparation time as your time guidelines allow and monitor the groups to make sure everyone knows what they're doing and is participating actively. Encourage them to use the **Useful expressions** in their presentations and to rehearse if they have time.

Start and finish each presentation with applause and encourage questions if there is time.

21ST CENTURY SKILLS

Read through the text with students and ask what kinds of connections they have already made in preparing the presentation of the invention (for example, matching consumer needs with inventions they can think of to meet them).

→ See pages 28-29 **21st century skills**

Evaluation

Before students discuss the questions in pairs (or in their groups if you prefer), give them time to prepare notes about their experience during the project. Remind students to be supportive and give constructive feedback to each other and say which things they thought they did well and which they found most difficult. Monitor discussions, adding your own feedback where appropriate and noting common observations to then convey to the class as a whole. You could round up the discussion by asking who thinks they can come up with the best invention by improving on or combining existing inventions.

Have a class discussion about what students have learnt from the project, reminding them of the unit objectives, the **Core values** and the **Learning to learn tools** in units 5 and 6, as well as the **21st century skills** section of the **Project** pages.

If you have decided to use the evaluation exercise as a springboard for a student self-assessment diary (see **Evaluation** page 77), give them time to do this now and remind them to refer to the **Reflect on your learning** section of the **Workbook** if they have one.

→ See pages 40-41 **Assessment**

Go beyond

Get students to scan the text to find the three inventions mentioned (Braille, the trampoline and a chemotherapy backpack). Ask them which invention impresses them most and why, and then get them discuss the questions. Ask round the class to find out which inventions students think have had the biggest impact in the world.

Remind students to do all the exercises in their notebook

7 TRAVEL THE WORLD

At the start of each unit and lesson, explain to the students what the objectives are.

Language objectives

Grammar

Present perfect with *already* and *yet*
- Students learn the present perfect to talk about the past with *already* and *yet*, in the negative and the affirmative.

Present perfect: questions with *ever* and *never*
- Students learn the present perfect to ask questions with *ever* and to answer them with *never*.

Vocabulary

Transport: *cruise ship, double decker bus, ferry, helicopter, hot air balloon, jet, limousine, lorry, submarine, train, tram, underground*
- Students use new vocabulary related to forms of transport.

Air travel: *abroad, airline, airport, announcement, arrivals, baggage, board, boarding pass, check-in, customers, delayed, departures, destination, disembark, first class, flight, gate, hand luggage, journey, land, passenger, passport, return, security, stopover, take off*
- Students use new vocabulary related to air travel.

Abstract nouns: *balance, happiness, health, meaning, pleasure, spirituality, truth*
- Students learn some important abstract nouns related to the **Core value - appreciation of beauty**.

Idioms and expressions

Transport: *be in the same boat, drive someone mad, be a backseat driver*
- Students look at idioms and expressions related to transport in the context of a conversation about a road trip.

Recycled language

Questions, Past simple

Skills objectives

Speaking

- Students discuss modes of transport and travel.
- Students share experiences and talk about things they would like to do in the future.
- Students discuss what happens when things go wrong with travel plans.
- Students talk about what they have and haven't done whilst on a trip.
- Students talk about favourite films and film locations.
- Students plan an imaginary road trip.

Pronunciation: Students practice words with the /f/ sound.

Pairwork: Students use various mediation techniques to ensure that a friend is prepared for an upcoming trip.

Listening

- Students listen in order to correct sentences about a travel writer.
- Students listen to complete sentences with *already* and *yet*.
- Students listen to match vocabulary with pictures.
- Students listen to complete dialogue in the context of a job interview.
- Students listen in order to answer questions about a holiday.

Reading

- Students read an account of a trip that went wrong.
- Students read about famous movies and the locations where they were filmed.
- Students read a diary entry about a holiday in Scotland.

Core values: Students discuss and quantify **appreciation of beauty**.

Writing

- Students write sentences about different types of beauty.
- Students, plan, write an check an entry in a travel diary.

Focus on sequencing: *finally, first, just, after, while, then*

Remind students to do all the exercises in their notebook

Learning to learn tools

SPEAKING TOOLS Students practise extending answers given in speaking tasks by adding extra, relevant information.	**LISTENING TOOLS** Students practise using the order of questions in a task to assist with listening comprehension.
READING TOOLS Students practise reading quickly to pick out specific information.	**WRITING TOOLS** Students practise appropriate use of exclamation marks.

VOCABULARY TOOLS Students practise correct use of *been* and *gone*.

Project objectives: Eco-tourism holiday

Task 1 Students discuss and define 'eco-tourism'.

Task 2 Students decide on the focus of their eco-holiday village and write a quiz for potential customers.

Task 3 Students design a plan for how to spend a day in their holiday village and decide how to present this information to customers.

Audiovisual objectives

Vlog: Students watch and listen to Sarah talk about holidays.

Culture: Students watch and listen to Sarah talk about modes of transport.

Grammar animations: Students are presented with visual presentations of the unit grammar.

Key competences

LC **Linguistic**
pages 64-71

MST **Mathematical and Science and Technology**
pages 64-65, 68

DC **Digital**
pages 64-65, 67, 71

SCC **Social and Civic**
pages 69, 71

CAE **Cultural awareness and expression**
pages 64-71

LL **Learning to learn**
pages 65, 67-68, 70-71

IE **Sense of initiative and entrepreneurship**
pages 65, 67, 70

→ See pages 42-43 **Key competences**

CEFR Mediation

7.1 Collaborating to construct meaning
Can make simple remarks and ask questions to show that he/she is following.

7.2 Processing text in writing
Can pick out and reproduce key words and phrases from a spoken text.

7.3 Relaying specific information in writing
Can relay in writing specific information in simple texts on familiar subjects.

7.4 Processing text in writing
Can pick out and reproduce key words and phrases from a short written text.

7.5 Facilitating collaborative interaction with peers
Can ask what others think, make suggestions and understand responses.

Project Collaborating to construct meaning
Can ask group members for reasons for their views and can check for mutual understanding.

Unit review Facilitating collaborative interaction with peers
Can ask what others think, make suggestions and understand responses.

Pairwork Processing text in speech
Can summarise the main points in short informational texts.

→ See pages 30-33 **Mediation**

Remind students to do all the exercises in their notebook

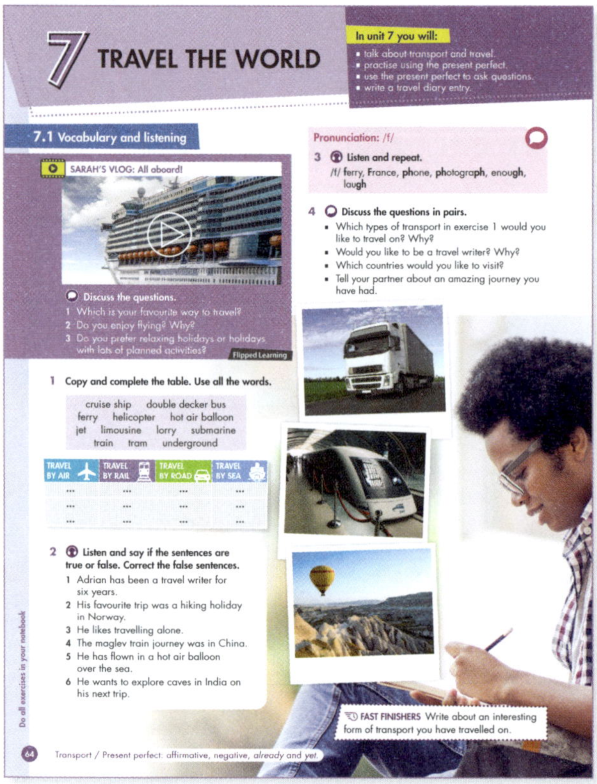
7 TRAVEL THE WORLD

In unit 7 you will:
- talk about transport and travel.
- practise using the present perfect.
- use the present perfect to ask questions.
- write a travel diary entry.

7.1 Vocabulary and listening

SARAH'S VLOG: All aboard!

Discuss the questions.
1 Which is your favourite way to travel?
2 Do you enjoy flying? Why?
3 Do you prefer relaxing holidays or holidays with lots of planned activities?

Flipped Learning

1 Copy and complete the table. Use all the words.

cruise ship double decker bus ferry helicopter hot air balloon jet limousine lorry submarine train tram underground

TRAVEL BY AIR	TRAVEL BY RAIL	TRAVEL BY ROAD	TRAVEL BY SEA
...	...	...	...
...	...	...	...
...	...	...	...

2 Listen and say if the sentences are true or false. Correct the false sentences.
1 Adrian has been a travel writer for six years.
2 His favourite trip was a hiking holiday in Norway.
3 He likes travelling alone.
4 The maglev train journey was in China.
5 He has flown in a hot air balloon over the sea.
6 He wants to explore caves in India on his next trip.

Pronunciation: /f/
3 Listen and repeat.
/f/ ferry, France, phone, photograph, enough, laugh

4 Discuss the questions in pairs.
- Which types of transport in exercise 1 would you like to travel on? Why?
- Would you like to be a travel writer? Why?
- Which countries would you like to visit?
- Tell your partner about an amazing journey you have had.

FAST FINISHERS Write about an interesting form of transport you have travelled on.

Do all exercises in your notebook

64 Transport / Present perfect: affirmative, negative, already and yet

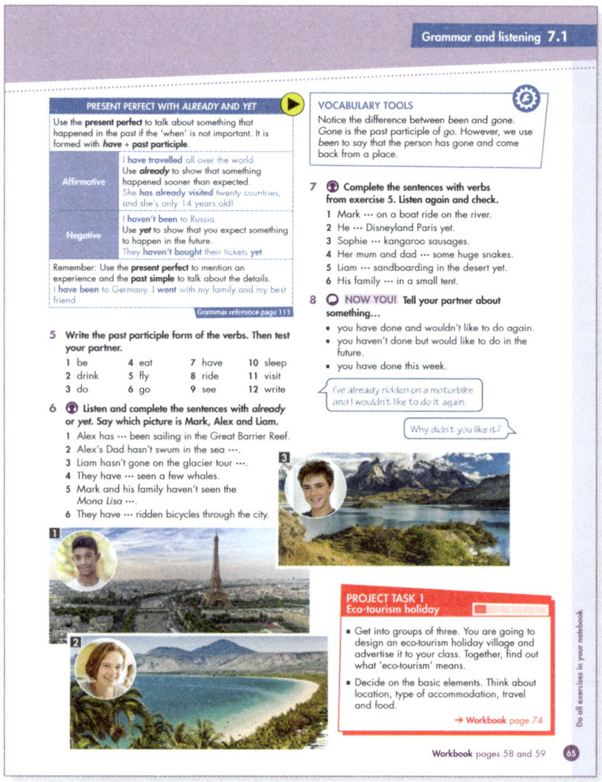
Grammar and listening 7.1

PRESENT PERFECT WITH ALREADY AND YET

Use the present perfect to talk about something that happened in the past if the 'when' is not important. It is formed with have + past participle.

Affirmative	I have travelled all over the world. Use already to show that something happened sooner than expected. She has already visited twenty countries, and she's only 14 years old!
Negative	I haven't been to Russia. Use yet to show that you expect something to happen in the future. They haven't bought their tickets yet.

Remember: Use the present perfect to mention an experience and the past simple to talk about the details. I have been to Germany. I went with my family and my best friend.

Grammar reference page 113

VOCABULARY TOOLS
Notice the difference between been and gone. Gone is the past participle of go. However, we use been to say that the person has gone and come back from a place.

5 Write the past participle form of the verbs. Then test your partner.
1 be 2 drink 3 do 4 eat 5 fly 6 go 7 have 8 ride 9 see 10 sleep 11 visit 12 write

6 Listen and complete the sentences with already or yet. Say which picture is Mark, Alex and Liam.
1 Alex has ··· been sailing in the Great Barrier Reef.
2 Alex's Dad hasn't swum in the sea ···.
3 Liam hasn't gone on the glacier tour ···.
4 They have ··· seen a few whales.
5 Mark and his family haven't seen the Mona Lisa ···.
6 They have ··· ridden bicycles through the city.

7 Complete the sentences with verbs from exercise 5. Listen again and check.
1 Mark ··· on a boat ride on the river.
2 He ··· Disneyland Paris yet.
3 Sophie ··· kangaroo sausages.
4 Her mum and dad ··· some huge snakes.
5 Liam ··· sandboarding in the desert yet.
6 His family ··· in a small tent.

8 NOW YOU! Tell your partner about something...
- you have done and wouldn't like to do again.
- you haven't done but would like to do in the future.
- you have done this week.

I've already ridden on a motorbike and I wouldn't like to do it again.

Why didn't you like it?

PROJECT TASK 1
Eco-tourism holiday
- Get into groups of three. You are going to design an eco-tourism holiday village and advertise it to your class. Together, find out what 'eco-tourism' means.
- Decide on the basic elements. Think about location, type of accommodation, travel and food.

→ Workbook page 74

Do all exercises in your notebook

Workbook pages 58 and 59 65

ANSWER KEY

Pages 64-65

1

Travel by air	Travel by rail	Travel by road	Travel by sea
hot air balloon helicopter jet	train tram underground	lorry limousine double decker bus	ferry cruise ship submarine

2 **1** False. He has been a travel writer for seven years.
2 False. His favourite trip was a cruise in Norway
3 False. It can get very lonely travelling alone.
4 True
5 True
6 True

3 *Student's own answers*

4 *Student's own answers*

5 **1** been **2** drunk **3** done **4** eaten **5** flown **6** gone **7** had **8** ridden **9** seen **10** slept **11** visited **12** written

6 **1** already **2** yet **3** yet **4** already **5** yet **6** already

7 **1** has been **2** hasn't visited **3** has eaten **4** have seen **5** hasn't done **6** have slept

8 *Student's own answers*

Remind students to do all the exercises in their notebook

LESSON FOCUS

Grammar Present perfect with *already* and *yet*

Vocabulary Transport

Listening Correcting sentences about a travel writer; Completing sentences with the correct form of the verb

Speaking Discussing forms of transport; Talking about travel experiences

Project task 1 Discuss and define 'eco-tourism'

Resources

Teacher's i-solutions, Student's Book audio, Vlog and worksheet

Flipped Learning

SARAH'S VLOG: All aboard!

- Make sure to set up the **Flipped Learning** work with the students beforehand. **See pages 20-23 for complete Flipped Learning guidelines.**
- Ask students to put the **Flipped Learning worksheets** on their desks and walk around to check how many have completed the Flipped task.
- In pairs or small groups, ask students to compare and check the *Before you watch...* and *While you watch...* exercises on the worksheet.
- Show students **Sarah's Vlog** and ask volunteers to provide correct answers and clarify any doubts other students may have.
- Choose three or four students to read aloud their answers to the *After you watch...* exercises on the worksheet and encourage some class discussion.
- Move straight to exercise 1 on page 64.

Warmer

Watch Sarah's Vlog and discuss the questions with the whole class. If you don't have video facilities, simply discuss the questions.

1 Write the four headings on the board: *Air, Rail, Road, Sea*. Complete the task as a class.

2 2.11 (See page 175 for transcripts) Before completing the exercise, ask students if there is any vocabulary they do not understand, and tell them to note it down. After listening to the audio, check to see if the definitions are clearer.

Pronunciation

3 2.12 (See page 175 for transcripts) Practise the individual sound before getting students to repeat the words.

4 After completing the exercise, discuss which form of transport was the most popular and why.

FAST FINISHERS Students can complete this exercise alone or in pairs.

Flipped Learning

PRESENT PERFECT WITH *ALREADY* AND *YET*

Draw students' attention to the **Grammar table**. Remind students that they can use this as a quick reference while completing the exercises.

Show students the **Grammar animation** and/or refer students to the **Grammar reference** on page 113 for further information on form and use.

→ See page 23 for how to flip the **grammar lesson**

5 Remind students that they can use the **Grammar reference** at the back of their **Student's Book** if they need guidance, and they can also look over the notes that they took for exercise 2.

6 2.13 (See page 175 for transcripts) Remind students to utilise the **Grammar table** for assistance with this exercise.

VOCABULARY TOOLS

Draw students' attention to the **Vocabulary tool**. It is important that they learn the difference between *been* and *gone* so that that their use of English is accurate and sounds natural.

7 2.14 (See page 176 for transcripts) Before completing the exercise, students can check again in pairs that their answers to exercise 5 were accurate.

8 NOW YOU! Once they have completed the exercise, the students can remain in their pairs. Student A should give Student B a clue using the present perfect. Student B then tries to guess the answer to the clue by asking a question using the present perfect. For example:

Student A: 'I have already ridden on something that has a motor and two wheels'

Student B: 'Have you already ridden on a motorbike?'

PROJECT TASK 1
Eco-tourism holiday

Organise students into teams of three. Tell them that they will first need to research the definition of 'eco-tourism' to make sure that their holiday village is fully eco-friendly. They then need to decide on the basic design of the holiday village and what they will offer customers. Remind students that they need to keep their project notes together in their **Workbook** (page 74) or in their own notebook.

→ See pages 24-27 **Projects**

FURTHER PRACTICE

Workbook pages 58-59
- **Grammar reference and practice** pages 90 and 96
- **Wordlist and exercises** pages 101 and 104

Remind students to do all the exercises in their notebook

CONTINUOUS ASSESSMENT Students can talk about transport and use the present perfect with *already* and *yet*.

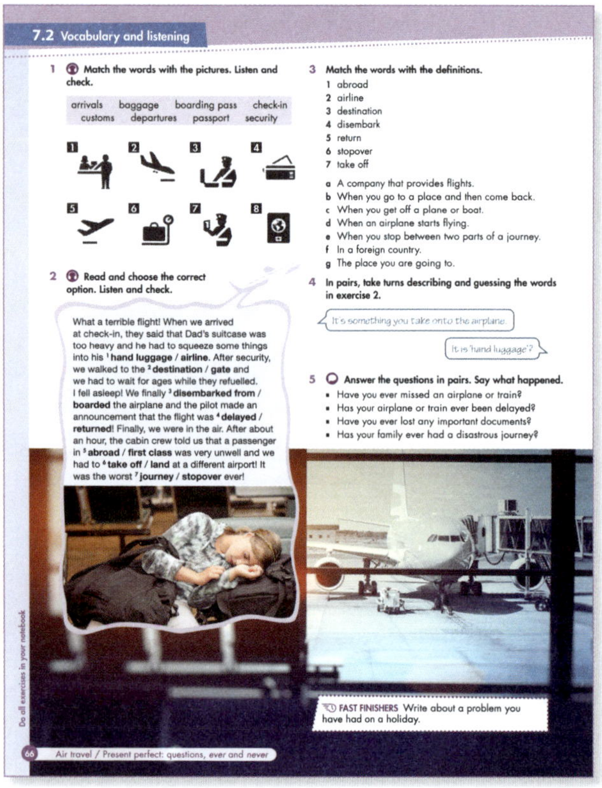

1 Match the words with the pictures. Listen and check.

arrivals baggage boarding pass check-in customs departures passport security

2 Read and choose the correct option. Listen and check.

What a terrible flight! When we arrived at check-in, they said that Dad's suitcase was too heavy and he had to squeeze some things into his [1] **hand luggage / airline**. After security, we walked to the [2] **destination / gate** and we had to wait for ages while they refuelled. I fell asleep! We finally [3] **disembarked from / boarded** the airplane and the pilot made an announcement that the flight was [4] **delayed / returned**! Finally, we were in the air. After about an hour, the cabin crew told us that a passenger in [5] **abroad / first class** was very unwell and we had to [6] **take off / land** at a different airport! It was the worst [7] **journey / stopover** ever!

3 Match the words with the definitions.

1 abroad
2 airline
3 destination
4 disembark
5 return
6 stopover
7 take off

a A company that provides flights.
b When you go to a place and then come back.
c When you get off a plane or boat.
d When an airplane starts flying.
e When you stop between two parts of a journey.
f In a foreign country.
g The place you are going to.

4 In pairs, take turns describing and guessing the words in exercise 2.

5 Answer the questions in pairs. Say what happened.

- Have you ever missed an airplane or train?
- Has your airplane or train ever been delayed?
- Have you ever lost any important documents?
- Has your family ever had a disastrous journey?

FAST FINISHERS Write about a problem you have had on a holiday.

Do all exercises in your notebook

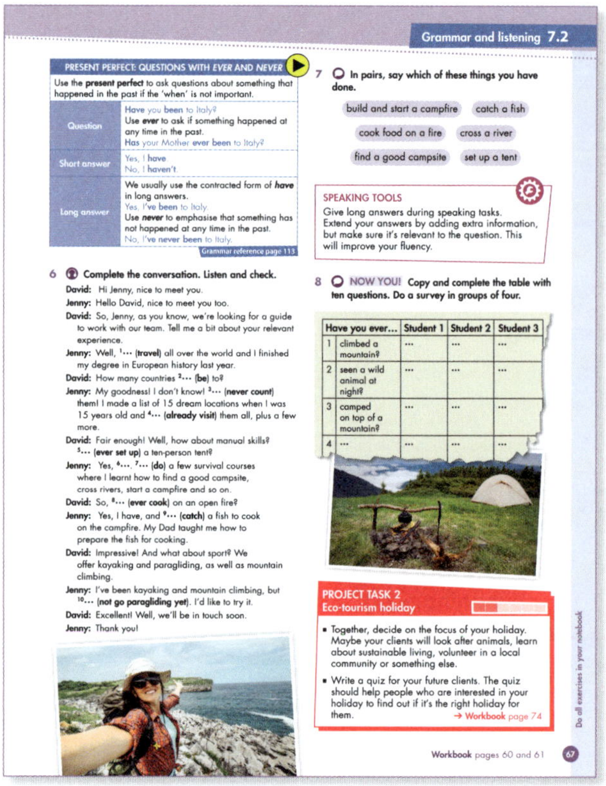

PRESENT PERFECT: QUESTIONS WITH *EVER* AND *NEVER*

Use the **present perfect** to ask questions about something that happened in the past if the 'when' is not important.

Question	**Have** you **been** to Italy? Use **ever** to ask if something happened at any time in the past. **Has** your Mother **ever been** to Italy?
Short answer	Yes, I **have**. No, I **haven't**.
Long answer	We usually use the contracted form of ***have*** in long answers. Yes, I**'ve been** to Italy. Use ***never*** to emphasise that something has not happened at any time in the past. No, I**'ve never been** to Italy.

Grammar reference page 113

6 Complete the conversation. Listen and check.

David: Hi Jenny, nice to meet you.
Jenny: Hello David, nice to meet you too.
David: So, Jenny, as you know, we're looking for a guide to work with our team. Tell me a bit about your relevant experience.
Jenny: Well, [1]… **(travel)** all over the world and I finished my degree in European history last year.
David: How many countries [2]… **(be)** to?
Jenny: My goodness! I don't know! [3]… **(never count)** them! I made a list of 15 dream locations when I was 15 years old and [4]… **(already visit)** them all, plus a few more.
David: Fair enough! Well, how about manual skills? [5]… **(ever set up)** a ten-person tent?
Jenny: Yes, [6]…. [7]… **(do)** a few survival courses where I learnt how to find a good campsite, cross rivers, start a campfire and so on.
David: So, [8]… **(ever cook)** on an open fire?
Jenny: Yes, I have, and [9]… **(catch)** a fish to cook on the campfire. My Dad taught me how to prepare the fish for cooking.
David: Impressive! And what about sport? We offer kayaking and paragliding, as well as mountain climbing.
Jenny: I've been kayaking and mountain climbing, but [10]… **(not go paragliding yet)**. I'd like to try it.
David: Excellent! Well, we'll be in touch soon.
Jenny: Thank you!

7 In pairs, say which of these things you have done.

build and start a campfire catch a fish cook food on a fire cross a river find a good campsite set up a tent

SPEAKING TOOLS
Give long answers during speaking tasks. Extend your answers by adding extra information, but make sure it's relevant to the question. This will improve your fluency.

8 NOW YOU! Copy and complete the table with ten questions. Do a survey in groups of four.

	Have you ever…	Student 1	Student 2	Student 3
1	climbed a mountain?	…	…	…
2	seen a wild animal at night?	…	…	…
3	camped on top of a mountain?	…	…	…
4	…	…	…	…

PROJECT TASK 2
Eco-tourism holiday

- Together, decide on the focus of your holiday. Maybe your clients will look after animals, learn about sustainable living, volunteer in a local community or something else.
- Write a quiz for your future clients. The quiz should help people who are interested in your holiday to find out if it's the right holiday for them. → Workbook page 74

Do all exercises in your notebook

ANSWER KEY

Pages 66-67

1
1 check-in
2 arrivals
3 security
4 boarding pass
5 departures
6 baggage
7 customs
8 passport

2
1 hand luggage
2 gate
3 boarded
4 delayed
5 first class
6 land
7 journey

3
1 f
2 a
3 g
4 c
5 b
6 e
7 d

4 *Student's own answers*

5 *Student's own answers*

6
1 I have travelled
2 have you been
3 I have never counted
4 I have already visited
5 have you ever set up
6 I have
7 I have done
8 have you ever cooked
9 I have caught
10 I have not been paragliding yet

7 *Student's own answers*

8 *Student's own answers*

Remind students to do all the exercises in their notebook

LESSON FOCUS

Grammar Present perfect: questions with *ever* and *never*

Vocabulary Air travel

Listening Choose the correct options related to air travel; complete a conversation from a job interview

Speaking Talking about previous travel experiences

Project task 2 Decide on the focus of the eco-holiday village and write a quiz for potential customers

Resources

Teacher's i-solutions, Student's Book audio

Preparation Blank postcards, or postcard sized pieces of paper

Warmer

Hand out postcard-sized pieces of paper. Give students five minutes to write a postcard to a friend telling them about an imaginary trip they are on. Tell them to include something negative and something positive. After they have finished, ask them to 'deliver' their postcard to another student. Ask some students to read out the postcards they have received.

1 2.15 (See page 176 for transcripts) Cover the wordpool and ask students to quickly shout out what the drawings represent, then let them listen and complete the exercise.

2 2.16 (See page 176 for transcripts) Ask students to scan the text and then a second time whilst they concentrate on choosing the right answer.

3 In pairs, tell students to cover the words and try to guess the definitions, then to look and see how many they got right.

4 Get students to check their understanding of the vocabulary before they start the exercise. They can use a dictionary if they are unsure of any of the words.

5 Round up with a class discussion and ask students to share any unusual experiences.

FAST FINISHERS Students can complete this exercise alone or in pairs.

Flipped Learning

PRESENT PERFECT: QUESTIONS WITH *EVER* AND *NEVER*

Draw students' attention to the **Grammar table**. Remind students that they can use this as a quick reference while completing the exercises.

Show students the **Grammar animation** and/or refer students to the **Grammar reference** on page 113 for further information on form and use.

→ See page 23 for how to flip the **grammar lesson**

6 2.17 (See page 176 for transcripts) Remind students to look back over their notes from the last lesson on the past perfect with *already* and *yet* and to make use of the **Grammar reference** at the back of their **Student's Book**.

7 Round up with a class discussion. Ask students what other activities can be done when camping and whether they have done any of these as well.

SPEAKING TOOLS

Draw students' attention to the **Speaking tool**. They can use new knowledge and new vocabulary when employing this **Speaking tool** but remind them that the extra information they give must be relevant to the context of the conversation.

8 NOW YOU! Encourage students to look back over the **Unit** so far to help them write the questions.

PROJECT TASK 2
Eco-tourism holiday

Ask students to decide which element of their eco-holiday they will focus on and to design a quiz for potential customers so that they can find out if the holiday village is the right place for them. Remind students that they need to keep their project notes together in their **Workbook** (page 74) or in their own notebook.

→ See pages 24-27 **Projects**

FURTHER PRACTICE

Workbook pages 60-61

- Grammar reference and practice pages 90 and 95
- Wordlist and exercises pages 101 and 104

Vocabulary and Grammar worksheets available to download and edit from the

Richmond *Learning* **Platform**

→ See pages 38-39 **Mixed-ability classes**

Remind students to do all the exercises in their notebook

CONTINUOUS ASSESSMENT Students can talk about air travel and ask and answer questions in the present perfect with *ever* and *never*.

1 Write down your five favourite films. In pairs, say where you think they were filmed. Have you been to the places? Would you like to go?

READING TOOLS
In order to scan a text for information quickly, look only for the information you need. Don't stop to make notes on other things.

2 Scan the article to find the names of the films shown in the five photos. How many of them have you seen?

3 Read the article again and answer the questions.
1 What three types of transport are mentioned in the paragraph on Paris?
2 What two musical connections does Salzburg have?
3 Which location is a famous archaeological site?
4 What effect did *The Lord of the Rings* film series have on New Zealand tourism?
5 What can you do at King's Cross Station that is linked to the *Harry Potter* films?

4 Find these words and expressions in the text and classify them as related to either film or travel.

canal car chase come out go on a tour picturesque scene set tourist destination

IT'S JUST LIKE IT IS IN THE MOVIES!

Tourists who have been to New York City often say it's like walking through a big film set.

That's not surprising; New York has some of the most cinematic locations in the world, including Coney Island, Times Square and the most filmed location of all time – Central Park. Here are five other places that are closely associated with films.

The romantic charms of Paris have appeared in lots of films, from love stories to thrillers. The 2018 action spy film *Mission: Impossible – Fallout* shows car chases through its boulevards, a speedboat chase along its canals and a helicopter flight over the Eiffel Tower. If there's one thing better than a good action scene, it's a good action scene in a beautiful setting.

PARIS, FRANCE

The picturesque Austrian city of Salzburg is the birthplace of Mozart, but probably more tourists come to see locations from the musical *The Sound of Music*. Here you can go on a tour that follows in the footsteps of Maria and the Von Trapp family, and even sing 'Do Re Mi' in the famous Mirabell Gardens.

SALZBURG, AUSTRIA

Do all exercises in your notebook

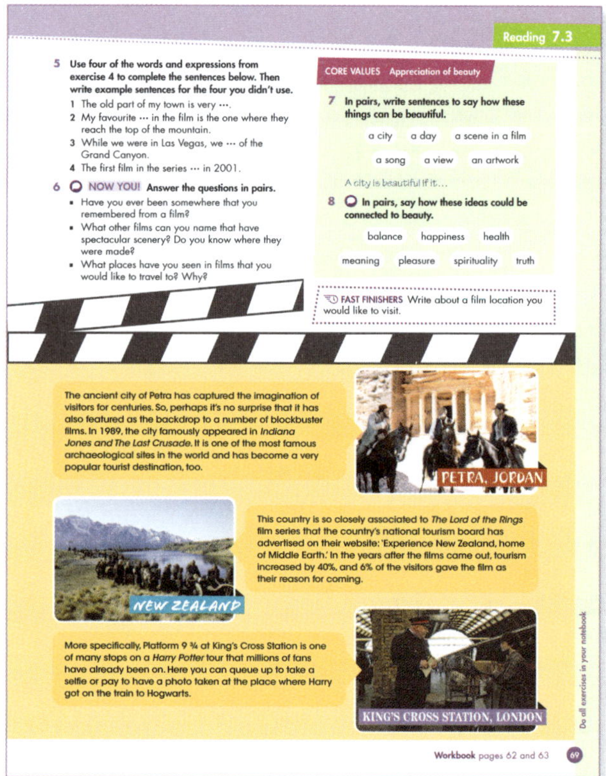

5 Use four of the words and expressions from exercise 4 to complete the sentences below. Then write example sentences for the four you didn't use.
1 The old part of my town is very ···.
2 My favourite ··· in the film is the one where they reach the top of the mountain.
3 While we were in Las Vegas, we ··· of the Grand Canyon.
4 The first film in the series ··· in 2001.

6 NOW YOU! Answer the questions in pairs.
- Have you ever been somewhere that you remembered from a film?
- What other films can you name that have spectacular scenery? Do you know where they were made?
- What places have you seen in films that you would like to travel to? Why?

CORE VALUES Appreciation of beauty

7 In pairs, write sentences to say how these things can be beautiful.

a city a day a scene in a film a song a view an artwork

A city is beautiful if it…

8 In pairs, say how these ideas could be connected to beauty.

balance happiness health meaning pleasure spirituality truth

FAST FINISHERS Write about a film location you would like to visit.

The ancient city of Petra has captured the imagination of visitors for centuries. So, perhaps it's no surprise that it has also featured as the backdrop to a number of blockbuster films. In 1989, the city famously appeared in *Indiana Jones and The Last Crusade*. It is one of the most famous archaeological sites in the world and has become a very popular tourist destination, too.

PETRA, JORDAN

NEW ZEALAND

This country is so closely associated to *The Lord of the Rings* film series that the country's national tourism board has advertised on their website: 'Experience New Zealand, home of Middle Earth.' In the years after the films came out, tourism increased by 40%, and 6% of the visitors gave the film as their reason for coming.

More specifically, Platform 9 ¾ at King's Cross Station is one of many stops on a *Harry Potter* tour that millions of fans have already been on. Here you can queue up to take a selfie or pay to have a photo taken at the place where Harry got on the train to Hogwarts.

KING'S CROSS STATION, LONDON

Do all exercises in your notebook

ANSWER KEY

Pages 68-69

1 *Student's own answers*

2 **Paris:** *Mission: Impossible – Fallout*
Salzburg: *The Sound of Music*
Petra: *Indiana Jones and the Last Crusade*
New Zealand: *The Lord of the Rings film series*
King's Cross Station, London: *Harry Potter*

3 **1** car, speedboat and helicopter
2 It's the birthplace of Mozart and the location for *The Sound of Music.*
3 Petra, Jordan
4 Tourism increased by 40%.
5 Pay to have a photo taken at Platform 9 ¾, where Harry got on the train to Hogwarts.

4 **Film:** set, car chase, scene, come out
Travel: canal, picturesque, tourist destination, go on a tour

5 **1** picturesque
2 scene
3 went on a tour
4 came out

6 *Student's own answers*

7 *Student's own answers*

8 *Student's own answers*

Remind students to do all the exercises in their notebook

LESSON FOCUS

Language in context Abstract nouns

Core values Appreciation of beauty

Resources

Teacher's i-solutions, Student's Book audio

Preparation Print photos of New York city.

→ See pages 36-37 **Literature**

Warmer

Show students the photos of New York city, but don't tell them where it is. Ask them to guess. Then ask them why they think directors often choose to shoot their films in New York city. Ask students if they have any favourite films that were set in New York.

1 In pairs, see how many favourite films students have in common. They should tell each other why the films they have in common are their favourites. If they do not have any in common, they can tell each other about their favourite and why they like it so much.

READING TOOLS

Draw students' attention to the **Reading tool**. This will help them to pick out key information quickly in exams.

2 2.18 (See page 176 for transcripts) When they have completed the exercise, ask students to tell you whether they have been to any of the film locations mentioned in the text.

3 After completing the exercise, get students to check their answers in pairs.

4 Write 'Film' and 'Travel' on the board and classify the words as a class. Leave the words up so students can use them for the remainder of the class.

5 Ask students to share one of their example sentences with the class.

6 NOW YOU! After the dicussion, ask volunteers to tell the class what films they came up with and what answers to the last question anyone had in common with their partner.

CORE VALUES Appreciation of beauty

7 For inspiration for this task, encourage students to look back at their work from unit 3 on art forms.

8 Round up with a class discussion. Find out which points students agree on and which they don't.

FAST FINISHERS Students can complete this exercise alone or in pairs.

FURTHER PRACTICE

Workbook pages 62-63

Remind students to do all the exercises in their notebook

CONTINUOUS ASSESSMENT Students can understand a text about film locations and talk about abstract nouns related to beauty.

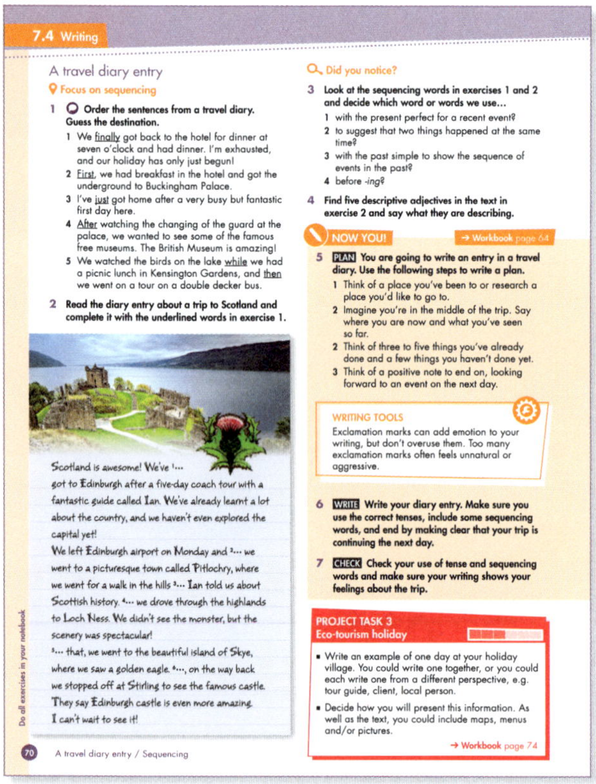

7.4 Writing

A travel diary entry

Focus on sequencing

1 Order the sentences from a travel diary. Guess the destination.

1 We finally got back to the hotel for dinner at seven o'clock and had dinner. I'm exhausted, and our holiday has only just begun!
2 First, we had breakfast in the hotel and got the underground to Buckingham Palace.
3 I've just got home after a very busy but fantastic first day here.
4 After watching the changing of the guard at the palace, we wanted to see some of the famous free museums. The British Museum is amazing!
5 We watched the birds on the lake while we had a picnic lunch in Kensington Gardens, and then we went on a tour on a double decker bus.

2 Read the diary entry about a trip to Scotland and complete it with the underlined words in exercise 1.

Scotland is awesome! We've [1]... got to Edinburgh after a five-day coach tour with a fantastic guide called Ian. We've already learnt a lot about the country, and we haven't even explored the capital yet!
We left Edinburgh airport on Monday and [2]... we went to a picturesque town called Pitlochry, where we went for a walk in the hills [3]... Ian told us about Scottish history. [4]... we drove through the highlands to Loch Ness. We didn't see the monster, but the scenery was spectacular!
[5]... that, we went to the beautiful island of Skye, where we saw a golden eagle. [6]..., on the way back we stopped off at Stirling to see the famous castle. They say Edinburgh castle is even more amazing. I can't wait to see it!

Did you notice?

3 Look at the sequencing words in exercises 1 and 2 and decide which word or words we use...
1 with the present perfect for a recent event?
2 to suggest that two things happened at the same time?
3 with the past simple to show the sequence of events in the past?
4 before *-ing*?

4 Find five descriptive adjectives in the text in exercise 2 and say what they are describing.

NOW YOU! → Workbook page 64

5 PLAN You are going to write an entry in a travel diary. Use the following steps to write a plan.
1 Think of a place you've been to or research a place you'd like to go to.
2 Imagine you're in the middle of the trip. Say where you are now and what you've seen so far.
2 Think of three to five things you've already done and a few things you haven't done yet.
3 Think of a positive note to end on, looking forward to an event on the next day.

WRITING TOOLS
Exclamation marks can add emotion to your writing, but don't overuse them. Too many exclamation marks often feels unnatural or aggressive.

6 WRITE Write your diary entry. Make sure you use the correct tenses, include some sequencing words, and end by making clear that your trip is continuing the next day.

7 CHECK Check your use of tense and sequencing words and make sure your writing shows your feelings about the trip.

PROJECT TASK 3
Eco-tourism holiday
- Write an example of one day at your holiday village. You could write one together, or you could each write one from a different perspective, e.g. tour guide, client, local person.
- Decide how you will present this information. As well as the text, you could include maps, menus and/or pictures.

→ Workbook page 74

Do all exercises in your notebook

70 A travel diary entry / Sequencing

ANSWER KEY

Page 70

1 3, 2, 4, 5, 1
London

2 **1** just **2** first **3** while **4** Then **5** After **6** Finally

3 **1** just **2** while **3** first, then, finally **4** after

4 awesome – Scotland
picturesque – Pitlochry
spectacular – the scenery on the drive through the highlands to Loch Ness
beautiful – the island of Skye
amazing - Edinburgh castle

5 *Student's own answers*

6 *Student's own answers*

7 *Student's own answers*

FURTHER PRACTICE

Workbook page 64

LESSON FOCUS

Focus on Sequencing: *finally, first, just, after, while, then*

Writing A travel diary entry

Project task 3 Design a plan for how to spend a day in the holiday village and decide how to present this information to customers

Resources

Teacher's i-solutions

Warmer

Tell students about the last trip or holiday you went on and use as many sequencing words as possible.

Focus on sequencing

1 After students have finished the exercise, draw a horizontal line on the board and get students to help you to add the sequencing words, from what happened first to what happened last. Ask students if they know of any other sequencing words and add these to the timeline as well.

2 Students can use the timeline on the board to help with this exercise. After they have finished ask three students to read a paragraph each out loud. Correct pronunciation where necessary.

Did you notice?

3 Encourage students to make a note of all the sequencing words from this exercise, and from exercises 1 and 2, to use in the writing task.

4 After students have finished, brainstorm more examples of descriptive adjectives as a class and write them on the board.

5 PLAN Students can discuss their ideas with a partner if they need inspiration for their plan.

WRITING TOOLS

Draw students' attention to the **Writing tool** and remind them that all punctuation should be used accurately, not just the exclamation mark, because otherwise the entire meaning of a sentence can change.

6 WRITE Before students write, make a list on the board of content elements they should keep in mind: structure, language, style, etc.

7 CHECK Once students have checked their own diary entry, they can swap work with a partner and check theirs.

PROJECT TASK 3
Eco-tourism holiday

Tell students to write an example day plan for their customers, including what activities they can do and in what order. They will then need to decide how to present this to customers to persuade them to come to the holiday village. Tell students that they need to keep their project notes together in their **Workbook** (page 74) or in their own notebook.

→ See pages 24-27 **Projects**

Remind students to do all the exercises in their notebook

 CONTINUOUS ASSESSMENT Students can use sequencing words to write a travel diary entry.

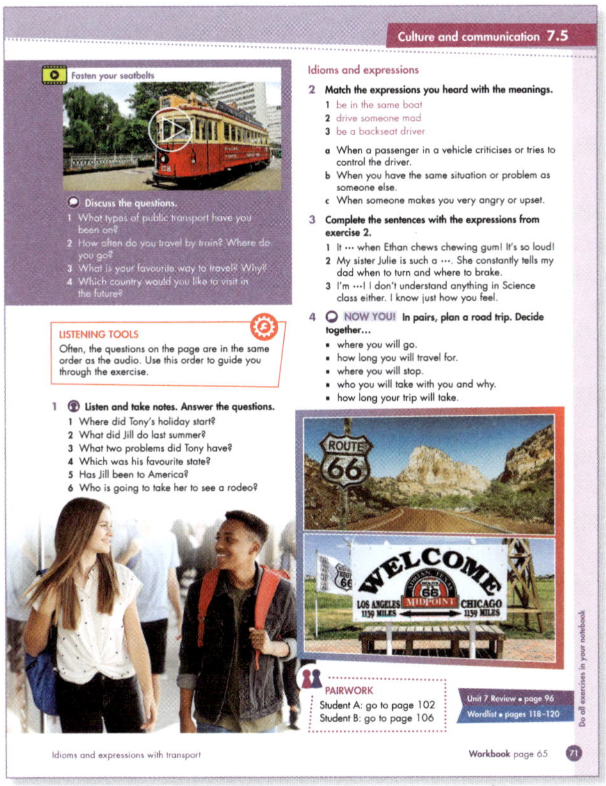

Culture and communication 7.5

Fasten your seatbelts

Discuss the questions.

1 What types of public transport have you been on?
2 How often do you travel by train? Where do you go?
3 What is your favourite way to travel? Why?
4 Which country would you like to visit in the future?

LISTENING TOOLS
Often, the questions on the page are in the same order as the audio. Use this order to guide you through the exercise.

1 Listen and take notes. Answer the questions.
1 Where did Tony's holiday start?
2 What did Jill do last summer?
3 What two problems did Tony have?
4 Which was his favourite state?
5 Has Jill been to America?
6 Who is going to take her to see a rodeo?

Idioms and expressions

2 Match the expressions you heard with the meanings.
1 be in the same boat
2 drive someone mad
3 be a backseat driver

a When a passenger in a vehicle criticises or tries to control the driver.
b When you have the same situation or problem as someone else.
c When someone makes you very angry or upset.

3 Complete the sentences with the expressions from exercise 2.
1 It ··· when Ethan chews chewing gum! It's so loud!
2 My sister Julie is such a ···. She constantly tells my dad when to turn and where to brake.
3 I'm ···! I don't understand anything in Science class either. I know just how you feel.

4 NOW YOU! In pairs, plan a road trip. Decide together…
- where you will go.
- how long you will travel for.
- where you will stop.
- who you will take with you and why.
- how long your trip will take.

PAIRWORK
Student A: go to page 102
Student B: go to page 106

Unit 7 Review • page 96
Wordlist • pages 118–120

Do all exercises in your notebook

Idioms and expressions with transport

Workbook page 65 71

LESSON FOCUS

Idioms and expressions Transport
Listening Listen and answer questions
Speaking Plan a road trip

Resources

Teacher's i-solutions, Student's Book audio, Culture video and worksheet

Fasten your seatbelts

Video and worksheet available on the RichmondLearningPlatform

- In pairs, ask students to complete the *What I know…* exercises on the **Culture video worksheet**.
- Show students the **Culture video** and ask them to complete the *What I learned…* exercises on the worksheet.
- In pairs, students compare answers.
- In small groups, tell students to complete the *What I wonder…* exercises on the worksheet.

Warmer

Watch the culture video and discuss the questions with the whole class. If you don't have video facilities, simply discuss the questions.

LISTENING TOOLS

Draw students' attention to the **Listening tool**. They can practise the advice given in the next exercise.

1 2.19 (See page 176 for transcripts) Tell students to familiarise themselves with the questions and the key words before listening.

Idioms and expressions

2 Ask students if they can think of any other expressions related to transport and, if not, to invent their own.

3 When students have completed the exercise, ask them to write three more sentences of their own using the expressions in exercise 2.

4 NOW YOU! Ask a few students to share their plans and itinerary with the class and explain why they chose that particular destination.

ANSWER KEY

Page 71

1
1 Chicago
2 Went camping with her family
3 His brother drove him mad and his dad was a backseat driver
4 Texas
5 Yes
6 Her uncle

2
1 b
2 c
3 a

3
1 drives me mad
2 backseat driver
3 in the same boat

4 *Student's own answers*

FURTHER PRACTICE AND UNIT ASSESSMENT

Unit 7 Review Student's Book page 96
Workbook page 65
- **Reflect on your learning** page 65
- **Grammar reference and practice** pages 90 and 96
- **Wordlist and exercises** pages 101 and 104

Tests available to download and edit from the **RichmondLearningPlatform**

→ See pages 40-41 **Assessment**

PAIRWORK **Student's Book** pages 102 and 106
See **Teacher's Book** page xxx for more information.
→ See pages 30-33 **Mediation**

Remind students to do all the exercises in their notebook

CONTINUOUS ASSESSMENT Students can use idioms and expressions with transport.

Unit 7 Review

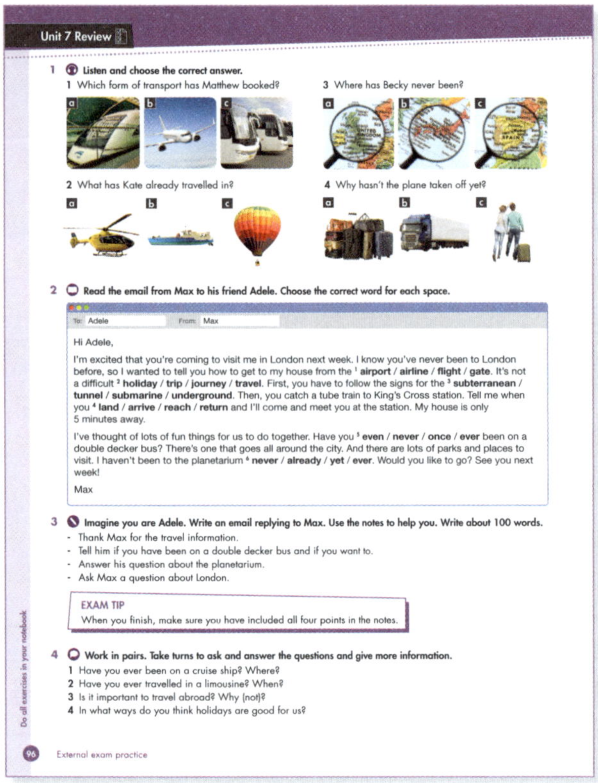

Unit 7 Review

1 Listen and choose the correct answer.

1 Which form of transport has Matthew booked?

a b c

2 What has Kate already travelled in?

a b c

3 Where has Becky never been?

a b c

4 Why hasn't the plane taken off yet?

a b c

2 Read the email from Max to his friend Adele. Choose the correct word for each space.

To: Adele From: Max

Hi Adele,

I'm excited that you're coming to visit me in London next week. I know you've never been to London before, so I wanted to tell you how to get to my house from the [1] **airport / airline / flight / gate**. It's not a difficult [2] **holiday / trip / journey / travel**. First, you have to follow the signs for the [3] **subterranean / tunnel / submarine / underground**. Then, you catch a tube train to King's Cross station. Tell me when you [4] **land / arrive / reach / return** and I'll come and meet you at the station. My house is only 5 minutes away.

I've thought of lots of fun things for us to do together. Have you [5] **even / never / once / ever** been on a double decker bus? There's one that goes all around the city. And there are lots of parks and places to visit. I haven't been to the planetarium [6] **never / already / yet / ever**. Would you like to go? See you next week!

Max

3 Imagine you are Adele. Write an email replying to Max. Use the notes to help you. Write about 100 words.

- Thank Max for the travel information.
- Tell him if you have been on a double decker bus and if you want to.
- Answer his question about the planetarium.
- Ask Max a question about London.

EXAM TIP
When you finish, make sure you have included all four points in the notes.

4 Work in pairs. Take turns to ask and answer the questions and give more information.

1 Have you ever been on a cruise ship? Where?
2 Have you ever travelled in a limousine? When?
3 Is it important to travel abroad? Why (not)?
4 In what ways do you think holidays are good for us?

Do all exercises in your notebook

96 External exam practice

Student's Book page 96

ANSWER KEY

See page 181 for transcripts

1 2.43

1 a
2 c
3 b
4 b

2

1 airport
2 journey
3 underground
4 arrive
5 ever
6 yet

3 *Student's own answers*

4 *Student's own answers*

Pairwork

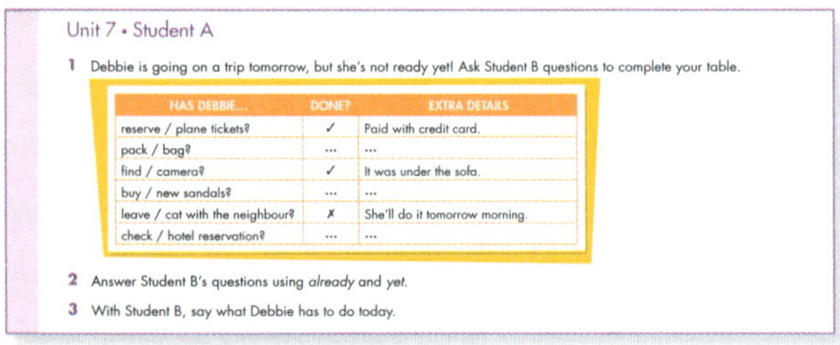

Unit 7 • Student A

1 Debbie is going on a trip tomorrow, but she's not ready yet! Ask Student B questions to complete your table.

HAS DEBBIE...	DONE?	EXTRA DETAILS
reserve / plane tickets?	✓	Paid with credit card.
pack / bag?	...	...
find / camera?	✓	It was under the sofa.
buy / new sandals?	...	...
leave / cat with the neighbour?	✗	She'll do it tomorrow morning.
check / hotel reservation?	...	...

2 Answer Student B's questions using *already* and *yet*.

3 With Student B, say what Debbie has to do today.

Student's Book page 102

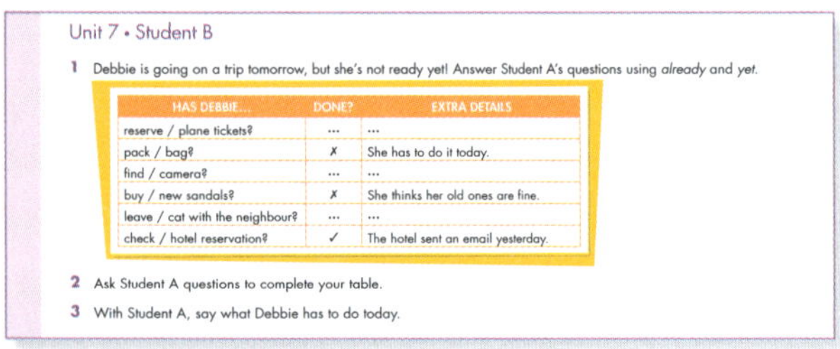

Unit 7 • Student B

1 Debbie is going on a trip tomorrow, but she's not ready yet! Answer Student A's questions using *already* and *yet*.

HAS DEBBIE...	DONE?	EXTRA DETAILS
reserve / plane tickets?	...	...
pack / bag?	✗	She has to do it today.
find / camera?	...	...
buy / new sandals?	✗	She thinks her old ones are fine.
leave / cat with the neighbour?	...	...
check / hotel reservation?	✓	The hotel sent an email yesterday.

2 Ask Student A questions to complete your table.

3 With Student A, say what Debbie has to do today.

Student's Book page 106

CEFR MEDIATION DESCRIPTOR

- **Overall mediation**
  Students can convey the main points involved in short, simple conversations or texts on everyday subjects of immediate interest.

- **Requesting information**
  Tell students that they each have different information about a friend called Debbie who is leaving to go on a trip tomorrow. Students must figure out between them what Debbie needs to do in order to be able to go on the trip.

Remind students to do all the exercises in their notebook

Grammar reference

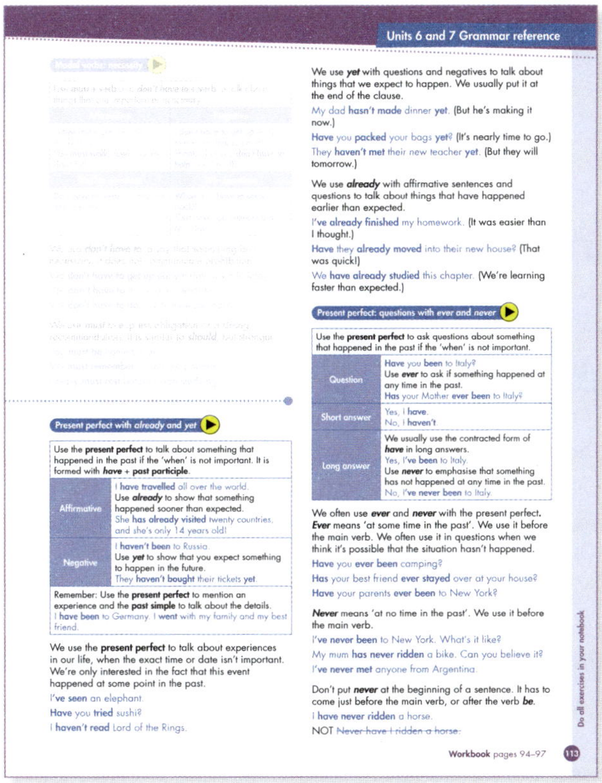

Units 6 and 7 Grammar reference

Present perfect with *already* and *yet*

Use the **present perfect** to talk about something that happened in the past if the 'when' is not important. It is formed with ***have*** + **past participle**.	
Affirmative	I **have travelled** all over the world. Use ***already*** to show that something happened sooner than expected. She **has already visited** twenty countries, and she's only 14 years old!
Negative	I **haven't been** to Russia. Use ***yet*** to show that you expect something to happen in the future. They **haven't bought** their tickets **yet**.
Remember: Use the **present perfect** to mention an experience and the **past simple** to talk about the details. I **have been** to Germany. I **went** with my family and my best friend.	

We use the **present perfect** to talk about experiences in our life, when the exact time or date isn't important. We're only interested in the fact that this event happened at some point in the past.

I**'ve seen** an elephant.

Have you **tried** sushi?

I **haven't read** Lord of the Rings.

We use ***yet*** with questions and negatives to talk about things that we expect to happen. We usually put it at the end of the clause.

My dad **hasn't made** dinner **yet**. (But he's making it now.)

Have you **packed** your bags **yet**? (It's nearly time to go.)

They **haven't met** their new teacher **yet**. (But they will tomorrow.)

We use ***already*** with affirmative sentences and questions to talk about things that have happened earlier than expected.

I**'ve already finished** my homework. (It was easier than I thought.)

Have they **already moved** into their new house? (That was quick!)

We **have already studied** this chapter. (We're learning faster than expected.)

Present perfect: questions with *ever* and *never*

Use the **present perfect** to ask questions about something that happened in the past if the 'when' is not important.	
Question	**Have** you **been** to Italy? Use ***ever*** to ask if something happened at any time in the past. **Has** your Mother **ever been** to Italy?
Short answer	Yes, I **have**. No, I **haven't**.
Long answer	We usually use the contracted form of ***have*** in long answers. Yes, I**'ve been** to Italy. Use ***never*** to emphasise that something has not happened at any time in the past. No, I**'ve never been** to Italy.

We often use ***ever*** and ***never*** with the present perfect. ***Ever*** means 'at some time in the past'. We use it before the main verb. We often use it in questions when we think it's possible that the situation hasn't happened.

Have you **ever been** camping?

Has your best friend **ever stayed** over at your house?

Have your parents **ever been** to New York?

Never means 'at no time in the past'. We use it before the main verb.

I**'ve never been** to New York. What's it like?

My mum **has never ridden** a bike. Can you believe it?

I**'ve never met** anyone from Argentina.

Don't put ***never*** at the beginning of a sentence. It has to come just before the main verb, or after the verb ***be***.

I **have never ridden** a horse.

NOT ~~Never have I ridden a horse.~~

Do all exercises in your notebook

Workbook pages 94–97 113

Student's Book page 113

Wordlist

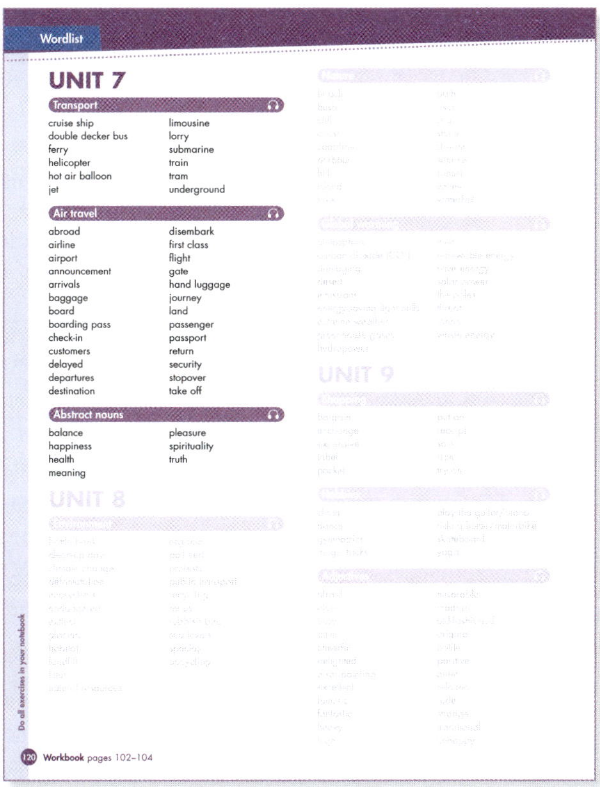

Wordlist

UNIT 7

Transport

cruise ship
double decker bus
ferry
helicopter
hot air balloon
jet
limousine
lorry
submarine
train
tram
underground

Air travel

abroad
airline
airport
announcement
arrivals
baggage
board
boarding pass
check-in
customers
delayed
departures
destination
disembark
first class
flight
gate
hand luggage
journey
land
passenger
passport
return
security
stopover
take off

Abstract nouns

balance
happiness
health
meaning
pleasure
spirituality
truth

Do all exercises in your notebook

120 **Workbook** pages 102–104

Student's Book page 120

2.64 2.65 2.66

Remind students to do all the exercises in their notebook

8 OUR WORLD

At the start of each unit and lesson, explain to the students what the objectives are.

Language objectives

Grammar

Zero and first conditional

- Students practise the zero and the first conditional to talk about general truths and real future possibilities.

Future with *going to*

- Students practise using *going to* for talking about plans and intentions.

Vocabulary

Environment: *bottle bank, clean-up days, climate change, deforestation, ecosystems, endangered, extinct, glaciers, habitat, landfill, litter, natural resources, organic, polluted, protests, public transport, recycling, reuse, rubbish bins, sea levels, species, upcycling*

- Students practise vocabulary related to the environment.

Nature: *beach, bush, cliff, coast, coastline, harbour, hill, island, lake, path, river, sea, stone, stream, sunrise, sunset, valley, waterfall*

- Students practise vocabulary related to nature.

Global warming: *atmosphere, carbon dioxide (CO_2), damaging, desert, emissions, energy-saving light bulb, extreme weather, greenhouse gases, hydropower, melt, renewable energy, save energy, solar power, the poles, threat, tonne, waste energy*

- Students practise vocabulary related to global warming.

Idioms and expressions

Taking action: *to make a stand, actions speak louder than words, to think outside the box*

- Students look at idioms and expressions related to taking action in the context of three short talks.

Recycled language

Present simple, Present continuous, Future with *will*

Skills objectives

Speaking

- Students agree and disagree with statements about the environment.
- Students complete conditional sentences about the environment with their own ideas.
- Students discuss opinions about the future of the environment.
- Students discuss what different groups of people can do to help fight global warming.
- Students complete sentences about the environment with their own ideas.

Pronunciation: Students practise the /aʊ/ sound in different words.

Pairwork: Students use various mediation techniques to develop ideas about how to educate parents on environmentally friendly behaviour.

Listening

- Students listen to short statements to match key words with pictures.
- Students listen to match parts of zero conditional sentences.
- Students listen to complete first conditional sentences.
- Students listen to complete a conservationist's weekly plan and answer questions.
- Students listen to complete texts about a family's plans to help look after the environment.
- Students listen to complete three texts from people taking different stands to protect the environment.

Reading

- Students skim an article to match headings with paragraphs.
- Students read in detail to answer multiple-choice questions.
- Students scan a text to find words to complete other sentences.

Core values: Students consider what some specific research suggests about **solidarity**.

Writing

- Students look at some ways of expressing cause and effect.
- Students plan, write and check a leaflet about the environment.

Focus on indefinite pronouns: *every, some, any, no*

Remind students to do all the exercises in their notebook

Learning to learn tools

SPEAKING TOOLS Students practise consolidating new structures by practising them with a range of vocabulary.	LISTENING TOOLS Students focus on taking effective notes to make sure they get as much important information as possible.
READING TOOLS Students develop their ability to retain statistical information from texts.	WRITING TOOLS Students practise using a question/ answer format to help write more clearly and engagingly.

VOCABULARY TOOLS Students develop their understanding of English spelling and pronunciation by noticing silent letters and different spelling patterns with the same pronunciation.

Project objectives: Eco-tourism holiday

Task 4 Students make a list of the classes and activities they will offer.

Task 5 Students plan a week of activities and excursions.

Task 6 Students invent feedback from previous clients.

Audiovisual objectives

Vlog: Students watch and listen to George talk about environmental action.

Culture: Students watch and listen to George talk about the seaside village of Fairbourne.

Grammar animations: Students are presented with visual presentations of the unit grammar.

Key competences

LC **Linguistic**
pages 72-79

MST **Mathematical and Science and Technology**
pages 72-79

DC **Digital**
pages 72-73, 75, 79

SCC **Social and Civic**
pages 72-73, 75-79

CAE **Cultural awareness and expression**
pages 72-73, 75, 78-79

LL **Learning to learn**
pages 74-76, 78-79

IE **Sense of initiative and entrepreneurship**
pages 73, 75, 78

→ See pages 42-43 **Key competences**

CEFR Mediation

8.1 Collaborating to construct meaning
Can ask group members for reasons for their views and can check for mutual understanding.

8.2 Relaying specific information in writing
Can write specific information from spoken texts.

8.3 Facilitating collaborative interaction with peers
Can ask what others think, make suggestions and understand responses.

8.4 Adapting language
Can repeat the main point of a message using different words.

8.5 Relaying specific information in writing
Can write specific information from spoken texts.

Project Collaborating to construct meaning
Can ask group members for reasons for their views and can check for mutual understanding.

Unit review Encouraging conceptual talk
Can ask what somebody thinks of a certain idea.

Pairwork Encouraging conceptual talk
Can ask questions to invite people to clarify their reasoning.

→ See pages 30-33 **Mediation**

Remind students to do all the exercises in their notebook

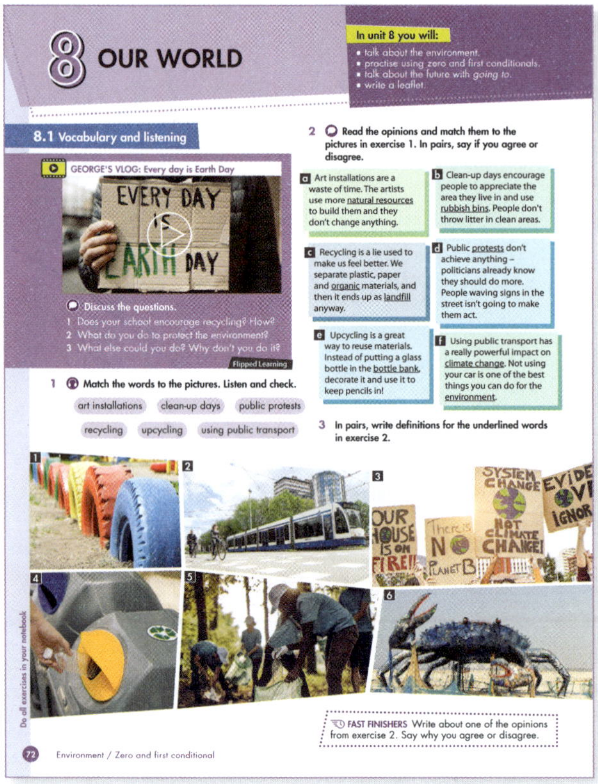

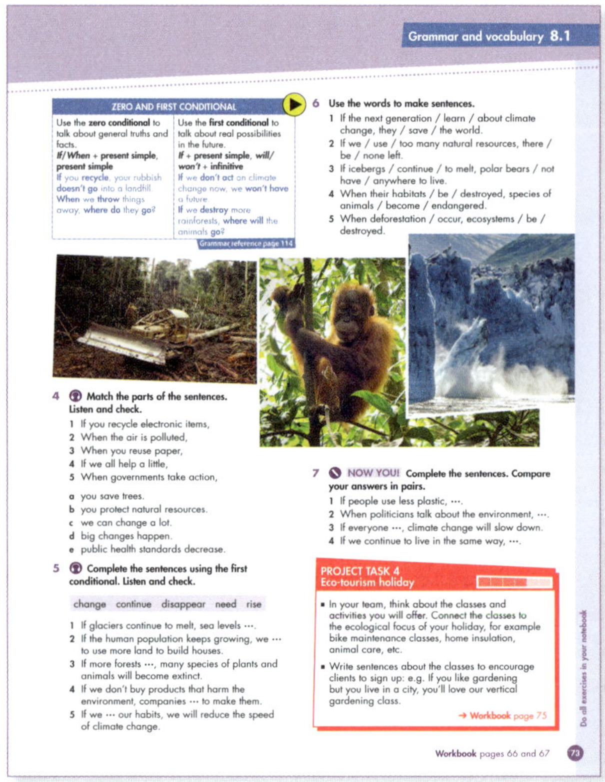

ANSWER KEY

Pages 72-73

1
1 upcycling
2 using public transport
3 public protests
4 recycling
5 clean-up days
6 art installations

2
a 6; *Student's own answers*
b 5; *Student's own answers*
c 4; *Student's own answers*
d 3; *Student's own answers*
e 1; *Student's own answers*
f 2; *Student's own answers*

3 *Student's own answers*

4
1 b
2 e
3 a
4 c
5 d

5
1 will rise
2 will need
3 disappear
4 won't continue
5 change

6
1 If the next generation learn about climate change, they will save the world.
2 If we use too many natural resources, there will be none left.
3 If icebergs continue to melt, polar bears won't have anywhere to live.
4 When their habitats are destroyed, species of animals become endangered.
5 When deforestation occurs, ecosystems are destroyed.

7 *Student's own answers*

Remind students to do all the exercises in their notebook

LESSON FOCUS

Grammar Zero and first conditional

Vocabulary Environment

Listening Matching short statements to key words with pictures; Matching and completing zero and first conditional sentences

Speaking Agreeing and disagreeing with statements about the environment; Completing conditional sentences about the environment with students' own ideas

Project task 4 Make a list of the classes and activities on offer

Resources

Teacher's i-solutions, Student's Book audio, Vlog and worksheets

Flipped Learning

GEORGE'S VLOG: Every day is Earth Day

- Make sure to set up the **Flipped Learning** work with the students beforehand. **See pages 20-23 for complete Flipped Learning guidelines.**
- Ask students to put the **Flipped Learning worksheets** on their desks and walk around to check how many have completed the **Flipped** task.
- In pairs or small groups, ask students to compare and check the *Before you watch…* and *While you watch…* exercises on the worksheet.
- Show students **George's Vlog** and ask volunteers to provide correct answers and clarify any doubts other students may have.
- Choose three or four students to read aloud their answers to the *After you watch…* exercises on the worksheet and encourage some class discussion.
- Move straight to exercise 1 on page 72.

Warmer

Watch George's Vlog and discuss the questions with the whole class. If you don't have video facilities, discuss the questions.

1 2.20 (See page 177 for transcripts) Tell students they will hear definitions for the words and phrases. Play the audio again if necessary.

2 Ask the students if they think the comments are realistic, idealistic or cynical.

3 Encourage students to guess unfamiliar vocabulary from the context and check their definitions.

FAST FINISHERS Students can complete this exercise alone or in pairs.

Flipped Learning

ZERO AND FIRST CONDITIONAL

Draw students' attention to the **Grammar table**. Remind students that they can use this as a quick reference while completing the exercises.

Show students the **Grammar animation** and/or refer students to the **Grammar reference** on page 114 for further information on form and use.

→ See page 23 for how to flip the **grammar lesson**

4 2.21 (See page 177 for transcripts) Tell the students that all the matched sentences are expressed in the zero conditional. If necessary, students can complete the exercise in pairs.

5 2.22 (See page 177 for transcripts) Refer students to the **Grammar table** as they do the exercise. When they have completed it, get them to match the pictures with sentences from this exercise.

6 Tell students that they are making first conditional sentences. When students have finished, ask how much they agree with the statements.

7 NOW YOU! Encourage students to give reasons for their answers, and agree or disagree with each other. Tell them you will ask for a summary of their discussion on one of the points after they've finished.

PROJECT TASK 4
Eco-tourism holiday

Put students in their teams to continue the **Project**. Remind students that they need to keep their project notes together in their **Workbook** (page 75) or in their own notebook.

→ See pages 24-27 **Projects**

FURTHER PRACTICE

Workbook pages 66-67

- **Grammar reference and practice** pages 91 and 96
- **Wordlist and exercises** pages 101 and 104

Remind students to do all the exercises in their notebook

CONTINUOUS ASSESSMENT Students can talk about the environment, and use zero and first conditional.

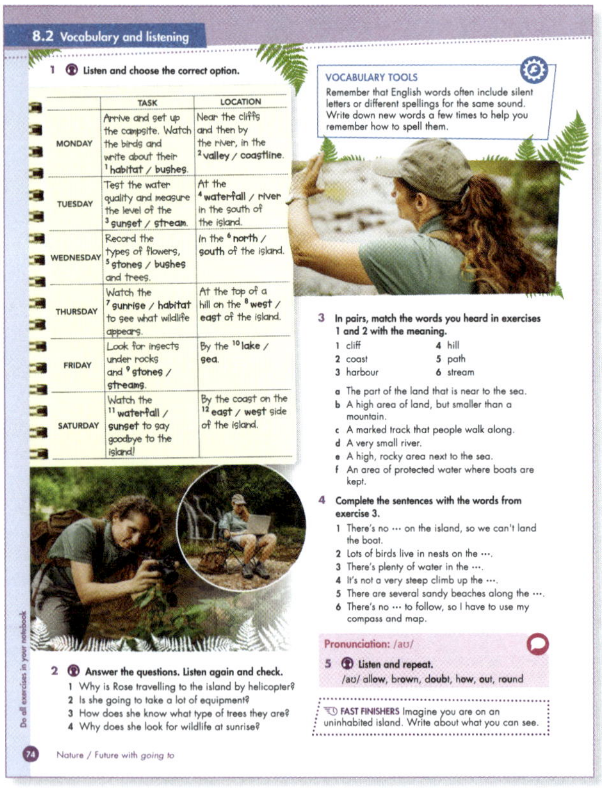

8.2 Vocabulary and listening

1 Listen and choose the correct option.

	TASK	LOCATION
MONDAY	Arrive and set up the campsite. Watch the birds and write about their [1] habitat / bushes.	Near the cliffs and then by the river, in the [2] valley / coastline.
TUESDAY	Test the water quality and measure the level of the [3] sunset / stream.	At the [4] waterfall / river in the south of the island.
WEDNESDAY	Record the types of flowers, [5] stones / bushes and trees.	In the [6] north / south of the island.
THURSDAY	Watch the [7] sunrise / habitat to see what wildlife appears.	At the top of a hill on the [8] west / east of the island.
FRIDAY	Look for insects under rocks and [9] stones / streams.	By the [10] lake / sea.
SATURDAY	Watch the [11] waterfall / sunset to say goodbye to the island!	By the coast on the [12] east / west side of the island.

VOCABULARY TOOLS
Remember that English words often include silent letters or different spellings for the same sound. Write down new words a few times to help you remember how to spell them.

2 Answer the questions. Listen again and check.
1 Why is Rose travelling to the island by helicopter?
2 Is she going to take a lot of equipment?
3 How does she know what type of trees they are?
4 Why does she look for wildlife at sunrise?

3 In pairs, match the words you heard in exercises 1 and 2 with the meaning.
1 cliff 2 coast 3 harbour 4 hill 5 path 6 stream
a The part of the land that is near to the sea.
b A high area of land, but smaller than a mountain.
c A marked track that people walk along.
d A very small river.
e A high, rocky area next to the sea.
f An area of protected water where boats are kept.

4 Complete the sentences with the words from exercise 3.
1 There's no ··· on the island, so we can't land the boat.
2 Lots of birds live in nests on the ···.
3 There's plenty of water in the ···.
4 It's not a very steep climb up the ···.
5 There are several sandy beaches along the ···.
6 There's no ··· to follow, so I have to use my compass and map.

Pronunciation: /aʊ/
5 Listen and repeat.
/aʊ/ allow, brown, doubt, how, out, round

FAST FINISHERS Imagine you are on an uninhabited island. Write about what you can see.

Do all exercises in your notebook

74 Nature / Future with going to

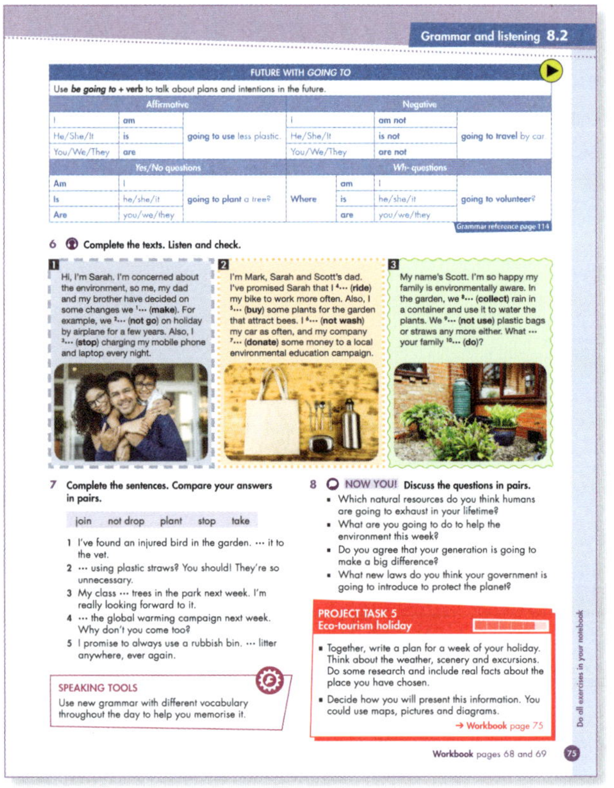

Grammar and listening 8.2

FUTURE WITH GOING TO
Use be going to + verb to talk about plans and intentions in the future.

Affirmative			Negative		
I	am	going to use less plastic.	I	am not	going to travel by car.
He/She/It	is		He/She/It	is not	
You/We/They	are		You/We/They	are not	
Yes/No questions			Wh- questions		
Am	I	going to plant a tree?	Where am	I	going to volunteer?
Is	he/she/it		is	he/she/it	
Are	you/we/they		are	you/we/they	

Grammar reference page 114

6 Complete the texts. Listen and check.

1 Hi, I'm Sarah. I'm concerned about the environment, so me, my dad and my brother have decided on some changes we [1]··· (make). For example, we [2]··· (not go) on holiday by airplane for a few years. Also, I [3]··· (stop) charging my mobile phone and laptop every night.

2 I'm Mark, Sarah and Scott's dad. I've promised Sarah that I [4]··· (ride) my bike to work more often. Also, I [5]··· (buy) some plants for the garden that attract bees. I [6]··· (not wash) my car as often, and my company [7]··· (donate) some money to a local environmental education campaign.

3 My name's Scott. I'm so happy my family is environmentally aware. In the garden, we [8]··· (collect) rain in a container and use it to water the plants. We [9]··· (not use) plastic bags or straws any more either. What ··· your family [10]··· (do)?

7 Complete the sentences. Compare your answers in pairs.
join not drop plant stop take
1 I've found an injured bird in the garden. ··· it to the vet.
2 ··· using plastic straws? You should! They're so unnecessary.
3 My class ··· trees in the park next week. I'm really looking forward to it.
4 ··· the global warming campaign next week. Why don't you come too?
5 I promise to always use a rubbish bin. ··· litter anywhere, ever again.

SPEAKING TOOLS
Use new grammar with different vocabulary throughout the day to help you memorise it.

8 NOW YOU! Discuss the questions in pairs.
- Which natural resources do you think humans are going to exhaust in your lifetime?
- What are you going to do to help the environment this week?
- Do you agree that your generation is going to make a big difference?
- What new laws do you think your government is going to introduce to protect the planet?

PROJECT TASK 5
Eco-tourism holiday
- Together, write a plan for a week of your holiday. Think about the weather, scenery and excursions. Do some research and include real facts about the place you have chosen.
- Decide how you will present this information. You could use maps, pictures and diagrams.
→ Workbook page 75

Do all exercises in your notebook

Workbook pages 68 and 69 75

ANSWER KEY

Pages 74-75

1
1 habitat
2 valley
3 stream
4 waterfall
5 bushes
6 north
7 sunrise
8 east
9 stones
10 lake
11 sunset
12 west

2
1 There's nowhere for a boat to dock safely (there's no harbour and the waves are too strong).
2 No, she travels light (she only takes only what she needs).
3 By looking at the leaves
4 Because it's easier for her to hide from the animals and observe them in their natural habitat.

3
1 e
2 a
3 f
4 b
5 c
6 d

4
1 harbour
2 cliff
3 stream
4 hill
5 coast
6 path

5 *Student's own answers*

6
1 are going to make
2 aren't going to go
3 am going to stop
4 am going to ride
5 am going to buy
6 am not going to wash
7 is going to donate
8 are going to collect
9 aren't going to use
10 is; going to do?

7
1 I am going to take
2 Are you going to stop
3 is going to plant
4 I am going to join
5 I am not going to drop

8 *Student's own answers*

Remind students to do all the exercises in their notebook

LESSON FOCUS

Grammar Future with *going to*

Vocabulary Nature

Listening Completing the weekly plan of a conservationist and answering questions; Completing texts about a family's plans to help look after the environment

Speaking A discussion of opinions about the future of the environment

Project task 5 Plan a week of activities and excursions

Resources

Teacher's i-solutions, Student's Book audio

Warmer

Think of a country with distinctive landscapes that students may know and describe it for them to guess. For example: *This country is very big. It's got deserts, famous beaches on the west coast, national parks with huge forests, one state that's very cold and one that's an island in the Pacific Ocean* (the USA). Students can continue the exercise in pairs or small groups.

1 2.23 (See page 177 for transcripts) Tell students that they are going to listen to a woman's travel itinerary for a trip to a remote island. Tell them to answer the questions and compare their answers. They can then play the audio again if they need to.

2 2.24 (See page 177 for transcripts) Tell students you will now play an interview with the same woman from exercise 1. Tell them to answer the questions and compare their answers. They can then play the audio again if they need to.

VOCABULARY TOOLS

Get students to read the **Vocabulary tool** and ask which of the nature words in the Nature **Wordlist** on page 120 has a silent letter (island).

3 Write the sentences from the audio to help them guess the words from context.

4 After students complete the exercise, ask them to use the words to describe places they know to each other.

Pronunciation

5 2.25 (See page 177 for transcripts) Remind students of the **Vocabulary tool** and ask which patterns make the same sound here ('ow' and 'ou') and which letter is silent in which word (the 'b' in doubt).

FAST FINISHERS Students can complete this exercise alone or in pairs.

FUTURE WITH *GOING TO*

Flipped Learning

Draw students' attention to the **Grammar table**. Remind students that they can use this as a quick reference while completing the exercises.

Show students the **Grammar animation** and/or refer students to the **Grammar reference** on page 114 for further information on form and use.

→ See page 23 for how to flip the **grammar lesson**

6 2.26 (See pages 177-178 for transcripts) Ask students to scan the texts to identify who is who in the photo (Sarah, Mark – her dad – and Scott – her brother). Refer them to the **Grammar table** to complete the texts before they listen to check.

7 Extend and personalise the exercise by asking student to write their own environmental resolutions.

SPEAKING TOOLS

Ask students to read the **Speaking tool** and encourage them to write more resolutions for themselves.

8 NOW YOU! Help students with any vocabulary they might need so that they can give developed personal answers to the questions.

PROJECT TASK 5
Eco-tourism holiday

Put students in their teams to continue the **Project**. Remind students that they need to keep their project notes together in their **Workbook** (page 75) or in their own notebook.

→ See pages 24-27 **Projects**

FURTHER PRACTICE

Workbook pages 68-69
- **Grammar reference and practice** pages 91 and 96
- **Wordlist and exercises** pages 101 and 104

Vocabulary and Grammar worksheets available to download and edit from the **Richmond** *Learning* **Platform**

→ See pages 38-39 **Mixed-ability classes**

Remind students to do all the exercises in their notebook

CONTINUOUS ASSESSMENT Students can talk about nature and use *going to* for the future.

8.3 Reading

1 Identify the environmental issues in the pictures. In pairs, say what problems they cause and how they can be stopped.

2 Read the article and complete it with the headings.
a Set an example.
b Drive and fly less.
c Be energy smart.
d Eat less meat.

READING TOOLS
Pay attention to numbers and statistics in reading texts. There will often be questions about them.

Global warming
Can we make a difference?

There are many threats to our environment, but most scientists agree that the biggest is global warming, and that we are mostly responsible. That is because we have filled the air with greenhouse gases: methane, nitrous oxide and especially carbon dioxide (CO_2), which trap heat in the atmosphere. We are seeing its effects already: melting glaciers, growing deserts and more frequent and severe extreme weather events. If this continues, ice near the poles will melt too. If that happens, sea levels will rise dramatically and many parts of the world will be underwater. What can we can do?

1…
Around 15% of human greenhouse gas emissions come from farmed animals. People who eat no meat save nearly a tonne of CO_2 a year. That's about a fifth of what the average person produces in a year. If we all reduce our meat consumption, we can make a big difference.

2…
Choosing not to use a car can reduce your emissions by 2.5 tonnes, but just using public transport more often also saves an enormous amount. Flying produces a lot of CO_2 too – about half a tonne for a five-hour flight.

3…
Energy is the biggest contributor to greenhouse gases. Households can make a big difference by using renewable energy, like solar, wind or hydropower. If a typical house uses solar power, it can save almost a tonne of CO_2 a year. But that's not an easy change for everyone to make. There are many ways to reduce the energy you use at home. Use energy-saving light bulbs, take shorter showers, put on warm clothes instead of turning on the heating, and turn things off when you're not using them.

4…
Some people don't believe that one person can make a difference. Others say they don't want to tell people what to do. But maybe you don't have to. Research shows that people tend to imitate each other. So, just by doing what you can, you're inspiring those around you to do the same.

Do all exercises in your notebook

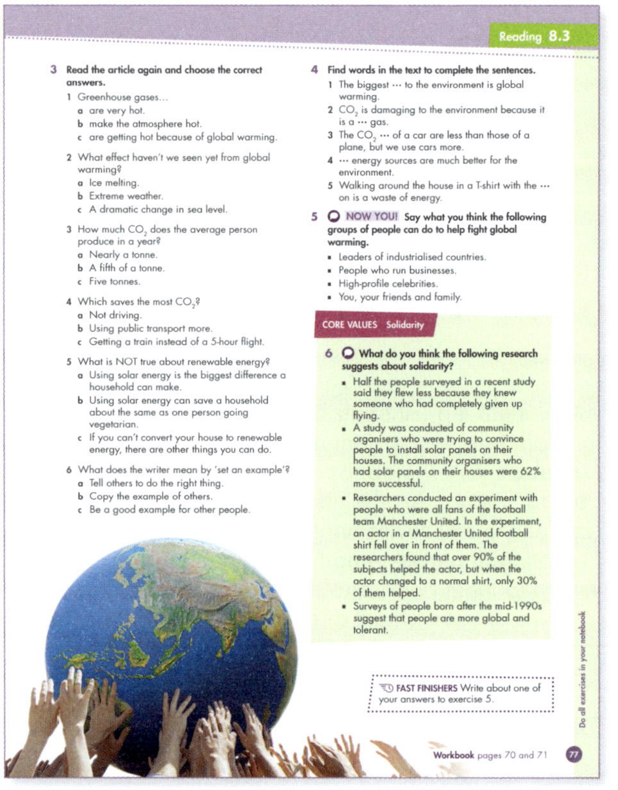

3 Read the article again and choose the correct answers.
1 Greenhouse gases…
a are very hot.
b make the atmosphere hot.
c are getting hot because of global warming.
2 What effect haven't we seen yet from global warming?
a Ice melting.
b Extreme weather.
c A dramatic change in sea level.
3 How much CO_2 does the average person produce in a year?
a Nearly a tonne.
b A fifth of a tonne.
c Five tonnes.
4 Which saves the most CO_2?
a Not driving.
b Using public transport more.
c Getting a train instead of a 5-hour flight.
5 What is NOT true about renewable energy?
a Using solar energy is the biggest difference a household can make.
b Using solar energy can save a household about the same as one person going vegetarian.
c If you can't convert your house to renewable energy, there are other things you can do.
6 What does the writer mean by 'set an example'?
a Tell others to do the right thing.
b Copy the example of others.
c Be a good example for other people.

4 Find words in the text to complete the sentences.
1 The biggest ··· to the environment is global warming.
2 CO_2 is damaging to the environment because it is a ··· gas.
3 The CO_2 ··· of a car are less than those of a plane, but we use cars more.
4 ··· energy sources are much better for the environment.
5 Walking around the house in a T-shirt with the ··· on is a waste of energy.

5 NOW YOU! Say what you think the following groups of people can do to help fight global warming.
- Leaders of industrialised countries.
- People who run businesses.
- High-profile celebrities.
- You, your friends and family.

CORE VALUES Solidarity

6 What do you think the following research suggests about solidarity?
- Half the people surveyed in a recent study said they flew less because they knew someone who had completely given up flying.
- A study was conducted of community organisers who were trying to convince people to install solar panels on their houses. The community organisers who had solar panels on their houses were 62% more successful.
- Researchers conducted an experiment with people who were all fans of the football team Manchester United. In the experiment, an actor in a Manchester United football shirt fell over in front of them. The researchers found that over 90% of the subjects helped the actor, but when the actor changed to a normal shirt, only 30% of them helped.
- Surveys of people born after the mid-1990s suggest that people are more global and tolerant.

FAST FINISHERS Write about one of your answers to exercise 5.

Do all exercises in your notebook

ANSWER KEY

Pages 76-77

1
1 Litter
Suggested answer: It pollutes our streets, parks and beaches, and some of the rubbish can be dangerous. People should take their litter home with them and recycle as much as possible, and they should be penalised enough to stop them doing it.
2 Air pollution or smog
Suggested answer: It causes serious health problems. We need to reduce our use of cars and try to use less polluting energy sources.
3 Industrial pollution
Suggested answer: It pollutes water sources, for example. There need to be bigger penalties to stop companies doing this.

2
1 d
2 b
3 c
4 a

3
1 b
2 c
3 c
4 a
5 a
6 c

4
1 threat
2 greenhouse
3 emissions
4 Renewable
5 heating

5 *Student's own answers*

6 *Student's own answers*

Remind students to do all the exercises in their notebook

LESSON FOCUS

Language in context Global warming

Core values Solidarity

Resources

Teacher's i-solutions, Student's Book audio

→ See pages 36-37 **Literature**

Warmer

Mime preparing for an activity and get students to guess what it is. For example, make your way past people seated at a cinema to find your seat (you're going to watch a film) put on a cap and goggles (you're going to go swimming), etc. Students can continue the activity in pairs or small groups.

1 After the discussion in pairs, elicit ideas that students came up with and discuss them as a class.

2 2.27 (See page 178 for transcripts) Ask students what environmental issue the text is about (global warming) and what answer it gives to the question it poses in the title (yes). Then get them to do the exercise and point out that the headings are all answers to the question at the end of the introduction.

READING TOOLS

Get students to read the **Reading tool** and get them to look ahead and see which question in exercise 3 asks for a number (question 3). Point out that statistics also help strengthen arguments.

3 Put students in pairs to compare answers. Check that they find evidence for their answers and against the other options in the text.

4 Before students start the exercise, ask if there is any unfamiliar vocabulary in the texts and ask them to help each other guess meaning from context. To extend the exercise, get them to find other vocabulary that they think is useful and write sentences with gaps to test each other.

5 NOW YOU! Encourage them to think of specific things that some people already do that others should do as well.

CORE VALUES Solidarity

6 Possible conclusions are that people, as the text suggests, tend to imitate each other, that it's more effective to lead by example, that people feel more inclined to help others if they feel they are similar to them in some way. Point out that younger generations have become less tribal and have a greater sense of the global community.

FAST FINISHERS Students can complete this exercise alone or in pairs.

FURTHER PRACTICE

Workbook pages 70-71

Remind students to do all the exercises in their notebook

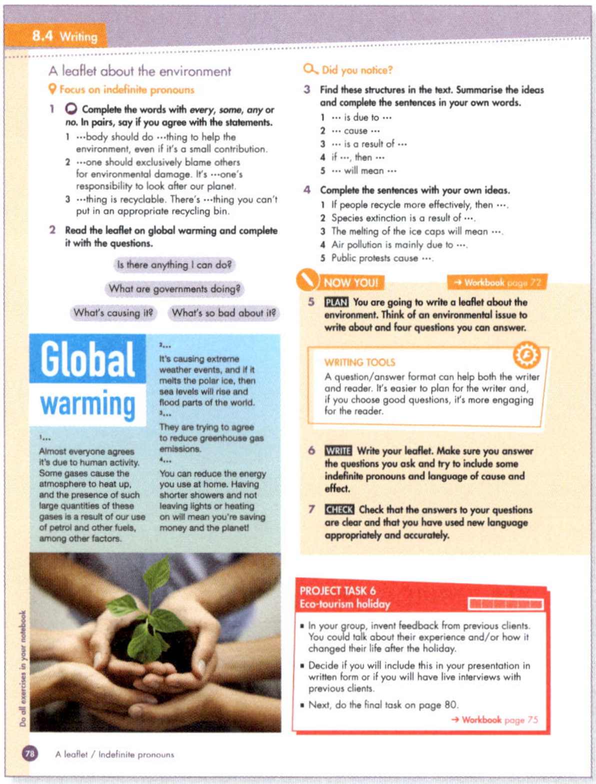
8.4 Writing

A leaflet about the environment

Focus on indefinite pronouns

1 Complete the words with *every, some, any* or *no*. In pairs, say if you agree with the statements.
1 …body should do …thing to help the environment, even if it's a small contribution.
2 …one should exclusively blame others for environmental damage. It's …one's responsibility to look after our planet.
3 …thing is recyclable. There's …thing you can't put in an appropriate recycling bin.

2 Read the leaflet on global warming and complete it with the questions.

Is there anything I can do? / What are governments doing? / What's causing it? / What's so bad about it?

Global warming

1… Almost everyone agrees it's due to human activity. Some gases cause the atmosphere to heat up, and the presence of such large quantities of these gases is a result of our use of petrol and other fuels, among other factors.

2… It's causing extreme weather events, and if it melts the polar ice, then sea levels will rise and flood parts of the world.

3… They are trying to agree to reduce greenhouse gas emissions.

4… You can reduce the energy you use at home. Having shorter showers and not leaving lights or heating on will mean you're saving money and the planet!

Did you notice?

3 Find these structures in the text. Summarise the ideas and complete the sentences in your own words.
1 … is due to …
2 … cause …
3 … is a result of …
4 if …, then …
5 … will mean …

4 Complete the sentences with your own ideas.
1 If people recycle more effectively, then ….
2 Species extinction is a result of ….
3 The melting of the ice caps will mean ….
4 Air pollution is mainly due to ….
5 Public protests cause ….

NOW YOU! → Workbook page 72

5 PLAN You are going to write a leaflet about the environment. Think of an environmental issue to write about and four questions you can answer.

WRITING TOOLS
A question/answer format can help both the writer and reader. It's easier to plan for the writer and, if you choose good questions, it's more engaging for the reader.

6 WRITE Write your leaflet. Make sure you answer the questions you ask and try to include some indefinite pronouns and language of cause and effect.

7 CHECK Check that the answers to your questions are clear and that you have used new language appropriately and accurately.

PROJECT TASK 6
Eco-tourism holiday
- In your group, invent feedback from previous clients. You could talk about their experience and/or how it changed their life after the holiday.
- Decide if you will include this in your presentation in written form or if you will have live interviews with previous clients.
- Next, do the final task on page 80.

→ Workbook page 75

Do all exercises in your notebook

78 A leaflet / Indefinite pronouns

ANSWER KEY

Page 78

1
1 Every; some
2 No; every
3 Any; no

2
1 What's causing it?
2 What's so bad about it?
3 What are governments doing?
4 Is there anything I can do?

3 *Student's own answers*

4 *Student's own answerss*

5 *Student's own answers*

6 *Student's own answers*

7 *Student's own answers*

FURTHER PRACTICE

Workbook page 72

LESSON FOCUS

Focus on Indefinite pronouns
Writing A leaflet about the environment
Project task 6 Invent feedback from previous clients
Resources
Teacher's i-solutions

Warmer

Write the groups of people mentioned in exercise 5 on page 77 on the board. Say some things one of the groups should do and have students guess which group you are describing. Students can continue the activity in pairs.

Focus on indefinite pronouns

1 Get students to compare answers in pairs and check their answers before they say if they agree.

2 After students complete the exercise, check that they understand all the vocabulary and ask if they think the leaflet is missing any important information that they would have included.

Did you notice?

3 Ask students which expressions have the cause at the beginning of the sentence and the effect at the end (cause, if…then, will mean).

4 Get students to compare answers in pairs and elicit popular class answers.

5 **PLAN** Put students in pairs or small groups to brainstorm possible environmental issues to write about. Get them to plan individually and then check each other's plans.

WRITING TOOLS

Get students to read the **Writing tool** and encourage them to use the format in their leaflet.

6 **WRITE** Before students start writing, make a checklist on the board of any elements related to content, structure, language and style that they should bear in mind.

7 **CHECK** Once students have checked their own leaflets, they can swap with a partner and check each other's.

PROJECT TASK 6
Eco-tourism holiday

Put students in their teams to continue the **Project**. Remind students that they need to keep their project notes together in their **Workbook** (page 75) or in their own notebook.

→ See pages 24-27 **Projects**

Remind students to do all the exercises in their notebook

 CONTINUOUS ASSESSMENT Students can use indefinite pronouns appropriately to write a leaflet about the environment.

Culture and communication 8.5

Disappearing villages

Discuss the questions.

1 What do you think will happen to the environment in the next 50 years?
2 What is your community doing to protect the environment?
3 What should your government do?
4 Who is responsible for stopping climate change, people or governments?

LISTENING TOOLS
When you have to write a difficult word in a listening task, don't worry about the spelling. Listen and write the word as well as you can, then correct the spelling when the audio has finished.

1 Listen and complete the texts.

1 KATIE
To solve big problems, we have to think outside the [1]···. Some people don't like the idea of genetically modified [2]···, but I believe that it's the best way to solve world [3]···. If we can [4]··· plants so they can adapt to difficult conditions, people will be able to [5]··· their own food.

2 DEREK
I go door to door and ask people to [1]··· petitions and [2]··· to politicians. I believe that [3]··· really do speak louder than words. If lots of people get [4]···, the government will talk about the idea. It doesn't always mean the laws will change, but it shows the politicians that people are interested in [5]··· issues.

3 EMMA
If we really want to [1]··· a stand against climate change, we have to [2]··· the next generation correctly. If people understand the effect their [3]··· has on the planet, society will change. So, education is the most important tool in the fight against [4]··· warming. By improving their [5]···, we can help our children to make a difference.

2 In pairs, say if you agree or disagree with the opinions in exercise 1.

Idioms and expressions

3 Match the expressions you heard with the meanings.
1 make a stand
2 actions speak louder than words
3 think outside the box

a When we imagine unusual solutions to a problem, or have new or original ideas.
b When we protest about or fight for something we believe in.
c Real change is a result of people taking action.

4 NOW YOU! Complete the sentences with your own ideas. Compare your sentences in pairs.
- If we really want to make a stand against plastic use, we ···.
- Actions speak louder than words, so we should ···.
- Governments need to think outside the box. For example, ···.

PAIRWORK
Student A: go to page 102
Student B: go to page 106

Unit 8 Review • page 97
Wordlist • pages 118–120

Do all exercises in your notebook

Idioms and expressions about taking action

Workbook page 73

79

ANSWER KEY

Page 79

1

1	2	3
1 box	**1** sign	**1** make
2 food	**2** letters	**2** educate
3 hunger	**3** actions	**3** behaviour
4 modify	**4** involved	**4** global
5 grow	**5** environmental	**5** understanding

2 *Student's own answers*

3 **1** b
2 c
3 a

FURTHER PRACTICE AND UNIT ASSESSMENT

Unit 8 Review **Student's Book** page 97
Workbook page 73
- Reflect on your learning Workbook page 73
- Grammar reference and practice pages 91 and 97
- Wordlist and exercises pages 101 and 104

Tests available to download and edit from the **Richmond** *Learning* **Platform**

➔ See pages 40-41 on **Assessment**

LESSON FOCUS

Idioms and expressions Taking action
Listening Completing three texts from people taking different stands to protect the environment
Speaking Completing sentences about the environment with students' own ideas

Resources
Teacher's i-solutions, Student's Book audio, Culture video worksheet

Disappearing villages

Video and worksheet available on the Richmond *Learning* **Platform**

- In pairs, ask students to compare/complete the *What I know...* exercises on the **Culture video worksheet**.
- Show students the **Culture video** and ask them to check/complete the *What I learned...* exercises on the worksheet. If students are completing the exercises for the first time, they will need to watch the video twice.
- In pairs, students compare answers.
- In small groups, tell students to complete/discuss the *What I wonder...* exercises on the worksheet.

Warmer

Watch the **Culture video** and discuss the questions with the whole class. If you don't have video facilities, simply discuss the questions.

LISTENING TOOLS

Get students to read the **Listening tool** and tell them to apply it in the next exercise.

1 2.28 (See page 178 for transcripts) Give students time to read the texts and guess answers. Play the audio, get them to compare answers and spelling in pairs and play it again if necessary before checking answers.

2 Monitor discussions and help with any new vocabulary. Bring up any comments students make that you think are of interest to the class.

Idioms and expressions

3 Get students to find the expressions in the texts to help them guess meanings.

4 NOW YOU! Ask around the class to find sentences that you think express important truths and that are original and interesting.

PAIRWORK **Student's Book** pages 102 and 106
See **Teacher's Book** page 152 for more information.
➔ See pages 30-33 **Mediation**

Remind students to do all the exercises in their notebook.

CONTINUOUS ASSESSMENT Students can use idioms and expressions about taking action.

Unit 8 Review

Unit 8 Review

1 Listen to 14-year-old Sarah talking about her Nature Clean-up project on her school radio and choose the correct answer.

1 Sarah organised a clean-up day because
  a there was a lot of plastic on the beach.
  b she did a project about pollution at school.
  c she was worried about climate change.

2 Nature Clean-up has become famous because
  a Sarah put notices asking for help.
  b Sarah talked about them on the local news.
  c Sarah writes a blog about the environment.

3 When they collect the litter
  a they put it all in rubbish bins.
  b they recycle as much as they can.
  c they put it in landfill away from the beach.

4 In the next few days, Sarah is going to
  a organise a protest to stop climate change.
  b make a suggestion to the local government.
  c try to save energy at home.

2 **Work in pairs. Your friend David is very interested in the environment, and it's his birthday next week. Talk about these ideas for a present and decide which you are going to buy him.**

> EXAM TIP
> Discuss ideas together and make suggestions. The language you use is more important than your ideas.

- a book about renewable energy
- a solar-powered light
- energy-saving light bulbs
- a visit to a local recycling plant
- a ticket to a talk about climate change
- a jacket made of upcycled materials

3 **Read and choose the correct sentences for gaps 1 to 4. There are two sentences you don't need.**

I didn't use to think about recycling or saving energy at home, but everything changed when I started learning about climate change at school. [1]… I talked to my mum and dad and we started recycling.

I also try to save energy at home. [2]… When I clean my teeth, I turn the tap off to save water. When it's not too cold, I walk to school because if you use the car less, you create less carbon dioxide. We also have a compost bin in the garden for all our organic waste. We use the compost to feed plants in the garden. [3]… That's really good for biodiversity.

I have a lot of ideas about how to protect the planet. I think it's really important to use renewable energy. Next month we're going to install a solar panel on the roof. [4]… There's an old bike in the garage that I'm going to make into a cool clock! I'm going to put it on my bedroom wall.

a If we don't stop deforestation, there won't be any trees left.
b I turn off the lights when I leave a room so I don't waste energy.
c I'm going to see a documentary about the melting glaciers on Friday.
d If you have flowers in your garden, they attract bees and other insects.
e I realised there were a lot of environmentally friendly things I could do at home.
f I'm also going to start reusing old items around the house.

Do all exercises in your notebook

External exam practice 97

Student's Book page 97

ANSWER KEY See page 181 for transcripts

1 2.44
1 a **2** c **3** b **4** b

2 *Student's own answers*

3 **1** e **2** b **3** d **4** f

Pairwork

Unit 8 • Student A

1 There is a competition at your school to find the best way to encourage environmentally friendly behaviour. Your team wants to start an education scheme for children so that they can educate their parents too. Use the headings and make notes about your idea.
How What Where Who Why

2 Present your idea to Student B and answer their questions.
My team is going to …

3 Listen to Student B's presentation and ask them questions about their idea.
What will you do if people don't change their behaviour?

4 Defend your idea. Tell Student B why your idea should win the competition. After you have both spoken, decide whose idea is the most effective.

Student's Book page 102

Unit 8 • Student B

1 There is a competition at your school to find the best way to encourage environmentally friendly behaviour. Your team wants to start a scheme that promotes using environmentally friendly transport. Use the headings and make notes about your idea.
How What Where Who Why

2 Listen to Student A's presentation and ask them questions about their idea.
What will you do if people don't change their behaviour?

3 Present your idea to Student A and answer their questions.
My team is going to …

4 Defend your idea. Tell Student A why your idea should win the competition. After you have both spoken, decide whose idea is the most effective.

Student's Book page 106

CEFR MEDIATION DESCRIPTOR

- **Facilitating collaborative interaction with peers**
  Students can collaborate in simple, practical tasks, asking what others think, making suggestions and understanding responses.

- **Defending ideas**
  Tell students that they have the same task and read it through with them. Give them time to work on their own and then encourage them to challenge each other's ideas constructively before trying to reach consensus on which they like more.

Remind students to do all the exercises in their notebook

Grammar reference

Unit 8 Grammar reference

Zero and first conditional

Use the **zero conditional** to talk about general truths and facts.	Use the **first conditional** to talk about real possibilities in the future.
***If/When* + present simple, present simple**	***If* + present simple, *will/won't* + infinitive**
If you **recycle**, your rubbish **doesn't go** into a landfill.	**If** we **don't act** on climate change now, we **won't have** a future.
When we **throw** things away, **where do** they **go**?	**If** we **destroy** more rainforests, **where will** the animals **go**?

We use the **first conditional** to talk about things that are likely to happen, and their possible consequences. It has two parts: ***If* + present simple, *will/won't* + infinitive.**

If I **eat** all this ice cream, I**'ll be** ill.

If it **doesn't rain** tomorrow, we**'ll go** to the park.

I**'ll call** you on my mobile **if** I'm late.

We can put either the ***if*** part or the ***will/won't*** part first. When the ***if*** part is first, we use a comma to separate the parts of the sentence.

If I have time, **I'll go** to the party.

OR

I'll go to the party **if I have** time.

The **zero conditional** is used to express absolute truths or facts. We often use to it talk about things that are certain to happen.

If you eat too much, **you put on** weight.

Babies cry when **they are** hungry.

If you touch the fire, **you get** burned.

Future with *going to*

Use ***be going to* + verb** to talk about plans and intentions in the future.

Affirmative			Negative		
I	am	**going to use** less plastic.	I	**am not**	**going to travel** by car.
He/She/It	is		He/She/It	**is not**	
You/We/They	are		You/We/They	**are not**	

Yes/No questions			Wh- questions			
Am	I	**going to plant** a tree?	**Where**	am	I	**going to volunteer**?
Is	he/she/it			is	he/she/it	
Are	you/we/they			are	you/we/they	

We use ***be going to*** to talk about future intentions.

I'**m going to finish** school and then study at university.

We'**re going to save** money for our holidays.

He'**s going to be** a lawyer when he grows up.

We can also use ***be going to*** for future predictions based on what we can see.

Watch out! That glass is **going to fall** over.

Oh no! The ball is **going to break** the window.

You're **going to have** an accident if you're not careful.

The choice of which future form to use is not always clear, and often more than one choice is appropriate with only small or even insignificant changes in meaning. Compare the following sentences.

Kelly **will probably win** the talent show.

Kelly **is probably going to win** the talent show.

(Very similar – ***be going to*** emphasises that the prediction is based on what we can see now.)

I'**m going to see** my cousins at the weekend.

I'**m seeing** my cousins at the weekend.

(Very similar – ***be going to*** suggests there may not be an arrangement with the cousins yet.)

I think it **will rain**.

It **might rain**.

(Very similar – both ***I think*** and ***might*** suggest uncertainty.)

Do all exercises in your notebook

114 **Workbook** pages 94–97

Student's Book page 114

Wordlist

Wordlist

UNIT 8

Environment

bottle bank
clean-up days
climate change
deforestation
ecosystems
endangered
extinct
glaciers
habitat
landfill
litter
natural resources
organic
polluted
protests
public transport
recycling
reuse
rubbish bins
sea levels
species
upcycling

Nature

beach
bush
cliff
coast
coastline
harbour
hill
island
lake
path
river
sea
stone
stream
sunrise
sunset
valley
waterfall

Global warming

atmosphere
carbon dioxide (CO_2)
damaging
desert
emissions
energy-saving light bulb
extreme weather
greenhouse gases
hydropower
melt
renewable energy
save energy
solar power
the poles
threat
tonne
waste energy

Do all exercises in your notebook

120 **Workbook** pages 102–104

Student's Book page 120

2.67 2.68 2.69

Remind students to do all the exercises in their notebook

PROJECT: Eco-tourism holiday

RECAP

- In this project, you have created and developed an eco-tourism holiday.
- In **units 7 and 8**, you practised using the present perfect. You also used zero and first conditionals and talked about the future with *going to*. You learnt vocabulary for transport, travel and the environment and you wrote a travel diary entry and a leaflet.
- Now you are ready to present your eco-tourism holiday to your class!

TASK 1 Define the basic elements of your holiday village.
TASK 2 Identify a focus and write a quiz for possible clients.
TASK 3 Write an example of a day at the holiday village.
TASK 4 Make a list of the classes and activities you will offer.
TASK 5 Plan a week of activities and excursions.
TASK 6 Invent feedback from previous clients.

FINAL TASK: Present your eco-tourism holiday

- In your group, look over the information you have created about your eco-tourism holiday. Check, correct and improve your texts.
- If you haven't already chosen one, think of a name for your holiday village.
- Decide how you are going to present your ideas to the class. You could include live interviews, pictures, maps, posters, timetables, etc.
- Together, think about who from your team will present which part of the information. Think about your role at the holiday village and create a personality for yourselves.
- When you are ready, present your eco-tourism holiday to the class.

USEFUL EXPRESSIONS

- Hello, we're the team from…
- We'd like to tell you all about…
- In this picture, you can see…
- This is a truly incredible experience because…
- As you will see, our feedback is always excellent!
- We hope to see you at … soon!

21ST CENTURY SKILLS

Flexibility

Often, being flexible can improve our relationships with others and the world around us. Although change can be scary, being flexible helps us to grow and learn. It can help us to see the world in new ways and find creative solutions.

Do all exercises in your notebook

EVALUATION

Answer the questions in your group.

1 Which presentation did you like the most? Why?
2 Which was the most environmentally friendly holiday?
3 Would you like to go on any of these holidays? Which one?
4 Do you think your family holiday habits might change in the future?

GO BEYOND

Staycations

We all know that travelling by airplane is bad for the environment, but we all need a holiday from time to time, so what should we do?

Every year, more and more people choose to have a 'staycation' or 'holistay'. This means going on holiday in your own country, or simply staying at home and acting like a tourist in your hometown. If you choose to stay in your own home, the trick is to totally change your normal routine. You could sleep in a tent in the garden, or even do an expensive extreme sport; you'll be saving lots of money on flights and hotels anyway! It's true that most people don't often visit the tourist attractions in their own town. There are also probably interesting places in the towns right next to yours. Why don't you find out?

Answer the questions in pairs.

1 Do you prefer to travel abroad or stay at home?
2 Would you like to have a staycation? Why?
3 Where in your country would be a good place to go on holiday?
4 Have you visited all of the tourist attractions where you live?

Do all exercises in your notebook

Workbook project task notes

PROJECT: Eco-tourism holiday

Team members

______ ______ ______

TASK 1

Eco-tourism definition: ______

Basic elements of our holiday village: ______

→ Student's book page 65

TASK 2

Focus of our holiday village: ______

Ideas for quiz: ______

→ Student's book page 67

TASK 3

One day in our holiday village: ______

Display ideas: ______

→ Student's book page 70

TASK 4

Classes and activities: ______

→ Student's book page 73

TASK 5

A week in our holiday village: ______

Display ideas: ______

→ Student's book page 75

TASK 6

Feedback ideas: ______

→ Student's book page 78

FINAL TASK

Name for our holiday village: ______

Presentation ideas: ______

My task: ______

→ Student's book page 80

Remind students to do all the exercises in their notebook

PROJECT FOCUS

→ See pages 24-27 **Projects**

Skills

- Collaborate to decide on the basic elements of an eco-tourism holiday
- Research online to make the holiday seem realistic
- Write a quiz to identify potential clients
- Write about a typical day at the village
- Write sentences to encourage clients to participate
- Write a week-long itinerary
- Write comments or interviews from imaginary clients
- Present the holiday
- Discuss evaluations of the project
- Read and discuss a text related to the project

CEFR mediation

Encouraging conceptual talk

Can ask group members for reasons for their views and can check for mutual understanding.

→ See pages 30-33 **Mediation**

Preparation Remind students to bring the elements they created in tasks 1-6 and their notes from **Workbook** project task notes pages 74-75. Get them to bring in their self-assessment diaries if they are writing them.

Recap

Put students in their groups and read through the **Recap** as a class. Draw their attention to the project tasks and the unit objectives and ask which task helped achieve which objectives. Make sure they have all the materials and notes that they need (see **Preparation**) for the **Final task**.

Final Task: Present your eco-tourism holiday

Tell students they are now going to present their eco-tourism holiday. Put them in their groups and direct their attention to the **21st century skill** (see next column).

Students will have a range of different materials and various options of how to present them. Make sure they know what resources they can use and how long they have to give the presentations before they start planning. Encourage them to use the **Useful expressions** as a guide and to make sure that the ways they choose to present the materials will be effective: visuals should be clear and visible to everyone; texts should be engaging; audience participation (e.g. quiz questions) should be considered; the presentation should be structured logically. Remind them that they are trying to sell their holidays!

Give them a time limit for preparation and for each presentation to ensure that they all have enough time and monitor them in preparation to make sure everyone is collaborating somehow. For each presentation, encourage audience responses where appropriate.

21ST CENTURY SKILLS

Read through the text with the students. Remind them that effective negotiating skills (see the first **project**) involve compromise and flexibility, and ask them to consider in what ways they have been flexible in this project so far. Tell them that effective collaboration requires each group member to contribute and defend their ideas, but also to listen to those of others and be prepared to concede at times.

→ See pages 28-29 **21st century skills**

Evaluation

Before students discuss the questions in their groups, give them time to prepare notes about their experience in the project. Remind students to be supportive and give constructive feedback to each other, and say which things they thought they did well and which they found most difficult. Monitor discussions, adding your own feedback where appropriate, and noting common observations to then convey to the class as a whole.

Have a class discussion about what students have learnt from the project, reminding them of the unit objectives, the **Core values** and the **Learning to learn tools** sections of units 7 and 8, as well as the **21st century skills** section of the **Project** pages.

If you have decided to use the evaluation exercise as a springboard for a student self-assessment diary (see **Evaluation** notes on page 77), give them time to do this now and remind them to refer to the **Reflect on your learning** section of the **Workbook** if they have one.

→ See pages 40-41 **Assessment**

Go beyond

Before students read the text, ask them what a *staycation* is and ask them to find the answer in the text if they don't already know. Then get them to discuss the questions below the text in pairs and listen to share any answers you think the whole class might be interested in.

Remind students to do all the exercises in their notebook

9 FARAWAY FRIENDS

At the start of each unit and lesson, explain to the students what the objectives are.

Language objectives

Grammar

Too* and *enough

- Students practise *too* and *enough* to talk about excess and sufficiency.

Can* and *be able to

- Students practise *can* and *be able to* to talk about ability.

Comparatives and superlatives

- Students practise comparing things, people and places.

Vocabulary

Shopping: *bargain, exchange, expensive, label, pocket, put on, receipt, sale, size, try on*

- Students practise vocabulary for shopping.

Hobbies: *chess, dance, gymnastics, magic tricks, play the guitar/piano, ride a horse/motorbike, skateboard, yoga*

- Students use vocabulary related to hobbies.

Adjectives: *afraid, alone, busy, calm, cheerful, delighted, disappointing, excellent, famous, fantastic, heavy, high, miserable, modern, old-fashioned, original, polite, positive, quiet, relaxed, rude, strange, traditional, unhappy*

- Students practise a range of adjectives for describing people and human experience.

Idioms and expressions

Telling lies: *tell a white lie, bend the truth, lie through your teeth*

- Students look at idioms and expressions in the context of three short monologues.

Recycled language

Adjectives with *-ing* and *-ed* endings, Infinitives, Questions with modal verbs, Linking expressions

Skills objectives

Speaking

- Students discuss their abilities.
- Students ask and answer questions using comparatives and superlatives.
- Students compare hobbies according to different criteria.
- Students compare opinions and experiences of lies.

Pronunciation: Students practise the /j/ sound individually and in words with different spellings.

Pairwork: Students use various mediation techniques to compare fact files about three pet dogs.

Listening

- Students listen to a monologue and a conversation between friends about shopping to answer questions and choose the correct options.
- Students listen to a girl comparing her abilities to a friend's to complete a text.
- Students listen to a girl talk about a cousin who has gone to live in another country.
- Students listen to three short monologues about lies.

Reading

- Students skim a text to offer an opinion based on its content.
- Students read in detail to find and correct false sentences.
- Students read to find linking expressions in context and determine their function.

Core values: Students reflect on the **core value** of **accepting differences** by speculating about reasons why people might like things that they don't like.

Writing

- Students focus on common language in informal emails.
- Students plan, write and check an email to a friend.

Focus on informal language

Learning to learn tools

SPEAKING TOOLS Students practise giving extended answers in speaking tasks to help develop their spoken English.	**LISTENING TOOLS** Students learn a technique to distinguish between *can* and *can't* at natural speed.
READING TOOLS Students practise recording useful vocabulary from texts for their own productive use.	**WRITING TOOLS** Students practise keeping lists of useful expressions at hand for when they write.

VOCABULARY TOOLS Students are reminded of the difference between *-ing* and *-ed* endings in adjectives.

Review task objectives: Flip cards

Review Task 1 Students make flip cards for each **grammar point** in the **Student's Book** and write cues on the front of each.

Review Task 2 Students complete the information on the back of their flip cards.

Review Task 3 Students use their flip cards with a friend.

Audiovisual objectives

Vlog: Students watch and listen to Emma talk about an old friend who's moved far away.

Culture: Students watch and listen to Emma talk about a mysterious, talented amateur photographer.

Grammar animations: Students are presented with visual presentations of the unit grammar.

Key competences

LC **Linguistic**
pages 82-89

MST **Mathematical and Science and Technology**
pages 85-87

DC **Digital**
pages 82-83, 85, 89

SCC **Social and Civic**
pages 83-89

CAE **Cultural awareness and expression**
pages 82-89

LL **Learning to learn**
pages 83-84, 87, 89

IE **Sense of initiative and entrepreneurship**
pages 83, 85, 88

→ See pages 42-43 **Key competences**

CEFR Mediation

9.1 Relaying specific information in writing
Can write specific information in short spoken texts.

9.2 Explaining data in writing
Can interpret and write about data in simple charts.

9.3 Facilitating communication in delicate situations and disagreements
Can recognise when difficulties occur in interaction and seek compromise and agreement.

9.4 Processing text in writing
Can pick out and reproduce key words and phrases from a short text.

9.5 Encouraging conceptual talk
Can ask what somebody thinks of a certain idea.

Review Encouraging conceptual talk
Can ask people to elaborate on points and check understanding of concepts.

Unit review Relaying specific information in writing
Can write specific information in short spoken texts.

Pairwork Note-taking
Can make simple notes with familiar subject matter and with the possibility of clarification.

→ See pages 30-33 **Mediation**

Remind students to do all the exercises in their notebook

9 FARAWAY FRIENDS

In unit 9 you will:
- talk about activities and places.
- use too, enough, can and be able to.
- practise using comparatives and superlatives.
- write an email.

9.1 Vocabulary and grammar

EMMA'S VLOG: Old friends

Discuss the questions.
1 Who do you know that lives in a different country?
2 Do you ever keep in touch with people you meet on holiday? Why?
3 What common free time activities are there in your country?

Flipped Learning

1 Listen and answer the questions.
1 How did Jane and Taylor meet?
2 How do they keep in touch?
3 What activities do they do together?
4 What did Jane buy yesterday?
5 Which item of clothing was very cheap?

2 Listen and choose the correct words.
1 The price isn't on the **sale** / **label**. I'll ask the shop assistant.
2 That's too **exchange** / **expensive**. I don't have enough money.
3 I love **putting on** / **trying on** clothes, even if I don't buy them!
4 I don't think that's the right **size** / **bargain** for you. It looks too small.
5 If you want to take it back, just keep the **pocket** / **receipt**.

TOO AND ENOUGH

Use **too** to say that something is more than needed. It goes before an adjective. These shoes are **too** small. Don't buy it. It's **too** expensive.	Use **enough** to say that something is or isn't sufficient. It can go before a noun or after an adjective. These trousers aren't long **enough**. Yes, we have **enough** money.

Grammar reference page 115

3 Complete the sentences with *too* or *enough*.
1 You can't wear shorts this weekend; it's not ··· **(hot)**.
2 These shoes are massive! They're ··· **(big)** for me.
3 The shop is going to close! We don't have ··· **(time)**.
4 You can reach it; you're ··· **(tall)**.
5 I can't take the T-shirt off! It's ··· **(small)**!
6 These jeans are ··· **(short)**.

FAST FINISHERS Write about the last time you went shopping. What did you buy?

Do all exercises in your notebook

82 Shopping / Too and enough / Hobbies / Can and be able to

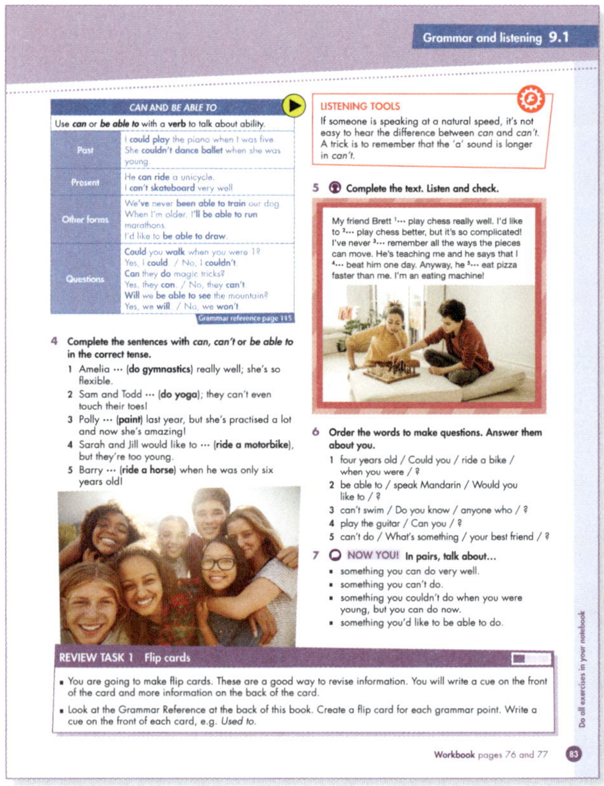

Grammar and listening 9.1

CAN AND BE ABLE TO

Use *can* or *be able to* with a verb to talk about ability.

Past	I **could play** the piano when I was five. She **couldn't dance** ballet when she was young.
Present	He **can ride** a unicycle. I **can't skateboard** very well.
Other forms	We've never **been able to train** our dog. When I'm older, I'**ll be able to run** marathons. I'd like to **be able to draw**.
Questions	**Could** you walk when you were 1? Yes, I **could**. / No, I **couldn't**. **Can** they do magic tricks? Yes, they **can**. / No, they **can't**. **Will** we **be able to** see the mountain? Yes, we **will**. / No, we **won't**.

Grammar reference page 115

4 Complete the sentences with *can*, *can't* or *be able to* in the correct tense.
1 Amelia ··· **(do gymnastics)** really well; she's so flexible.
2 Sam and Todd ··· **(do yoga)**; they can't even touch their toes!
3 Polly ··· **(paint)** last year, but she's practised a lot and now she's amazing!
4 Sarah and Jill would like to ··· **(ride a motorbike)**, but they're too young.
5 Barry ··· **(ride a horse)** when he was only six years old!

LISTENING TOOLS

If someone is speaking at a natural speed, it's not easy to hear the difference between *can* and *can't*. A trick is to remember that the 'a' sound is longer in *can't*.

5 Complete the text. Listen and check.

My friend Brett [1]··· play chess really well. I'd like to [2]··· play chess better, but it's so complicated! I've never [3]··· remember all the ways the pieces can move. He's teaching me and he says that I [4]··· beat him one day. Anyway, he [5]··· eat pizza faster than me. I'm an eating machine!

6 Order the words to make questions. Answer them about you.
1 four years old / Could you / ride a bike / when you were / ?
2 be able to / speak Mandarin / Would you like to / ?
3 can't swim / Do you know / anyone who / ?
4 play the guitar / Can you / ?
5 can't do / What's something / your best friend / ?

7 NOW YOU! In pairs, talk about...
- something you can do very well.
- something you can't do.
- something you couldn't do when you were young, but you can do now.
- something you'd like to be able to do.

REVIEW TASK 1 Flip cards
- You are going to make flip cards. These are a good way to revise information. You will write a cue on the front of the card and more information on the back of the card.
- Look at the Grammar Reference at the back of this book. Create a flip card for each grammar point. Write a cue on the front of each card, e.g. *Used to*.

Do all exercises in your notebook

Workbook pages 76 and 77 83

ANSWER KEY

Pages 82-83

1
1 Jane was visiting her grandparents.
2 They message each other and chat online.
3 They like to listen to music and go shopping.
4 She bought a jacket.
5 A skirt

2
1 label
2 expensive
3 trying on
4 size
5 receipt

3
1 hot enough
2 too big
3 enough time
4 tall enough
5 too small
6 too short

4
1 can do gymnastics
2 can't do yoga
3 couldn't paint
4 be able to ride a motorbike
5 could ride a horse

5
1 can
2 be able to
3 been able to
4 will be able to
5 can't

6
1 Could you ride a bike when you were four years old?
Student's own answers
2 Would you like to be able to speak Mandarin?
Student's own answers
3 Do you know anyone who can't swim?
Student's own answers
4 Can you play the guitar?
Student's own answers
5 What's something your best friend can't do?
Student's own answers

7 *Student's own answers*

Remind students to do all the exercises in their notebook

LESSON FOCUS

Grammar *Too* and *enough*; *Can* and *be able to*
Vocabulary Shopping; hobbies
Listening A conversation between friends about shopping; A girl comparing her abilities to a friend's
Speaking A discussion of students' abilities
Review task 1 Make flip cards for each grammar point in the Student's Book

Resources
Teacher's i-solutions, Student's Book audio, Vlog and worksheet

Preparation Cards for each student to make flip cards for each grammar point (21 cards each)

Flipped Learning

EMMA'S VLOG: Old friends

- Make sure to set up the **Flipped Learning** work with the students beforehand. **See pages 20-23 for complete Flipped Learning guidelines.**
- Ask students to put the **Flipped Learning worksheets** on their desks and walk around to check how many have completed the Flipped task.
- In pairs or small groups, ask students to compare and check the *Before you watch…* and *While you watch…* exercises on the worksheet.
- Show students **Emma's Vlog** and ask volunteers to provide correct answers and clarify any doubts other students may have.
- Choose three or four students to read aloud their answers to the *After you watch…* exercises on the worksheet and encourage some class discussion.
- Move straight to exercise 1 on page 82.

Warmer

Watch Emma's Vlog and discuss the questions with the whole class. If you don't have video facilities, simply discuss the questions.

1 2.29 (See page 178 for transcripts) Tell students they are going to listen to a girl talking about a close friend. Ask them what the two girls are doing in the photo. Give them time to read the questions before playing the audio so that they can check their answers.

2 2.30 (See page 178 for transcripts) Let students read the sentences and choose the options they think are correct before playing the audio.

Flipped Learning

TOO AND ENOUGH

Draw students' attention to the **Grammar table**. Remind students that they can use this as a quick reference while completing the exercises.

Show students the **Grammar animation** and/or refer students to the **Grammar reference** on page 115 for further information on form and use.

→ See page 23 for how to flip the **grammar lesson**

3 Refer students to the **Grammar table** as they do the exercise. Tell them to be careful with word order. Give them more practice by asking them to write a list of various types of things (clothing brands, singers, TV shows, foods, etc.) that they don't like and say why using *too* or *enough*.

FAST FINISHERS Students can complete this exercise alone or in pairs.

Flipped Learning

CAN AND BE ABLE TO

Draw students' attention to the **Grammar table**. Remind students that they can use this as a quick reference while completing the exercises.

Show students the **Grammar animation** and/or refer students to the **Grammar reference** on page 115 for further information on form and use.

→ See page 23 for how to flip the **grammar lesson**

4 Refer students to the **Grammar table** as they do the exercise.

LISTENING TOOLS

Get students to read the **Listening tool**. Say sentences with *can* and *can't* at natural speed and get them to tell you which you said.

5 2.31 (See page 178 for transcripts) Ask students what the two friends are doing in the photo (playing chess). Encourage them to look for textual clues like infinitives, auxiliaries and time expressions to help them decide which verb form to use.

6 Check the questions as a class before putting students into pairs to answer them.

7 NOW YOU! After students have finished the exercise, ask volunteers to choose one thing to talk about and have the class guess which it is. Encourage the class to ask further questions.

REVIEW TASK 1 Flip cards

Tell students they will do this exercise alone and later exchange cards. Hand out the cards and point them to the **Grammar reference** pages at the back of the **Student's Book** for their cues.

FURTHER PRACTICE

Workbook pages 76-77
- **Grammar reference and practice** pages 92-93 and 97
- **Wordlist and exercises** pages 101 and 104

Remind students to do all the exercises in their notebook

CONTINUOUS ASSESSMENT Students can talk about shopping and hobbies, and use *too*, *enough*, *can* and *be able to*.

9.2 Listening and vocabulary

1 Listen and choose the correct answer.
1 How did Julie feel when her cousin left England?
a Afraid and alone.
b Calm but unhappy.
c Cheerful and positive.
2 What hobbies do they both have?
a They both like hanging out at home.
b They both like sunbathing and barbecues.
c They both like eating pizza.
3 What was amazing about the photo?
a It was the same, but it looked lighter.
b It was the same bridge, but longer.
c The weather was so nice!
4 How does John feel in his new city?
a He loves living there.
b He hates living there.
c He's starting to enjoy living there.

Pronunciation: /j/
2 Listen and repeat.
/j/ uniform, useful, year, yes, you, young

3 In pairs, match the adjectives to their opposites.

1	excellent	a	old-fashioned
2	delighted	b	disappointing
3	modern	c	polite
4	rude	d	quiet
5	busy	e	miserable

VOCABULARY TOOLS
Remember that adjectives that end in *-ing* describe things, and adjectives that end in *-ed* describe emotions. You probably mean to say *I am bored*, not *I am boring*!

4 Use the words below to complete the sentences.

famous fantastic heavy high original relaxed strange traditional

1 I feel ··· when I'm with my best friend. We laugh a lot and I feel totally ···.
2 The buildings in my town are very ···, with long windows and really ··· roofs.
3 The bridge in my city is really ···. It was difficult to build because it's so ···.
4 There's a sculpture in my aunt's city. It's really ··· and ···. Not many people like it!

FAST FINISHERS Describe how you feel today and what you can see around you.

Do all exercises in your notebook

84 Adjectives / Comparatives and Superlatives

Grammar and vocabulary 9.2

COMPARATIVES AND SUPERLATIVES

Use **comparative** + **than** to compare two things, people, places. I am **taller than** my best friend.	Use **the** + **superlative** to compare three or more things, people or places. My brother is **the tallest** person in my family.

Comparatives and superlatives: spelling

	Comparatives	Superlatives
One syllable	add *-er* cheap → cheaper	add *-est* cheap → cheapest
One syllable ending in *-e*	add *-r* nice → nicer	add *-st* nice → nicest
One syllable ending in vowel + consonant	double consonant and add *-er* big → bigger	double consonant and add *-est* big → biggest
Two syllables ending in *-y*	delete *-y* and add *-ier* happy → happier	delete *-y* and add *-iest* happy → happiest
Three or more syllables	add *more* more expensive	add *most* most expensive
Irregular forms	good → better bad → worse	good → best bad → worst

Grammar reference page 116

5 Copy and complete the table.

Adjective	Comparative	Superlative
delicious	more delicious than	the most delicious
heavy	···	···
large	···	···
slow	···	···
hot	···	···
amazing	···	···

6 Complete the sentences. Listen and check.

bad beautiful dark good long old tall

1 My friend Tammy is a little ··· than me; she's 15 years old.
2 My hair is ··· than hers, but her hair is ··· than mine.
3 She lives in Cologne, in Germany. The weather there is ··· than in my town!
4 I live in Lincoln, in England. I think it's the ··· city in the world.
5 Cologne and Lincoln both have cathedrals, but the cathedral in her city is ···.
6 I was so sad when she moved away from England. It was the ··· day ever!

7 Use the information to write sentences about the two landmarks.

Lincoln Cathedral was taller than Cologne Cathedral

LINCOLN CATHEDRAL	COLOGNE CATHEDRAL
Building started: 1072	**Building started:** 1248
Tallest building in the world: 1311–1548 (238 years)	**Tallest building in the world:** 1880–1884 (4 years)
Number of steps to viewing platform: 338	**Number of steps to viewing platform:** 533
Size: 5,000 m²	**Size:** 8,000m²
Visitors: 210,000 people a year	**Visitors:** 6,000,000 people a year
Height: 83m (160m before the spire fell)	**Height:** 157m

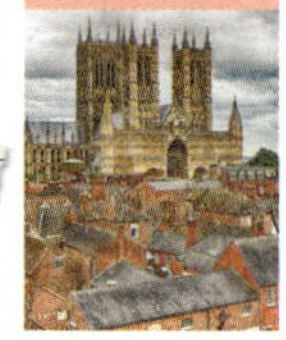

8 NOW YOU! Complete the questions and answer them in pairs.
- Who / tall / person in your class?
- Where / quiet / room in your house?
- Who / funny / friend?
- Which sport / popular / in your school?

REVIEW TASK 2 Flip cards
- Now you are going to complete the information on the back of your flip cards. Include example sentences and information about how and when to use the grammar point. Read the information a few times to memorise it.
- Think about how you can display the information. Use timelines, pictures, sentences and/or words to summarise the most important information.

Do all exercises in your notebook

Workbook pages 78 and 79 85

ANSWER KEY

Pages 84-85

1 **1** a **2** c **3** b **4** c

2 *Student's own answers*

3 **1** b **2** e **3** a **4** c **5** d

4
1 fantastic; relaxed
2 traditional; high
3 famous; heavy
4 strange; original

5

Adjective	Comparative	Superlative
delicious	more delicious than	the most delicious
heavy	heavier than	the heaviest
large	larger than	the largest
slow	slower than	the slowest
hot	hotter than	the hottest
amazing	more amazing than	the most amazing

6
1 older
2 darker; longer
3 better
4 most beautiful
5 taller
6 worst

7 *Student's own answers*

8 *Student's own answers*

Remind students to do all the exercises in their notebook

LESSON FOCUS

Grammar Comparatives and superlatives

Vocabulary Adjectives

Listening Answering multiple-choice questions about a boy who has gone to live in another country

Speaking Asking and answering questions using comparatives and superlatives

Review task 2 Complete the information on the back of the flip cards

Resources

Teacher's i-solutions, Student's Book audio

Preparation Students' own flip cards

Warmer

Put students in pairs. Tell them you are going to give them an adjective and they have to write a synonym and an antonym as quickly as possible. Continue with more adjectives.

1 2.32 (See page 178 for transcripts) Tell students they are going to listen to a girl talking about her cousin. Get them to read the questions, look at the pictures and guess what has happened. Play the audio for them to answer the questions and check their guesses.

Pronunciation

2 2.33 (See page 179 for transcripts) Point out that the tongue doesn't touch the palate when we make this sound but that it goes slightly higher than for an 'i' sound.

3 When students have done the exercise, ask them to find adjectives from exercise 1 and see if they can find opposites (e.g. *afraid/fearless, alone/accompanied, calm/anxious, unhappy/cheerful, positive/negative*).

VOCABULARY TOOLS

Get students to read the **Vocabulary tool** and ask them to find examples of three similar words about things or emotions in exercises 3 and 4 (*delighted, disappointing* and *relaxed*).

4 When students have completed the exercise, ask them to write personal sentences about themselves using any new adjectives in their notebooks.

FAST FINISHERS Students can complete this exercise alone or in pairs.

Flipped Learning

COMPARATIVES AND SUPERLATIVES

Draw students' attention to the **Grammar table**. Remind students that they can use this as a quick reference while completing the exercises.

Show students the **Grammar animation** and/or refer students to the **Grammar reference** on page 116 for further information on form and use.

→ See page 23 for how to flip the **grammar lesson**

5 Get students to refer to the **Grammar table** as they do the exercise.

6 2.34 (See page 179 for transcripts) Get students to pencil in possible answers before you play the audio for them to check their answers.

7 Get students to compare their sentences with a partner to see how many they have in common.

8 NOW YOU! Check students' questions are correct before they ask and answer them in pairs.

REVIEW TASK 2 Flip cards

You could put students in pairs or small groups to brainstorm ideas of what to include and how, but make sure they each produce their own flip cards and encourage them to do it in a way that supports their learning style.

FURTHER PRACTICE

Workbook pages 78-79
- **Grammar reference and practice** pages 92-93 and 97
- **Wordlist and exercises** pages 101 and 104

Vocabulary and Grammar worksheets available to download from the **Richmond***Learning***Platform**

→ See page 38-39 **Mixed-ability classes**

Remind students to do all the exercises in their notebook

CONTINUOUS ASSESSMENT Students can use adjectives and their comparative and superlative forms.

9.3 Reading

1 Match the hobbies with the pictures. In pairs, say which you like and which you think is the most popular.

birdwatching crafts fishing playing music reading

2 Read about the three hobbies and say which you think is the most unusual.

3 Read the article again and decide if the sentences are true or false. Correct the false ones.

1 Air guitar is a way of playing guitar.
2 There is more than one criterion in the air guitar world championship.
3 Trainspotters note and share information about trains.
4 Trainspotters now mostly take computers to note the details of the trains they spot.
5 The winner of the Wisconsin mooing competition is the one who moos the loudest.
6 The mooing competition probably advantages some people over others.

Do all exercises in your notebook

86 Language in context / Linking language

UNUSUAL HOBBIES

Air guitar

This may seem more like something everyone does sometimes when we're at home listening to music and we think no one is watching. All you do is pretend to play the guitar while you listen to music. In fact, for some people it's a very serious hobby, and there is even a world championship every year in Finland. The winner is the person who looks the most realistic and shows the most charisma and art in their 'playing'. And the prize is, of course, a real electric guitar. So why not start training? It's very easy – anyone can do it. And it's absolutely free!

MOOING

Can you moo like a cow? Well, if you're good enough at it, maybe you can go to the US state of Wisconsin, where they have contests of who can moo most like a real cow. Although perhaps it's not as varied or artistic as air guitar, the prizes can still be generous. In 2010, ten-year-old Austin Siok beat 80 contestants to win $1000. Not surprisingly, these contests take place in rural areas with lots of cows, so if you're a city kid it'll probably be a bit more difficult for you. But in an age where you can find all sorts of strange videos on the internet, maybe you'll be able to find some good 'mooers' to copy.

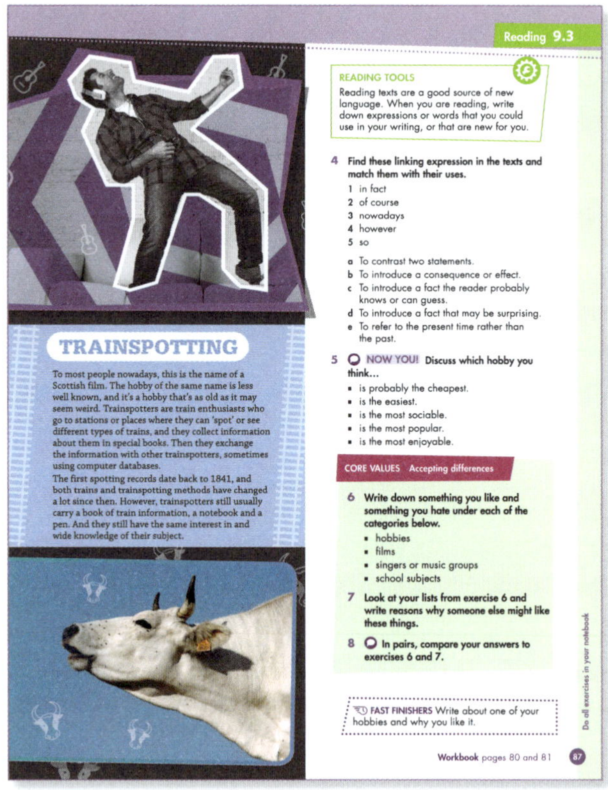

Reading 9.3

TRAINSPOTTING

To most people nowadays, this is the name of a Scottish film. The hobby of the same name is less well known, and it's a hobby that's as old as it may seem weird. Trainspotters are train enthusiasts who go to stations or places where they can 'spot' or see different types of trains, and they collect information about them in special books. Then they exchange the information with other trainspotters, sometimes using computer databases.

The first spotting records date back to 1841, and both trains and trainspotting methods have changed a lot since then. However, trainspotters still usually carry a book of train information, a notebook and a pen. And they still have the same interest in and wide knowledge of their subject.

READING TOOLS

Reading texts are a good source of new language. When you are reading, write down expressions or words that you could use in your writing, or that are new for you.

4 Find these linking expression in the texts and match them with their uses.

1 in fact
2 of course
3 nowadays
4 however
5 so

a To contrast two statements.
b To introduce a consequence or effect.
c To introduce a fact the reader probably knows or can guess.
d To introduce a fact that may be surprising.
e To refer to the present time rather than the past.

5 NOW YOU! Discuss which hobby you think…

- is probably the cheapest.
- is the easiest.
- is the most sociable.
- is the most popular.
- is the most enjoyable.

CORE VALUES Accepting differences

6 Write down something you like and something you hate under each of the categories below.

- hobbies
- films
- singers or music groups
- school subjects

7 Look at your lists from exercise 6 and write reasons why someone else might like these things.

8 In pairs, compare your answers to exercises 6 and 7.

FAST FINISHERS Write about one of your hobbies and why you like it.

Workbook pages 80 and 81 87

Do all exercises in your notebook

ANSWER KEY

Pages 86-87

1 **1** playing music
2 reading
3 fishing
4 crafts
5 birdwatching

2 *Student's own answers*

3 **1** False. It's pretending to play the guitar while listening to music.
2 True
3 True
4 False. They still usually use a notebook and a pen, though they sometimes record the information on computer databases to exchange it.
5 False. It's the one who can moo most like a real cow.
6 True

4 **1** d **2** c **3** e **4** a **5** b

5 *Student's own answers*

6 *Student's own answers*

7 *Student's own answers*

8 *Student's own answers*

Remind students to do all the exercises in their notebook

LESSON FOCUS

Language in context Linking language

Core values Accepting differences

Resources

Teacher's i-solutions, Student's Book audio

Preparation Bring in a survey of most popular hobbies that includes those in exercise 1

→ See pages 36-37 **Literature**

Warmer

Think of different categories of hobbies and put students in pairs to list as many as they can in a limited time, for example: artistic hobbies, things people collect, non-competitive sports, hobbies that require no equipment, etc.

1 Once they've decided which they think is the most popular, read out the results of the survey you have brought in and ask them if they can think of an explanation for any of the results that they find surprising.

2 2.35 (See page 179 for transcripts) Get students to look first at the pictures and guess what the hobbies are. Then let them read to check their guesses and decide which they think is the most unusual.

3 Get students to compare their answers in pairs.

READING TOOLS

Get students to read the **Reading tool** and ask if there are any words or expressions they particularly like in the text.

4 Students may know the expressions without having to look at the text, but highlight them in the text to show how they fit into sentences.

5 NOW YOU! After students finish discussing their ideas, elicit answers and ask if they would like to try any of the hobbies. Ask them what other unusual hobbies they know of.

CORE VALUES Accepting differences

6 You could get students to come up with ideas in pairs but encourage them to write their own choices.

7 Encourage students to think of more than one reason for each.

8 Ask students to help each other think of reasons why someone might like the things they said they hated. Point out that trying to understand why someone might like something that you really do not like can help us to accept differences. Explain that this can help us to fulfil and enjoy our roles in a diverse and global society.

FAST FINISHERS Students can complete this exercise alone or in pairs.

FURTHER PRACTICE

Workbook pages 80-81

Remind students to do all the exercises in their notebook

CONTINUOUS ASSESSMENT Students can understand a text about unusual hobbies.

9.4 Writing

An email to a friend

Focus on informal language

1 Look at the expressions and decide if they normally go at the beginning or the end of an email.

1 Looking forward to seeing you!
2 I hope all's well with you and your family.
3 Hope to hear from you soon.
4 Sorry for not writing earlier.
5 Anyway, that's all for now.
6 Glad to hear you're all well.

2 Read the email and say why Sophie is writing.

To: Juana From: Sophie

Hi Juana,

It was great to hear from you! I had a fantastic time at that sports camp, and I was really glad to get your email. So you're coming to Brussels?

The hotel you sent the link for is right near our house, so if you like, my Dad and I can meet you there on Saturday and show you the sights. Brussels is probably a bit smaller than Madrid, so we'll be able to see most of it in one day. Then we could have 'moules-frites' for dinner – that's mussels with chips, and it's one of our most famous dishes.

Anyway, I'm glad you're coming. I think you'll love Brussels! Let me know if there's anything specific you want to do or see, and I'll see if we can arrange it.

Bye for now,

Sophie

Did you notice?

3 Which words or expressions does Sophie use to…

1 react to receiving Juana's email?
2 check understanding of news from Juana's email?
3 introduce an offer of help?
4 introduce a suggestion for something for them to do together?
5 mark the return to an earlier idea or to start the end of a conversation?
6 show pleasure on hearing some news?
7 ask for information?
8 sign off?

4 Say what the purpose of each paragraph is.

NOW YOU! → Workbook page 82

5 PLAN You are going to write an email to a friend who's coming to visit. Think of a name for your friend and where they're from so you can write your email. Then think of some things you can do to help and suggestions for their visit.

WRITING TOOLS
Make a list of useful common expressions for emails. Keep it next to your computer to help you when you're writing.

6 WRITE Write your email. Use the list of expressions from exercises 1 and 3 and make sure your final comments make it clear what the next communication will be.

7 CHECK Check that you have used the expressions correctly and ask yourself: would your friend feel happy and informed on reading your email?

REVIEW TASK 3 Flip cards

- Use your flip cards with a friend. They will show you only the cue on the front of the card. You have to remember as much of the information from the back of the card as you can.
- Your friend should tell you if you are correct and help you remember the parts you have forgotten. This is a great activity to do before an exam.

Do all exercises in your notebook

88 An email / Informal language

ANSWER KEY

Page 88

1 **Beginning:** 2, 4, 6
End: 1, 3, 5

2 To reply to an email from Juana saying she's coming to Brussels to visit.

3
1 It was great to hear from you!
2 So you're coming to Brussels?
3 So, if you like…
4 Then we could
5 Anyway
6 I'm glad
7 Let me know
8 Bye for now

4
1 React to email and respond to news
2 Offer help and make suggestions
3 Repeat response to news and offer more help

5 *Student's own answers*

6 *Student's own answers*

7 *Student's own answers*

FURTHER PRACTICE

Workbook page 82

LESSON FOCUS

Focus on Informal language
Writing An email to a friend
Review task 3 Use the flip cards with a friend

Resources
Teacher's i-solutions, Student's Book audio

Preparation Pieces of paper for each student to write a short note.

Warmer

Hand the pieces of paper out to students, get them to write 'Hi' and their own first name on their paper and then collect them and distribute them randomly. Ask students to write a short note to the person whose name is at the top of their paper, introducing themselves like a pen pal, but signing off with a made-up name. When they have finished, collect the notes again and hand them out for the addressees to guess who wrote to them.

Focus on informal language

1 Before students do the exercise, highlight any good informal language they used in their notes.

2 Give students a time limit to answer the question so that they have to practise skimming the text.

Did you notice?

3 You could put students in pairs to do this and the next exercise so they can compare ideas. Encourage them to ask you about any unfamiliar vocabulary.

4 After completing the exercise, ask students what they think of Sophie's suggestions.

5 **PLAN** Once students have finished their plan, encourage them to talk it through with a partner.

WRITING TOOLS

Get students to read the **Writing tool**. Suggest they keep a separate section of their notebooks for this.

6 **WRITE** Before students start writing, get them to make a checklist of things they know they need to consider.

7 **CHECK** Once students have checked their own emails, they can swap with a partner and check each other's.

REVIEW TASK 3 Flip cards

Put students in pairs to practise using their flip cards to revise.

Remind students to do all the exercises in their notebook

CONTINUOUS ASSESSMENT Students can use informal language appropriately to write an email to a friend.

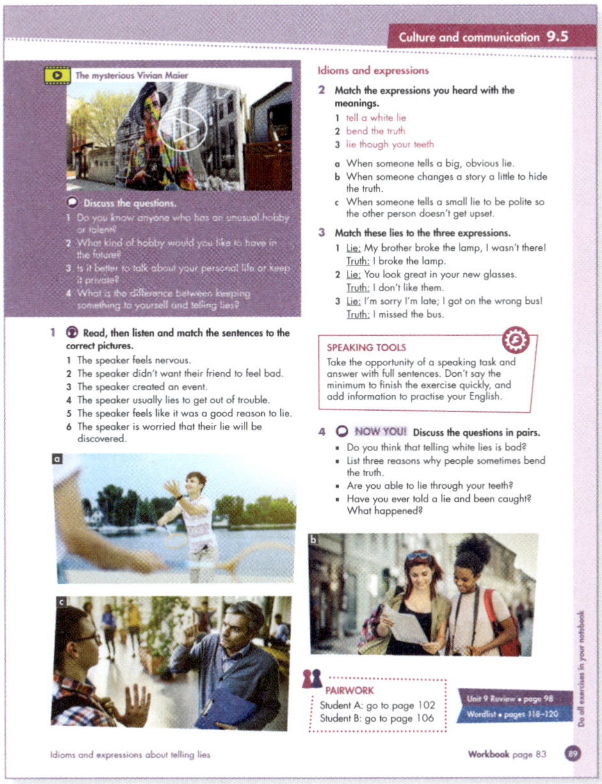

Culture and communication 9.5

The mysterious Vivian Maier

Discuss the questions.

1 Do you know anyone who has an unusual hobby or talent?
2 What kind of hobby would you like to have in the future?
3 Is it better to talk about your personal life or keep it private?
4 What is the difference between keeping something to yourself and telling lies?

1 Read, then listen and match the sentences to the correct pictures.

1 The speaker feels nervous.
2 The speaker didn't want their friend to feel bad.
3 The speaker created an event.
4 The speaker usually lies to get out of trouble.
5 The speaker feels like it was a good reason to lie.
6 The speaker is worried that their lie will be discovered.

a

c

Idioms and expressions

2 Match the expressions you heard with the meanings.

1 tell a white lie
2 bend the truth
3 lie though your teeth

a When someone tells a big, obvious lie.
b When someone changes a story a little to hide the truth.
c When someone tells a small lie to be polite so the other person doesn't get upset.

3 Match these lies to the three expressions.

1 Lie: My brother broke the lamp, I wasn't there! Truth: I broke the lamp.
2 Lie: You look great in your new glasses. Truth: I don't like them.
3 Lie: I'm sorry I'm late; I got on the wrong bus! Truth: I missed the bus.

SPEAKING TOOLS

Take the opportunity of a speaking task and answer with full sentences. Don't say the minimum to finish the exercise quickly, and add information to practise your English.

4 NOW YOU! Discuss the questions in pairs.

- Do you think that telling white lies is bad?
- List three reasons why people sometimes bend the truth.
- Are you able to lie through your teeth?
- Have you ever told a lie and been caught? What happened?

b

PAIRWORK
Student A: go to page 102
Student B: go to page 106

Unit 9 Review • page 98
Wordlist • pages 118–120

Do all exercises in your notebook

Idioms and expressions about telling lies

Workbook page 83

89

LESSON FOCUS

Idioms and expressions Telling lies
Listening Matching sentences to pictures
Speaking Comparing opinions and experiences of lies

Resources

Teacher's i-solutions, Student's Book audio, Culture video and worksheet

The mysterious Vivian Maier

Video and worksheet available on the Richmond Learning Platform

- In pairs, ask students to complete the *What I know...* exercises on the **Culture video worksheet.**
- Show students the **Culture video** and ask them to complete the *What I learned...* exercises on the worksheet.
- In pairs, students compare answers.
- In small groups, tell students to complete the *What I wonder...* exercises on the worksheet.

Warmer

Watch the Culture video and discuss the questions with the whole class. If you don't have video facilities, simply discuss the questions.

1 2.36 (See page 179 for transcripts) Tell students that neither the pictures nor the sentences are in order. Play the audio twice and suggest they first order the pictures and then match the sentences.

Idioms and expressions

2 Remind students of the contexts before they match the meanings.

3 Encourage them to answer with full sentences using the expressions.

SPEAKING TOOLS

Get students to read the **Speaking Tool** and to put it into practice in the next exercise.

4 NOW YOU! Tell students you will ask some of them to tell the class about their partner's answers after the exercise.

ANSWER KEY

Page 89

1 1 a
2 b
3 c
4 c
5 b
6 a

2 1 c
2 b
3 a

3 1 lie through your teeth
2 tell a white lie
3 bend the truth

4 *Student's own answers*

FURTHER PRACTICE AND UNIT ASSESSSMENT

Unit 9 Review **Student's Book** page 98
Workbook page 83
- Reflect on your learning page 83
- Grammar reference and practice pages 92-93 and 97
- Wordlist and exercises pages 101 and 104

Tests available to download and edit from the **Richmond Learning Platform**

→ See pages 40-41 **Assessment**

PAIRWORK **Student's Book** pages 102 and 106
See **Teacher's Book** page 164 for more information.

→ See page 30-33 **Mediation**

Remind students to do all the exercises in their notebook

CONTINUOUS ASSESSMENT Students use idioms and expressions about telling lies.

Unit 9 Review

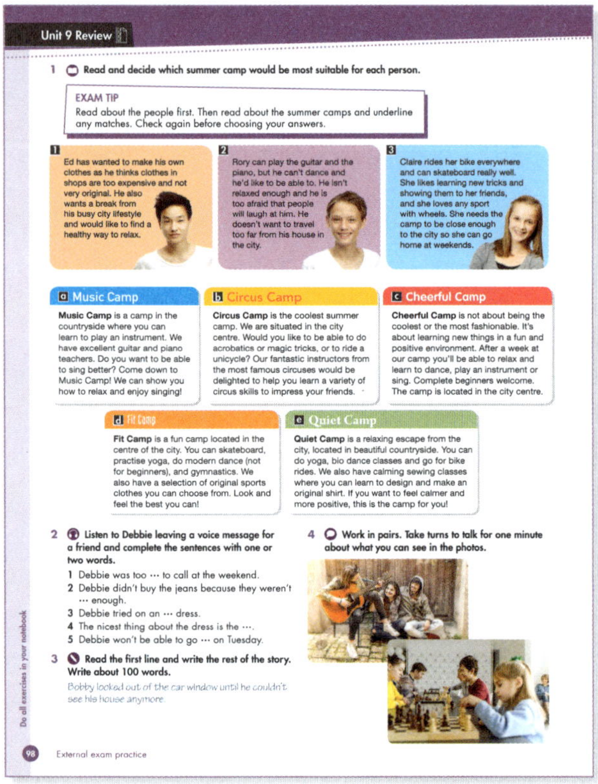

Unit 9 Review

1 Read and decide which summer camp would be most suitable for each person.

EXAM TIP
Read about the people first. Then read about the summer camps and underline any matches. Check again before choosing your answers.

1 Ed has wanted to make his own clothes as he thinks clothes in shops are too expensive and not very original. He also wants a break from his busy city lifestyle and would like to find a healthy way to relax.

2 Rory can play the guitar and the piano, but he can't dance and he'd like to be able to. He isn't relaxed enough and he is too afraid that people will laugh at him. He doesn't want to travel too far from his house in the city.

3 Claire rides her bike everywhere and can skateboard really well. She likes learning new tricks and showing them to her friends, and she loves any sport with wheels. She needs the camp to be close enough to the city so she can go home at weekends.

a Music Camp
Music Camp is a camp in the countryside where you can learn to play an instrument. We have excellent guitar and piano teachers. Do you want to be able to sing better? Come down to Music Camp! We can show you how to relax and enjoy singing!

b Circus Camp
Circus Camp is the coolest summer camp. We are situated in the city centre. Would you like to be able to do acrobatics or magic tricks, or to ride a unicycle? Our fantastic instructors from the most famous circuses would be delighted to help you learn a variety of circus skills to impress your friends.

c Cheerful Camp
Cheerful Camp is not about being the coolest or the most fashionable. It's about learning new things in a fun and positive environment. After a week at our camp you'll be able to relax and learn to dance, play an instrument or sing. Complete beginners welcome. The camp is located in the city centre.

d Fit Camp
Fit Camp is a fun camp located in the centre of the city. You can skateboard, practise yoga, do modern dance (not for beginners), and gymnastics. We also have a selection of original sports clothes you can choose from. Look and feel the best you can!

e Quiet Camp
Quiet Camp is a relaxing escape from the city, located in beautiful countryside. You can do yoga, bio dance classes and go for bike rides. We also have calming sewing classes where you can learn to design and make an original shirt. If you want to feel calmer and more positive, this is the camp for you!

2 Listen to Debbie leaving a voice message for a friend and complete the sentences with one or two words.
1 Debbie was too ··· to call at the weekend.
2 Debbie didn't buy the jeans because they weren't ··· enough.
3 Debbie tried on an ··· dress.
4 The nicest thing about the dress is the ···.
5 Debbie won't be able to go ··· on Tuesday.

3 Read the first line and write the rest of the story. Write about 100 words.
Bobby looked out of the car window until he couldn't see his house anymore.

4 Work in pairs. Take turns to talk for one minute about what you can see in the photos.

Do all exercises in your notebook

98 External exam practice

Student's Book page 98

ANSWER KEY

See page 181 for transcripts

1 **1** e **2** c **3** b

2 2.45
1 busy
2 long
3 original
4 pockets
5 horse riding

3 *Student's own answers*

4 *Student's own answers*

Pairwork

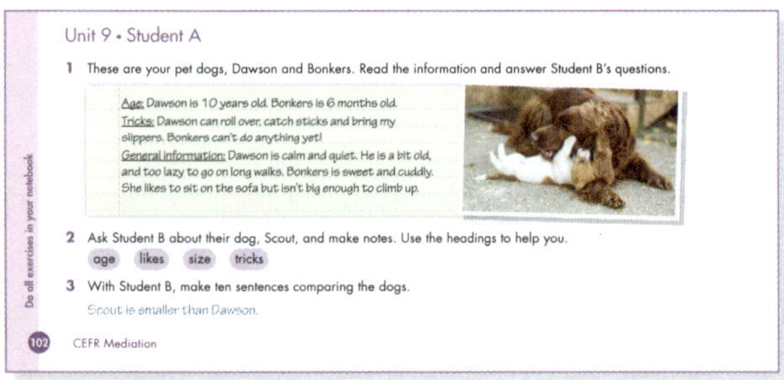

Unit 9 • Student A

1 These are your pet dogs, Dawson and Bonkers. Read the information and answer Student B's questions.

Age: Dawson is 10 years old. Bonkers is 6 months old.
Tricks: Dawson can roll over, catch sticks and bring my slippers. Bonkers can't do anything yet!
General information: Dawson is calm and quiet. He is a bit old, and too lazy to go on long walks. Bonkers is sweet and cuddly. She likes to sit on the sofa but isn't big enough to climb up.

2 Ask Student B about their dog, Scout, and make notes. Use the headings to help you.
age likes size tricks

3 With Student B, make ten sentences comparing the dogs.
Scout is smaller than Dawson.

Do all exercises in your notebook

102 CEFR Mediation

Student's Book page 102

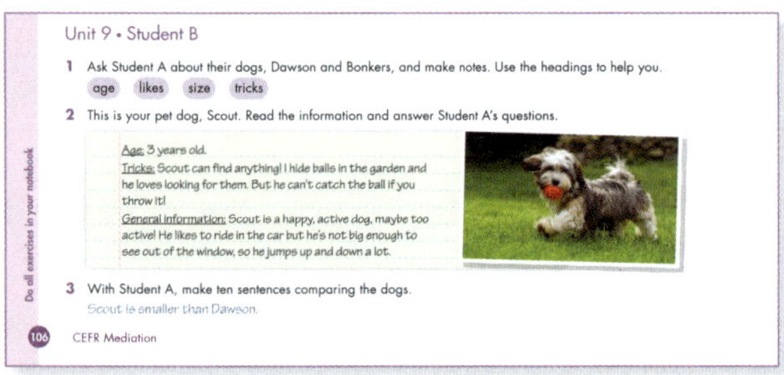

Unit 9 • Student B

1 Ask Student A about their dogs, Dawson and Bonkers, and make notes. Use the headings to help you.
age likes size tricks

2 This is your pet dog, Scout. Read the information and answer Student A's questions.

Age: 3 years old.
Tricks: Scout can find anything! I hide balls in the garden and he loves looking for them. But he can't catch the ball if you throw it!
General information: Scout is a happy, active dog, maybe too active! He likes to ride in the car but he's not big enough to see out of the window, so he jumps up and down a lot.

3 With Student A, make ten sentences comparing the dogs.
Scout is smaller than Dawson.

Do all exercises in your notebook

106 CEFR Mediation

Student's Book page 106

CEFR MEDIATION DESCRIPTOR

- **Overall mediation**
  Students can convey relevant information contained in clearly-structured, short, simple, informational texts.

- **Comparing information**
  Tell students they have different pet dogs to ask and answer questions about and to compare.

Remind students to do all the exercises in their notebook

Grammar reference

Too and enough

Use ***too*** to say that something is more than needed. It goes before an adjective. These shoes are **too** small. Don't buy it. It's **too** expensive.	Use ***enough*** to say that something is or isn't sufficient. It can go before a noun or after an adjective. These trousers aren't long **enough**. Yes, we have **enough** money.

We use ***too much*** and ***too many*** to say that we have more than necessary.

We've got **too much food** here. We'll never eat it all.

There are **too many people**. We need more chairs.

He has **too many tasks**. Don't give him any more.

In the negative, we use ***not enough*** to say that we have less than necessary.

We **haven't got enough time** to wrap the presents now. We'll do it later.

There **aren't enough cars**. Some people will have to walk.

We **don't have enough money** to buy the bicycle. it's very expensive.

Remember:

too much + uncountable nouns

too many + plural countable nouns

not enough + countable/uncountable nouns

Can and be able to

Use ***can*** or ***be able to*** with a **verb** to talk about ability.

Past	I **could play** the piano when I was five. She **couldn't dance ballet** when she was young.
Present	He **can ride** a unicycle. I **can't skateboard** very well.
Other forms	We**'ve** never **been able to train** our dog. When I'm older, I**'ll be able to run** marathons. I'd like to **be able to draw**.
Questions	**Could** you **walk** when you were 1? Yes, I **could**. / No, I **couldn't** **Can** they **do** magic tricks? Yes, they **can**. / No, they **can't**. **Will** we **be able to see** the mountain? Yes, we **will**. / No, we **won't**.

Sometimes we need to use ***be able to*** instead of ***can/could*** because ***can*** is a modal verb and doesn't have infinitives, gerunds or participles.

I'd like **to be able to sing**.

NOT ~~I'd like to can sing~~.

Being able to make your own decisions is very satisfying.

NOT ~~Canning to make…~~

My dad's never **been able to ride** a bike.

NOT ~~My dad's never could ride…~~

The past simple of ***can/can't*** is normally ***could/couldn't***.

I **could swim** when I was five.

Julia **couldn't come** because she was ill.

They ***couldn't believe*** it!

However, when we want to talk about ability or possibility on a specific occasion in the past, we use ***was able to***.

I **was able to finish** the exam with ten minutes left over.

NOT ~~I could finish the exam…~~

Do all exercises in your notebook

Student's Book page 115

Wordlist

UNIT 7

UNIT 8

UNIT 9

Shopping

bargain	put on
exchange	receipt
expensive	sale
label	size
pocket	try on

Hobbies

chess	play the guitar/piano
dance	ride a horse/motorbike
gymnastics	skateboard
magic tricks	yoga

Adjectives

afraid	miserable
alone	modern
busy	old-fashioned
calm	original
cheerful	polite
delighted	positive
disappointing	quiet
excellent	relaxed
famous	rude
fantastic	strange
heavy	traditional
high	unhappy

Do all exercises in your notebook

Student's Book page 120

2.70 2.71 2.72

Remind students to do all the exercises in their notebook

Track 1.1 Get started! page 7, exercise 1

Sports camp was brilliant this summer. We did the usual sports and also some new activities, like water polo. I'm glad I brought my swimsuit! We also designed our own football strip, it was stripy, of course! Anyway, the sports centre is great, there is a new running track and there are a few basketball hoops, too. I wore my new jacket at the party on the last night. I'm glad I brought that, too!

Track 1.2 Get started! page 8, exercise 1

This summer was quiet; we didn't go away, but I wasn't bored! We didn't go on holiday, but some people moved into the house next door. We're really happy because it's been empty for a long time. Also, our new neighbours, Sylvia and Gordon, are lovely! They have travelled all over the world and they have lots of interesting stories to tell. I could look at Sylvia's photo albums all day; it's better than watching a film!

Track 1.3 Get started! page 9, exercise 1

This summer was absolutely amazing. We went on holiday to Seoul, the capital of South Korea! There are so many interesting buildings to see and cool things to do, but my favourite thing was the food. It's so healthy, and delicious! There's usually a bowl of kimchi on the table. Kimchi is a spicy cabbage dish. Often, there isn't any dairy in Korean food, but there's nearly always some rice, even for breakfast!

Track 1.4 Unit 1, page 10, exercise 1

1

Hi, my name is Jenny. This is my budgie. Isn't he colourful? His name is Yakyak because he's so noisy! He's really energetic. He loves flying around the house!

2

I'm called Adam and this is my lizard, a bearded dragon called Dracky. She's curious and she likes to investigate, but she's a bit lazy. She likes to lie in the sun all day long.

3

Hello, I'm Kathleen, but you can call me Kath. This is my pet rat, Clark. Some people don't like rats, but actually they are very clever animals. They can learn some really cool tricks, too!

4

Hiya, my name's Matt but my nickname is MJ. My turtle is Tim. He's not very big but he is heavy! He's a bit slow of course, but he's a wonderful pet.

Track 1.5 Unit 1, page 11, exercise 3

Bearded dragon lizards are from Australia. They eat small insects and also vegetables. It's important to give them a bath once a week. A bath helps you to care for the lizard's skin properly. Bearded dragons are curious and like to explore. If a lizard feels frightened, it puffs out its 'beard'. When lizards are looking for food, they hold up their tails.

Track 1.6 Unit 1, page 11, exercise 4

Turtles live in the water and also on the land. Some types of turtles come out of the water to 'bask' in the sun. However, they spend most of their time in the water and they are excellent swimmers. A young turtle likes to eat plants, insects and small fish, but an older turtle eats more vegetables and less meat.

Track 1.7 Unit 1, page 11, exercise 6

Listen and repeat.

/eə/ care, hairy, their, there, wear, where

/ɪə/ beard, ear, deer, hear, here, near

Track 1.8 Unit 1, page 12, exercise 1

Ellie: OK, are you ready for the interview questions?

Tamara: Sure!

Ellie: First question: do you have a nickname?

Tamara: Well, some of my friends call me Tam.

Ellie: And... do you have a pet?

Tamara: Yup, I have a dog called Jimmy. He's energetic and a bit silly.

Ellie: Ha! True. What's your favourite food?

Tamara: Umm, sausages, I think.

Ellie: Yum! What kind of music do you like?

Tamara: Erm, I like pop, but I listen to chillout music when I draw.

Ellie: Ah ha! That's the next question. What do you do in your free time?

Tamara: Well, you know I love drawing, but I also enjoy reading comics and watching action films. I collect stamps and models of superheroes, too! Superman is my favourite.

Ellie: Hmm, I prefer Spiderman. So, do you draw every day?

Tamara: Yes! My dream is to be a cartoonist one day. There aren't many female superheroes, so I'm creating one.

Ellie: Cool! What's her superpower?

Tamara: I'm not sure yet, but she is very strong and she has X-ray vision.

Ellie: I can't wait to see the film one day!

Track 1.9 Unit 1, page 13, exercise 5

Speaker 1: Where is Superman from?

Speaker 2: He's from the planet Krypton.

Speaker 1: Where does he live?

Speaker 2: He lives in America, in a fictional city called Metropolis.

Speaker 1: Does he have a secret identity?

Speaker 2: Yes, he does. It's Clark Kent, a reporter at the Daily Planet newspaper.

Speaker 1: Which superpowers does he have?

Speaker 2: He has a lot! For example, he has X-ray vision, a fantastic memory and he's

very strong. He flies really fast, too.

Speaker 1: Who is his enemy?

Speaker 2: His enemy is Lex Luthor. Lois Lane is his girlfriend and Jimmy Olsen is his friend.

Track 1.10 Unit 1, page 14, exercise 3

What makes you who you are?

We live in an age of social media. We post selfies and links to things we like. We look at other people's social media pages to see what they look like, who they're with, where they go and what they like. Many people have hundreds of online 'friends'. But how well do we know them, and how well do they know us? And where does the digital age leave our sense of identity?

Firstly, it's very public. You put something online and everyone can see it. This means it's important to be very careful with what we post. Secondly, the digital identities we create can be superficial. You are much more than the sum of your selfies, your posts and your hobbies.

So, what makes us who we are? There's no simple answer to that question. We are a complex mix of genes, influences and experiences. These things affect our emotional reactions, our behaviour and our view of the world we live in. On top of that, we often project a different public image to how we really are. We also choose to show different parts of our personalities to different people. And our personalities are unique because we combine the main traits in different ways: agreeable, extroverted, conscientious, open to experiences, neurotic. We change over time and the way we see ourselves can be quite different from how other people see us.

There is an important lesson in all of this. Your identity doesn't just exist on its own; it exists in the context of everyone you have contact with. They compare you with others and sometimes they even judge you by what you do, especially what you do for them.

How do you think about the people in your life?

Track 1.11 **Unit 1, page 17, exercise 1**

1

I'm Megan and this is my brother, Matt. We're like chalk and cheese but he's my best friend. We live in a small town, but we are never bored. We have a dog and we play music together. I play keyboard and he plays the guitar. Our dream is to be in a famous band one day.

2

Hi, I'm James and these are my two best friends, Liz and Ross. From the moment we met, we got on like a house on fire. We go skateboarding together every day. We live in a big city, so there is always something to do. Our dream is to be PE teachers.

3

I'm Tom and this is Alex. He's been my best friend for years. We live next door to each other. We usually see eye to eye but any problems we have are solved quickly. We go skateboarding together. Our dream is to be famous scientists.

Track 1.12 **Unit 2, page 18, exercise 2**

Hi, my name's Nick. My routine is quite normal. I eat my breakfast in the kitchen at 7. We rarely use the dining room, only for special occasions. On Tuesdays I have football practice after school. I am supposed to put my kit in the washing machine in the utility room, but I have to say that I often forget! If I don't have football, I like to sit on the porch because it has a nice view of the garden. At 5pm I do my homework. We have a study, but I hardly ever do homework in there. I prefer to do it in the kitchen, so I can ask my dad questions while he is cooking. My house is nice, but I wish we had a basement so that I could have a drumkit! Even though my dad recently bought a new car, he doesn't spend much time in the garage. He is usually on the rooftop terrace. He has a telescope and he likes to look at the stars.

Track 1.13 **Unit 2, page 19, exercise 5**

Listen and repeat.

/æ/ adverb, bag, has, have, magazine, match

Track 1.14 **Unit 2, page 19, exercise 6**

Interviewer: Hello Nick, hello Terry! Thanks for helping me with my survey. So, my first question is for Nick... can you tell me how often you tidy your room?

Nick: Well, my parents tell me I should tidy it every day, but I don't really have time so I tidy it several times a week instead. That's more often than Terry. He only tidies his room on Saturdays!

Terry: Hey!

Interviewer: OK, OK. I'm sure you are both very tidy. Terry, do you listen to music when you are at home?

Terry: I rarely listen to music at home. I like watching films instead.

Nick: I do! I listen to music three times a week. I listen to recordings of famous drummers. I want to buy a drumkit one day!

Interviewer: You both have lots to keep you busy at home. When you are in class, do you get bored?

Terry: I hardly ever get bored because I like learning new things. I usually ask my teacher a lot of questions as well.

Nick: I am bored all the time. I would rather be at home learning the drums!

Terry: He never stops talking about the drums, but his playing doesn't improve!

Interviewer: I can see that although you are both different, you are still good friends. Do you walk to school together?

Nick: I always walk to school because I live nearby.

Terry: I usually get the bus or sometimes my mum will take me to school in the car.

Interviewer: And the last question: are you late for school?

Terry: That's the only thing about us that is the same - we are always late!

Track 1.15 **Unit 2, page 20, exercise 1**

1

Hello everyone! I'm Billy. My home is a converted windmill. I love living here because it is so unusual. The only bad thing is that the windmill is made of wood, so it is very cold and I have to get dressed quickly in the mornings! When I get home from school, around seven o'clock, I water the plants in the garden. Then I often read a book until it´s time to go to bed.

2

Emily here! I live in a caravan, although some people call it a motorhome because it is a home on wheels! I wake up every day at 7:00, but I don´t get up until 7:30 because I like to hit the snooze button a few times. I'm not in a rush anyway. I always have to wait for my sister to finish brushing her teeth before I can use the bathroom. The sink is tiny! My dad makes lunch for us every day, but I like to help. I love cooking and trying out new recipes. After school I relax for a while. I like to sit outside the caravan in the fresh air.

3

I'm Steven and my home floats on water. That's right, it's a boat! I wake up every day at 6:30 because that´s when the ducks start making noise! I don't have a shower in the morning. I usually wait until the evening because the water tank takes a long time to heat up. My parents are very busy, so they arrive home at a different time every day, but we always wait to have dinner at the same time because it´s important to eat together. After dinner I play video games at the back of the boat, near the generator. That´s where it's warmest!

Track 1.16 Unit 2, page 20, exercise 2
See previous track

Track 1.17 Unit 2, page 21, exercise 6
Sophie: Hello?
Jane: Hey, it's me.
Sophie: Jane! This is a strange phone number.
Jane: Oh. I have a new French phone.
Sophie: Ah! Well thanks for phoning. We miss you!
Jane: I miss you too! But I am having a great time.
Sophie: Cool! So, what are you doing right now?
Jane: I am talking to you!
Sophie: Don't be silly…
Jane: Sorry. Well, right now I am waiting for my host family.
Sophie: What are they doing?
Jane: They are buying sandwiches for a picnic this afternoon.
Sophie: Sounds great. How often do you have picnics?
Jane: We have a picnic about twice a week.
Sophie: That sounds wonderful. I love picnics.
Jane: Oh! I can see them now. They are coming back. I've got to go!
Sophie: Have fun and take care.
Jane: OK! Speak soon.

Track 1.18 Unit 2, page 22, exercise 2
Five students, five continents
Europe.
This is Miia. She's preparing the ice to go skating on a lake near her house. Miia lives in Finland. She goes to school every day at 8:00am, even in winter when it's sometimes -30°C and dark all day. But the lessons are fun and they finish at 1:00pm.
South America.
This is Renata. She's practising sandboarding. Renata lives in Florianopolis, in the south of Brazil. Her school has a morning and an afternoon session, and she goes to the afternoon session, from 12:00pm to 5:00pm. In the morning, she hardly ever misses an opportunity to go the beach.
Africa.
This is Azibo. She's washing her hands before lunch at school. Azibo lives in a village in Malawi. She gets up every morning at 5:00am and does some housework before the 12km walk to school. School finishes at 5:00pm and she walks home, does her homework and is usually in bed by 8:00pm.
Asia.
This is Hyeun Jung. He's chatting with his friends. He uses social media a lot. Hyeun Jung lives in Seoul, in South Korea. After his normal school day, Hyeun Jung goes to an academy called a 'hagwon' every day until 10:00pm. And that's before he starts his homework!
Oceania.
This is David. He lives on a cattle farm in Western Australia. It's 170km to the nearest big town, so he has lessons via satellite! He studies in the morning, and then he usually spends the afternoon riding horses and looking after the cattle.

Track 1.19 Unit 2, page 25, exercise 1
1
Hi, I'm Sam! I'm so happy – I slept like a log last night! I often can't get to sleep and I also wake up a lot in the night. I recently tried to change my routine and I started going to bed earlier. I went to bed at 9:30 last night and it worked!
2
Alex here. I am an early bird. I think the best time of the day is the morning and I usually wake up before my alarm. Last night I went to bed at 8:30. Well, you know what they say: the early bird gets the worm!
3
I'm Charlie and I am a real night owl. I don't feel creative until late at night. To get to sleep I need total silence. Once I am asleep I am usually a heavy sleeper. I didn't go to bed until eleven o'clock last night.

Track 1.20 Unit 2, page 25, exercise 2
See previous track

Track 1.21 Unit 3, page 28, exercise 1
Here you can see three oil paintings. They are all portraits of women, but the paintings are very different. Portraits required the models to sit still for long periods of time. Because the artists and the models spent so much time together some artists fell in love with the people in their portraits.
Picture 1
In 1506 Rafael created the 'Portrait of Young Woman with Unicorn'. The painting is in the High Renaissance style. High Renaissance painters were inspired by beauty and harmony. This period of time was often referred to as the most important moment in western painting.
Picture 2
Mary Cassatt painted 'The Cup of Tea' in 1880, in the Impressionist style. Cassatt did not make political statements about women in her work, but she was inspired by women's social and private lives. These were not subjects widely represented in art at that time. Artists often held strong political views and female painters in particular fought hard to be recognised by art lovers and society as a whole.
Picture 3
The 'Portrait of Madame Josette Gris' is by the Cubist painter Juan Gris. He completed it in 1916. Cubist painters were inspired by mathematics and the use of geometric shapes in their work made their paintings abstract. Artists like Pablo Picasso helped the Cubist style to become famous. However, this modern style of painting was not popular at first and many artists died before the public and critics recognised their work.

Track 1.22 Unit 3, page 29, exercise 7
Presenter: Antoni Gaudí's buildings are famous all over the world. Seven of his works are protected by UNESCO as World Heritage Sites. Let's find out more about this mysterious and very talented man. Dr Jenkins, did Antoni Gaudí have a nickname?
Expert: Yes. Because of his incredible talent and interest in religion, he was known as 'God's architect'.
Presenter: Did he finish the Sagrada Familia?

Expert: No. The Sagrada Familia is probably his most famous work, but it is still unfinished today.
Presenter: Where did he find inspiration? As well as in religion, he found a lot of his inspiration in nature. You can see that clearly in his work.
Presenter: Did he like drawing plans? No, he didn't. He preferred to make 3-dimensional models, and used lots of different materials, especially natural materials to make them.
Presenter: When did he die? He died in 1926. Sadly, his work wasn't very popular until the 1950s. Now there are plans to finish the Sagrada Familia for the centenary of his death, in 2026.

Track 1.23 **Unit 3, page 30, exercise 1**
In this picture, you can see the stage and the actors. It looks similar to a modern theatre, but going to see a play used to be a very different experience in the 1500s. There was no roof over the main 'pit', and audiences didn't used to sit in rows. Rich people sat in the galleries and poorer people stood up in the 'pit'. Plays also used to be more interactive because people in the audience used to shout at the actors. People would meet friends and eat food during the interval.

Track 1.24 **Unit 3, page 30, exercise 4**
Listen and repeat.
Yes/No questions:
Did he like the music?
Did they visit the theatre?
Wh- questions:
Who went to the show?
Which artists did you meet?

Track 1.25 **Unit 3, page 31, exercise 6**
Lily: Since I was very young, I wanted to be an actor. My aunt used to take me to the theatre every weekend. Before I went to acting classes I didn't use to have a lot of confidence, but now I'm the star of the school show! The only thing I don't like about acting class is that we have to wear black. I used to like wearing colourful clothes.
David: I used to go and see concerts with my grandpa and I always wanted to play the trumpet. At first, I used to play my grandpa's trumpet, but now I play in the school orchestra so I have my own. I didn't use to travel to my music classes by car, but I have a new teacher and she lives far away.
Sharon: I didn't use to do so much exercise and I always used to feel bored at the weekends. My sister and I just stayed home and watched a lot of TV. Now I have dance classes three times a week and I'm never bored.

Track 1.26 **Unit 3, page 31, exercise 7**
See previous track

Track 1.27 **Unit 3, page 32, exercise 2**
Turning points in the arts
From the first cave paintings over 40,000 years ago to interactive multi-media artistic experiences today, art has a long and dynamic history. Let's take a look at some of the important moments in the history of the arts.
Literature
The biggest change in the history of literature was the development of writing. People used to tell stories and perform plays from memory, and many famous classical texts come from stories passed down orally over generations. The invention of the printing press in 1440 meant that literature became available to nearly everybody, so many more people learnt to read (although literacy rates in Europe were still less than 50%). Interestingly, one form of literature that's becoming more popular now is performance poetry.
Music
The printing press was also important for music, as it meant that we could print sheet music and distribute it for everyone to play. And in 1700, Bartolomeo Cristofori invented an instrument that quickly became the most popular to compose for, and is still the most popular to play: the piano. But probably the biggest change in music was digital audio files. Now we can listen to any piece of music whenever we want!
Visual Arts
The visual arts used to refer mainly to drawing, painting, sculpture and architecture. One important development in painting was the discovery of linear perspective in the Renaissance period. This is the technique of creating the illusion of 3D space, and it led to more realistic and detailed paintings. Then came the Modern Art revolution of the 19th and 20th centuries, where visual art became more about experimentation and abstraction. The biggest modern changes have been the development of new art forms such as photography, cinema and computer art. Who knows what the future holds?

Track 1.28 **Unit 3, page 35, exercise 1**
1
I'm crazy about sculptures. I like really big ones. Every time I go on holiday, I find out where the best sculptures are before I go. My favourite is called 'Cloud Gate' and it's in Millennium Park, Chicago. That's in the United States. It's so huge it took two years to finish. Work started in 2004 and ended in 2006. The sculpture's surface reflects sky. I think it's beautiful.
2
I can't stand Shakespeare. At school they used to make me study his plays over and over again; it was terrible! He died a long time ago, in the year 1616, so I don't understand anything he wrote! I just can't stand that everyone thinks he's wonderful.
3
Abstract art isn't my cup of tea. It's all blobs and colours. I think it's ugly. I prefer paintings of people, with a story, that's much more interesting. My uncle used to take me to art galleries when I was younger and he taught me him about the history of painting and what the paintings meant. I like learning about history.

Track 1.29 **Unit 4, page 36, exercise 1**
It was my brother's birthday this weekend, we had a barbecue in the garden. There were burgers and sausages but my aunt is vegetarian, so there was a big pasta salad, too. For dessert there were biscuits and a big birthday cake with seventeen candles. He couldn't blow out the candles because there were so many! After we ate, my brother opened his presents. There weren't gift tags on some of the presents, and we still don't know who they were from!

Track 1.30 Unit 4, page 36, exercise 3
Listen and repeat.
/a:/ barbecue, card, garden, guitar, party, start

Track 1.31 Unit 4, page 37, exercise 5
Chloe: Hi, Jenny. How was your birthday party?
Jenny: Hey, it was great! It's sad you couldn't be there.
Chloe: I know! Tell me all about it.
Jenny: There was a big table under the trees. My little cousins helped with the decorations. There were colourful balloons and tiny flags all over the garden!
Chloe: It sounds lovely. Who was at the party? Anyone from our class?
Jenny: No, there weren't any friends from school at the party, it was just for family.
Chloe: Ahh. So, what kinds of food were there?
Jenny: There was a huge salad and a big cheese and mushroom pizza. There were mini-sandwiches, too.
Chloe: Was there anything for dessert?
Jenny: Of course! There were tiny cupcakes and biscuits on the table. There was also a massive cake with cream and fruit on top, but there wasn't any ice cream this year.
Chloe: That all sounds lovely! I hope I can come next year!

Track 1.32 Unit 4, page 38, exercise 1
1
Last weekend I went to a concert at the new stadium. The tickets were expensive, but my mum bought me a backstage pass for Christmas. After the show, I met the band! I was so nervous, I was shaking!
2
Yesterday we went to a fancy restaurant for my mum's birthday. We were eating our starters and suddenly, my favourite singer walked in! Later, the waiter told me that I could go and meet her. She signed my napkin; it was so exciting!
3
Three weeks ago, I won two tickets to an amusement park in a competition at school. I took my best friend and we had a wonderful day. When we were leaving, they gave us a photo of us screaming on the roller coaster. It's brilliant!
4
Last summer, I was snorkelling in the sea on holiday with my brother. One of my flippers fell off my foot, so I looked down and I saw a turtle! It was swimming right under us! I couldn't believe my eyes!

Track 1.33 Unit 4, page 38, exercise 2
See previous track

Track 1.34 Unit 4, page 39, exercise 5
Adventure Camp
Monday: Urgh. When we arrived today, it was raining! I was wearing my T-shirt and shorts. Bad idea!
Tuesday: Today Jim was taking a photo next to the river and Simon pushed him in! Mr Matthews was not laughing, but we were, even Jim!
Wednesday: Mr Matthews played the guitar today while we were eating lunch. It was really nice; he's good! While we weren't looking, Jim threw Simon's shoes on the roof. Mr Matthews was so angry!
Thursday: We were waiting in line to get on the zip wire today and we saw a huge spider! Everyone was screaming - it was so funny afterwards, but not at the time! The zip wire was brilliant.
Friday: The sun was shining today! Good weather on the day we were leaving! Anyway, it was a great week.

Track 1.35 Unit 4, page 40, exercise 2
What are we celebrating?
Wherever you go in the world, there are festivals and celebrations of different kinds. Some are solemn and serious, others loud and colourful. Although the ways we celebrate vary, the things we celebrate are similar.
Almost all cultures have a New Year's celebration. Western cultures celebrate New Year's Eve, the 31st of December, with fireworks displays and small family gatherings or big parties. In Brazil, people run to the beach to jump over waves and make wishes for the New Year. In China, they celebrate a Lunar New Year, which is in late January or February. Many cultures also have spring festivals, like Holi, an Indian festival in March. People cover each other with coloured powder and have water fights. People in the UK celebrate a festival on the 1st of May called May Day by dancing around a pole. The Christian festival of Easter also has elements from ancient pagan spring rituals, like eggs and the Easter Bunny. Historically, eggs were a symbol of new life and rabbits were a symbol of fertility. The word 'Easter' comes from the old Saxon goddess of fertility, Eostre.
There are also many autumn celebrations to honour the dead. The most famous is Halloween, on the 31st of October. Like Easter, it's a mixture of Christian and pagan festivals. It coincides with the night before All Saints' Day, but now it has more in common with the ancient Celtic festival of Samhain, in which people used to dress up as pagan gods or fairies and visit houses asking for offerings. Sound familiar? Mexicans celebrate it as the Day of the Dead by visiting the graves of departed loved ones and leaving gifts. A lot of celebrations are more local and less universal, but they all have one important thing in common: the idea of bringing communities together.

Track 1.36 Unit 4, page 43, exercise 1
Tracy: Last month I entered a competition for the best young writer of the year. The organisers invited me to an award ceremony and I went with my brother. I was already feeling happy just to be there. I wasn't expecting to win anything. We were all waiting nervously for them to announce the winner, and when they said my name my jaw dropped. I could hardly hold the trophy, my hands were shaking so much!
Adam: We only started raising money for the local hospital six months ago, but we're doing very well. We make bags and hats to sell at markets and organise events every two weeks. The hospital's really grateful for the amount of money we've raised. But the award for rising stars in philanthropy came out of the blue.
Ross: I didn't have a great start to the season, but then I improved as time went on and won a gold medal and a bronze medal in two different races. Unfortunately, I had a bad knee so I couldn't run in the final race. But I was watching from the finish line when my friend Sam got the silver medal! It took my breath away! He only started running a few months ago.

Track 1.37 Unit 4, page 43, exercise 2
See previous track

Track 1.38 Unit 5, page 46, exercise 1
Dad: This looks so cool! What is it?
Tina: It's a 3D printer, Dad.
Dad: How do you switch it on?
Jeff: You turn it on and off with this button, here.
Dad: What are you printing?
Jeff: The parts we need for our robotics class.
Tina: We downloaded the instructions from a website we found.
Dad: Is it difficult?
Tina: No, but there's a video clip that explains the process. I'll put it on.
Dad: I can't hear it.
Jeff: You right-click there to turn it up.
Dad: Ahh, ok. This is so exciting!

Track 1.39 Unit 5, page 47, exercise 4
Rachel: Hi?
Granny Jean: Hello my darling!
Rachel: Granny Jean, is that you?
Granny Jean: Yes! I'm calling you from my new smart telephone!
Rachel: Ha ha, well done! Is it easy to use?
Granny Jean: Yes my love, it's wonderful! I feel like an IT expert.
Rachel: Oh Granny Jean, that's great.
Granny Jean: Well, there is one thing that I can't do.
Rachel: What is it? Maybe I can help you.
Granny Jean: I'd like to take a self-photograph, but I don't know how.
Rachel: A selfie? OK. Do you have the selfie stick I sent you?
Granny Jean: The long pole? Yes dear. I connected the phone to the pole ... erm, I mean selfie-stick but when I take a photograph the phones switches off.
Rachel: Ah! I think you are using the wrong button. Are you pushing the one at the end of the selfie stick?
Granny Jean: No, I was using the button on the side of the phone.
Rachel: Oh, don't do that Granny Jean! Push the button on the selfie stick. Call me back if it doesn't work.

Track 1.40 Unit 5, page 47, exercise 5
First, turn the phone on.
Open the message and click on the link I sent you.
Choose the track that you want to hear.
Click on the 'play' symbol.
Remember to plug in the headphones.
Use the + and – buttons to turn the volume up or down.
Turn it off when you're finished.

Track 1.41 Unit 5, page 48, exercise 1
Mr Evans: Eric, Chris - how is the project going?
Eric: Hello, Mr Evans. Well, we need to change the hardware. The hardware isn't very attractive, but it needs to be strong!
Chris: I agree, but the strength isn't as important as the software. The problem is that we can't update the software for free.
Teacher: Hmm, I see. Can you change the design?
Eric: We already made that decision. The original idea was to make a robot that could find your mobile phone.
Chris: But we don't know enough about electronics.
Eric: So now we are making a robot that throws a ball to your dog – that's why it needs to be strong!
Teacher: Well, keep working hard. I'm sure you will reach a conclusion! Katie and Jim, tell me about your invention.
Katie: Our invention collects data from its environment. It's a special alarm clock that makes sure you get up in the morning.
Jim: Yes, it hides from you and makes a loud noise! You insert a memory card into the slot, here. That's where the different noises are stored.
Katie: Our original idea was to make a robot that protects your bedroom. But we changed it because this is more useful.
Jim: And because Katie usually wakes up late!
Katie: Ha ha, it's true. I really need this robot. At the moment though, it's dangerous because it gets too hot.
Jim: But we are trying to solve the problem. The connection between the wheels and the circuit isn't working well.
Mr Evans: Very good! And Katie don't be late to class tomorrow!

Track 1.42 Unit 5, page 48, exercise 2
1 The hardware isn't very attractive, but it needs to be strong!
2 The problem is that we can't update the software for free.
3 But we don't know enough about electronics.
4 Our invention collects data from its environment.
5 You insert a memory card into the slot, here.
6 The connection between the wheels and the circuit isn't working well.

Track 1.43 Unit 5, page 48, exercise 3
Listen and repeat.
/d/ change, dangerous, edge, general, intelligence, original
/ʒ/ conclusion, decision, genre, usually, vision, visual

Track 1.44 Unit 5, page 49, exercise 6
James: Sarah's idea to organise a science fair in the school cafeteria is great!
David: I know! I will ask the head teacher if she likes the idea.
Sarah: Who else will help us? Will Jane help?
David: Jane won't want to help us. She hates Science class.
James: Alexa will help, but she will arrive late. She has extra classes.
Sarah: I will call her today after lunch, at 1:30pm.
David: Great! You call Alexa and we will make the posters.
Sarah: My dad will love the idea.
David: And mine! He will help with setting up the tables.
James: I will borrow my brother's camera. I will take photographs to put on the school blog.
Sarah: We won't have much time to organise everything...
James: That's true. We won't be able to use the cafeteria after next week. It will be closed for repairs.
Sarah: We will have to work fast!

Track 1.45 Unit 5, page 49, exercise 7
See previous track

Track 1.46 Unit 5, page 50, exercise 2
A whole new world
In 1901, English science fiction writer H.G. Wells made a series of predictions for the next one hundred years in a book called Anticipations. He predicted the success of cars and trains and their effects on cities, the industrialisation of war and the establishment of a European Union. Now you can find the theories of 'futurologists' all over the internet. Here are some of their predictions.
The future of transport will be interesting. Many big car companies are developing self-driving and electric vehicles, so they will probably become more common. In fact, we are already seeing privately owned and shared electric cars on our city streets. Several countries are also experimenting with 'hyperloops', capsules that carry passengers along magnetised tubes with very little friction. They say hyperloops will reach speeds of over 1,000 km/h.
There are also some exciting predictions for medicine. Researchers are studying ways to locate and edit defective genes, and that could lead to the eradication of some of the world's most lethal diseases. Advances in nanotechnology could also give us nanobots that patrol our bodies and destroy diseased cells. Some experts even predict that we will have brain-computer interfaces so we can artificially increase our mental capacity.
A prediction everyone agrees on is the increased connectivity of everything. We already have smart houses, where security, heating, and entertainment systems connect to create more comfortable living spaces. Experts also talk of smart factories and even smart cities, with different technologies all working together to make everything run efficiently.
Most of these predictions involve humans trusting technology and giving up a lot of our control. Fans of science fiction know that this could end badly. Some technology experts suggest that governments dedicate more resources to investigating the dangers of new technologies, especially artificial intelligence (AI). As tech entrepreneur Sam Altman says, 'In the next few decades we are either going to head toward self-destruction or toward humans colonising the universe.'

Track 1.47 Unit 5, page 53, exercise 1
1
Alice: Sandra, I don't have a clue what I'm doing. I'm so confused!
Sandra: And me! That's why we chose this topic though, remember?
Alice: Yeah, I know. We chose it because we don't know anything about it and we thought it would be interesting.
Sandra: Exactly. Really, I prefer biology!
Alice: And I prefer creating computer programmes on my laptop, but here I am investigating chemical structures instead!
2
Tony: My name's Tony. I'm working on this project alone because I will get better marks that way. My project is to develop an interactive guide about how machines work. I chose it because my mum works with machines in a factory and she knows them like the back of her hand. She has promised she will give me a tour of the factory. I'm excited.
3
Sally: Mark, will your parents be home soon? I've made such a mess!
Mark: Don't worry, Sally. We are working at my house because my parents don't mind the mess.
Sally: Ah yes. I forgot. I'm bored, Mark. I thought creating a computer from parts would be more difficult!
Mark: Me too, but really it isn't rocket science.

Track 1.48 Unit 5, page 53, exercise 2
See previous track

Track 2.1 Unit 6, page 54, exercise 1
1
Last week I had a horrible earache. My head was spinning and I felt dizzy all the time. It was so difficult to hear when people were talking. The doctor looked in my ear and said that I had an infection. She gave me some medicine and said that I shouldn't go swimming for at least two weeks. I feel a lot better now. I think I've almost completely recovered.
2
I had lots of bad headaches, so I had a check-up at the doctors. She told me to make an appointment for an eye test. Sure enough, I need glasses! That's why I was getting lots of headaches! The doctor also told me I should rest my eyes after every hour on the computer.
3
I had an appointment with the doctor yesterday. I went because I had a sore throat and a cough. Sometimes my chest hurt and it was hard to breathe as well. She checked and I had a temperature, too! I'm taking medicine now and I should feel a lot better soon.

Track 2.2 Unit 6, page 54, exercise 2
See previous track

Track 2.3 Unit 6, page 55, exercise 6
Rose: Hello, can I come in?
Doctor: Yes, you can. What's the problem?
Rose: My chest hurts and it's difficult to breathe.
Doctor: OK, let me listen to your lungs. Breathe in, please. Breathe out. Ah, you have a chest infection.
Rose: A chest infection?! Oh no, can I go running?
Doctor: No. Until you've recovered, you can't do any exercise. It's best to stay indoors.
Rose: Urgh! So, I can't do anything!
Doctor: Well, you can rest!

Track 2.4 Unit 6, page 56, exercise 1
My brother and I are not very lucky at the moment! I broke a bone in my wrist while I was skateboarding and he has a bad sprain from falling off the climbing wall! I have to wear a plaster cast for about six weeks. It's annoying and it itches a lot. I have to scratch my arm by poking a pencil down inside the plaster cast. I have to wear a sling too, to hold my arm up because the plaster cast is really heavy. But it's my left wrist and I'm right-handed, so I don't have to change my routine much. My brother has to use crutches for 12 weeks though, and a special boot to protect his ankle. Using crutches to get around isn't easy. He has blisters on his hands, and his back aches too. He mustn't stand on it, so he's really slow and grumpy!

Track 2.5 Unit 6, page 56, exercise 3
Listen and repeat.
/m/ appointment, from, medicine, must, temperature, thumb
/n/ infection, know, nose, nurse, runny, when

Track 2.6 Unit 6, page 56, exercise 5
It was my birthday last week and I got a new pair of rollerblades from my aunt! I was so excited. The new rollerblades felt big around the ankles, but I couldn't wait to go out, so I sped off down the road! I saw a friend from school and I waved at her. I didn't see there was something slippery on the pavement. I fell and hit my elbow hard. It really hurt! My friend ran to my house to get help. My parents called the paramedics because I felt very dizzy and they were worried that I had concussion. The doctors and nurses at the hospital were very nice to me. I have an appointment next week to check my elbow is healing well. Everyone told me that I mustn't use my rollerblades for a while! And before I do, I'll get some proper protection so it doesn't happen again!

Track 2.7 Unit 6, page 57, exercise 7
If you twist or sprain a joint in your body, you should follow the RICE method.
Rest: Often, your body can heal itself with a little rest. If it's not a serious injury, you can use the damaged joint again after 24–48 hours.
Ice: Keeping the area cold reduces pain, but you don't have to use ice; a packet of peas from the freezer is better! You must put the ice on the area for 20 minutes, six times a day.
Compression: Use a bandage to stop swelling. Remember, you mustn't wrap the bandage too tight. If the area turns blue, you have to see a doctor.
Elevation: Keeping the injured part of the body above the heart reduces pain and swelling.

Track 2.8 Unit 6, page 58, exercise 2
Jobs in healthcare
When we think of healthcare, we think of doctors. But there are many different types of healthcare professionals. Let's take a look at some of them and what they do.
Doctor: You and your family should have a doctor you go to regularly. They're called a general practitioner, or GP, and they know you and your medical history best. They can diagnose and treat you themselves, or refer to you a specialist.
Nurse: These people work very closely with patients, especially in hospitals. They test and monitor them, and they follow doctors' instructions to help patients recover effectively.
Pharmacist: When your doctor prescribes you medication, these are the people you have to take the prescription to. They can answer questions about prescribed medications, and give you advice on medicine that you don't need a prescription for.
Therapist: These healthcare specialists don't have to have the same full medical training as doctors, and there are lots of different types. One of the best known are physiotherapists. They can help you recover from injuries or manage back pain, for example. You don't have to have a referral from your GP to see a physiotherapist.
Paramedic: When you call an ambulance, these are the healthcare professionals who arrive at the scene. They have training in emergency medicine and can do things like resuscitate people who have stopped breathing and immobilise people who may have spinal injuries to transport them safely to hospital.
Dentist: Most of us know we should brush our teeth at least twice a day, but surveys show that in the UK 3 out of 10 adults, and 1 out of 4 children, don't. We also know we should see one of these healthcare professionals at least every two years, but many of us don't like going. Maybe that's why statistics say that almost 100% of adults worldwide have some tooth decay!

Track 2.9 Unit 6, page 61, exercise 1
I woke up at 6:45am. I felt tired and a bit under the weather. Around noon I was coughing a lot and I had a frog in my throat. My mum said I should drink tea with lemon and honey, but I said no. In the afternoon I had to go home from school, I was sick as a dog! I went to bed very early and am feeling a bit better now.

Track 2.10 Unit 6, page 61, exercise 2
See previous track

Track 2.11 Unit 7, page 64, exercise 2
Interviewer: Today we are talking to Adrian. Adrian is a travel writer and he has been travelling the world for seven years! So, tell us - do you have a favourite destination?
Adrian: Well, I have seen lots of amazing things, but I have to say my favourite trip was to Norway. I travelled in a cruise shop down the fjords. A fjord is a narrow stretch of water, usually between cliffs, so the scenery was beautiful. I also saw the Northern Lights. It was unforgettable.
Interviewer: Wow! That really sounds really picturesque. Do you usually travel with a friend or in a group of people?
Adrian: It can get very lonely travelling around the world on your own. However, sometimes I need to visit some strange places! So, for that reason, I prefer to travel alone.
Interviewer: You must have used a lot of different forms of transport, which has been the most unusual?
Adrian: Great question! In China I travelled on the Shanghai maglev train. It´s just like a normal train, but it operates using magnets! There are only three in the world, so that makes it quite unusual. But the most memorable has to be when I flew over the sea in a hot air balloon. It was scary, but exciting!
Interviewer: And my last question… Where have you planned to visit next?
Adrian: My next trip is to India. I have already spent time in New Delhi, so this time I will ride to the Ajanta Caves in a helicopter and sleep there for a few nights.

Track 2.12 Unit 7, page 64, exercise 3
Listen and repeat.
/f/ ferry, France, phone, photograph, enough, laugh

Track 2.13 Unit 7, page 65, exercise 6
1 Alex has already been sailing in the Great Barrier Reef.
2 Alex's dad hasn't swum in the sea yet.
3 Liam hasn't gone on the glacier tour yet.
4 They have already seen a few whales.
5 Mark and his family haven't seen the Mona Lisa yet.
6 They have already ridden bicycles through the city.

Track 2.14 **Unit 7, page 65, exercise 7**

1 Mark has been on a boat ride on the river.
2 He hasn't visited Disneyland Paris yet.
3 Sophie has eaten kangaroo sausages.
4 Her mum and dad have seen some huge snakes.
5 Liam hasn't done sandboarding in the desert yet.
6 His family have slept in a small tent.

Track 2.15 **Unit 7, page 66, exercise 1**

1 Check-in
2 Arrivals
3 Security
4 Boarding pass
5 Departures
6 Baggage
7 Customs
8 Passport

Track 2.16 **Unit 7, page 66, exercise 2**

What a terrible flight! When we arrived at check-in, they said that Dad's suitcase was too heavy and he had to squeeze some things into his hand luggage. After security, we walked to the gate and we had to wait for ages while they refuelled. I fell asleep! We finally boarded the airplane and the pilot made an announcement that the flight was delayed! Finally, we were in the air. After about an hour, the cabin crew told us that a passenger in first class was very unwell and we had to land at a different airport! It was the worst journey ever!

Track 2.17 **Unit 7, page 67, exercise 6**

David: Hi Jenny, nice to meet you.
Jenny: Hello David, nice to meet you too.
David: So, Jenny, as you know, we're looking for a guide to work with our team. Tell me a bit about your relevant experience.
Jenny: Well, I have travelled all over the world and I finished my degree in European history last year.
David: How many countries have you been to?
Jenny: My goodness! I don't know! I have never counted them! I made a list of 15 dream locations when I was 15 years old and I have already visited them all, plus a few more.
David: Fair enough! Well, how about manual skills? Have you ever set up a ten-person tent?
Jenny: Yes, I have. I have done a few survival courses where I learnt how to find a good campsite, cross rivers, start a campfire and so on.
David: So, have you ever cooked on an open fire?
Jenny: Yes, I have, and I have caught a fish to cook on the campfire. My dad taught me how to prepare the fish for cooking.
David: Impressive! And what about sport? We offer kayaking and paragliding, as well as mountain climbing.
Jenny: I've been kayaking and mountain climbing, but I have not been paragliding yet. I'd like to try it.
David: Excellent! Well, we'll be in touch soon.
Jenny: Thank you!

Track 2.18 **Unit 7, page 68, exercise 2**

It's just like it is in the movies!

Tourists who have been to New York City often say it's like walking through a big film set. That's not surprising; New York has some of the most cinematic locations in the world, including Coney Island, Times Square and the most filmed location of all time – Central Park. Here are five other places that are closely associated with films.

Paris, France

The romantic charms of Paris have appeared in lots of films, from love stories to thrillers. The 2018 action spy film Mission: Impossible – Fallout shows car chases through its boulevards, a speedboat chase along its canals and a helicopter flight over the Eiffel Tower. If there's one thing better than a good action scene, it's a good action scene in a beautiful setting.

Salzburg, Austria

The picturesque Austrian city of Salzburg is the birthplace of Mozart, but probably more tourists come to see locations from the musical The Sound of Music. Here you can go on a tour that follows in the footsteps of Maria and the Von Trapp family, and even sing 'Do Re Mi' in the famous Mirabell Gardens.

Petra, Jordan

The ancient city of Petra has captured the imagination of visitors for centuries. So, perhaps it's no surprise that it has also featured as the backdrop to a number of blockbuster films. In 1989, the city famously appeared in Indiana Jones and the Last Crusade. It is one of the most famous archaeological sites in the world and has become a very popular tourist destination, too.

New Zealand

This country is so closely associated to The Lord of the Rings film series that the country's national tourism board has advertised on their website: 'Experience New Zealand, home of Middle Earth.' In the years after the films came out, tourism increased by 40%, and 6% of the visitors gave the film as their reason for coming.

King's Cross Station, London

More specifically, Platform 9 ¾ at King's Cross Station is one of many stops on a Harry Potter tour that millions of fans have already been on. Here you can queue up to take a selfie or pay to have a photo taken at the place where Harry got on the train to Hogwarts.

Track 2.19 **Unit 7, page 71, exercise 1**

Jill: You're back! How was your holiday?
Tony: Hey! Oh, it was great, thanks.
Jill: Where have you been?
Tony: We did a road trip from Chicago to Los Angeles. Now I can say I've been on Route 66!
Jill: That's so cool!
Tony: Yeah, it's been my mum's dream for years.
Jill: I've never been on a road trip, what was it like?
Tony: It was amazing, but it's a long time to be stuck with your family. My brother
drove me mad! Especially when we got stuck in traffic.
Jill: Ha ha, I know how that feels, I was in the same boat last summer on our camping trip. I love my family, but after three weeks in a tent together, everybody was driving me mad!
Tony: Yeah? My dad was pretty annoying too. He's such a backseat driver! Whenever my mum was driving, he kept telling her what to do.

Jill: Anyway, what was your favourite part?
Tony: Well, my favourite state was Texas.
Jill: Oh! I've been there a few times! My aunt lives near Dallas.
Tony: Cool! Have you ever been to a Rodeo?
Jill: No, I haven't seen a Rodeo yet, but my uncle said he'll take me next time we visit.
Tony: You should definitely go; it's amazing! Anyway, I have to get to class, but I'll show you the photos later!
Jill: Great, see you later!

Track 2.20 **Unit 8, page 72, exercise 1**

1

Upcycling is when you reuse an object in a new way, for example when you change, repair or decorate something so that it's even more practical or beautiful.

2

Public transport is the system of buses, trains and trams, for example, that the government runs. If more people use public transport, there will be less traffic and less pollution.

3

When people get together in the street to raise awareness of an issue or to object to something, this is called a public protest.

4

Recycling is when we collect materials like glass, plastic, paper or even clothing so they can be reused instead of being thrown into a landfill.

5

Clean-up days are when people get together to clean up a public area, picking up litter and waste to make it safer and more attractive. Usually this takes place in a natural area, such as a park or a riverbank.

6

With a bit of imagination, you can make rubbish into art. Then you can put it in a public place for all to enjoy. This is called an art installation. Art installations can help raise awareness of the importance of taking care of the environment.

Track 2.21 **Unit 8, page 73, exercise 4**

1 If you recycle electronic items, you protect natural resources.
2 When the air is polluted, public health standards decrease.
3 When you reuse paper, you save trees.
4 If we all help a little, we can change a lot.
5 When governments take action, big changes happen.

Track 2.22 **Unit 8, page 73, exercise 5**

1 If glaciers continue to melt, sea levels will rise.
2 If the human population keeps growing, we will need to use more land to build houses.
3 If more forests disappear, many species of plants and animals will become extinct.
4 If we don't buy products that harm the environment, companies won't continue to make them.
5 If we change our habits, we will reduce the speed of climate change.

Track 2.23 **Unit 8, page 74, exercise 1**

Monday

Task: Arrive and set up the campsite. Watch the birds and write about their habitat. Location: Near the cliffs and then by the river, in the valley.

Tuesday

Task: Test the water quality and measure the level of the stream. Location: At the waterfall in the south of the island.

Wednesday

Task: Record the types of flowers, bushes and trees. Location: In the north of the island.

Thursday

Task: Watch the sunrise to see what wildlife appears. Location: At the top of a hill on the east of the island.

Friday

Task: Look for insects under rocks and stones. Location: By the lake.

Saturday

Task: Watch the sunset to say goodbye to the island! Location: By the coast on the west side of the island.

Track 2.24 **Unit 8, page 74, exercise 2**

Interviewer: Today we are talking Rose Oakes. Rose is a biologist and tomorrow she is going to travel to a local island to do a study of the wildlife there. Why are you going to the island by helicopter?
Rose: I know, it´s not exactly public transport! However, I'm going to arrive by helicopter because there's no harbour and the waves are too strong. If I go by boat, it will smash against the cliffs!
Interviewer: Oh no! A helicopter is the best way to travel then. Are you going to take a lot of equipment?
Rose: No, I travel light. I am going to take what I need. There are a lot of hills on the island and I am going to walk a lot.
Interviewer: As well as wildlife, you are going to study plants and trees. How do you know what type of trees there are going to be on the island?
Rose: I studied forestry, so I can identify trees by looking at the leaves.
Interviewer: And finally, why do you look for wildlife at sunrise and not sunset?
Rose: Ah! That's because it's easier for me to hide from the animals and observe them in their natural habitat.

Track 2.25 **Unit 8, page 74, exercise 5**

Listen and repeat.

/aʊ/ allow, brown, doubt, how, out, round

Track 2.26 **Unit 8, page 75, exercise 6**

1

Hi, I'm Sarah. I'm concerned about the environment, so me, my dad and my brother have decided on some changes we are going to make. For example, we aren't going to go on holiday by airplane for a few years. Also, I am going to stop charging my mobile phone and laptop every night.

2

I'm Mark, Sarah and Scott's dad. I've promised Sarah that I am going to ride my bike to work more often. Also, I am going to buy some plants for the garden that attract bees.

I am not going to wash my car as often, and my company is going to donate some money to a local environmental education campaign.

3

My name's Scott. I'm so happy my family is environmentally aware. In the garden, we are going to collect rain in a container and use it to water the plants. We aren't going to use plastic bags or straws any more either. What is your family going to do?

Track 2.27 **Unit 8, page 76, exercise 2**

Global warming, can we make a difference?

There are many threats to our environment, but most scientists agree that the biggest is global warming, and that we are mostly responsible. That is because we have filled the air with greenhouse gases: methane, nitrous oxide and especially carbon dioxide (CO2), which trap heat in the atmosphere. We are seeing its effects already: melting glaciers, growing deserts and more frequent and severe extreme weather events. If this continues, ice near the poles will melt too. If that happens, sea levels will rise dramatically and many parts of the world will be underwater. What can we do?

Eat less meat.

Around 15% of human greenhouse gas emissions come from farmed animals. People who eat no meat save nearly a tonne of CO2 a year. That's about a fifth of what the average person produces in a year. If we all reduce our meat consumption, we can make a big difference.

Drive and fly less.

Choosing not to use a car can reduce your emissions by 2.5 tonnes, but just using public transport more often also saves an enormous amount. Flying produces a lot of CO2 too – about half a tonne for a five-hour flight.

Be energy smart.

Energy is the biggest contributor to greenhouse gases. Households can make a big difference by using renewable energy, like solar, wind or hydropower. If a typical house uses solar power, it can save almost a tonne of CO2 a year. But that's not an easy change for everyone to make. There are many ways to reduce the energy you use at home. Use energy-saving light bulbs, take shorter showers, put on warm clothes instead of turning on the heating, and turn things off when you're not using them.

Set an example.

Some people don't believe that one person can make a difference. Others say they don't want to tell people what to do. But maybe you don't have to. Research shows that people tend to imitate each other. So, just by doing what you can, you're inspiring those around you to do the same.

Track 2.28 **Unit 8, page 79, exercise 1**

Katie

To solve big problems, we have to think outside the box. Some people don't like the idea of genetically modified food, but I believe that it's the best way to solve world hunger. If we can modify plants so they can adapt to difficult conditions, people will be able to grow their own food.

Derek

I go door to door and ask people to sign petitions and letters to politicians. I believe that actions really do speak louder than words. If lots of people get involved, the government will talk about the idea. It doesn't always mean the laws will change, but it shows the politicians that people are interested in environmental issues.

Emma

If we really want to make a stand against climate change, we have to educate the next generation correctly. If people understand the effect their behaviour has on the planet, society will change. So, education is the most important tool in the fight against global warming. By improving their understanding, we can help our children to make a difference.

Track 2.29 **Unit 9, page 82, exercise 1**

Hey, I'm Jane. My friend Taylor and I are really close, but we met by chance! I was visiting my grandparents in the town where they live and Taylor moved in next door to them. We can't see each other during the week, so we keep in touch by messaging and chatting online. At the weekend we like to listen to music and go shopping. We mostly go shopping with Taylor's friends because the shops are better where she lives. Yesterday I bought a really cool jacket. Taylor bought a skirt. The skirt was cheaper than my jacket because it was on sale.

Track 2.30 **Unit 9, page 82, exercise 2**

Jane: Look, Taylor! Aren't these jeans nice?!

Taylor: Oh yes, they look really good!

Jane: The price isn't on the label. I'll ask the shop assistant. Excuse me, could you tell me how much these jeans cost?

Shop Assistant: They're 60 pounds. The brand is Italian.

Jane: That's too expensive. I don't have enough money. I can't afford them.

Taylor: Can you ask your mum if you don't have enough money?

Jane: It doesn't matter. I love trying on clothes, even if I don't buy them!

Taylor: Umm, what do you think of this skirt?

Jane: It's nice, but... I don't think that's the right size for you. It looks too small. I'll go and find you a bigger one.

Taylor: Thanks, Jane!

Taylor: What do you think?

Jane: I think you should buy it! If you want to take it back, just keep the receipt.

Taylor: You're right. I'm going to buy it!

Track 2.31 **Unit 9, page 83, exercise 5**

My friend Brett can play chess really well. I'd like to be able to play chess better, but it's so complicated! I've never been able to remember all the ways the pieces can move. He's teaching me and he says that I will be able to beat him one day. Anyway, he can't eat pizza faster than me. I'm an eating machine!

Track 2.32 **Unit 9, page 84, exercise 1**

When my cousin John left Newcastle and went to live in Sydney, I told him I was cheerful because he was positive about moving. But really I felt afraid and alone. We used to hang out together with our friends after school a lot and sometimes go for a slice of pizza. We both love pizza.

He sends me lots messages and photos, though. He says Sydney is a very modern city compared to Newcastle, and everyone loves sunbathing and having barbecues. I thought that sounds excellent, but he thinks sunbathing's boring and he doesn't care much about barbecues.

He emailed me a photograph he took of the Sydney Harbour Bridge. It looked just like the Tyne Bridge in Newcastle! The Tyne Bridge is shorter and the Sydney Harbour Bridge is more famous, but they look the same. We were shocked! When he first arrived in Sydney, John was a bit disappointed. He thought the kids at school would be friendlier, and he said there were times he hated being there, but now he's making friends and things are getting better. He doesn't love it, but he's starting to enjoy living there. And one day, I'm going to go and visit him!

Track 2.33 **Unit 9, page 84, exercise 2**
Listen and repeat.
/j/ uniform, useful, year, yes, you, young

Track 2.34 **Unit 9, page 85, exercise 6**

1 My friend Tammy is a little older than me; she's 15 years old.
2 My hair is darker than hers, but her hair is longer than mine.
3 She lives in Cologne, in Germany. The weather there is better than in my town!
4 I live in Lincoln, in England. I think it's the most beautiful city in the world.
5 Cologne and Lincoln both have cathedrals, but the cathedral in her city is taller.
6 I was so sad when she moved away from England. It was the worst day ever!

Track 2.35 **Unit 9, page 86, exercise 2**
Unusual hobbies

Air Guitar: This may seem more like something everyone does sometimes when we're at home listening to music and we think no one is watching. All you do is pretend to play the guitar while you listen to music. In fact, for some people it's a very serious hobby, and there is even a world championship every year in Finland. The winner is the person who looks the most realistic and shows the most charisma and art in their 'playing'. And the prize is, of course, a real electric guitar. So why not start training? It's very easy – anyone can do it. And it's absolutely free!
Trainspotting: To most people nowadays, this is the name of a Scottish film. The hobby of the same name is less well known, and it's a hobby that's as old as it may seem weird. Trainspotters are train enthusiasts who go to stations or places where they can 'spot' or see different types of trains, and they collect information about them in special books. Then they exchange the information with other trainspotters, sometimes using computer databases. The first spotting records date back to 1841, and both trains and trainspotting methods have changed a lot since then. However, trainspotters still usually carry a book of train information, a notebook and a pen. And they still have the same interest in and wide knowledge of their subject.
Mooing: Can you moo like a cow? Well, if you're good enough at it, maybe you can go to the US state of Wisconsin, where they have contests of who can moo most like a real cow. Although perhaps it's not as varied or artistic as air guitar, the prizes can still be generous. In 2010, ten-year-old Austin Siok beat 80 contestants to win $1000. Not surprisingly, these contests take place in rural areas with lots of cows, so if you're a city kid it'll probably be a bit more difficult for you. But in an age where you can find all sorts of strange videos on the internet, maybe you'll be able to find some good 'mooers' to copy.

Track 2.36 **Unit 9, page 89, exercise 1**

Girl: I just came back from a holiday with my friend Amy. On the last day I told her that I had a stomach ache and I couldn't leave the hotel. In fact, I was tired of sightseeing and walking around the city every day. I was exhausted! It was only a white lie because I didn't want her to feel bad.
Boy 1: I told my cousin that I'm the school badminton champion. I said that I'm the best the school has ever seen! I'm pretty good, but not that good. I was bending the truth because I wanted to impress her, but now I'm stuck with the lie. I'm worried she might my ask parents if it's true!
Boy 2: Yesterday I was meant to finish an important project for school. My teacher was furious! So I lied through my teeth and said that my dog had run away and I spent the whole night looking for him. I lie to my teacher all the time, but this is the biggest one I've ever told.

Track 2.37 **Unit 1 Review, page 90, exercise 4**

Annabel: Hi Scott, is that your cat? She's enormous!
Scott: Yes, it is. Her name's Curly. I'm taking her to the vet. I take her once a year to
make sure she's healthy. She wakes me up every morning. She meows outside my
bedroom door and she's really noisy!
Annabel: Oh no! I love animals. I have two pets.
Scott: What pets do you have?
Annabel: I have a lizard called Rufus. He lives in a tank but he comes out to play every
day. He's energetic. I thought lizards were slow but he's fast.
Scott: That's cool! What's your other pet?
Annabel: I've got a hamster called Heather. She's slow and lazy; she sleeps all day! She's not like Rufus. They're like chalk and cheese. Do you have any other pets?
Scott: Yes, I do. I've got a rabbit called Fluffy, too.
Annabel: Do your pets see eye to eye?
Scott: Curly the cat and Fluffy play together. Fluffy's curious. She explores and Curly follows her. They get on like a house on fire! Fluffy like to sit on my lap, too. It's nice, she's pretty light.
Annabel: Aren't pets wonderful?

Track 2.38 **Unit 2 Review, page 91, exercise 1**

1. Where does Layla usually do her homework?
Boy: Hi Layla. What are you doing in the living room?
Girl: I'm doing my homework.
Boy: Why aren't you doing it in the study like you usually do?
Girl: Mum is working in the study. I can't concentrate! I'm going to my bedroom.
2. Which TV programme is Will watching?
Woman: Will, are you watching that programme about lizards?
Boy: No, Mum. I'm watching one about how to build your own house. A family are building a house in the countryside. The main bedroom is amazing!
Woman: That sounds interesting. I'm coming to watch too.
Boy: And tomorrow there's a programme about sleeping. It's called early birds and night owls.
3. Where does Sarah always put her bike?
Girl: Where's my bike, Dad? I'm looking for it but I can't find it!

Man: I don't know. Where did you leave it?
Girl: I always leave it in the porch because it's easy to get but it's not there now.
Man: Well, it's raining a lot. Maybe your mum moved it into the garage.
Girl: Oh, here it is! It's in the utility room.
4. What time does John wake up every morning?
Girl: Hi John. How are you? You look tired.
Boy: Yes, I am. I always wake up at eight o'clock. But today my baby brother woke me up at six! He sometimes cries in the mornings.
Girl: Are you coming to the cinema? The film starts at seven.
Boy: Yes, I am. We only go once a month and I can sleep later.

Track 2.39 Unit 3 Review, page 92, exercise 2

1 Two friends are talking about an art gallery. What did the gallery use to be?
Boy: What did you do at the weekend?
Girl: I went to that new art gallery in the city centre called Art Now! It opened last month. They had some amazing photographs of famous local artists in their studios and a short film about them on an enormous cinema screen.
Boy: Cool! Oh, I know that place. I used to see plays and ballet there with my mum before it became a gallery.
2 Peter is talking to his grandma. What did she use to do when she was a child?
Old woman: That's a lovely drawing, Peter.
Boy: Did you use to be creative when you were young, Grandma?
Old woman: Well, I used to go to the theatre with my auntie and I fell in love with the ballerinas. They were so beautiful. I wasn't very good at dancing, but I learnt to play the violin and I used to play in an orchestra. I was quite good!
3 Ellen, an artist, is talking about her art. What did she make a sculpture of last year?
Woman: I used to make a lot of sculptures of insects. I think I was inspired by Louise Bourgeois' big spider sculptures. I was crazy about them! Then I started making giant owls. Now, I make sculptures of people. A year ago, I made a glass ballerina for a theatre exhibition.
4 Owen and Lisa are talking about an arts festival they went to last week. What did Owen really like?
Boy: Hi Lisa. I had a lot of fun at the arts festival last weekend.
Girl: Me too, Owen. I loved the silent films with the jazz band playing live. I'm crazy about jazz now. I listened to my mum's jazz collection last night. She used to play in a jazz band!
Boy: I thought the jazz was OK, but it's not really my cup of tea. I really liked the photographs of famous people with their pets. They were brilliant!

Track 2.40 Unit 4 Review, page 93, exercise 4

Boy: Hi Rachel. I'm sorry I missed your birthday party last weekend. I made you these birthday biscuits. Did you have a good time?
Girl: Thanks very much! Yes, I did. It was a surprise party. We had a barbecue. There weren't any burgers but there were delicious sausages. My auntie was barbecuing all afternoon!
Boy: Yum! What decorations were there?
Girl: Our house looked amazing! There were coloured napkins on the table. There weren't any balloons but there were photos of me on the walls. There was one of me when I was seven. I was wearing a clown's nose!
Boy: That's funny. What presents did you get?
Girl: There were a lot of presents. There was a snorkel and some cool pink flippers from my dad. I lost a flipper when I was snorkelling at the beach last summer. The best present was from my mum. It had a gift tag in the shape of a guitar.
Boy: That's cool. Was there a guitar inside?
Girl: No, there wasn't. There were two tickets to go and see my favourite band play, and to go backstage and meet them after the concert! Do you want to come?
Boy: Wow! Yes please! Was there any music at your party?
Girl: Yes, there was. Everybody was dancing. There was a karaoke competition too. Oh, and there was an amazing chocolate cake. People were singing and I was blowing out the candles. Suddenly, it got very windy and the wind carried our parasol over the side of the roof terrace!
Boy: Oh no! Was there anybody in the street?
Girl: No, there wasn't, surprisingly. It's usually very busy. Nobody was hurt. Napkins were flying everywhere and my cousins were trying to catch them.

Track 2.41 Unit 5 Review, page 94, exercise 2

Woman: Last year at Tech Camp we gave courses on how to use a digital camera and a 3D printer. This summer we're offering a course on robotics. We'll teach you how to build and program a robot.
Tech Camp is for teenagers between thirteen and fifteen years old. It starts on the twenty-second of June and finishes on the third of July. In August there will be an exhibition on our website with video clips of the robots.
You'll work in small teams of five students. We'll provide laptops and all the materials. There are only thirty places on the course. The course costs seventy pounds per person.
Go to our website to reserve a place. Click on the robot icon on the homepage and download a form to complete. Email us the completed form before the thirty-first of May and tell us why you want to do the course. Please don't attach photos.
To finish the course, our futurologist Maggie Martin will give a talk. I'm sure you've heard of driverless cars and smart homes, but Maggie will tell us her predictions about nanobots. How will they help us? How will they change us? Look on our website for more information!

Track 2.42 Unit 6 Review, page 95, exercise 1

1 Harry is telling Amanda about a health problem. Who has he got an appointment with?
Girl: Hi Harry. Are you OK?
Boy: Not really. My teeth really hurt but my dentist said there's nothing wrong with them.
Girl: That's strange.
Boy: Yes, I know. I've got an appointment with our family doctor later today.
Girl: Maybe it's because of the way you eat. My mother had something similar and she has to have physiotherapy.
2 Jake has hurt his wrist. What does the paramedic say he has to wear now?
Woman: Hi Jake. Can you tell me what happened?
Boy: I was playing tennis and I've injured my wrist. It's bleeding and I feel a bit dizzy.
Woman: OK, calm down. There's a lot of swelling. You mustn't move your arm. I'll put a sling on it for you. You have to wear it until you get to the hospital.
Boy: Will I need a plaster cast or a bandage?

Woman: I don't know. At the hospital they will give you an X-ray to see if the bone is broken.

3 Lucy tells her dad she's feeling unwell. What does her dad say Lucy should do?

Girl: Dad, I'm not feeling very well.

Man: What's wrong?

Girl: I've got a sore throat and a runny nose and I'm really hot.

Man: Hmm… I think you've got a temperature. I don't think you should go to school today and it would be a good idea to see the doctor. I'll make an appointment now.

Girl: OK, Dad. Can I take a paracetamol?

Man: Yes, you can. I'll get you one from the first aid kit.

4 Bella is talking to a friend about work. What job does she think she should do?

Boy: What job do you want to do, Bella?

Girl: Well, I want to help people. At first, I thought I should work as a therapist, but I can't find a course I like. Then I thought I should become a paramedic like my dad. He loves his job, but he has to work at night and I wouldn't like that. I'd like to work in a health centre and give vaccinations to help children.

Boy: What about nursing? You could help lots of people that way, and we always need more nurses.

Girl: Good idea!

Track 2.43 **Unit 7 Review, page 96, exercise 1**

1 Which form of transport has Matthew booked?

Man: I looked at flights like we agreed, but the truth is the airport is very far away from where we're staying. And it would take a long time to get there by bus. So then I had a look at the maglev train. It looks great. The station is near our hotel and the journey only takes two hours. I reserved two tickets. I've never travelled by high-speed train before. I'm excited!

2 What has Kate already travelled in?

Boy: Hi Kate. Are you having a nice holiday?

Girl: Yes, I am. We're staying on an island. We've done a lot of things. Yesterday, we went in a hot air balloon.

Boy: Wow! I've been in a helicopter but I've never been in a hot air balloon. What was it like?

Girl: It was amazing. We saw the island from really high up. Tomorrow we're going to the mainland on a ferry. Have you ever been on one?

Boy: No, I haven't.

3 Where has Becky never been?

Boy: Have you ever been to Spain, Becky?

Girl: Yes, I have. I went on holiday to Majorca with my family last summer. It's much hotter in summer than the United Kingdom! Have you ever been?

Boy: No, I've never been abroad. Have you visited a lot of countries?

Girl: Yes, I have. I've already been to China, Russia and Mexico. In October I'm going to Japan for the first time.

Boy: Wow!

4 Why hasn't the plane taken off yet?

Woman: Good afternoon, this is your captain speaking. I'd like to apologise on behalf of the airline for the delayed flight today. This was because there was a lorry parked on the runway. Airport staff have already moved the lorry and we should be taking off soon. All passengers please remain in your seats for take-off. Please put hand luggage under the seat in front of you. Thank you and enjoy your flight.

Track 2.44 **Unit 8 Review, page 97, exercise 1**

Boy: I'm talking to Sarah Green, who started the environmental project Nature Clean-up last year. Can you tell us about the project and how it started, Sarah?

Girl: Well, Nature Clean-up is a team of volunteers. We pick up litter in natural areas like beaches, rivers and lakes. I'd studied about climate change and pollution at school but I really got the idea for the project on a trip to the coast last summer with my family. I was shocked by all the plastic on the sand and in the water.

Boy: Nature Clean-up now has over 5000 volunteers. Why do you think that is?

Girl: I think people can see that nature is being destroyed and if we don't act now, it will be too late to save it. At first, I put notices all along the cliffs and beaches asking people to volunteer. About twenty people came to help. Then I started a blog with pictures of the beaches, and that reached a lot more people. Next week I'm going to be interviewed on Channel Three!

Boy: What happens to the litter you collect?

Girl: When we do a clean-up, we organise the litter into different categories. If something can be recycled, we take it to the recycling bins. If it can't, it goes into a rubbish bin. That rubbish then goes to a landfill, but at least it isn't on the beach.

Boy: That's true. And it doesn't end up polluting the sea and endangering marine life. What are your plans for the future?

Girl: Tomorrow, I'm going to go on a protest against climate change in the city. On Saturday, I'm going to meet with local politicians to talk about installing recycling containers and bottle banks on the path that goes to the beach. I have a lot of energy and I want to save the planet! If we act now, we can make a difference.

Track 2.45 **Unit 9 Review, page 98, exercise 2**

Girl: Sorry I didn't call you at the weekend. I was really busy! On Saturday, I went to gymnastics class and then I went clothes shopping with my auntie. When I got home I was too tired to watch TV! On Sunday we had a barbeque, but the weather was too miserable to be able to sit in the garden.

Anyway, I wanted to get some bargains in the sales but I couldn't find many things I liked enough. Well, I tried on some fantastic jeans but they were too short, which was disappointing. I like jeans to be long enough to cover my socks. And the most amazing thing I saw was a beautiful jacket but they didn't have my size. All the ones they had weren't big enough. I couldn't put them on!

My auntie wanted to buy me a pink shirt and a black hat but they were too old-fashioned. They were the worst! Then I tried on a dress. It's really original! It was in the sales and it wasn't too expensive so I bought it.

The dress is a beautiful blue colour and it has flowers on it. I think the pockets are the best thing about it. They're bigger than a bag! I will be able to put a lot of things in them.

I'm happy because I'll be able to wear the dress to the party next Friday. I don't know if I'll look the most original or the strangest. Oh yes, on Tuesday I'm going to go to yoga class so I can't go horse riding with you. Can you go on Wednesday instead? Let me know…

Track 2.46 Wordlist, page 118, unit 1, Adjectives

big
brainy
clever
colourful
cool
curious
energetic
enormous
heavy
inquisitive
lazy
noisy
slow
vibrant
weighty
wonderful

Track 2.47 Wordlist, page 118, unit 1, Interests

collecting
drawing
hobbies
instrument
models
playing the guitar/violin
reading comics
watching films

Track 2.48 Wordlist, page 118, unit 1, Personality traits

active
agreeable
careless
cautious
challenging
compassionate
confident
conscientious
consistent
detached
easy-going
efficient
extroverted
friendly
inventive
nervous
neurotic
open to experiences
organised
outgoing
reserved
secure
sensitive
solitary

Track 2.49 Wordlist, page 118, unit 2, Home

attic
basement
bathroom
bedroom
flat
garage
kitchen
living room
main bedroom
porch
rooftop terrace
study
utility room
washing machine

Track 2.50 Wordlist, page 118, unit 2, Daily routine

brush your teeth
cook breakfast/lunch/dinner
do homework
eat something for breakfast/lunch/dinner
finish school
get dressed
get home
get up
go for a run
go to bed
have a break
have a nap
have a shower
have/eat breakfast/lunch/dinner
leave the house
play videogames
read a book
ride your bike
study
tidy your room
wake up
walk the dog
water the plants

Track 2.51 Wordlist, page 118, unit 2, World geography

Africa
Antarctica
Asia
continent
country
Europe
lake
landmass
North America
Oceania
South America

Track 2.52 Wordlist, page 118, unit 3, Irregular verbs

became
fell
fought
gave
had
made
met
say
sat
took

Track 2.53 Wordlist, page 118, unit 3, Culture

act
audience
ballerina
dance
interval
orchestra
perform
performance
performer
play
row
screen
stage
star

Track 2.54 Wordlist, page 118, unit 3, Art forms

architecture
cinema
digital art
drawing
literature
music
novel
performing arts
painting
photography
poetry
sculpture
short story
theatre
visual arts

Track 2.55 Wordlist, page 119, unit 4, Parties

balloons
barbecue
birthday
biscuits
blow out
burgers
cake
candles
gift
gift tags
cupcakes
decorations
presents
sausages

Track 2.56 Wordlist, page 119, unit 4, Entertainment

adventure
amusement park
backstage
camp
competition
concert
fancy restaurant
live music
roller coaster
snorkelling
ticket
zip wire

Track 2.57 Wordlist, page 119, unit 4, Festivals and celebrations

Easter
fireworks
gathering
graves
Halloween
make wishes
New Year
New Year's Eve
offerings
pagan
pole
powder
ritual
The Easter Bunny
water fights

Track 2.58 Wordlist, page 119, unit 5, Technology

Technology I
alarm clock
attach
charge
click
connection
digital platform
download
drag
homepage
laptop
machine
main menu
password
printer
right-click
track
type
video clip
Technology II
camera
computer programme
circuit
connection
data
electronics
hardware
insert
memory card
mobile phone
robot
software
update
wire

Track 2.59 Wordlist, page 119, unit 5, Phrasal verbs

log in/out
plug in (opposite: unplug)
sign in/out
switch on/off
turn on/off
turn up/down

Track 2.60 Wordlist, page 119, unit 5, Future technologies

artificial intelligence (AI)
driverless cars
electric cars
futurologist
genetic research
nanobot
nanotechnology
robotics in medicine
self-driving vehicle
smart factory
smart home

Track 2.61 Wordlist, page 119, unit 6, Health and illness

a cold
allergy
appointment
check-up
cough
dizzy
earache
eye test
hay fever
headache
infection
patient
runny nose
sneeze
sore throat
temperature
the flu
unwell
virus

Track 2.62 Wordlist, page 119, unit 6, Accidents

ankle
bandage
bone
break
bruise
bump
burn
chin
compression
concussion
crutches
elbow
first aid kit
heal
hurt
ice
injure
itch
nosebleed
pain
plaster cast
scratch
sling
sprain
wound
wrist

Track 2.63 Wordlist, page 119, unit 6, Healthcare professionals

dentist
doctor
nurse
paramedic
pharmacist
physiotherapist
specialist
therapist

Track 2.64 Wordlist, page 120, unit 7, Transport

cruise ship
double decker bus
ferry
helicopter
hot air balloon
jet
limousine
lorry
submarine
train
tram
underground

Track 2.65 Wordlist, page 120, unit 7, Air travel

abroad
airline
airport
announcement
arrivals
baggage
board
boarding pass
check-in
customers
delayed
departures
destination
disembark
first class
flight
gate
hand luggage
journey
land
passenger
passport
return
security
stopover
take off

Track 2.66 Wordlist, page 120, unit 7, Abstract nouns

balance
happiness
health
meaning
pleasure
spirituality
truth

Track 2.67 Wordlist, page 120, unit 8, Environment

bottle bank
clean-up days
climate change
deforestation
ecosystems
endangered
extinct
glaciers
habitat
landfill
litter
natural resources
organic
polluted
protests
public transport
recycling
reuse
rubbish bins
sea levels
species
upcycling

Track 2.68 Wordlist, page 120, unit 8, Nature

beach
bush
cliff
coast
coastline
harbour
hill
island
lake
path
river
sea
stone
stream
sunrise
sunset
valley
waterfall

Track 2.69 Wordlist, page 120, unit 8, Global warming

atmosphere
carbon dioxide (CO2)
damaging
desert
emissions
energy-saving light bulb
extreme weather
greenhouse gases
hydropower
melt
renewable energy
save energy
solar power
the poles
threat
tonne
waste energy

Track 2.70 Wordlist, page 120, unit 9, Shopping

bargain
exchange
expensive
label
pocket
put on
receipt
sale
size
try on

Track 2.71 Wordlist, page 120, unit 9, Hobbies

chess
dance
gymnastics
magic tricks
play the guitar/piano
ride a horse/motorbike
skateboard
yoga

Track 2.72 Wordlist, page 120, unit 9, Adjectives

afraid
alone
busy
calm
cheerful
delighted
disappointing
excellent
famous
fantastic
heavy
high
miserable
modern
old-fashioned
original
polite
positive
quiet
relaxed
rude
strange
traditional
unhappy

Get started!

Page 6

1 *Student's own answers*

2 1 interesting
2 lots of
3 a few
4 tennis

3 1 didn't go
2 stayed
3 are
4 broke
5 had

4 1 holiday
2 culture
3 aware
4 fascinating
5 perfect

5 *Student's own answers*

6 *Student's own answers.*

Page 7

1 1 swimsuit
2 stripy
3 there is
4 a few
5 jacket

2 1 Are there; there aren't
2 There is
3 There are
4 Are there; there are
5 Is there; there isn't

3 1 shorts – you wear the others in the winter
2 cap – you wear the others on your legs
3 yellow – the others are patterns
4 jumper – the others are accessories
5 suit – the others go on your feet

4 1 many; seven
2 much; a little
3 many; few
4 many; 50
5 much; lot of

5 *Student's own answers*

6 *Student's own answers*

Page 8

1 1 bored
2 it's
3 our
4 They
5 interesting

2 1 morning
2 well
3 introduce
4 meet
5 lovely

3 1 my
2 their
3 her
4 its
5 his

4 1 d
2 a
3 b
4 e
5 c

5 1 She
2 We
3 It
4 He
5 They

6 *Student's own answers*

Page 9

1 1 many
2 healthy
3 bowl of
4 any
5 some

2 1 any
2 isn't
3 are
4 some
5 a

3 1 e 2 b 3 d 4 a 5 c

4 1 These
2 This
3 Those
4 That
5 This

5 *Student's own answers*

6 *Student's own answers*

Unit 1

Page 10

1 1 colourful; noisy; energetic
2 curious; lazy
3 clever; cool
4 heavy; slow; wonderful

2 **1** e iii
2 a iv
3 d v
4 c i
5 b ii

Page 11

3 **1** eat
2 helps
3 like
4 feels
5 hold

4 **1** live
2 spend
3 are
4 likes
5 eats

5 *Suggested answers:*
1 True
2 True
3 False
4 False
5 True
6 False

6 *Student's own answers*

7 *Student's own answers*

Page 12

1 **1** nickname
2 pet
3 music
4 free time
5 enjoy
6 prefer
7 dream
8 not sure

2 **1** Tam
2 energetic and silly
3 pop or chill-out
4 drawing, reading comics, watching action films, collecting stamps and models of superheroes
5 every day
6 to be a cartoonist

3 *Student's own answers*

Page 13

4 **1** a **2** b **3** b **4** a **5** c

5 *Student's own answers*

6 *Student's own answers*

Page 14

1 *Student's own answers*

2 *Student's own answers*

3 *Suggested answers:*
Question 1: Where does the digital age leave our sense of identity?
Answer sentences: Firstly, it's very public. Secondly, it can be very superficial.
Question 2: So, what makes us who we are?
Answer sentence: We are all a complex mix of genes and experience that influence our emotional reactions, our behaviour and our view of the world we live in.

4 **1** To see what they look like, who they're with, where they go and what they like.
2 Because they're not necessarily real friends.
3 Because everyone can see it.
4 Genes, influences and experiences.
5 We project a different public image to how we really are, we show different sides of our personality to different people.
6 *Suggested answer:* Our identities don't exist on their own, they are affected by the people we come into contact with and how we treat them.

Page 15

5 **Technology:** link, online, post, selfie, social media
Psychology: behaviour, emotional reactions, experience, genes, personality

6 *Student's own answers*

7 *Student's own answers*

8 *Student's own answers*

Page 16

1 **1** Ellen DeGeneres
2 Jackie Chan
3 Cate Blanchett
4 Bruno Mars

2 **1** as well as, too, also, and
2 but, although
3 including, like, such as

3 **1** Combating poverty and disease, promoting fair trade.
2 They help make the world a fairer place and inspire others to do the same.

4 1, 3, 4

5 *Student's own answers*

6 *Student's own answers*

7 *Student's own answers*

Page 17

1 1 **Name:** Megan and Matt
Hobby: Playing keyboard / guitar.
Dream: Be in a famous band.
2 **Name:** James, Liz, Ross.
Hobby: Skateboarding.
Dream: Be PE teachers
3 **Name:** Tom and Alex.
Hobby: Skateboarding
Dream: Be famous scientists

2 **1** c **2** a **3** b

3 **1** are like chalk and cheese
2 see eye to eye
3 got on like a house on fire

4 *Student's own answers*

Unit 2

Page 18

1 **a** study
b bedroom
c rooftop terrace
d main bedroom
e bathroom
f utility room
g porch
h living room
i kitchen
j garage
k basement

2 **1** He eats his breakfast in the kitchen at 7:00.
2 He sometimes puts his football kit in the washing machine.
3 He sits on the porch every day.
4 Nick does his homework in the kitchen at 17:00.
5 He wishes that there was a basement in his house.
6 Nick's Dad spends lots of time on the rooftop terrace.

3 *Student's own answers*

Page 19

4 always
usually
often
sometimes
rarely / hardly ever
never

5 *Student's own answers*

6

How often...	Nick	Terry
do you tidy your room?	several times a week	every Saturday
do you listen to music?	three times a week	rarely
are you bored in class?	all the time	hardly ever
do you walk to school?	always	never
are you late for school?	always	always

7 **1** Nick tidies his room several times a week.
2 Terry rarely listens to music.
3 Nick is bored in class all the time.
4 Terry never walks to school.
5 They are always late for school.

8 *Student's own answers*

Page 20

1 **1** b **2** c **3** a **4** b **5** c **6** b

2 **1** Around 7:00.
2 It's cold in the mornings.
3 Her dad.
4 Because the sink is small.
5 At the back of the boat.
6 At 6:30.

3 *Student's own answers*

4 *Student's own answers*

Page 21

5 **1** am studying
2 eat
3 do
4 go
5 is having
6 are riding

6 **1** have
2 am having
3 are you doing
4 am talking
5 am waiting
6 are buying
7 do you have
8 have
9 love
10 see
11 are coming

7 **1** lives
2 is visiting
3 eats
4 are having
5 is buying
6 decides
7 is
8 is calling

8 *Student's own answers*

Page 22

1 *Suggested answers:*
1 Asia, Africa, North America, South America, Antarctica and Europe.
2 Oceania.
3 Egypt (in Africa and Asia), Russia, Turkey, Kazakhstan and Azerbaijan (all in both Europe and Asia).
4 Asia (2,310) and Europe (286).
5 All the land or earth (Pan meaning 'all' and Gaia meaning 'land' or 'earth').

2
Name: Miia
Country: Finland
How their routine is unusual: It's sometimes -30°C and dark all day. She finishes school at 1pm.

Name: Renata
Country: Brazil
How their routine is unusual: She goes to the beach most mornings and only has classes in the afternoon.

Name: Azibo
Country: Malawi
How their routine is unusual: She walks 12 km to school.

Name: Hyeun Jung
Country: South Korea
How their routine is unusual: He studies until after 10pm.

Name: David
Country: Australia
How their routine is unusual: He has lessons via satellite.

3 1 Hyeun Jung
2 Azibo
3 David
4 Renata
5 Miia
6 Hyeun Jung
7 David

4 1 housework
2 whip
3 cattle
4 (ice) skating
5 sandboarding

5 *Student's own answers*

6 1 give; feel
2 get; makes
3 have; don't like
4 make; don't need
5 means
6 help

7 *Student's own answers*

Page 24

1

Punctuation	Uses	Examples from profile
Apostrophes	possessives	friend's
	contractions	name's
Capital letters	place names	Colombia
	nationalities and languages	Spanish
Commas	separating clauses	, but she doesn't really like sport
	separating items in a list	reading, going to the cinema and dancing

2 1 My friend's name's Gerry.
2 He's from Ireland and he speaks English and Irish.
3 He's really interested in hip-hop, rock and reggae music, and he writes his own songs.

3 *Suggested answer:*
He's Paul, a boy from Middlesbrough in the north-east of England. He's playing roller hockey. His other interests are other sports, like football, basketball and judo, and playing computer games and hanging out with friends.

4 1 Paragraph 2   3 Paragraph 2   5 Paragraph 3
2 Paragraph 1   4 Paragraph 1   6 Paragraph 1

5 *Student's own answers*

6 *Student's own answers*

7 *Student's own answers*

Page 25

1 1 Sam   2 Charlie   3 Alex

2 1 Alex   3 Charlie   5 Charlie
2 Sam   4 Sam   6 Alex

3 1 b   2 c   3 a

4 *Student's own answers*

Unit 3

Page 28

1 **Painter:** Raphael
Style: Renaissance
Inspired by: Beauty and harmony
Created: 1506

2 **Painter:** Mary Cassatt
Style: Impressionist
Inspired by: Women's social and private lives
Created: 1880

3 **Painter:** Juan Gris
Style: Cubist
Inspired by: Mathematics
Created: 1916

2

become	became
die	died
fall	fell
fight	fought
have	had
sit	sat

3 **1** sat
2 fell
3 fought
4 died; became
5 had

4 *Student's own answers*

Page 29

5 **1** developed
2 did not have / didn't have
3 met; photographed
4 gave; created
5 took

6 **1** was
2 created
3 made
4 didn't finish
5 don't like; say

7 **1** Did Antoni Gaudí have a nickname?
2 Did he finish the Sagrada Familia?
3 Where did he find inspiration?
4 Did he like drawing plans?
5 When did he die?

8 *Student's own answers*

Page 30

1 **1** stage
2 play
3 rows
4 audience
5 interval

2 **1** d **2** c **3** a **4** e **5** b

3 **1** the Royal Ballet
2 at the age of 4
3 Yes, and also in England
4 15 minutes

4 *Student's own answers*

5 *Suggested answer:*
Verbs: act, perform, dance, play
Nouns: audience, ballerina, ballet, orchestra, performance, performer, screen, stage
Both: play, act

Page 31

6 *See table 1 below*

7 **1** didn't use to have
2 used to wear
3 used to play
4 didn't use to travel
5 didn't use to do
6 used to feel

8 *Suggested answers:*
1 David used to go to the cinema with his cousin.
2 David and his cousin used to eat in a fast food restaurant.
3 David's cousin used to live in England.
4 David didn't use to watch films at home.
5 David used to go to the cinema every Tuesday.
6 David didn't use to go to the cinema with his friends.

Page 32

1 *See table 2 below*

2
Literature: The development of writing
Music: Digital audio files
Visual arts: The development of new art forms, such as photography, cinema and computer art

1

	Lily	David	Sharon
In the past…	she used to go to the theatre every weekend.	he used to go to see concerts with his grandpa.	she used to watch a lot of TV.
With…	her aunt.	his grandpa.	her sister.
Now…	she is the star of the school show.	he plays in the school orchestra.	she has dance class three times a week.

2

Visual arts	Performing arts	Literature
painting photography sculpture Suggested added forms: illustration, ceramics, architecture, cinema, etc	ballet music theatre Suggested added forms: opera, other types of dance, mime, etc	poetry novels short stories Suggested added forms: drama, essays, novellas, etc

3 **1** True
2 True
3 False. Nearly everybody had access to books but less than 50% of Europeans could read.
4 True
5 False. He was inventor of the piano, the most popular instrument to compose for at the time.
6 False. They became more realistic in the Renaissance with the discovery of perspective, and then more abstract in the 19th and 20th centuries.

4 **1** cave paintings **2** the printing press **3** performance poetry **4** sheet music **5** digital audio file **6** sculpture

5 *Student's own answers*

6 **1** d **2** a **3** c **4** b

7 *Student's own answers*

Page 34

1 **1** b; Student's own answers
2 a; Student's own answers
3 d; Student's own answers
4 c; Student's own answers

2 *Student's own answers*

3 **Artist's name:** Wassily Kandinsky
Name of work: On White II
Type of art: abstract painting
Meaning of the painting: how fragile our lives are
Characteristics of the work: colourful geometric shapes and abstract forms, two sharp black lines cutting diagonally through them, a white background

4 **1** colourful geometric shapes
2 attractive abstract forms
3 sharp black lines
the descriptive adjective comes before the classifying one.

5 3, 2, 1

6 *Student's own answers*

7 *Student's own answers*

8 *Student's own answers*

Page 35

1 **1** Cloud Gate
2 2006
3 because she was forced to study Shakespeare at school
4 1616
5 paintings of people
6 his uncle

2 **1** b **2** c **3** a

3 **1** is crazy about **2** can't stand **3** not my cup of tea

4 *Student's own answers*

Unit 4

Page 36

1 **1** barbecue **2** burgers **3** sausages **4** biscuits **5** candles **6** blow out **7** presents **8** gift tags

2 **1** present **2** burger **3** sausage **4** blow out **5** candle **6** barbecue **7** gift tag **8** biscuit

3 *Student's own answers*

4 *Student's own answers*

Page 37

5 **1** there was **2** there were **3** there weren't **4** were there **5** There was **6** there were **7** Was there **8** there were **9** There was **10** wasn't

6 **1** There were decorations.
2 There weren't any people from her class.
3 There was one pizza.
4 There was a massive birthday cake.
5 There wasn't any ice cream.

7 **1** There was a big table under the trees
2 There were colourful balloons and tiny flags all over the garden
3 There was a cheese and mushroom pizza
4 Yes, there were cupcakes and biscuits
5 No, there was not chocolate on top of the cake

8 *Student's own answers*

Page 38

1

Tom	Sally	Megan	Will
Picture: b	Picture: d	Picture: c	Picture: a
concert, backstage	starter, napkin	competition, roller coaster	snorkelling, flipper

2 **1** **1** stadium **2** band
2 **1** singer **2** waiter
3 **1** amusement **2** photo
4 **1** holiday **2** swimming

3 **1** False
2 False
3 True
4 True
5 False
6 False

4 *Student's own answers*

Page 39

5 **1** was raining
2 was wearing
3 was taking
4 wasn't laughing
5 were eating
6 weren't looking
7 were waiting
8 was screaming
9 was shining
10 were leaving

6 **1** T-shirt and shorts
2 Mr Matthews
3 Next to the river
4 Because Simon pushed Jim into the river
5 To get on the zip wire
6 No, it was sunny

7 *Student's own answers*

Page 40

1 **1** People covering each other with coloured powder in India; Holi
2 People dancing around a maypole; May Day
3 Fireworks; New Year's Eve
4 Painted eggs; Easter
5 People visiting the graves of departed loved ones and leaving gifts; the Day of the Dead

2 *Student's own answers*

3 **1** c
2 c
3 b
4 b
5 a

Page 41

4 **1** e
2 h
3 d
4 f
5 g
6 a
7 c
8 b

5 *Student's own answers*

6 *Suggested answers:*
A historical re-enactment group: encourages the learning of history, encourages imagination and empathy.
A music group: you can work together to make something that is very beautiful and inspiring, much better than the sum of its parts.
A sports teams: you push each other to play better and learn from each other, help each other get and stay fit.
An environmental action group: you can achieve more by working together and have a stronger sense that what you're fighting for is worthwhile and that you're getting somewhere.
An online community: you meet people from very different backgrounds with similar interests, make people who don't fit into their immediate physical environments feel less alone
Your neighbourhood: you can meet people regularly in person and you can help each other more easily.
General benefits: make us feel less alone, help us grow and learn, make us feel better about ourselves

Page 42

1 d, b, a, c

2

Frequency	once; every year
Manner	carefully; suddenly
Sequencing	then; finally
Time	two years ago; last weekend

3 *Student's own answers*

4 *Student's own answers*

5

Frequency	every summer
Manner	brightly
Sequencing	at last
Time	last June

6 **1** invitation
2 fancy dress
3 wig
4 wardrobe
5 make-up
6 costume

7 *Student's own answers*

8 *Student's own answers*

9 *Student's own answers*

Page 43

1 1 b 2 c 3 a

2 1 Her brother
2 No
3 The local hospital
4 Make and sell bags and hats, and organise events
5 He had a bad knee
6 He was happy and amazed

3 1 a
2 c
3 b

4 *Student's own answers*

Unit 5

Page 46

1 1 printer
2 downloaded
3 video clip
4 right-click

2 1 homepage
2 log in
3 password
4 digital platform
5 upload
6 drag
7 clicking

3 1 c
2 b
3 a
4 b
5 a

Page 47

4 1 a smart phone
2 take a selfie
3 she doesn't know how to do it
4 the button on the side of the phone
5 push the button on the selfie stick

5 c, a, d, e, g, b, f

6 1 b
2 d
3 e
4 a
5 c

7 *Suggested answers:*
1 Plug it into the wall
2 Turn the volume down
3 Turn it off
4 Log out
5 Drag and drop it
6 Switch it off

8 *Student's own answers*

Page 48

1 1 c 2 a 3 c 4 a 5 a 6 b

2 1 hardware
2 update
3 electronics
4 data
5 insert
6 connection

3 *Student's own answers*

4 *Student's own answers*

5 1 c 2 f 3 b 4 a 5 d 6 e

Page 49

5 1 will
2 won't
3 either
4 will
5 either
6 won't

6 1 will 2 won't 3 will 4 will 5 will 6 won't

7 1 In the school cafeteria
2 She has extra classes
3 At 1:30PM
4 He will help with setting up the tables
5 His brother's camera
6 The school cafeteria will closed for repairs soon

8 *Student's own answers*

Page 50

1 1 smart homes; *Student's own answers*
2 driverless cars; *Student's own answers*
3 robotics in medicine; *Student's own answers*
4 artificial intelligence; *Student's own answers*

2 1 e 2 d 3 b 4 c 5 a

3 1 is an early example of successful 'futurology'.
2 use electricity and don't need human drivers.
3 eradicate lethal diseases.
4 will connect everything and make it run efficiently.
5 either destroy themselves or colonise the universe.

Page 51

4 **1** smart factory
2 nanobot
3 hyperloop

5 *Student's own answers*

6 *Student's own answers*

7 *Student's own answers*

Page 52

1 **1** password
2 video clip
3 download
4 right-click

2 *Student's own answers*

3 **Liked:** strength, added battery life
Didn't like: weight, you can't plug earphones into it

4 **1** battery case
2 battery life
3 drawbacks
4 earphones

5 **1** In general, all in all
2 The main thing is
3 The only drawbacks are
4 I'd recommend it

6 *Student's own answers*

7 *Student's own answers*

8 *Student's own answers*

Page 53

1

1
Name(s): Alice and Sandra
Project: Investigating chemical structures
How they feel: Confused

2
Name(s): Tony
Project: Developing an interactive guide to how machines work
How they feel: Excited

3
Name(s): Mark and Sally
Project: Creating a computer from parts
How they feel: Bored

2 **1** They didn't know anything about it and they wanted to learn something new
2 Biology
3 In a factory
4 He prefers working alone instead of in a team
5 At Mark´s house
6 She thought the project would be more difficult

3 **1** c **2** a **3** b

4 **1** don't have a clue
2 not rocket science
3 like the back of my hand

5 *Student's own answers*

Unit 6

Page 54

1
1 dizzy, earache, infection
2 appointment, eye test, headache
3 cough, sore throat, temperature

2 **1** go swimming
2 a lot better, almost recovered
3 glasses
4 after using the computer
5 yesterday
6 that she had a temperature

3 **1** b **2** d **3** a **4** e **5** c

Page 55

4 *Suggested answers:*
1 You should make a doctor's appointment.
2 You should take your temperature.
3 You should sit down.
4 You should drink hot lemon and honey.
5 You should take a nap.
6 You should try and do exercise every day.

5 **1** ill
2 fever
3 throat
4 indoors
5 rest
6 cough
7 chest infection

6 **1** can I come
2 you can
3 can I go
4 you can't do
5 I can't do
6 you can rest

7 *Student's own answers*

Page 56

1
- 1 wrist
- 2 sprain
- 3 plaster cast
- 4 itches
- 5 scratch
- 6 sling
- 7 crutches
- 8 ankle
- 9 blisters
- 10 aches

2 *Student's own answers*

3 *Student's own answers*

4 *Student's own answers*

5 *Student's own answers*

Page 57

6
- 1 You have to wear a helmet.
- 2 You musn't use headphones.
- 3 You musn't ignore road signs and traffic lights.
- 4 You have to cycle in the same direction as the cars.
- 5 You musn't cycle on the pavement.
- 6 You have to use hand signals to tell drivers you are going to turn.

7
- 1 should
- 2 can
- 3 don't have to
- 4 must
- 5 mustn't
- 6 have to

8 *Student's own answers*

Page 58

1
- 1 Doctor
- 2 Paramedic
- 3 Therapist
- 4 Nurse
- 5 Dentist
- 6 Pharmacist

2
- 1 Doctors
- 2 Nurses
- 3 Pharmacists
- 4 Therapists
- 5 Paramedics
- 6 Dentists

Page 59

3
- 1 Nurses
- 2 Paramedics
- 3 Doctors
- 4 Dentists
- 5 Therapists
- 6 Pharmacists

4
- 1 healthcare professionals
- 2 general practitioner, or GP
- 3 diagnose
- 4 recover
- 5 prescription
- 6 physiotherapists
- 7 resuscitate
- 8 tooth decay

5 *Student's own answers*

6 *Suggested answers:*
- 1 your possessions.
- 2 have a healthy mind.
- 3 enjoy ourselves and get lots of rest.
- 5 cure an illness after it after happens.

Page 60

1 *Suggested answers:*
- 1 a broken leg
- 2 a fever
- 3 gastroenteritis
- 4 headache
- 5 hayfever

2 have to, make sure, should, try, could

3 fruit, vegetables, wholegrain bread, pasta, rice, salmon, sardines and other fish

4
- 1 should, make sure
- 2 eat, try
- 3 experts recommend, studies suggest that
- 4 it's a good idea

5 *Student's own answers*

6 *Student's own answers*

7 *Student's own answers*

Page 61

1 a, c, b

2
- 1 True
- 2 False
- 3 True
- 4 False
- 5 False
- 6 True

3
- 1 c
- 2 a
- 3 b

4
- 1 was feeling under the weather
- 2 had a frog in his throat
- 3 was sick as a dog

5 *Student's own answers*

6 *Student's own answers*

Unit 7

Page 64

1 *See table at the bottom of page 195.*

2
- 1 False. He has been a travel writer for seven years.
- 2 False. His favourite trip was a cruise in Norway
- 3 True
- 4 True
- 5 True
- 6 True

3 *Student's own answers*

4 *Student's own answers*

Page 65

5
1 been
2 drunk
3 done
4 eaten
5 flown
6 gone
7 had
8 ridden
9 seen
10 slept
11 visited
12 written

6
1 already
2 yet
3 yet
4 already
5 yet
6 already

7
1 has been
2 hasn't visited
3 has eaten
4 have seen
5 hasn't done
6 have slept

8 *Student's own answers*

Page 66

1
1 check-in
2 arrivals
3 security
4 boarding pass
5 departures
6 baggage
7 customs
8 passport

2
1 hand luggage
2 gate
3 boarded
4 delayed
5 first class
6 land
7 journey

3 **1** f **2** a **3** g **4** c **5** b **6** e **7** d

4 *Student's own answers*

5 *Student's own answers*

Page 67

6
1 I have travelled
2 have you been
3 I have never counted
4 I have already visited
5 have you ever set up
6 I have
7 I have done
8 have you ever cooked
9 I have caught
10 I have not been paragliding yet

7 *Student's own answers*

8 *Student's own answers*

Page 68

1 *Student's own answers*

2

Paris: *Mission: Impossible – Fallout*
Salzburg: *The Sound of Music*
Petra: *Indiana Jones and the Last Crusade*
New Zealand: *The Lord of the Rings film series*
King's Cross Station, London: the *Harry Potter* film series

3
1 cars, speedboats and a helicopter
2 It's the birthplace of Mozart and the location for *The Sound of Music.*
3 Petra, Jordan
4 Tourism increased by 40%.
5 Pay to have a photo taken at Platform 9 ¾, where Harry got on the train to Hogwarts.

4 **Film:** set, car chase, scene, come out
Travel: canal, picturesque, tourist destination, go on a tour

Page 69

5
1 picturesque
2 scene
3 went on a tour
4 came out
Student's own answers

6 *Student's own answers*

7 *Student's own answers*

8 *Student's own answers*

Page 70

1 3, 2, 4, 5, 1
London

2
1 just
2 first
3 while
4 Then
5 After
6 Finally

3
1 just
2 while
3 first, then, finally
4 after

Travel by air	Travel by rail	Travel by road	Travel by sea
hot air balloon helicopter jet	train tram underground	lorry limousine double decker bus	ferry cruise ship submarine

4 awesome – Scotland
picturesque – Pitlochry
spectacular – the scenery on the drive through the highlands to Loch Ness
beautiful – the island of Skye
amazing - Edinburgh castle

5 *Student's own answers*

6 *Student's own answers*

7 *Student's own answers*

Page 71

1 **1** Chicago
2 Went camping with her family
3 His brother drove him mad and his dad was a backseat driver
4 Texas
5 Yes
6 Her uncle

2 **1** b **2** c **3** a

3 **1** drives me mad
2 backseat driver
3 in the same boat

4 *Student's own answers*

Unit 8

Page 72

1 **1** upcycling
2 using public transport
3 public protests
4 recycling
5 clean-up days
6 art installations

2 **a** 6; *Student's own answers*
b 5; *Student's own answers*
c 4; *Student's own answers*
d 3; *Student's own answers*
e 1; *Student's own answers*
f 2; *Student's own answers*

3 *Student's own answers*

Page 73

4 **1** b **2** e **3** a **4** c **5** d

5 **1** will rise
2 will need
3 disappear
4 won't continue
5 change

6 **1** If the next generation learn about climate change, they will save the world.
2 If we use too many natural resources, there will be none left.
3 If icebergs continue to melt, polar bears won't have anywhere to live.
4 When their habitats are destroyed, species of animals become endangered.
5 When deforestation occurs, ecosystems are destroyed.

7 *Student's own answers*

Page 74

1 **1** habitat
2 valley
3 stream
4 waterfall
5 bushes
6 north
7 sunrise
8 east
9 stones
10 lake
11 sunset
12 west

2 **1** There's nowhere for a boat to dock safely (there's no harbour and the waves are too strong).
2 No, she travels light (she only takes only what she needs).
3 By looking at the leaves
4 Because it's easier for her to hide from the animals and observe them in their natural habitat

3 **1** e **2** a **3** f **4** b **5** c **6** d

4 **1** harbour
2 cliff
3 stream
4 hill
5 coast
6 path

5 *Student's own answers*

Page 75

6 **1** are going to make
2 aren't going to go
3 am going to stop
4 am going to ride
5 am going to buy
6 am not going to wash
7 is going to donate
8 are going to collect
9 aren't going to use
10 is; going to do?

7 **1** I am going to take
2 Are you going to stop
3 is going to plant
4 I am going to join
5 I am not going to drop

8 *Student's own answers*

Page 76

1 **1 Litter**
Suggested answer: it pollutes our streets, parks and beaches, and some of the rubbish can be dangerous. People should take their litter home with them and recycle as much as possible, and they should be penalised enough to stop them doing it.
2 Air pollution or smog
Suggested answer: it causes serious health problems. We need to reduce our use of cars and try to use less polluting energy sources.
3 Industrial pollution
Suggested answer: it pollutes water sources, for example. There need to be bigger penalties to stop companies doing this.

2 **1** d **2** b **3** c **4** a

Page 77

3 **1** b **2** c **3** c **4** a **5** a **6** c

4 **1** threat
2 greenhouse
3 emissions
4 Renewable
5 heating

5 *Student's own answers*

6 *Student's own answers*

Page 78

1 **1** Every; some **2** No; every **3** Any; no

2 **1** What's causing it?
2 What's so bad about it?
3 What are governments doing?
4 Is there anything I can do?

3 *Student's own answers*

4 *Student's own answers*

5 *Student's own answers*

6 *Student's own answers*

7 *Student's own answers*

Page 79

1 **1** box
2 food
3 hunger
4 modify
5 grow

2 **1** sign
2 letters
3 actions
4 involved
5 environmental

3 **1** make
2 educate
3 behaviour
4 global
5 understanding

2 *Student's own answers*

3 **1** b
2 c
3 a

Unit 9

Page 82

1 **1** Jane was visiting her grandparents.
2 They message each other and chat online.
3 They like to listen to music and go shopping.
4 She bought a jacket.
5 A skirt.

2 **1** label
2 expensive
3 trying on
4 size
5 receipt

3 **1** hot enough
2 too big
3 enough time
4 tall enough
5 too small
6 too short

Page 83

4 **1** can do gymnastics
2 can't do yoga
3 couldn't paint
4 be able to ride a motorbike
5 could ride a horse

5 **1** can
2 be able to
3 been able to
4 will be able to
5 can't

6 **1** Could you ride a bike when you were four years old?
2 Would you like to be able to speak Mandarin?
3 Do you know anyone who can't swim?
4 Can you play the guitar?
5 What's something your best friend can't do?

7 *Student's own answers*

Page 84

1 **1** a **2** c **3** b **4** c

2 *Student's own answers*

3 **1** b **2** e **3** a **4** c **5** d

4 **1** fantastic; relaxed
2 traditional; high
3 famous; heavy
4 strange; original

Page 85

5

Adjective	Comparative	Superlative
delicious	more delicious than	the most delicious
heavy	heavier than	the heaviest
large	larger than	the largest
slow	slower than	the slowest
hot	hotter than	the hottest
amazing	more amazing than	the most amazing

6 **1** older
2 darker; longer
3 better
4 most beautiful
5 taller
6 worst

7 *Student's own answers*

8 *Student's own answers*

Page 86

1 1 playing music
2 reading
3 fishing
4 crafts
5 birdwatching

2 *Student's own answers*

3 1 False. It's pretending to play the guitar while listening to music.
2 True.
3 True.
4 False. They still usually use a notebook and a pen, though they sometimes record the information on computer databases to exchange it.
5 False. It's the one who can moo most like a real cow.
6 True.

Page 87

4 1 d 2 c 3 e 4 a 5 b

5 *Student's own answers*

6 *Student's own answers*

7 *Student's own answers*

8 *Student's own answers*

Page 88

1 **Beginning:** 2, 4, 6
End: 1, 3, 5

2 To reply to an email from Juana saying she's coming to Brussels to visit.

3 1 It was great to hear from you!
2 So you're coming to Brussels?
3 So, if you like…
4 Then we could
5 Anyway
6 I'm glad
7 Let me know
8 Bye for now

4 1 React to email and respond to news
2 Offer help and make suggestions
3 Repeat response to news and offer more help

5 *Student's own answers*

6 *Student's own answers*

7 *Student's own answers*

Page 89

1 1 a 2 b 3 c 4 c 5 b 6 a

2 1 c 2 b 3 a

3 1 lie through your teeth
2 tell a white lie
3 bend the truth

4 *Student's own answers*

Unit reviews

Unit 1

1 1 c 2 a 3 b 4 a 5 b 6 c

2 *Student's own answers*

3 *Student's own answers*

4 1 enormous, noisy
2 energetic, fast
3 lazy, slow
4 curious, light

Unit 2

1 1 b 2 a 3 c 4 c

2 1 every
2 ever
3 am
4 once
5 terrace
6 sleep

3 *Student's own answers*

4 *Student's own answers*

Unit 3

1 1 b
2 c
3 c

2 1 b
2 c
3 a
4 b

3 *Student's own answers*

4 *Student's own answers*

Unit 4

1 1 b 2 c 3 a 4 c 5 b 6 b

2 *Student's own answers*

3 *Student's own answers*

4 **1** b
2 a
3 b
4 c
5 c

Unit 5

1 **1** c
2 b
3 b
4 a

2 **1** robot
2 June
3 30
4 photo
5 nanobots

3 *Student's own answers*

4 *Student's own answers*

Unit 6

1 **1** a
2 c
3 a
4 b

2 *Student's own answers*

3 **1** bruise
2 heal
3 to
4 crutches
5 scratch
6 can

4 *Student's own answers*

Unit 7

1 **1** a
2 c
3 b
4 b

2 **1** airport
2 journey
3 underground
4 arrive
5 ever
6 yet

3 *Student's own answers*

4 *Students' own answers*

Unit 8

1 **1** a
2 c
3 b
4 b

2 *Student's own answers*

3 **1** e
2 b
3 d
4 f

Unit 9

1 **1** e
2 c
3 b

2 **1** busy
2 long
3 original
4 pockets
5 horse riding

3 *Student's own answers*

4 *Student's own answers*

Track 1

Unit 1, page 4, exercise 3

Ben: Hi, can I sit here?

Mel: Sure. You're new here, aren't you? What's your name?

Ben: It's Ben. Ben Patterson. I've just moved here from Brighton. Today was my first day at school and it's my first time on the school bus.

Mel: Ah OK! My family moved here a few years ago so I know what's it's like to be the new student in class. My name's Melanie, but everyone calls me Mel. It's my nickname.

Ben: Nice to meet you, Mel. Are we in the same year at school? How old are you?

Mel: I'm fourteen. And you?

Ben: I was fifteen on the first of September.

Mel: My birthday is next week, on the 29th.

Ben: Ha! It's my dog's birthday then too!

Mel: Oh, you have a dog?

Ben: Yes, I do. I have a black dog called Harvey. He's really big and energetic.

Mel: He sounds gorgeous. I see you like sport too. Is that a basketball in your bag?

Ben: No, it's a football. My hobbies are football and drawing.

Mel: Really? What kind of thing do you like to draw?

Ben: Anything, really – Harvey, sometimes!

Mel: Well, then you have to come to my birthday party. I love drawing too, so I'm thinking of having an art competition at my party. Oh, and I'm going to have a huge chocolate cake. You can bring your dog too if you like. I have a wonderful cat called Bess, she's really playful.

Ben: Will there be other dogs there?

Mel: Yeah, my sister Molly has a very lazy dog called Byron!

Ben: That sounds great. What time is the party?

Mel: It's at a quarter to six on Saturday.

Ben: Saturday at five forty-five, let me write that down.

Mel: Great! This is my stop. Bye!

Ben: OK, see you next Saturday… Wait, what's your address?!

Track 2

Unit 1, page 4, exercise 4

See previous track

Track 3

Unit 1, page 6, exercise 3

Larry: Err Fabiana? Why is your bag moving? What's in there?

Fabiana: It's my pet, Eric. It's pet day at school today, remember?

Larry: Oh no! I didn't remember! I'm frightened of animals.

Fabiana: Don't worry. Eric is very small. He is a wonderful pet and he's very clever. He recognises his own name and he really likes people too. Would you like to hold him? He's not heavy.

Larry: Wait. What kind of animal is Eric?

Fabiana: He's a rat. Here, say hello, Eric!

Larry: A RAT!? ARGH! Don't let it near me! Rats are really dirty animals. I hate them!

Fabiana: Actually Larry, that's not true. Rats are very clean and they make great pets. And they are very playful and they love to learn new tricks. Watch this. Eric, stand!

Larry: Look at that! He's standing on two legs! Just like a person. Cool!

Fabiana: He can do a lot more too. Look! Eric, touch my finger with your nose.

Larry: Wow, he is clever! What does he eat?

Fabiana: His favourite food is vegetables, just like me! He shouldn't eat meat or cheese though. They're not good for him because they're fatty. Did you know that a rat's teeth never stop growing?

Larry: Erm, no, I didn't.

Fabiana: What about you, Larry? Do you have a pet at home?

Larry: Of course not! Nobody in my family likes animals, not even dogs. I prefer collecting stamps or playing my guitar.

Fabiana: I like playing the guitar too! And making model planes, but I couldn't live without my pets.

Larry: So, Eric isn't your only pet?

Fabiana: No. I have two snakes, three goats and a horse. I want to get a pig too. Pigs are very clever animals too.

Larry: Yuck! Snakes!? Two?! I really hope nobody brings a snake to school today!

Fabiana: Oh Larry…

Track 4

Unit 1, page 6, exercise 4

See previous track

Track 5

Unit 1, page 8, exercise 3

What pet matches your personality?

Rob, Canada

I have a big, brown Labrador called Jack. He's really energetic and honestly, if you want a dog, you must be energetic too. I walk him twice a day, once in the morning and again in the evening. He is the perfect pet for me because he's very clever and I love teaching him. He learns new tricks really easily. He is also very loyal. He always knows how I'm feeling and if I'm sad about something, he comes and sits next to me.

He really is my best friend.

Marguerite, France

I have a horse called Sally and she is my perfect pet. She's ten years old now. Horses are great for people who like being outside. Taking care of horses takes a lot of time, so you have to be very responsible and organised. You have to clean out the stables, feed them and exercise them for hours every day. They also need to spend time with other horses because they are sociable animals. It's a lot of work but it's also great fun.

Simon, Germany

Snakes make cool pets. My snake Betty is a corn snake. She's really curious and colourful. She's quite heavy but she's not very long. Corn snakes can live for twenty years, so it's important to be aware of this when buying your first snake. Snakes also need special equipment like a tank and special lights to keep them warm. Snakes are quite solitary and cautious animals. They mainly eat rats and mice. I'd recommend this pet to people who are patient and who are not easily frightened.

Track 6

Unit 2, page 12, exercise 4

1 Mark

Where do I like to relax? Hmm… that's a good question. Well, I spend a lot time in the kitchen, cooking food for my family.

But that's not where I like to relax because cooking is fun, but it can also be hard work at times. It's not the utility room, because that's where I wash my clothes. I suppose my favourite place to relax is my study. I write my books there when the children are sleeping in the evening. I sit there for hours by the fire, listening to music. It really helps me to be creative.

2 Penny

I feel relaxed on the rooftop terrace. I know it's not really a room but I love spending time there in the evenings. It's much better than my bedroom. I have tea there every day and water the flowers once a week. I sometimes draw pictures, or paint too. My friends love it. When they come over, we always spend a lot of time there. My parents love it too. In fact, we spend a lot of time there together in the summer, playing games or talking. It's great.

3 Rachel

I love relaxing in my bedroom. I have a lot of brothers and sisters. Six, in fact! They are always talking, so I need a quiet place where I can go when it's noisy in the living room. I have a TV too. It was a present from my aunt at Christmas. I am the youngest child so I can't always watch what I want in the living room. But in my bedroom, I can. Or sometimes, I read and enjoy the silence!

4 Fern

OK, this might sound strange… but I love spending time in the utility room. I know! I don't like doing chores around the house and I hate washing the dishes. But I think the sound of the washing machine is so relaxing. I like to just sit there listening to it. I also love the smell of clean clothes! So yes, for me, the utility room is the place where I feel the most relaxed!

Track 7

Unit 2, page 12, exercise 5

See previous track

Track 8

Unit 2, page 14, exercise 3

Henry: Hello? Hi Mum. It's Henry.

Mum: Hi Henry! How is summer camp going?

Henry: It's great! I love it. It's just as good as last year.

Mum: Oh wonderful. Now, tell me about your daily routine. What's that like?

Henry: Well, we usually get up at seven o'clock. We have twenty minutes to brush our teeth and then get dressed. We all meet in the hall to have breakfast.

Mum: Oh, that's early for you! Do you like the food?

Henry: It's not bad. We usually have cereal, toast and an omelette for breakfast. Oh, and orange juice. We have chocolate pancakes once a week. I wish we had them every day!

Mum: Hmm, lovely. And what activities do you do every day?

Henry: We do lots of stuff! We play sports like tennis, football and rugby several times a week, after breakfast. We have competitions every day, but I hardly ever win. You know I'm not very good at sport.

Mum: It's OK – you can't be good at everything. What other things do you do? What's your favourite activity?

Henry: I love the English classes. We have them every afternoon. And we have Italian classes twice a week. Our teacher is really nice. She rarely gives us homework. You know I don't like doing homework!

Mum: Yes, I do know that. What about drama?

Henry: Yes, that's my favourite class. We have drama class every Tuesday and Thursday. I love acting. I have decided that I want to be an actor when I'm older.

Mum: That's great! And do you do anything in the evening?

Henry: We play board games or read every evening. Video games are not allowed. Oh and thank you for the book. I love it. We sometimes have to do jobs too, like water the plants or tidy our rooms, but you know…

Mum: Yes, I know that you don't like chores Henry! You never tidy your room at home!

Track 9

Unit 2, page 14, exercise 4

See previous track

Track 10

Unit 2, page 16, exercise 2

Teenage lives: city vs. countryside

Jake, 15 - city

What do you like about your city?

There are a lot of things for teenagers to do. You can go to the park when it's sunny, or to the cinema to see the latest films. I have art classes several times a week after school, and tennis and swimming lessons at the local sports centre every Saturday.

What do you do on a typical day?

I wake up at eight o'clock. I eat breakfast and then I get the bus to school. It stops very near my house. I usually get home from school at four o'clock. I do my homework and then I play video games online or watch fims. I go to bed at ten o'clock.

Maya, 15 - countryside

What do you like about your area?

I live in a very remote place by the sea. There are a lot of big, open spaces and spectacular scenery. I love living with nature on my doorstep.

What do you do on a typical day?

I wake up at six o'clock. After I get dressed and have breakfast, I help my parents. We live on a farm, so there is always something to do. I'm hardly ever bored. At half past eight, I start school. There are only five students in my class, and in winter it can be difficult to get there because of the weather, so we sometimes study at home. After school, I have piano lessons. I also have English classes online twice a week in the evenings. I have dinner at half past seven.

Track 11

Unit 3, page 22, exercise 2

Meg: Oh, look. There's a message on the school website about our next school trip.

Silvia: Really, Meg? Where are we going this time? I hope it's an adventure park.

Tom: And I hope it's not to another science museum.

Meg: No it isn't, Tom. We're going to a modern art gallery. I really like modern art.

Silvia: How boring. I don't really understand modern art. I'd prefer to go to the cinema and watch a film. What do you think, Tom?

Tom: I agree with you, Silvia. I'd prefer to visit the zoo or go for a walk in the mountains. But I suppose anything is better than studying for exams. What time is the trip?

Meg: We have to be at school at a quarter to eight. The bus leaves at eight o'clock and it takes an hour to get there. The museum opens at nine and it's quite far away.

Tom: Oh, that's so early! I usually get up at eight!

Silvia: Yes, it's very early for me too. I need time to get ready in the morning. It takes me twenty minutes to have a shower and ten minutes to get dressed. Then I need half an hour for breakfast. I really don't want to go now.

Meg: Come on guys! It'll be fun. It says that we can meet young artists and learn about some famous paintings in the gallery. And there's an art class at the end where we can create our own work of art!

Tom: Really? That sounds interesting. How much is the class?

Meg: It's free. It usually costs £50.00 but it's included in the price of the trip and that's only £15.00.

Tom: Cool! Maybe it isn't such a bad idea after all!

Silvia: I'd still prefer to see a film at the cinema.

Track 12

Unit 3, page 22, exercise 3

See previous track

Track 13

Unit 3, page 24, exercise 3

Deb: Hi Pooja. I'm just calling to say that I can't meet you for lunch today. I'm really sorry.

Pooja: What a shame! Are you OK?

Deb: Not really. I had a terrible day yesterday.

Pooja: Oh no, what happened?

Deb: Well, in the morning, I went to the art gallery by the park with Tom, my friend from school. We got the bus there together.

Pooja: Yes?

Deb: Well, while we were looking at the paintings, I noticed that my new watch was missing. I'm not sure where I lost it, but it was either on the bus or at the gallery.

Pooja: Oh, that's terrible!

Deb: I know. My aunt gave it to me for my birthday last weekend, remember?

Pooja: Yes, I do. It was beautiful. I'm so sorry.

Deb: I know. I really liked that watch. We looked in the gallery but it wasn't there.

Pooja: What happened then?

Deb: Well, I was very upset, so Tom bought tickets to see the new play at the theatre. That made me feel better.

Pooja: Yes, that was really nice of him.

Deb: It was… except…

Pooja: What happened?

Deb: Well, I was so happy at first. We sat in the front row, next to the orchestra and the stage. It was like being at a concert! But at the interval, I left my wallet on the seat and when I went back, it was gone. I had £100 in it!

Pooja: Oh no! £100! What did you do?

Deb: I looked in my bag and then talked to the manager, but he wasn't very helpful, so we left. But that wasn't the end of my bad day.

Pooja: Oh no?

Deb: I fell on the way out of the theatre and I broke my arm. I had to go to hospital. In fact, I'm still here now.

Pooja: Oh Deb! That's terrible. What a horrible day.

Track 14

Unit 3, page 24, exercise 4

See previous track

Track 15

Unit 3, page 26, exercise 2

Three reasons why the arts are good for you

I used to think that the arts were boring, and many of the students in my class felt the same. But when our school started the arts programme two years ago, we found that the opposite was true. Language isn't the only way to communicate. Through literature, music and visual arts, teenagers can express their feelings when they find it difficult to talk about them to an adult. I didn't use to tell anyone about things that made me sad. Now, I find it easier to do this by painting or writing about my feelings.

Trevor, Year 8

In the past, skills like creativity weren't considered important, but that has changed. Nowadays, thinking creatively and problem-solving are important skills for future careers in areas like digital media or marketing, sectors where there are more and more jobs. Joining dance, photography or poetry classes can help you to develop these skills for the future.

Kate, Year 8

I didn't use to think I was very creative, but then I joined the arts programme at my school and I discovered that I'm good at dancing. I go to performing arts classes every week. We do modern ballet and sometimes theatre. The classes help us to relax and forget about the stress of exams, or problems with family or friends. For example, I think I'm a lot less angry and worried than I was two years ago. In fact, all of us are happier as a group. I really recommend it.

Barry, Year 8

Track 16

Unit 4, page 30, exercise 3

1 Jennie

My name's Jennie and I'm fourteen years old. My last birthday was really special. I got lots of great presents from my friends and family. My grandmother gave me a beautiful necklace. I wear it all the time. The reason my birthday was so special was because I didn't know about the party. My mum organised a surprise party in my favourite restaurant and we had pizzas, my favourite chocolate cupcakes and a massive birthday cake for dessert! It was an amazing day. I really didn't expect it. I was so happy!

2 Kirsty

I'm Kirsty and my favourite memory of a special event was last Christmas. I went on holiday with my family to New Zealand. On Christmas day, we went to the beach because it's summer there at Christmas. We swam in the Pacific and played games on the sand. Later we had a traditional kind of barbecue outside. They made a hole in the ground and heated the barbecue with hot stones. They put sausages and hamburgers inside, then covered the hole to cook the meat. It was so special because I had the most delicious Christmas dinner of my life!

3 Mark

My name's Mark and last Saturday was my special day. Why? Because my football team won the final match of the season and we became the champions! We trained a lot all year and it was really hard work. I was nervous before the match because we played in the city stadium, and it's huge. There were a lot of people there too. And guess what? I scored two of the five goals. That's what made it so special. Afterwards the team had a celebration meal at an Italian restaurant, and we had massive plates of pasta. I'll never forget that day!

Track 17

Unit 4, page 30, exercise 4

See previous track

Track 18

Unit 4, page 32, exercise 3

1

Ann: How was your weekend, Megan? Did you and your family go to see the concert?

Megan: No, we didn't. I forgot to buy tickets!

Ann: Oh no! So, what did you do?

Megan: Well, we wanted to go to the amusement park in town. The one with the massive rollercoaster.

Ann: Great! What was it like?

Megan: I don't know. When we got there, there were a lot of people and we were waiting to buy tickets when it started to rain. It was really wet and cold. I was wearing a coat, but we didn't have an umbrella. So, we left.

Ann: Oh dear. What a disaster!

Megan: Not completely. In the end, we went to the new restaurant on Church Street and the food was delicious.

2

Barry: Hey Rachel! How was your holiday?

Rachel: It wasn't that great, to tell you the truth.

Barry: Why, what happened?

Rachel: Well, my brother wanted to go to the beach. My dad wanted to go on a cruise for a week and I wanted to go on a city break for three days to Berlin or Madrid.

Barry: Where did you go in the end?

Rachel: My brother got what he wanted, as usual. We spent 13 days on the beach. It was so boring! I spent my time snorkelling and reading, but I didn't go shopping because there were no good shops. And I didn't speak to my friends on the phone because the hotel didn't have internet.

Barry: Sounds like my perfect holiday!

3

Ava: Hey Linda. Happy birthday. How old were you? Wait, let me guess... 25?

Linda: Very funny! I was 15 on Saturday. I had a big party. There were 50 people there.

Ava: Wow! Who cooked the food?

Linda: My dad, but he forgot to buy half of it. I wanted pizza and a vegetarian dish because two of my friends are vegetarian. But Dad bought sausages and burgers and did a barbecue!

Ava: Oh dear!

Linda: Yes, those two friends only ate the cupcakes, and some of the birthday cake.

Track 19

Unit 4, page 32, exercise 4

See previous track

Track 20

Unit 4, page 34, exercise 2

A celebration of food

Food is a very important part of our lives, our culture and our celebrations. Here are some dishes from around the world each with their own special cultural significance.

Barmbrack

This bread is made with fruit and raisins and people traditionally eat it in Ireland, at Halloween. People put items such as peas, a piece of cloth, a coin or a ring inside the bread. Each item has a special meaning or superstition associated with it. The person who finds the coin, for example, will be rich. However, the person who finds a piece of cloth will have bad luck, or be poor.

Frappe

These Italian biscuits are made from pastry and icing sugar. Italians traditionally serve them at special gatherings such as weddings and at Christmas. The tasty snacks are a symbol of luck. People sometimes make wishes when they eat them.

Osechi Ryouri

This is a traditional dish from Japan and people eat it at New Year. It consists of chicken, salad, sushi and vegetables. Before the holiday, people prepare it so that they don't have to cook at the beginning of January. Each ingredient has a special meaning. Many people believe that the ritual of eating this dish brings good luck for the new year.

Russian Salad

Russians traditionally serve this salad at Christmas, birthday parties and other special gatherings. A chef from Russia started serving it in his restaurant in Moscow in the 1860s. They make it with potatoes, eggs, meat, apples, carrots and mayonnaise. Different regions of Europe have their own versions of this famous salad today. Caviar is another popular dish in Russia. They eat it on New Year's Eve because it is a symbol of wealth and good luck for the new year.

Track 21

Unit 5, page 40, exercise 3

Pete: Urgh, this is annoying!

Lily: Hi Pete, what's wrong?

Pete: Hi Lily. My tablet switches off all the time. And it's new! It worked on the first day, but then it started switching itself off. This is the third time today it's happened.

Lily: Don't worry. I'm good at technology. I'm sure I can help.

Pete: Really? Thank you. I'm usually good at these things too, but I don't know what's wrong.

Lily: Let's see. Hmm... Oh, I can see what the problem is.

Pete: What is it?

Lily: Look, the tablet isn't turned off. It's just locked, that's why the screen was dark. You push this button to unlock it. You can log in now. You just have to enter your password.

Pete: Oh! Thank you!

Lily: No problem. It's probably a good idea to change the settings though, so it doesn't do it so regularly.

Pete: Good idea!
James: Hi guys!
Pete/Lily: Hi James.
James: I was reading your technology blog this morning, Pete. It's great. There are some really useful tips.
Lily: Can you send me a link to your blog, Pete? I would like to read it too.
Pete: OK!
James: Speaking of technology. Do you guys have a minute? I have a problem.
Lily: What's wrong, James?
James: Well, I bought a new printer at the weekend, but I don't know how to use it.
Lily: Hmm, go on. What's the problem?
James: I'm not sure. I just press print, and nothing happens.
Lily: Right, you probably have to connect the printer to the laptop. Is there a user manual?
James: Yes, no, well - I threw it in the bin with the box by accident. Haven't you got a blog post about printers, Pete?
Pete: Yeah, but in this case we can just go to the company's website and download the manual from there.
James: Great idea! Thanks guys!

Track 22
Unit 5, page 40, exercise 4
See previous track

Track 23
Unit 5, page 42, exercise 2
Customer advisor: Hello, you're calling Tech Repairs. How can I help you?
Customer 1: Hello? Hello? Hello? I can't hear you!
Customer advisor: Madam, if you are calling from your laptop, make sure your headphones are plugged in.
Customer 1: Oh yes, that's much better.
Customer advisor: How can I help you today, madam?
Customer 1: Well, the thing is my printer isn't working. I bought it from your shop yesterday and I simply can't turn it on. Customer advisor:Madam, is it plugged in?
Customer 1: What?
Customer advisor: You need to plug in the machine. You'll need the charger. The charger is a piece of hardware that came with the printer.
Customer 1: Does it have a long black wire?
Customer advisor: Yes.
Customer 1: OK, and now?
Customer advisor: Press the big green button on the front of the machine.
Customer 1: It's working! Thank you so much.
Customer advisor: A pleasure to be of help. Have a good day, madam. Hello, you're calling Tech Repairs. How can I help you?
Customer 2: Yes, hello. Can you hear me?
Customer advisor: Yes, I can.
Customer 2: Oh, good. I'm talking on my new mobile phone and I'm still not sure how it works.
Customer advisor: How can I help you today, Sir?
Customer 2: It's my laptop. It's really slow. I'm getting messages telling me that I don't have enough space for my files and data.
Customer advisor: Ahh, I see. You need to update your software. This will give you more space for files and data and it will run faster.
Customer 2: How do I do that?
Customer advisor: Click on the menu symbol in the left-hand corner of the screen.
Customer 2: Yes. Now what?
Customer advisor: Type the word update in the search box. Do you see an option to update your software?
Customer 2: Yes, but is this safe? Will I lose information?
Customer advisor: It's perfectly safe, you won't lose information. All you need to do is...

Track 24
Unit 5, page 42, exercise 3
See previous track

Track 25
Unit 5, page 44, exercise 2
The advantages and disadvantages of technology for teenagers
Many of today's teens started using technology when they were three years old and are now digital experts. We look at the advantages and disadvantages of technology, and its effects on teenagers.
The skills we can develop
It is true that using technology from an early age can help young people learn important skills such as independence and decision-making. Many people predict that teens will be better prepared for work in the future due to the development of these skills from an early age. Teens can also develop natural talents for things such as playing a musical instrument, sports or writing by watching videos on digital platforms instead of paying for extra classes. However, using technology can also have a negative effect on creativity and imagination and also the ability to manage emotions like fear and anger.
A more connected world
Access to the internet allows teenagers to learn about different countries and cultures without having to travel. This creates a world that is more understanding and more open to differences. Apps, e-books and videos can also help to improve vocabulary and language comprehension skills. However, spending a lot of time on mobile phones, computers or social media can also make teens less socially active and sometimes make it difficult for them to make friends in real life.
The effects of technology on teen health
Teens can certainly learn more about their health and fitness thanks to thousands of websites and apps on the subject. However, spending a lot of time indoors isn't a good thing either. Research shows that using technology as part of their daily lives can encourage teens to sit more and move less. Spending a lot of time staring at a computer screen can also make their vision worse.

Track 26
Unit 6, page 48, exercise 3
Mum: Kids! It's time to get up or you'll be late for school.
Gabriella: Mum, I don't feel very well. I don't think I should go to school today.
Mum: What's wrong, Gabriella? You don't look unwell to me. In fact, you look very healthy!

Gabriella: I feel dizzy and I've got the worst… um… headache. I think I have a high temperature too. Look! Feel how hot I am!
Mum: Hmm. You look perfectly healthy to me. This isn't about your French test today, is it?
Gabriella: Err… no. Well, maybe. So, do I have to go to school?
Mum: Yes, you do. Get dressed and come down for breakfast. Raymond, Vincent, this is the third time I've called you. Come on!
Raymond: Mum, I don't feel very well.
Mum: What's wrong Raymond? Do you think you have a high temperature, too?
Raymond: No, my eyes are red and I have a runny nose. I can't stop coughing and sneezing.
Mum: Have you got a headache?
Raymond: No, my head is OK.
Mum: Then I think that you have hay fever. There are a lot of plants in your room.
Raymond: Oh no! I love them! What can I do?
Mum: Take the plants outside and then come to the kitchen to take some medicine.
Raymond: OK, Mum. But I want to go to school. I have a really important presentation today and I don't want to miss it.
Mum: Of course, you can go to school. And Vincent? Remember that you have a Maths test today. Wear your glasses; you always forget them. We don't want your eyes to get sore like last week.
Vincent: OK Mum.
Mum: Oh, and don't forget your doctor's appointment at 2:45pm, Vincent. I'll pick you up early from school. Now, everybody come downstairs and have some breakfast!

Track 27
Unit 6, page 48, exercise 4
See previous track

Track 28
Unit 6, page 50, exercise 3
Presenter: Welcome to Radio 40, live from London. I'm your host Dan Carling and it's very cold outside today! Here in the studio we some very helpful doctors who are going to tell us how to stay healthy in the winter. So, Doctor Gale, what are your top tips?
Dr Gale: Well Dan, the first thing you should do is eat healthily. That's true at all times of the year, of course, but it is even more important in the winter.
Presenter: What sort of food should we eat?
Dr Gale: We should eat lots of fruit because it contains vitamin C. You should drink hot water with lemon and honey if you feel unwell or have a sore throat. And it's important to drink a lot of water every day to look after your skin.
Presenter: Thanks for the tips! Doctor Desmond, what advice do you have to give?
Dr Desmond: I agree with Doctor Gale. I would also say that you should stay active and go for walks or for a run. But be careful of the snow and ice! If you get a concussion or break a bone, you should go straight to the hospital. Many people fall and break bones in the winter. And if you do fall and sprain your wrist or ankle you must rest. You shouldn't do any exercise until you've recovered.
Presenter: That's a good point. Anything else to add?
Dr Gale: I agree with Doctor Desmond, you shouldn't stay indoors all day. But you also shouldn't forget to use sun cream, to prevent sunburn. Even in winter!
Dr Desmond: True, and finally, don't forget to wash your hands regularly, because you kill the flu virus by doing that. You shouldn't eat anything without washing your hands.
Presenter: Thanks Doctors! That's all we have time for, folks. Tune in next week for…

Track 29
Unit 6, page 50, exercise 4
See previous track

Track 30
Unit 6, page 52, exercise 2
The professionals
This week Teen Time interviews paramedic Daniel Booth and dentist Cara Roberts to ask about their jobs in healthcare.
Daniel Booth
What's the best thing about your job?
I like the idea of helping people. In my job, we are usually the first people to get to an accident so the help we give can often save people's lives. That is very important to me. My job is different every day. Yesterday, I helped a man with a broken leg and this morning I helped an old lady with a concussion. Emergency medicine can be exciting, but there are also very hard moments. I work long hours and more than half of them are at night. Many people would find that difficult, but it's the best way to provide a good service to the community. And the job's never boring. I love talking to the patients because it helps them to keep calm. I also like driving the ambulance, and I certainly spend a lot of time doing it!
Why did you decide to do this job?
I didn't want to work in a hospital, but I wanted to make a difference to people's lives. Now I do, every day.
Cara Roberts
What is your daily routine like?
I get to work at nine o'clock. I usually have a lot of appointments in the morning. Many of my patients come just for dental check-ups, but some need to have procedures, like tooth extractions. Some people are scared of the dentist, but it's important to come because our teeth are essential for our general health. I see patients all morning, then I have lunch and have more appointments until I stop at 5 o'clock. Unlike other medical professionals, I work normal office hours from nine to five. It's quite a physical job and my arms hurt at the end of the day, especially if I have to extract a lot of teeth! It's the only negative thing about my job, however!
What did you study for this profession?
I did a degree in dentistry. It took five years to finish. Then I did a course in dental training and that was a year. It takes a long time, but it's worth it!

Track 31
Unit 7, page 58, exercise 3
1
Ben: Hi, Sarah. Isn't it your birthday tomorrow?
Sarah: It's today, actually. Guess what Dad bought me as a present. I'll give you a clue – it's related to transport.
Ben: A ride in a submarine? That would be amazing!

Sarah: No. A helicopter ride – this Friday!
Ben: But, don't you get sick when you travel? Remember that school trip to London? You were so sick, the driver of the double decker bus had to stop, and we all had to get off. We missed the trip to the theatre because of that. But it was funny…
Sarah: It wasn't funny, actually. I felt terrible. Anyway, that was two years ago. I'm fine with travelling now, thank you very much. But do you know what the best thing is? Dad said that I could invite two friends. I think I'll invite Gina and Lindsay.
Ben: But, I'd love to go on a helicopter.
Sarah: No, I've decided. I'm sorry, Ben.
Ben: I didn't mean it about the trip to London! You are a great traveller!
2
Denise: Did you know that more people use the underground in London than any **other method of transport, Sam?**
Sam: Really? I thought it was the tram.
Denise: No, trams don't carry as many people as the underground. And the tram system only opened in 2000. The first London underground railway opened in 1863. It **carried 38,000 passengers on its first day. And the first motor bus service in London only started in 1902.**
Sam: Wow! I didn't know that. How do you know so much about transport?
Denise: Oh, my grandad was a train driver, my aunt drives a bus and my dad is a lorry driver. Did you know that large lorries can't drive in parts of London on Sundays? It helps to make the roads safer and reduces traffic.
Sam: No, I didn't. I should learn more about driving and the roads though, because I want to buy a car soon!

Track 32
Unit 7, page 58, exercise 4
See previous track

Track 33
Unit 7, page 60, exercise 3
Mark: I can't believe we're going to Mexico! Are you excited, Elaine?
Elaine: Yes, I am. I'm not looking forward to the journey though. It's going to be a long flight. It will be 13 hours in total, and we have a stopover in Berlin.
Mark: I thought the stopover was in Germany.
Elaine: Berlin is in Germany, Mark! Hey, have you packed your bags yet?
Mark: Not yet.
Elaine: Mark! The flight's at 1pm. That means we have to be at the airport to board the plane by 12pm!
Mark: Oh no! I thought boarding time was 1pm.
Elaine: Well, hurry up. It's half past ten already. We can get there if we hurry. Don't forget your passport. And have you printed your boarding pass? … Right. There's security. We've only got hand luggage so we can go straight through.
Mark: Oh, good. Just think. Tomorrow we can be lying on the beach. Oh, and we have to go sailing. I've already made a list of things to do on our first day…
Elaine: And tonight we arrive at 9pm, so we can go straight out and try some amazing Mexican food. But for now, let's make sure we get on the flight! Have your passport and boarding pass ready for security. Then we have to run to the gate.
Mark: Let's see. Yes, here's my passport and my… oh no!
Elaine: What's wrong?
Mark: I've forgotten my boarding pass. I left it on the bed.
Elaine: Mark! Well, you'll have to go and check in. I'm going to go through security.
Mark: You're not going to wait for me?
Elaine: You're the one who made us late. If you go now, there's time. I'll see you at the gate. Or I'll see you when I get back on the 30th of October.
Mark: OK. I'll see you at the gate.

Track 34
Unit 7, page 60, exercise 4
See previous track

Track 35
Unit 7, page 62, exercise 2

Eco-tourism – what's it all about?
Tourism is very important for the economy of many countries. It can help create jobs for local people and bring money into the country. This money can be used to build hospitals and schools. It can also create better facilities for local communities, such as improved roads and airports, and more frequent buses and trains. It can also give remote communities an opportunity to learn more about other languages and cultures.
However, tourism can also have negative effects. Building luxury hotels and resorts often damages natural habitats like beaches and forests, and large cruise ships and airplanes pollute our oceans and the air we breathe. What's more, tourism can make things like food and local goods more expensive, as tourists will pay more for items. The business of tourism can also mean that the jobs created by this industry are seasonal, which means that they finish when the tourist season ends.
Eco-tourism is one solution to these problems as it allows travellers to get to different destinations without negatively affecting the environment or other people. However, this doesn't simply mean finding a good campsite, setting up a tent and catching fish for dinner. It's much more than that. It is a type of tourism that respects the natural and cultural environments of a tourist destination. It can be as simple as not buying souvenirs made from endangered animals. Or it can involve more committed actions, like choosing not to travel long distances by plane in order to reduce the amount of harmful carbon dioxide in the air. Some tourists only use public transport while on holiday.
Eco-tourism has many advantages, such as giving local communities control over how they spend the money earned from tourism and how to develop their area in an environmentally friendly way. It has many benefits for eco-tourists, such as learning about wildlife and different cultures. It also allows us to take part in protecting and conserving our natural resources. Most importantly, it has a positive effect on our planet and helps to protect our environment for future generations.

Track 36

Unit 8, page 66, exercise 3

Group of voices: Save our planet! Stop climate change now!
Chloe: Mark? Is that you? What are you doing?
Mark: Oh, hi Chloe. I'm a member of the Chorley Climate Change Coalition. We organise these protests every month. We want the government to do more to protect the environment.
Chloe: Wow! I've never been on a protest, but I saw you on TV last month, now I think about it. There are a lot more people here today.
Mark: Yes, more and more people are joining and that takes a lot of organisation. We have to think about things like location, time, signs and even what we are going to say. We all have to take part in organising the protests.
Chloe: Wow, that sounds like a of work. I try to recycle, and I use public transport a lot of the time, but I suppose organising public protests is very important, too.
Mark: Yes, it is. The government has to listen to us if we make enough noise! It's our responsibility to protect the Earth for future generations and teach people about the dangers of climate change.
Chloe: You're right. A lot of people don't worry about climate change because they don't have the information. I mean, we don't learn much about it at school.
Mark: I agree. And I think both young people and adults need to learn more about the consequences. Adults are not doing enough. It's their responsibility to combat climate change too.
Chloe: You're right. So, what can I do? I think I should do more to help.
Mark: Well, the protest today is finishing now. But how about helping with the clean-up day on Friday?
Chloe: Oh, no. I can't do this Friday. I have an exam.
Mark: Oh.
Chloe: When is the next protest?
Mark: Next month, on Saturday the 22nd.
Chloe: Oh no! I'm not here that weekend… Wait! I know. What about an upcycling day at school? I can ask students to bring used household items to school and help them to do something new with them.
Mark: That sounds great. Thanks, Chloe!

Track 37

Unit 8, page 66, exercise 4

See previous track

Track 38

Unit 8, page 68, exercise 3

1 Fergus
Hi, my name's Fergus and I live on a remote island. There isn't much to do, so I spend a lot of time outdoors enjoying nature. My favourite part of the island is a place that not a lot of people know about. That's probably why I like it. If you follow the path along the coastline, you come to a steep climb up a cliff. You have to be a very good climber and use professional climbing equipment to do this safely. At the top of the cliff, the views of the island are fantastic. You can see the birds' nests in the spring and lots of animals in their natural habitat. Up here, you feel like the only person in the world. It truly is a peaceful place.

2 Issy
Hi, I'm Issy and I live in a village in the west of the country, surrounded by forests. We get a lot of tourists here. People come to walk in the countryside and see the waterfalls, streams and lakes. The people who live here spend a lot of time outside, too. Most of them are farmers or outdoor activities instructors. My brother Sam, for example, is a professional canoeist and takes people on canoe trips in the area. We are total opposites. I can't wait to leave the area when I'm older and go and live in a big city. I want to work in an office.

3 Sarah
Hi there! My name's Sarah and I live near the beach. I spend a lot of time there with my family. We love sitting on the sand and watching the sunrise in the morning. I know I'm lucky to live in the south of the country. The coastline is beautiful and it's warm most of the year. It's not all positive, however. Our oceans are becoming more and more polluted. I can see the results of this every day because there is always plastic on the beach. I clean it up because the seagulls eat it, but if we don't all start looking after our natural resources, we will be in a lot of trouble very soon.

Track 39

Unit 8, page 68, exercise 4

See previous track

Track 40

Unit 8, page 70, exercise 3

Upcycling - reusing our waste creatively
In the past, we threw all of our waste in the rubbish. In fact, most people used the same rubbish bin for all types of waste, including paper, plastic and glass.
This resulted in large landfills that damage the environment. We now know that we need to change our habits in order to protect the environment. If we don't practise responsible waste management, we will destroy our planet. Reducing waste and recycling is everybody's obligation.
We can do more with our waste, however, than simply recycling it and buying something new to replace it. We can also think of completely new uses for our waste, and avoid throwing things away at all. This helps save energy and natural resources, and reduces air pollution. This is called upcycling.
Upcycling is a creative and intelligent approach to reusing our waste. There are many ways to upcycle and you can do it from the comfort of your own home. Painting old chairs and tables, or making new cushions for your sofa with material you have in the house, gives your furniture an original feel.
Finding different uses for items in the house also balances our consumption and can stop us from buying new products that we don't really need. You can find a lot of great ideas online, like making bookshelves from old ladders, using glass jars as vases, or giving an old vintage suitcase a new use as a table.
One of the best things about upcycling is that you don't need to spend a lot of money to do it. You probably have a lot of the materials that you need at home. The idea is to stop seeing waste and start seeing new ways to creatively reuse the things that you already own.
Upcycling also has health benefits: it means you have to move and think, which is good for your body and your mind. Additionally, when you create a unique item, it gives you a great sense of achievement.

So, what are you waiting for? If you take small steps to change your habits, you will contribute to reducing environmental damage. Start living sustainably today!

Track 41
Unit 9, page 77, exercise 5

Billy: What are you doing, Grandad?
Grandad: I'm just looking at some old photos from when I was young, Billy.
Billy: Cool! Can I see? Who is that on the horse?
Grandad: That's me! I could ride when I was four because we had a horse on the farm. I was very good. I won a horse-riding competition once.
Billy: Really? Could you jump as well?
Grandad: Yes. I was one of the best riders in the area. I wanted to become a jockey, but I couldn't because we were too poor. I had to start working on the farm when I was twelve.
Billy: I didn't know that! I'd like to be able to ride a horse.
Grandad: I can teach you, if you like. And you can teach me how to ride a bike!
Billy: That would be great! Can I see more photos? Is that you wearing the funny hat?
Grandad: Yes, it is. I really liked doing magic tricks when I was young, but I couldn't do them very well.
Billy: What about this one, Grandad?
Grandad: Let me see... Oh yes. That was the last game of the school chess competition. And I won it. I became the chess champion of the whole school. I could play really well. Nobody could beat me, not even the teachers.
Billy: Why don't you play anymore? I have never seen you play.
Grandad: There isn't anyone to play with now.
Billy: Can you teach me? I've never been able to understand chess. It looks so complicated.
Grandad: Of course, Billy. I'd love to be able play with someone again.
Billy: And what about this last photo? Is that you at a yoga class?
Grandad: No, it's a dance class. In those days, boys didn't take dance classes, but I wanted to. In the end, I only went to a dance school for a month. I was terrible at it!

Track 42
Unit 9, page 77, exercise 6

See previous track

Track 43
Unit 9, page 78, exercise 1

Presenter: Hello and welcome back to Oh My Word! On today's programme we are offering you the chance to win a trip to New York. Yes, that's right, the Big Apple! All you have to do is call in and tell us about your best friend and why they are special. And here is our first caller… hello?
Caller 1: I want to nominate my best friend Adam. A lot of people think he's old-fashioned because he doesn't wear modern clothes. I mean, I don't like wearing ties like he does, but I think he looks really original. Other people say he is miserable all the time, but he can be cheerful… sometimes. I'm a very positive person, but he's not. But he's never rude… Some people say…
Presenter: OK… thanks for telling us about Adam, but let's go to the next caller. Hi there. Tell us about your friend and why they should win.
Caller 2: I'd like to nominate my best friend Polly. She moved to South Africa last year, so I don't see her very often now. But we met at primary school, so we have been best friends for years. It's funny because I didn't like her very much at first because she's not an outgoing, cheerful person like me. But she is calm and quiet and she always listens. And we have the same hobbies. We both like gymnastics.
Presenter: Thanks for that story. OK, I think we have one more caller. Caller, tell us about your friend and why they should win.
Caller 3: I know it's not very original, but my mum, Naz, is my best friend. She is always cheerful, we have a lot of fun together. And she's calm in a crisis, so when I have a problem, I can always talk to her about it. She spends a lot of time and money on looking after me and my sisters. She's always busy, but she is never rude to anybody and she's an excellent cook. She really is the best mum in the world, and that's why I'd like to nominate her for this award.
Presenter: I think we have a winner! Congratulations!

Track 44
Unit 9, page 78, exercise 2

See previous track

Track 45
Unit 9, page 80, exercise 2

Live to work
Should you work to live or live to work? We interview three people who turned their hobbies into their professions.

Gina, restaurant owner
I spent all my free time cooking with my grandmother when I was a child. It was her hobby, too. She was very traditional and she always made every meal at home with love and care. She believed that home cooking was healthier, cheaper and more delicious than the ready-made meals from the supermarket. I started training to be a chef at the age of eighteen and my dream was to have my own restaurant. I finally opened Fresh Fare two years ago. Everything on my menu is organic and I buy my produce from local farms.

Fred, professional guitar player
It all started as a hobby when I was about seven. I spent hours of my free time practising in my room, until I was good enough to play in a band. I saw an advertisement in the newspaper for a guitarist and I decided to apply. My band and I have played together for ten years now. Having your passion as your career is fantastic! We aren't famous but that's better for me because I want to have a quiet life. When I'm not playing in the band, I give guitar classes at the local music school and look after my children at home.

Rick, craftsman
I have always been interested in creating things. I started making collages when I was five years old as presents for friends and family members. I used items I found around the house, like plastic bottles and paper tissues! My art teacher at school was fantastic and she really inspired me. She said my artwork was very original. She's the reason why I decided to make a profession out of my love for crafts. I have my own studio now and I still create things from recycled materials, but on a bigger scale. As an eco-conscious artist, I want to encourage people to use their waste creatively.

Track 46
Wordlist, page 99, Unit 1, Adjectives
See Student's Book transcript, Track 2.46

Track 47
Wordlist, page 99, Unit 1, Interests
See Student's Book transcript, Track 2.47

Track 48
Wordlist, page 99, Unit 1, Personality traits
See Student's Book transcript, Track 2.48

Track 49
Wordlist, page 99, Unit 2, Home
See Student's Book transcript, Track 2.49

Track 50
Wordlist, page 99, Unit 2, Daily routine
See Student's Book transcript, Track 2.50

Track 51
Wordlist, page 99, Unit 2, World geography
See Student's Book transcript, Track 2.51

Track 52
Wordlist, page 99, Unit 3, Irregular verbs
See Student's Book transcript, Track 2.52

Track 53
Wordlist, page 99, Unit 3, Culture
See Student's Book transcript, Track 2.53

Track 54
Wordlist, page 99, Unit 3, Art forms
See Student's Book transcript, Track 2.54

Track 55
Wordlist, page 100, Unit 4, Parties
See Student's Book transcript, Track 2.55

Track 56
Wordlist, page 100, Unit 4, Entertainment
See Student's Book transcript, Track 2.56

Track 57
Wordlist, page 100, Unit 4, Festivals and celebrations
See Student's Book transcript, Track 2.57

Track 58
Wordlist, page 100, Unit 5, Technology
See Student's Book transcript, Track 2.58

Track 59
Wordlist, page 100, Unit 5, Phrasal verbs
See Student's Book transcript, Track 2.59

Track 60
Wordlist, page 100, Unit 5, Future technologies
See Student's Book transcript, Track 2.60

Track 61
Wordlist, page 100, Unit 6, Health and illness
See Student's Book transcript, Track 2.61

Track 62
Wordlist, page 100, Unit 6, Accidents
See Student's Book transcript, Track 2.62

Track 63
Wordlist, page 100, Unit 6, Healthcare professionals
See Student's Book transcript, Track 2.63

Track 64
Wordlist, page 101, Unit 7, Transport
See Student's Book transcript, Track 2.64

Track 65
Wordlist, page 101, Unit 7, Air travel
See Student's Book transcript, Track 2.65

Track 66
Wordlist, page 101, Unit 7, Abstract nouns
See Student's Book transcript, Track 2.66

Track 67
Wordlist, page 101, Unit 8, Environment
See Student's Book transcript, Track 2.67

Track 68
Wordlist, page 101, Unit 8, Nature
See Student's Book transcript, Track 2.68

Track 69
Wordlist, page 101, Unit 8, Global warming
See Student's Book transcript, Track 2.69

Track 70
Wordlist, page 101, Unit 9, Shopping
See Student's Book transcript, Track 2.70

Track 71
Wordlist, page 101, Unit 9, Hobbies
See Student's Book transcript, Track 2.71

Track 72
Wordlist, page 101, Unit 9, Adjectives
See Student's Book transcript, Track 2.72

Unit 1

Page 4

1
- **1** curious
- **2** lazy
- **3** clever
- **4** wonderful
- **5** big

2
- **1** colourful
- **2** heavy
- **3** clever
- **4** noisy
- **5** curious
- **6** slow

3
- **1** c
- **2** a
- **3** b

4
- **1** F. Ben is a new student at school.
- **2** F. Ben's birthday is in September.
- **3** F. Ben's dog is big and energetic.
- **4** T.
- **5** T.

Page 5

5
- **1** aren't
- **2** holds
- **3** doesn't
- **4** don't
- **5** doesn't
- **6** is

6
- **1** don't need
- **2** don't want
- **3** find
- **4** am
- **5** don't have
- **6** are
- **7** don't like

7 **1** d **2** b **3** f **4** a **5** c **6** e

8 *Student's own answers*

Page 6

1
- **1** nickname
- **2** class
- **3** instrument
- **4** dream
- **5** hobbies
- **6** superhero

2
- **1** collecting
- **2** playing
- **3** watching
- **4** drawing
- **5** making
- **6** listening

3 **1 L** **2 E** **3 F**

4
- **1** clever
- **2** vegetables
- **3** teeth
- **4** stamps
- **5** pig
- **6** snake

Page 7

5 **1** e **2** d **3** c **4** f **5** a **6** b

6
- **1** Where are you from?
- **2** What class do you have after school today?
- **3** Who is your favourite singer?
- **4** What instrument do you play?
- **5** What is your best friend's name?
- **6** Do you have a pet/cat?

7
- **1** Do; have
- **2** Do; live
- **3** is
- **4** are
- **5** do; prefer
- **6** Do; draw
- **7** Do; know

8 *Student's own answers*

Page 8

1
- **1** friendly
- **2** reserved
- **3** compassionate
- **4** nervous
- **5** organised
- **6** curious

2 *Student's own answers*

3 **a**, c, e

4
- **1** You must be energetic.
- **2** You must be responsible and organised.
- **3** He says they are solitary and cautious.

5
- **1** D
- **2** S
- **3** S
- **4** D
- **5** H
- **6** H
- **7** S

6
- **1** d
- **2** e
- **3** a
- **4** c
- **5** b

Page 10

1 *Student's own answers*

2 *Student's own answers*

3 *Student's own answers*

Page 11

1 **1** see eye to eye
2 get on like a house on fire
3 are like chalk and cheese

2 **1** get on like a house on fire
2 see eye to eye
3 are like chalk and cheese

Unit 2

Page 12

1 **1** living room
2 kitchen
3 bedroom
4 attic
5 utility room
6 study

2 **1** c
2 a
3 e
4 d
5 b

3 **1** flat
2 garage
3 main bedroom
4 rooftop terrace
5 kitchen

4 **1** b **2** d **3** c **4** a

5 **1** c
2 b
3 a
4 c
5 a

Page 13

6 **1** every evening
2 sometimes
3 Once a year
4 often
5 never
6 hardly ever

7 **1** I hardly ever see Jen at school now. I hope she's OK.
2 We always see Mr Smith walking his dog in the mornings.
3 Rick sometimes tidies his bedroom and the living room on Saturdays.
4 That shop on the corner is rarely open.
5 My friends sometimes get the bus to school.
6 Hurry up! You are always late!

8 **1** I go to the cinema once a week.
2 She rarely eats dessert.
3 He drives his father's car twice a week.
4 They see their cousins once a year.
5 Students speak in English every day.

Page 14

1 1 finish school
2 go for a run
3 go to bed
4 brush your teeth
5 have breakfast
6 get home

2 **1** b
2 a
3 e
4 d
5 c

3 **a** 1
c 2
e 3
b 4
f 5
g 6
d 7

4 **1** 20
2 once
3 several times
4 every
5 rarely
6 reads
7 never
8 never

Page 15

5 **1** wakes up
2 gets up
3 has
4 eats
5 leaves
6 brushes
7 rides
8 walks
9 does
10 is not riding
11 is reading
12 is listening
13 is not doing
14 is relaxing

6 **1** What does John do every evening?
2 Is Emma reading (right now)?
3 What do you do after dinner?
4 Are you studying French (at the moment)?
5 Does Claire play tennis every day?
6 What time do you eat dinner?

7 **1** walk
2 doesn't like
3 Do you go
4 Are you having
5 aren't listening
6 have

8 *Student's own answers*

Page 16

1 **1** continents
2 Finland
3 landmass
4 languages
5 Oceania

2 b

3 **1** Jake wakes up at 8:00am.
2 Jake gets home from school at 4:00pm.
3 Jake goes to bed at 10:00pm.
4 Maya wakes up at 6:00am.
5 Maya starts school at 8:30am.
6 Maya has dinner at 7:30pm.

4 **1** T
2 F. The bus stops very near his house.
3 T
4 F. Maya lives in a very remote place.
5 F. Maya is hardly ever bored.
6 T.
7 T.
8 F. They both do schoolwork at home.

5 **1** hardly ever
2 every
3 usually
4 several
5 twice

Page 18
1 *Student's own answers*

2 *Student's own answers*

3 *Student's own answers*

Page 19
1 **1** slept like a log
2 early bird gets the worm
3 night owl

2 **1** night owl
2 sleeps like a log
3 early bird gets the worm

Unit 3
Page 22
1 **1** fell
2 drew
3 died
4 made
5 gave
6 became
7 took
8 sat

2 **1** M
2 S
3 T

3 **1** c **2** c **3** a **4** b **5** c **6** b

4 **1** Photography
2 Sculpture
3 painter
4 inspired
5 Drawing

Page 23
5 **1** had
2 took
3 met
4 visited
5 was
6 told
7 wasn't

6 **1** Did he create the sculpture; Yes, he did.
2 Did Lisa finish her book?; No, she didn't.
3 Did Jake make friends on holiday?; Yes, he did.
4 Did you draw that picture?; Yes, I did.
5 Did they visit the museum?; No, they didn't.
6 Did she develop documentary photography?; Yes, she did.

7 **1** did the artist finish the sculpture
2 did Harry create the company
3 did you make for dinner
4 did he go to France
5 did she give you for your birthday
6 did the artist die

8 *Student's own answers*

Page 24
1
Across
4 act
5 stage
6 row
7 audience
Down
1 play
2 interval
3 star
5 screen

2 **1** audience
2 stage
3 star
4 interval
5 orchestra
6 play
7 acts

3 2, 4, 6

4 **a** 1 **e** 2 **c** 3 **b** 4 **d** 5 **f** 6

Page 25
5 **1** to go
2 feel
3 use
4 didn't
5 use
6 to live

6
1 Children used to play outside, but now they play videogames.
2 People used to eat more fresh food, but now they eat lots of junk food.
3 Pete didn't use to wear glasses, but now he has glasses and a beard.
4 Almudena used to be a gymnast, but now she writes children's books.

7
1 didn't use to sit
2 didn't use to be
3 used to visit
4 used to go
5 used to be
6 used to write

8
1 Did people use to have mobile phones? Student's own answers
2 Did there use to be more traffic? Student's own answers
3 Did artists use to make more money? Student's own answers
4 Did people use to go to the cinema more often? Student's own answers
5 How else did life use to be different? Student's own answers

Page 26

1
1 ballet
2 photography
3 poetry
4 sculpture
5 literature

2 a 2 b 3 c 1

3 1 K 2 B 3 T 4 T 5 B 6 K

4
1 They thought the arts were boring.
2 By painting or writing.
3 Skills like creativity weren't considered important but now they are.
4 In digital media and marketing.
5 They help students to relax and forget about the stress of exams or problems with family or friends.
6 He used to feel angry and worried.

5
1 e
2 d
3 c
4 a
5 b

Page 28

1 *Student's own answers*

2 *Student's own answers.*

3 *Student's own answers.*

Page 29

1
1 not my cup of tea
2 can't stand
3 is crazy about it

2
1 am crazy about
2 can't stand
3 not my cup of tea

Unit 4

Page 30

1
1 candles
2 presents
3 cake
4 barbecue
5 gift tag
6 decorations

2
1 burgers
2 sausages
3 cupcakes
4 cake
5 balloons
6 candles

3
1 c
2 a
3 b

4
1 Her favourite restaurant.
2 Pizza, chocolate cupcakes and birthday cake.
3 Because it was a surprise.
4 New Zealand.
5 Sausages and hamburgers.
6 She had the most delicious Christmas dinner of her life.
7 The city stadium.
8 Massive plates of pasta.
9 He scored two of the five goals.

Page 31

5
1 There were
2 Were there
3 There wasn't
4 Were there
5 Was there
6 There was

6
1 there weren't
2 There weren't
3 there were
4 there weren't
5 there wasn't
6 There were
7 There wasn't
8 there were

7
1 Were there rock concerts when you were a teenager?
2 Was there internet when you were young?
3 Were there a lot of exams at your school?
4 What kind of videogames were there in the shop?
5 Were there any candles on the birthday cake?
6 Was there any money in your bank account?
7 Were there more people in the world ten years ago?
8 Was there enough milk in the fridge?

8 *Student's own answers*

Page 32

1
1 camp
2 concert
3 napkin
4 backstage
5 zip wire

2
1 snorkelling
2 flippers
3 competitions
4 adventure
5 roller coasters

3
1 c
2 a
3 a

4
1 Megan forgot to buy tickets for the concert.
2 Megan had a coat, but she didn't have an umbrella.
3 Rachel was on holiday for thirteen days.
4 Rachel spent her time snorkelling and reading on holiday.
5 Rachel didn't speak to her friends because the hotel didn't have an internet connection.
6 Linda's dad bought sausages and burgers for her birthday party.
7 Two of Linda's friends only ate the cupcakes at her party.

Page 33

5
1 It was raining so I brought my umbrella.
2 They were not dancing at the party.
3 We were eating lunch when my friend called.
4 You weren't listening during Maths class.
5 My mum was driving when it started to snow.
6 I was wearing my new shoes at the party.

6
1 was coming
2 were staying
3 were dancing
4 was playing
5 were clapping and cheering
6 was enjoying herself
7 was taking

7
1 No she wasn't. She was coming back from a school trip.
2 No they weren't. They were staying at their own house.
3 No they weren't. They were dancing to a song.
4 No they weren't. They were dancing to a song that was playing when they first met.
5 No, they weren't. They were clapping and cheering.
6 Yes, she was. She was enjoying herself.
7 Yes, he was. He was taking the photo.

8 *Student's own answers*

Page 34

1
1 fireworks
2 gatherings
3 a wish
4 Easter
5 fruit and raisins
6 biscuits
7 wealth
8 dish

2 2

3 a 3 b 4 c 1 d 2

4
1 They are eaten on a special occasion.
2 Peas, a piece of cloth, a coin or a ring.
3 Because they have a special meaning or superstition.
4 At special gatherings such as weddings and Christmas.
5 They sometimes make a wish when they eat frappe.
6 So that they don't have to cook at the beginning of January.
7 Potatoes, eggs, meat, apples, carrots and mayonnaise. No, it doesn´t contain caviar.
8 Because it's a symbol of wealth and good luck for the new year.

5 1 a 2 b 3 b

Page 36

1 *Student's own answers*

2 *Student's own answers*

3 *Student's own answers*

Page 37

1
1 my jaw dropped
2 came out of the blue
3 took our breath away

2
1 my jaw dropped
2 took our breath away
3 came out of the blue

Unit 5

Page 40

1

Across
2 homepage
4 password
5 right click
7 download

Down
1 printer
3 attachment
6 laptop/tablet

2
1 Click
2 homepage
3 type
4 upload
5 main menu
6 drag

3 **1** a **2** c **3** b

4 **1** b **2** c **3** a **4** a

Page 41

5 **1** Right-click
2 Download
3 Drag
4 Connect
5 Attach

6 **1** charge
2 plug it in
3 Press
4 Type
5 log in
6 download
7 Switch off

7 **1** log in
2 turn off
3 switch off
4 unplug

8 **1** c **2** f **3** d **4** a **5** b **6** e

9 *Student's own answers*

Page 42

1 **1** electronics
2 memory card
3 camera
4 data
5 robot
6 wires
7 software
8 update

2 **1**, 3

3 **1** headphones
2 plug in
3 hardware
4 wire
5 update
6 data
7 click
8 type

Page 43

4 **1** Will you go home after school today?
2 Will you come with me to the park?
3 She won't buy a laptop from that shop.
4 I won't watch that now, I don't have time.
5 I will be at work on Saturday and Sunday.
6 Will you update your software soon?

5 **1** No, it won't.
2 Yes, I will.
3 No, they won't.
4 Yes, he will.
5 No, she won't.
6 Yes, I will.

6 **1** What time will the fair start? / When will the fair start?
2 What will I need (to bring)?
3 Where will the fair take place?
4 What will we learn about?
5 Who will speak at the fair?

7 *Student's own answers*

Page 44

1 **1** driverless cars
2 smart homes
3 Artificial
4 Robots

2 **a** 3 **b** 1 **c** 2

3 *Suggested answers:*

Advantages of using technolog
1 help you learn important skills
2 better prepared for work
3 develop natural talents
4 learn about different countries and cultures
5 help improve vocabulary and comprehension skills
6 can learn more about health and fitness
Disadvantages of using technology
1 negative effect on creativity and imagination
2 affect ability to manage emotions
3 make you less socially active
4 make it difficult to make friends in real life
5 makes you sit more and move less
6 affect your vision

4 **1** b **2** c **3** c **4** a

5 **1** advantages
2 technology
3 screen
4 predict
5 websites

Page 46

1 *Student's own answers*

2 *Student's own answers*

3 *Student's own answers*

Page 47

1 **1** know
2 don't have
3 isn't

2 **1** don't have a clue
2 I know it like the back of my hand
3 isn't rocket science

Unit 6

Page 48

1 **1** runny nose
2 cough
3 headache
4 sore throat
5 earache

2 **1** Mark
2 Thalia
3 Steve
4 Carol
5 Thalia

3 **1** healthy
2 runny nose
3 a doctor's appointment

4 **1** T
2 F. She doesn't want to do her French test.
3 F. He loves them.
4 F. She tells him to take the plants outside.
5 T.
6 F. He always forgets them.
7 T.

Page 49

5 **1** shouldn't go
2 should listen
3 can borrow
4 can't spend
5 should help

6 **1** should
2 Can
3 shouldn't
4 can't
5 should

7 **1** You can't speak loudly.
2 You can't run around.
3 You can eat in the café.
4 You can ask the guide questions.
5 You can't touch the art.

8 **1** should go
2 should get
3 shouldn't leave
4 should take
5 should make
6 shouldn't do
7 should wait

9 *Student's own answers.*

Page 50

1

Part of the body	Health problem
ankle	bruise
bone	burn
chin	concussion
elbow	nosebleed
wrist	wound

2 **1** plaster cast
2 sling
3 itches
4 scratch
5 crutches
6 heal
7 bandage

3 **1** b **2** a **3** a **4** b

4 **1** fruit
2 lemon and honey
3 for walks
4 the hospital
5 any exercise
6 stay indoors
7 prevent sunburn
8 washing your hands

Page 51

5 **1** mustn't ignore
2 have to wear
3 must call
4 mustn't touch
5 have to change
6 don't have to do

6 *Student's own answers.*

7 **1** don't have to
2 must
3 mustn't
4 don't have to
5 mustn't
6 must

8 *Student's own answers*

Page 52

1 **1** c **2** e **3** d **4** a **5** f **6** b

2 **b**

3 **1** F. The job is different every day.
2 DS.
3 F. Only some need operations.
4 T.

4 **1** Paramedics.
2 The long hours and working at night.
3 It helps to keep them calm.
4 She sees patients.
5 At 5 o'clock.
6 She works normal office hours.
7 Her arms hurt at the end of the day.

5 **1** concussion
2 check-ups
3 healthcare
4 ambulance
5 procedures

Page 54

1 *Student's own answers*

2 *Student's own answers*

3 *Student's own answers*

Page 55

1 **1** b
2 a
3 b

2 **1** have a frog in my throat
2 am sick as a dog
3 feeling under the weather

Unit 7

Page 58

1 **1** a
2 b
3 b
4 b
5 a

2 **1** cruise ship
2 train/tram
3 helicopter
4 double decker bus
5 lorry

3 **1** a
2 c

4 **1** a **2** b **3** c **4** a **5** b **6** c

Page 59

5 **1** haven't written
2 haven't had
3 have already done
4 have visited
5 have seen
6 have ridden
7 has been
8 haven't swum yet
9 have already made
10 have eaten

6 **1** We haven't slept in our new house yet.
2 The students haven't visited the museum yet.
3 Sarah has already swum in the pool three times today.
4 I haven't flown on a jet yet but I really want to.
5 They have already ridden on the tram.
6 We haven't been to the theme park yet.

7 **1** have you been
2 haven't seen
3 have been
4 went
5 have wanted
6 have ridden
7 was
8 flew
9 took
10 haven't sent

8 *Student's own answers*

Page 60

1

Across
2 passport
5 security
7 stopover
8 delayed

Down
1 gate
2 customs
3 arrivals
4 take off / take-off
6 land

2 **1** journey
2 destination
3 check in
4 boarding pass
5 security
6 abroad
7 take-off / take off
8 lands
9 disembark

3 **1** T
2 F (He forgets his boarding pass)
3 T

4 **1** Mexico
2 13 hours
3 Berlin, Germany
4 1pm
5 9pm
6 30th October

Page 61

5 **1** Have you bought the plane tickets, Roy?
2 Have you packed your passport?
3 Have you checked in online?
4 Have you found a good hotel?
5 Have you got train tickets from the airport?
6 Have you learnt a few words of Italian?
7 Have you ever flown alone?

6 **1** ever heard
2 have never been
3 have never made
4 ever been
5 have never visited

7 1 Have you ever travelled first class? No, I haven't.
2 Have you ever travelled with only hand luggage? *Student's own answers.*
3 Have you ever slept in a tent? Student's own answers.
4 Have you been on holiday yet this year? Student's own answers.
5 Have you finished your homework yet? Student's own answers.

Page 62

1 1 picturesque
2 go on a tour
3 tourist destination
4 balance
5 pleasure

2 c, d, e

3 1 T.
2 F. It pollutes the air.
3 T.
4 F. It also respects its cultural environment.
5 F. Local communities decide how to spend it.
6 F. It teaches tourists about wildlife.

4 b

5 1 c
2 a
3 d
4 b

Page 64

1 *Student's own answers.*

2 *Student's own answers.*

3 *Student's own answers.*

Page 65

1 1 driving
2 be
3 are

2 1 drove me mad
2 were in the same boat
3 is a backseat driver

Unit 8

Page 66

1 1 Upcycling
2 protest
3 climate change
4 litter
5 bottle bank
6 a landfill
7 ecosystems

2 1 rubbish bin
2 recycle
3 landfill
4 protest
5 climate change
6 natural resources

3 1 At a protest.
2 No, she isn't.
3 Organise an upcycling day.

4 1 c
2 b
3 a
4 a
5 c

Page 67

5 1 become; has
2 protest; take
3 don't act; will be
4 continues; will get
5 recycle; create
6 will have; use

6 1 b 2 b 3 a 4 a 5 a 6 b

7 1 destroy; will happen
2 don't recycle; goes
3 protect; increase
4 melt; will rise

8 *Student's own answers*

Page 68

1 1 cliffs; c
2 habitat; b
3 path; a
4 sunset; f
5 stream; d
6 west coast, e

2 1 cliffs
2 west coast
3 sunset
4 habitat
5 stream
6 path

3 1 c
2 a
3 b

4 1 I 2 F 3 S 4 S 5 I 6 F 7 I

Page 69

5 1 are going to work
2 are going to buy
3 is going to plant
4 are going to organise
5 aren't going to use
6 is going to talk
7 are going to sell

6 **1** What is Jamie going to do on holiday?
2 When are you going to help at the clean-up?
3 Are you going to travel by public transport?
4 Is she going to organise a recycling campaign?
5 Who is Jane going to see tomorrow?
6 What are you going to do to help the planet?

7 *Students own answers*

Page 70

1 **a** emissions
b carbon dioxide
c damaging
d renewable
e threats

1 damaging
2 emissions
3 threats
4 carbon dioxide
5 renewable

2 *Student's own answers*

3 **1** c
2 a
3 b

4 **1** We threw it all in the same rubbish bin.
2 We will destroy our planet.
3 It saves energy and natural resources, and reduces air pollution.
4 Buying new products that we don't need.
5 Because you probably have a lot of the materials that you need at home.
6 Making bookshelves from old ladders, using glass jars as vases, or giving an old vintage suitcase a new use as a table.
7 It's good for your body and your mind.

5 **1** waste
2 vintage
3 habits
4 pollution
5 consumption

Page 72

1 *Student's own answers*

2 *Student's own answers*

3 *Student's own answers*

Page 73

1 **1** to make a stand
2 Actions speak louder than words.
3 to think outside the box

2 **1** actions speak louder than words
2 to make a stand
3 to think outside the box

Unit 9

Page 76

1 **1** exchange
2 sale
3 size
4 receipt
5 bargain
6 label

2 **1** enough
2 too
3 too
4 enough

3 **1** enough time
2 too expensive
3 enough money
4 too small
5 enough food
6 too tired
7 enough shops

Page 77

4 **1** a
2 a
3 b
4 b
5 b
6 a
7 b
5 4 and 6

6 **1** too poor
2 ride a bike
3 (school) chess competition
4 a month

7 **1** couldn't go
2 can't do
3 will be able to beat
4 couldn't play
5 can paint
6 can you meet

8 *Student's own answers*

Page 78

1 **1** c **2** a **3** b

2 **1** T
2 F. They have been best friends for years.
3 F. She didn't like her at first.
4 T
5 F. Naz spends a lot of money on her children.
6 F. The third caller wins the competition.

3 **1** busy
2 modern
3 polite
4 delighted
5 original
6 quiet
7 miserable

4 **1** Rude
2 positive
3 strange
4 Famous
5 disappointed

Page 79

5 **1** better
2 more expensive
3 more relaxed
4 hotter
5 more exciting
6 nicer
7 bigger
8 happier

6 **1** the oldest
2 the largest
3 the heaviest
4 the longest
5 the hottest
6 the highest

7 **a** biggest; 4
b earlier; 1
c hottest; closer; 5
d largest; bigger; 2
e highest; tallest; 6
f heavier; 3

8 *Student's own answers*

Page 80

1 **1** birdwatching
2 crafts
3 cooking
4 playing music
5 reading
6 fishing

2 c

3 **1** A
2 R
3 G
4 G
5 F

4 **1** It's healthier, cheaper and more delicious.
2 Local farms.
3 Ten years ago.
4 He wants a quiet life.
5 As presents for friends and family.
6 In his studio.

5 **1** original
2 advertisement
3 organic
4 apply
5 ready-made
6 waste

Page 82

1 *Student's own answers*

2 *Student's own answers*

3 *Student's own answers*

Page 83

1 **1** told a white lie
2 bending the truth
3 lying though her teeth

2 **1** lie through your teeth
2 bending the truth
3 tells a white lie

3 *Student's own answers*

Grammar practice

Unit 1

1 **1** My pet doesn't eat meat.
2 Fish don't live on land.
3 She plays the guitar and the violin. / She plays the violin and the guitar.
4 His mother is from Ireland.
5 Dan works as a volunteer in Africa.
6 Ed and I are in the same class.
7 I don't like fruit or vegetables.
8 Her hobby is collecting stamps.

2 **1** b
2 f
3 d
4 a
5 e
6 c

Unit 2

1 **1** I often have lunch at school.
2 I go to the cinema once a month.
3 I hardly ever read at night.
4 I am always nervous when I have an exam.
5 I play the guitar several times a week.

2 1 is working
2 go
3 doesn't like
4 Do you live
5 are you working
6 doesn't have

Unit 3

1 1 was
2 went
3 lived
4 fell
5 created
6 became
7 died

2 1 used to love
2 used to play
3 didn't use to have
4 did you use to go
5 did you use to play

Unit 4

1 1 There were
2 There wasn't
3 there weren't
4 There was
5 there were
6 Were there

2 1 was working
2 was decorating
3 were walking
4 were you going
5 wasn't listening

Unit 5

1 1 Don't give anyone your details.
2 Turn the music down. / Turn down the music.
3 Don't forget to buy a memory card.
4 Be careful. There's a car!
5 Switch your phone off. / Switch off your phone.

2 1 Don't worry, I'll help you.
2 I'll call you in five minutes.
3 I will see you very soon
4 Will you open the window please?
5 I think he will be famous.

Unit 6

1 1 b
2 a
3 b
4 b
5 b

2 1 mustn't
2 don't have to
3 mustn't
4 must
5 mustn't
6 don't have to

Unit 7

1 1 She hasn't bought her ticket yet.
2 I have already written 500 words.
3 I haven't travelled in a helicopter yet.
4 You haven't done your homework yet.
5 I've already been to Germany.
6 The flight has already left.

2 1 Have you ever travelled
2 I have flown
3 I have never been
4 Have you visited
5 I have already travelled
6 Have you ever camped
7 I have never stayed

Unit 8

1 1 heat; will boil
2 cut down; will die
3 recycle; help
4 don't pick up; will not look
5 will have; use
6 melts; don't put

2 1 am going to volunteer
2 Are you going to donate
3 is not going to wash
4 are going to start
5 are going to visit
6 am not going to buy

Unit 9

1 1 too
2 enough
3 too
4 enough
5 too

2 1 to be able to
2 been able to
3 could / was able to
4 can
5 will be able to

3 1 Villages are smaller than cities.
2 Tokyo is the biggest city in the world.
3 Wood is heavier than paper.
4 Gold is more expensive than aluminium.
5 Mount Everest is the highest mountain in the world.

Wordlist exercises

Unit 1

1
1 stamps
2 colourful
3 cool
4 drawing
5 curious
6 reading
7 hobbies
8 models
9 big

2
1 inventive
2 nervous
3 friendly
4 colourful
5 energetic

a nervous
b colourful
c inventive
d energetic
e friendly

Unit 2

1
1 c
2 a
3 b
4 d

2
1 get
2 have
3 go
4 walk
5 do

3
Across
1 Oceania
3 landmass
5 Europe
6 Asia
Down
2 Antarctica
4 Africa

Unit 3

1
1 theatre
2 photography
3 play
4 interval
5 stage
6 audience

2
1 met
2 fell
3 fought
4 became
5 made
6 went
7 had

Unit 4

1

Party food	Party items
barbecue	balloons
biscuits	candles
burgers	gift tags
sausages	decorations

2
1 ritual
2 camp
3 snorkelling
4 competition
5 gathering
6 firework

Unit 5

1
1 alarm clock
2 password
3 smart home
4 hardware
5 charge
6 video clip

2
1 switch off
2 log out
3 sign in
4 plug in
5 unplug

Unit 6

1
1 burn
2 allergy
3 plaster cast
4 bruise
5 sling
6 flu

2
1 doctor
2 dentist
3 paramedic
4 nurse
5 pharmacist

Unit 7

1

Sea	Air
cruise ship	helicopter
ferry	hot air balloon
Submarine	jet

2
1 gate
2 pleasure
3 announcement
4 destination
5 hand luggage

Unit 8

1
1 carbon dioxide
2 threat
3 atmosphere
4 sea levels
5 renewable
6 recycling

2
1 beaches
2 cliffs
3 waterfall
4 valleys
5 sunset

Unit 9

1
1 sale
2 size
3 receipt
4 chess
5 horse riding
6 bike

2
1 disappointing
2 excellent
3 miserable
4 polite
5 quiet

Richmond ®
58 St Aldates
Oxford OX1 1ST
United Kingdom

Publishing Director: María Lera
Managing Editor: Catherine Richards
Development Editor: Ben Pincus
Editorial Team: Joanne Fairgrieve, Natalie Krol, Jayne Marshall, Siobhàn O'Connor, Nicola Strutt

Video: MTJ Media
Audio: EFS Television Production Ltd. Motivation Sound Studios

Art Director: José Crespo
Art Coordination: Rosa Marín, Javier Tejeda
Cover: EMC Design Ltd.
Design and layout: ColART Design

Technical Director: Jorge Mira Fernández
Technical Coordination: Rocío Lominchar Romero
Photo Researcher: Amparo Rodríguez

Photos:
ARCHIVO SANTILLANA

Printed in Brazil
ISBN: 978-84-668-3401-8

The editors would like to thank all those teachers and consultants who provided invaluable help and insight with their participation in this book.